The Deacons for Defense

D1602964

The Deacons

ARMED

RESISTANCE

AND THE

CIVIL RIGHTS

MOVEMENT

Lance Hill

WITHDRAWN
Damaged, Obsolete, or Surplus
Jackson County Library Services

for Defense

The University of North Carolina Press   Chapel Hill and London

© 2004 The University of North Carolina Press
All rights reserved
Manufactured in the United States of America

Designed by Jacquline Johnson
Set in Charter
by Keystone Typesetting, Inc.

The paper in this book meets the guidelines for
permanence and durability of the Committee on
Production Guidelines for Book Longevity of the
Council on Library Resources.

Library of Congress Cataloging-in-Publication Data
Hill, Lance E. (Lance Edward), 1950–
The Deacons for Defense : armed resistance and the civil rights
movement / Lance Hill.
p. cm.
Includes bibliographical references and index.
ISBN-13: 978-0-8078-2847-2 (cloth : alk. paper)
ISBN-10: 0-8078-2847-5 (cloth : alk. paper)
ISBN-13: 978-0-8078-5702-1 (pbk. : alk. paper)
ISBN-10: 0-8078-5702-5 (pbk. : alk. paper)
1. Deacons for Defense and Justice—History. 2. African
American civil rights workers—Louisiana—Jonesboro—
History—20th century. 3. Self-defense—Political aspects—
Southern States—History—20th century. 4. Political violence—
Southern States—History—20th century. 5. Ku Klux Klan
(1915–)—History—20th century. 6. African Americans—Civil
rights—Southern States—History—20th century. 7. Civil rights
movements—Southern States—History—20th century.
8. Southern States—Race relations. 9. Louisiana—Race
relations. 10. Mississippi—Race relations. I. Title.
E185.615.H47 2004
323.1196′073′009046—dc22
2003021779

cloth: 08 07 06 05 04   5 4 3 2 1
paper: 10 09 08 07 06   5 4 3 2 1

THIS BOOK WAS DIGITALLY PRINTED.

For Eileen

Contents

A section of photographs appears after p. 107.

Acknowledgments

I FIRST LEARNED of the Deacons for Defense and Justice while attending a meeting of activists in Plaquemines Parish, Louisiana, in 1984. I had moved to rural Louisiana in 1979 and initially worked not far from Bogalusa as a welder and an industrial organizer. At the meeting in Plaquemines Parish—once the stronghold of arch-racist Leander Perez—I met one of the founders of the Deacons, Frederick Douglas Kirkpatrick. From my first meeting with Kirkpatrick, I decided that the history of this remarkable group of courageous men needed to be told.

Several people offered thoughtful and stimulating reactions to this book and deserve a great deal of thanks. Foremost is Lawrence N. Powell, for his indispensable advice, perceptive criticism, and steadfast encouragement. Adam Fairclough, Michael Honey, and Tim Tyson provided challenging criticisms and invaluable advice, which greatly benefited the final manuscript. Patrick Maney, Rosanne Adderley, and Kim Harris all read earlier drafts and offered many useful and illuminating insights. I have also learned much from long conversations over the years with my colleague Plater Robinson.

Tulane University's History Department made my research possible through several teaching assistantships and travel and research grants. I am especially indebted to Gwendolyn Midlo Hall for her professional assistance and expansive generosity. Gwen allowed me to consult her research papers on the Deacons for Defense and Justice at the Amistad Research Center, and has been an endless source of information on the left and black nationalist movements. Many friends and archivists aided me in obtaining materials, among them Tyler Bridges, Katherine Nachod, Annie Purnell Johnson, and Brenda Square. David Perry, Paula Wald, and Stevie Champion at the University of North Carolina Press made this book possible through their wise advice and skillful editing.

Writing a book about a semiclandestine organization poses some unique problems. The Deacons left no written records, and save for the FBI files and news reports, the real history of the organization resides in the collective memories of its members. This book would not have been possible had it not been for the members of the Deacons for Defense and Justice who shared with me their stories and wisdom.

My three children, Lisa, John, and Joel, admirably suffered a father who spent too many sunny days hunched over a dimly lit keyboard. My grandson Cody Robertson was an inspiration through his love of history—and diesel trucks. And my parents, Herbert and Gaye Hill, have always been accepting and supportive through trying times. Finally, I am deeply grateful to my wife, Eileen San Juan, who has provided years of intellectual companionship and moral support, and lent her critical eye to reading this manuscript. I have dedicated the book to her, though such a symbolic act is a pittance for her love and encouragement.

The Deacons for Defense

Introduction

PAUL FARMER HAD brought his pistol. The president of
the Washington Parish White Citizens Council was standing in the middle of
the street along with several other members of the council and the local Ku
Klux Klan. It was the autumn of 1966 in the small paper mill town of Bogalusa, Louisiana.

Royan Burris, a black barber and civil rights leader, knew why the Klansmen were there. They were waiting for the doors to open at Bogalusa Junior
High. The school had recently been integrated, and white students had been
harassing and brutalizing black students with impunity. "They were just
stepping on them, and spitting on them and hitting them," recalled Burris,
and the black students "wasn't doing anything back." In the past Burris had
counseled the black students to remain nonviolent. Now he advised a new
approach. "I said anybody hit you, hit back. Anybody step on your feet, step
back. Anybody spit on you, spit back."[1]

The young black students heeded Burris's advice. Fights between black
and white students erupted at the school throughout the day. Now Paul
Farmer and his band of Klansmen had arrived with guns, prepared to intervene. Their presence was no idle threat; whites had murdered two black
men in the mill town in the past two years, including a sheriff's deputy.

But Farmer had a problem. Standing in the street, only a few feet from the
Klan, was a line of grim, unyielding black men. They were members of the
Deacons for Defense and Justice, a black self-defense organization that had
already engaged the Klan in several shooting skirmishes. The two groups
faced off: the Klansmen on one side, the Deacons on the other.

After a few tense moments the police arrived and attempted to defuse the
volatile situation. They asked the Deacons to leave first, but the black men
refused. Burris recalled the Deacons' terse response to the police request.
"We been leaving first all of our lives," said Burris. "This time we not going in
peace." Infuriated by the Deacons' defiance, Farmer suddenly pulled his
pistol. In a reflex response, one of the Deacons drew his revolver, and in an

instant half a dozen pistols were waving menacingly in the air. Surveying the weapons arrayed against them, the Klansmen grudgingly pocketed their own guns and departed.[2]

The Deacons for Defense and Justice had faced death and never flinched. "From that day forward," said Burris, "we didn't have too many more problems."[3]

In 1964 a clandestine armed self-defense organization formed in the black community in Jonesboro, Louisiana, with the goal of protecting civil rights activists from the Ku Klux Klan and other racist vigilantes. After several months of relatively secret operations, the group publicly surfaced in February 1965 under the name "Deacons for Defense and Justice." By the end of 1966, the Deacons had grown to twenty-one chapters with several hundred members concentrated in Louisiana and Mississippi. The Deacons guarded marches, patrolled the black community to ward off night riders, engaged in shoot-outs with Klansmen, and even defied local police in armed confrontations. When the u.s. Justice Department faltered in enforcing the Civil Rights Act, the Deacons' militant politics and armed actions forced a pivotal showdown in Bogalusa between the government and southern segregationists.

Although the Deacons began as a simple self-defense guard to compensate for the lack of police protection, they soon developed into a highly visible political organization with a clear and compelling alternative to the pacifist strategies promoted by national civil rights organizations. They were not the first blacks to practice or advocate armed self-defense. Throughout the civil rights movement, African Americans frequently guarded themselves and their communities against vigilante assaults. But until the Deacons emerged, these armed self-defense efforts were almost always conducted by informal and disconnected covert groups that avoided open confrontations with authority and purposefully eschewed publicity—in part because they feared retaliation and in part because they wanted to maintain the illusion of nonviolence in the movement. It was this public image of a nonviolent movement that ensured white liberal support in the North. Civil rights leaders and activists also concealed armed self-defense for the same reasons. During the Montgomery Bus Boycott, one visitor to Martin Luther King's home was alarmed to find an "arsenal" of weapons and discovered that King himself had requested gun permits for his bodyguards. Yet publicly King adamantly opposed any open, organized armed self-defense activity. Similarly, Sally Belfrage, a northern volunteer in the Mississippi movement, deliberately omitted reference to armed self-defense in her memoir *Freedom Summer*

(1965). One local black activist in Mississippi had bluntly warned her, "If you write about the guns, we'll kill you." She took his advice.[4]

Invisible to the broader public, clandestine self-defense groups had little effect on the Ku Klux Klan or federal policy in the South. The Deacons, in contrast, consciously built a highly public, regional organization that openly defied local authorities and challenged the Klan—something that neither the Klan nor Washington could ignore. The Deacons boldly flouted the age-old southern code that denied blacks the right of open and collective self-defense, and by doing so they made an implicit claim to social and civil equality. By the summer of 1965 the Deacons for Defense had developed chapters throughout the South and generated considerable national publicity through major news stories in *Life* magazine, the *New York Times*, the *Wall Street Journal*, and the *Los Angeles Times*. Stories in *Newsweek*, *Time*, *Nation*, and *Business Week* followed in 1966. Influential black publications like *Ebony* carried the Deacons' story into thousands of black households, along with a widely read series of articles that appeared in *Jet* magazine— the premier weekly for the African American working class. Within a few months of their birth, the Deacons had become the talk of the movement and folk heroes to legions of African Americans in the Deep South. The publicity propelled the Deacons into the center of a national debate on the effectiveness of nonviolent direct action, and very soon they were at logger-heads with Dr. Martin Luther King Jr. and the mainstream nonviolent civil rights organizations.[5]

Not alone in their disenchantment with passive resistance, the Deacons reflected a growing disillusionment of working-class blacks with the pacifistic, legalistic, and legislative strategies proffered by national organizations. Many African Americans, men in particular, refused to participate in nonviolent protests because they believed that passive resistance to white violence simply reproduced the same degrading rituals of domination and submission that suffused the master/slave relationship. Moreover, many African Americans regarded passive resistance and love for one's oppressor as dubious antidotes for immobilizing fear and resignation. The fissure between civil rights leaders and their rank and file loomed large: by the summer of 1963 a Louis Harris poll showed that 22 percent of black respondents said that they thought they would have to resort to violence to win their rights—five times the percentage of black leaders polled. Moreover, a majority of those surveyed believed that blacks would win in this violent showdown with whites.[6]

The Deacons were a unique phenomenon among civil rights groups—the only independent working-class–controlled organization with national aspirations to emerge during the civil rights movement in the Deep South and the only indigenous African American organization in the South to pose a visible challenge to Martin Luther King and the nonviolent movement orthodoxy.[7] The Deacons were not the first organization to publicly defy the strictures of nonviolence—Robert F. Williams had pioneered the strategy several years earlier in Monroe, North Carolina, when he converted a local National Association for the Advancement of Colored People (NAACP) chapter into a redoubt for armed self-defense. But when the national NAACP drummed Williams out of the organization—with the help of Martin Luther King—he was left without an organizing framework. A riot in Monroe in 1961 caused Williams to flee to Cuba and ended his organizing days inside the United States. The Deacons took a different tact: they formed their own organization outside the mainstream nonviolent groups and mounted a vigorous campaign to expand it throughout the South.[8]

Reflecting class tensions within the African American community, the Deacons spearheaded a working-class revolt against the entrenched black middle-class leadership and its nonviolent reform ideology. In small towns throughout Louisiana, the Deacons assailed the traditional NAACP leaders, a social stratum forged in the old economic order of agricultural dependency and habituated to the politics of accommodation and tactical legalism. They were emblematic of the newly industrialized southern economy that had called into existence a black working class that was no longer the captive of sharecropper servitude. Their political strategy was confrontational, disdainful of nonviolence, and independent of white liberal control.

The Deacons were born in response to two significant developments in 1964: the emergence of a well-organized racist militia—the Ku Klux Klan—and the federal government's appalling failure to enforce the Civil Rights Act and uphold basic constitutional rights and liberties in the South. The Klan's resurgence in 1964 was a direct result of the failure of the Citizens Councils of America. Beginning with the U.S. Supreme Court's 1954 school desegregation decision, the Citizens Councils, dominated by respectable white civic and business leaders, led the opposition to integration efforts across the South. The Councils preferred legal and legislative strategies to violence and terror. But by the 1960s many ardent segregationists regarded the Councils' law-abiding and electoral strategy as an ignominious defeat; the Councils had failed to hold the line against the Yankee invaders.[9]

By 1964 the deteriorating position of the Councils and other old-line segregationists, coupled with the implementation of the Civil Rights Act, sparked a spectacular growth of Klan organizations that advocated terrorist violence and direct action to thwart enforcement of the new law.[10] In towns with large black working-class communities—independent of the old agricultural elite—terrorist violence replaced economic threats as the principal means of social control over blacks. Throughout slavery and Jim Crow, violence had been a major coercive instrument for maintaining white supremacy, and there was little reason to expect that African Americans could successfully avail themselves of the new civil rights laws as long as white violence went unchecked.

The rise of white supremacist violence in response to desegregation made armed self-defense a paramount goal for many local black organizing efforts. Beginning in 1960, the Deep South states blatantly ignored federal authority and openly flouted the Constitution and Bill of Rights. Civil rights activists were routinely beaten and illegally imprisoned with impunity. The First Amendment right of free expression disappeared into the smoke of burning crosses. By 1965 the Ku Klux Klan had, through a well-organized terrorist war, carved out a virtual "Klan nation" in southwestern Mississippi and neighboring southeastern Louisiana—often with the complicity of state and local law enforcement agencies. Within this territory a highly organized and well-disciplined Klan organization fought a successful guerrilla war to defend white caste privilege. The Klan governed the territory on all matters of race. They mobilized thousands of supporters, conducted scores of successful boycotts, published their own newspapers, and staged coups against recalcitrant local governments. It was manifest that there would be no racial progress in this region unless African Americans could devise a stratagem to break the back of white terror.[11]

A full year after passage of the 1964 Civil Rights Act, the Klan's terror campaign had succeeded in preventing enforcement of the law in the Deep South, and most small communities remained rigidly segregated in all public accommodations. President Lyndon Johnson, fearing a political backlash in the South, had avoided a showdown with southern law enforcement and the Klan. "Covenants, without the Sword, are but Words," said Thomas Hobbes, "and of no strength to compel a man at all." The Sword of the Covenant was nowhere to be found in the Deep South. And so the final act of the civil rights movement had been written, complete with a cast of menacing night riders, derelict sheriffs, dawdling federal authorities, and vulnerable African Americans. The fatal limits of nonviolence would soon become clear.[12]

Nonviolence is at the center of the Deacons' story. Much of the popular history of the civil rights era rests on the myth of nonviolence: the perception that the movement achieved its goals through nonviolent direct action. The myth posits that racial inequality was dismantled by a nonviolent movement that awakened the moral conscience of white America. In this narrative Martin Luther King Jr. serves as the "moral metaphor" of the age while black militants—advocates of racial pride and coercive force—are dismissed as ineffective rebels who alienated whites with Black Power rhetoric and violence.[13]

Recent accounts take issue with the idea that the movement relied on moral suasion, instead arguing that King and other civil rights leaders never placed much stock in Mohandas Gandhi's theory of redemptive suffering—the idea that if one suffered racist violence through nonviolent resistance, one could eventually change the hearts and minds of racists. These narratives argue that, even if King began his career believing that black suffering would awaken a sense of "moral shame" in white southern racists, he quickly came to terms with the political limitations of nonviolence and abandoned the strategy. The idealistic pacifist became a hard-nosed pragmatist and turned to a strategy that combined nonviolent tactics with direct action protest—winning reforms through coercion rather than persuasion.[14]

The truth is that King never abandoned his overriding strategy of moral suasion: he did, however, change his target audience. By 1963 King had given up any hope of appealing to the conscience of the white South and instead turned exclusively to the North for his moral appeals. This strategic course placed white liberals and armed self-defense at the center of a conflict that would deeply affect the evolution of the Deacons for Defense.

From the beginning of the modern civil rights movement, opposition to black armed self-defense was an article of faith for national organizations, including King's Southern Christian Leadership Conference (SCLC), the NAACP, the Congress on Racial Equality (CORE) and the Student Nonviolent Coordinating Committee (SNCC)—though SNCC and CORE moderated their official positions near the end of the movement. By opposing armed self-defense, the national civil rights organizations often placed themselves on a collision course with local movements. There were significant differences between the goals and strategies of national and local organizations and campaigns. Locally controlled movements frequently focused on immediate efforts to gain power over segregation, economic needs, and government services. And unrelenting police and vigilante terror compelled local movements to give substantial time and resources to counter violence and intimidation.[15]

In contrast, the national organizations were guided by the thinking that racial inequality—social, economic, and political—could be remedied only by national legislation that removed the civil barriers of segregation and discrimination. This civil rights legislation would be won by coalescing with northern liberals and applying pressure on Congress and the president. White liberals became an indispensable ally for the national civil rights organizations—for legislative reform as well as movement funding. King held to his belief that northern white liberals (and, to some degree, trade union leaders) could be morally persuaded to support the civil rights movement. Toward this end, he sought to gain their sympathy by employing tactics that provoked and exposed the raw white violence that lay under the surface of southern life. The strategy wielded both coercion and moral suasion: coercion against southern whites to create the circumstances for moral suasion in the North.[16]

But winning the sympathy of whites unavoidably meant appeasing white fears of black violence. In the 1950s many northern whites retained old stereotypes of blacks as violent, vengeful, and impulsive. They believed that blacks lacked internal psychological constraints and self-discipline, and that they were incapable of forgiveness and generosity. King was acutely aware of these white fears of violence, and in his first and most important book, *Stride toward Freedom*, published in 1958, he adamantly argued that the civil rights movement had to adopt nonviolence if it wanted to win over northern whites. "Only through a nonviolent approach can the fears of the white community be mitigated," argued King. "A guilt-ridden white minority lives in fear that if the Negro should ever attain power, he would act without restraint or pity to revenge the injustices and brutality. . . . Many white men fear retaliation. The job of the Negro is to show them that they have nothing to fear, that the Negro understands and forgives and is ready to forget the past." To underscore his point, King counseled blacks not to defend themselves against Klan assaults and bombings, but to wear down whites through redemptive suffering: "Bomb our homes and threaten our children; send your hooded perpetrators of violence into our communities and drag us out on some wayside road, beating us half dead, and we will still love you. But we will soon wear you down by our capacity to suffer." If the Klan bombed one home, King urged blacks to submit themselves by the hundreds to more bombings until the terrorists, "forced to stand before the world and his God splattered with the blood of his brother . . . will call an end to his self-defeating massacre."[17]

Sadly, that day of penitence never came for the inveterate racists. But King's early pronouncements on the importance of nonviolence in maintaining the black/liberal coalition set the course for the national movement in the years that followed. King continued to rely on a strategy that required blacks to suffer white violence to win liberal sympathy. During the 1965 Selma campaign King said that the movement was forcing its "oppressor to commit brutality openly—in the light of day—with the rest of the world looking on" and that white violence in Selma would lead "Americans of conscience in the name of decency [to] demand federal intervention and legislation." The movement could not afford to alienate whites. "We can't win our struggle with nonviolence and . . . cloak it under the name of defensive violence," King said in criticizing the Deacons. "The Negro must have allies to win his struggle for equality, and our allies will not surround a violent movement." Using force against the Klan "would only alienate our allies and lose sympathy for our cause."[18]

The position of a civil rights organization on armed self-defense became the litmus test for white liberal support. For an organization to embrace collective self-defense—a right that was taken for granted by whites—was to risk losing critically needed liberal funds and jeopardize the tenuous coalition with northern whites. Not surprisingly, the task of moral suasion ultimately determined the overarching strategy of the national civil rights movement. Major strategic initiatives were measured against the ability to win or retain white northern allies. It was a strategy that had its detractors in the African American community from the beginning. In the 1930s black moderates and conservatives first trumpeted Gandhian nonviolence in an effort to undermine the considerable appeal of Marxism among young blacks.[19] In the 1960s many critics suspected that the partisans of nonviolence once again had ulterior motives; that the exotic philosophical import from the East was merely a method of candy-coating the black revolution to make it palatable to white liberals. Noted black writer Lerone Bennett was among the skeptics. The dilemma for blacks, according to Bennett, was to oppose power but not appear to be rebelling against the status quo. "The history of the Negro in America," wrote Bennett in 1964, ". . . has been a quest for a revolt that was not a revolt—a revolt, in other words, that did not seem to the white power structure as a revolt." Martin Luther King had solved the dilemma, Bennett said, by "clothing a resistance movement in the comforting garb of love and forgiveness."[20]

Nonviolence was ultimately a coalition-based legislative strategy cloaked as religion. In their attempt to assuage white fears of black violence, the national organizations took a stand against self-defense that placed them at odds with local movements besieged by police and Klan violence and hobbled by passive stereotypes. By giving the luster of religious precept to a pragmatic stratagem to attract white liberals—while accommodating liberal fears of black violence—the national civil rights leadership took the high moral ground and made their critics look like nihilistic advocates of violence. In truth, defense groups like the Deacons used weapons to *avoid* violence. And they raised important and legitimate questions about a strategy that pinned its hopes on liberals, organized labor and the federal government. CORE activist Lincoln Lynch summed up the doubts of the dissenters from nonviolence: "History has shown that if you're really depending on the vast majority of whites to help, you're leaning on a very broken reed."[21]

The Deacons came to see nonviolence as a "broken reed" strategy that offered little support or protection. The nonviolent strategy had its strengths and made enormous accomplishments, but they came at a high price for many African American men in the South. This is not to second-guess the choices made by national civil rights organizations, but to understand the limitations of nonviolence and how it shaped the ultimate outcome of the movement—and continues to affect American racial politics to this day.[22]

The escalating attacks by the Ku Klux Klan in 1964 thrust the Deacons for Defense and Justice into the middle of a national debate on nonviolence. More than a defense group, the Deacons grew into a symbolic political organization that played a key role in the battle against nonviolent movement orthodoxy. They represented the black working class's fledgling attempt to create a new black consciousness. They preached self-reliance rather than dependence on the government for rights and freedom; they sought reform by force and coercion rather than by pacifism and moral suasion; and they repudiated the strategy of winning white approbation through suffering. Freedom was to be won through fear and respect, rather than guilt and pity. In short, they believed that *to be free* blacks had to act free.[23]

Beginnings

1

EARNEST THOMAS HAD been a fighter all his life. Born in Jonesboro, Louisiana, on 20 November 1935, Thomas was descended from a long line of independent tradesmen and farmers. He came of age in the Deep South under the system of segregation, yet he knew white people as well as his own folk. Racial segregation fought a relentless battle against human nature—against the instinctual longing for companionship and shared joy among members of the human race. The intimacy of everyday life tempted people to disregard the awkward rituals of segregation. In his youth Thomas had frequented the local swimming hole in Jonesboro, a gentle creek that wound its way through the pines. Its tranquil waters welcomed children of all colors. Here black and white children innocently played together, splashing and dunking. At a distance, colors disappeared into a shadow silhouette of bobbing heads, the languid summer air disturbed only by occasional shrieks of joy.[1]

Yet inevitably nature surrendered to the mean habits of adult society. Thomas recalled that sometimes the whites would band together and swoop down on a handful of frolicking blacks, claiming the waters as the spoils of war. On other occasions, Thomas would join a charging army of whooping black warriors as they descended on the stream, scattering a gaggle of unsuspecting white boys. The swimming hole wars of his youth provided Earnest Thomas with one enduring lesson: rights were secured by force more often than by appeals to reason and moral argument.

In the summer of 1964 Thomas was swept up in a new phase of the civil rights movement and became a leader of the founding chapter of the Deacons for Defense and Justice. How the most widely known armed self-defense organization in the Deep South came into existence in a remote Louisiana town, far removed from the movement centers and media limelight, in itself speaks volumes about a largely invisible conflict within the civil rights movement between the partisans of nonviolence that descended on the South and an emerging working-class movement that resisted pacifism in the face of police and vigilante terror.

In the nineteenth century the pine hills of North Louisiana were a hostile refuge for the poor and dispossessed. Following the Civil War, legions of starving and desperate whites were driven into the pine hills by destruction, drought, and depleted soil in the Southeast. They arrived to find the best alluvial land controlled by large landowners and speculators. The remaining soil was poorly suited for farming, rendered haggard and sallow by millennia of acidic pine needles deposited on the forest floor. The lean migrants scratched the worthless sandy soil, shook their heads, and resigned themselves to the unhappy fate of subsistence farming.

Upcountry whites eked out a living with a dozen acres of "corn and 'taters," a few hogs for fatback, trapping and hunting for game, and occasionally logging for local markets. Not until the turn of the century, when the large-scale lumber industry invaded the pines, did their hopes and prospects change. Even then, prosperity was fleeting. By the 1930s the lumber leviathans had stripped the pine woods bare, leaving a residue of a few paper and lumber mills. Those fortunate enough to find work in the pulp and paper industry watched helplessly in the 1950s and 1960s as even these remaining jobs were threatened by shrinking reserves and automation.[2]

These Protestant descendants of the British Isles were the latest in several generations of whites forced west by a slave-based economy that rapidly expended the very soil it arose from. With the end of the Civil War their plight was compounded by more than three million black freedmen surging across the South in search of work and land. Emancipation thrust blacks into merciless competition with whites for the dearth of work, land, and credit.

The freedmen also looked to the pines for deliverance. Blacks who remained on plantations lived in constant fear of new forms of bondage such as gang labor and sharecropping. Thousands of dusty, tattered black families packed their belongings and trekked into the hills to escape the indignities of debt peonage. Like their white competitors, the freedmen sought the dignity and independence conferred by a few acres of land and the freedom to sell their labor.

The pine hills were soon peopled by the most independent and self-sufficient African Americans: those willing to risk everything to escape economic bondage. Their passionate independence flourished in the hills as they worked as self-employed timber cutters and log haulers. By the middle of the twentieth century many of their descendants had left the land, drawn to the small industrial towns that offered decent wages in lumber and paper mills.

From the end of the Civil War through the 1960s these two fiercely independent communities, black and white, traveled separate yet parallel paths in the pine hills of North Louisiana. In the summer of 1964, in the small town of Jonesboro, these two worlds would finally cross paths—as well as swords.

Jonesboro was one of dozens of makeshift mill towns that sprang up as eastern businesses rushed to mine the vast timber spreads of Louisiana. Incorporated in 1903, the town was little more than an appendage to a sawmill—crude shacks storing the human machinery of industry.

By the 1960s Jonesboro lived in the shadow of the enormous Continental Can Company paper mill located in Hodge, a small town on the outskirts of Jonesboro. The New York–based company produced container board and kraft paper at the Hodge facility and employed more than 1,500 whites and 200 blacks. In addition, many blacks found employment at the Olin Mathieson Chemical Company. Those blacks who were not fortunate enough to find work in the paper mill labored as destitute woodcutters and log haulers on the immense timber landholdings owned by Continental Can.[3]

Almost one-third of Jonesboro's 3,848 residents were black. Though by southern standards Jonesboro's black community was prosperous, poverty and ignorance were still rampant. Nearly eight out of every ten black families lived in poverty. Ninety-seven percent of blacks over the age of twenty-five had never completed a high school education. The "black quarters" in Jonesboro and Hodge consisted of dilapidated clapboard shacks, with cracks in the walls that whistled in the bitter winter wind. Human waste ran into the dirt streets for want of a sewerage system. Unpaved streets with exotic names like "Congo" and "Tarbottom" served alternately as dust storms and impassable rivers of mud.[4]

Daily life in Jonesboro painstakingly followed the rituals and conventions of Jim Crow segregation. A white person walking downtown could expect blacks to obsequiously avert their eyes and step off the sidewalk in deference. Jobs were strictly segregated, with blacks allotted positions no higher than "broom and mop" occupations. The local hospital had an all-white staff, and the paper mill segregated both jobs and toilets. Blacks were even denied the simple right to walk into the public library.[5]

On the surface there appeared to be few diversions from the tedium and poverty. The ramshackle "Minute Spot" tavern served as the only legal drinking establishment for blacks. To Danny Mitchell, a black student organizer who arrived in Jonesboro in 1964, Jonesboro's African Americans appeared to take refuge in gambling and other unseemly pastimes. Mitchell, with a note of youthful piety, once reported to his superiors in New York that most of Jonesboro's black community "seeks enjoyment and relief from the frustrating life they endure through marital, extramarital, and inter-marital relationships."[6]

But there was more to Jonesboro than sex and dice. Indeed, segregation had produced a complex labyrinth of social networks and organizations in the black community. The relatively large industrial working class preserved the independent spirit that characterized blacks in the pine woods. As in many other small mill towns, blacks in Jonesboro had created a tightly knit community that revolved around the institutions of church and fraternal orders. In the post–World War II era, black men in the South frequently belonged to several fraternal orders and social clubs, such as the Prince Hall Masons and the Brotherhood for the Protection of Elks. These formal and informal organizations provided a respite from the oppressive white culture. They offered status, nurtured mutual bonds of trust, and served as schools for leadership for Jonesboro's black working and middle classes.[7]

In the period of increased activism following World War II, most of Jonesboro's civil rights leadership emerged from the small yet significant middle class of educators, self-employed craftsmen, and independent business people (religious leaders were conspicuously absent from the ranks of the reformers). While segregation denied blacks many opportunities, it also created captive markets for some enterprising blacks, particularly in services that whites refused to provide them. There were twenty-one black-owned businesses in Jonesboro in 1964, including taxi companies, gas stations, and a popular skating rink.[8]

The black Voters League of Jonesboro drew its leadership primarily from the ranks of businessmen and educators, such as W. C. Flannagan, E. N. Francis, J. W. Dade, and Fred Hearn. Flannagan, who led the league in the early 1960s, was a self-employed handyman who also published a small newsletter. Francis owned several businesses, including a funeral home, grocery store, barber shop, and dry-cleaning store. Dade was, by local standards, a man of considerable wealth. He taught mathematics at Jackson High School and supplemented his teaching salary with income from a dozen rental houses. Hearn was also a teacher and worked as a farmer and installed and cleaned water wells.[9]

Jackson Parish (county), where Jonesboro is located, had had a small but well-organized chapter of the National Association for the Advancement of Colored People (NAACP) since the 1940s. In 1956 the Louisiana NAACP was gravely damaged by a state law that required disclosure of membership.

Rather than divulge members' names and expose them to harassment, many chapters replaced the NAACP with "civic and voters leagues." Such was the case in Jackson Parish, where the NAACP became the "Jackson Parish Progressive Voters League." From its inception, the Voters League concentrated on voter registration and enjoyed some success. When the White Citizens Council and the Registrar of Voters conspired to purge blacks from the registration rolls in 1956, the Voters League retaliated with a voting rights suit initiated by the Justice Department. The Voters League prevailed and federal courts eventually forced the registrar to cease discriminating against blacks, to report records to the federal judiciary, and to assist black applicants in registering to vote. By 1964 nearly 18 percent of the parish voters were black, a remarkably high percentage for the rural South.[10]

The Voters League never commanded enough votes to win elective office for a black candidate. For the most part, the league was limited to delivering the black vote to white candidates in exchange for political favors. Although political patronage offered some benefits to the black community at large, it more frequently created opportunities for personal aggrandizement. At its worse, patronage disguised greed as public service. Some Voters League critics felt that its leaders were principally interested in gaining personal favors from politicians, and there was credence to the charge.[11]

In truth, the white political establishment offered a tempting assortment of patronage rewards to compliant black leaders in an effort to discourage them from conducting disruptive civil rights protests. Inducements included positions in government and public education, ranging from school bus drivers to school administrators. White political patronage bought influence and loyalty in the black community. The practice testified to the fact that white domination rested on more than repression and fear: it depended on consent by a segment of the black middle class. Conflicts over segregation were to be resolved by gentlemen behind closed doors. Time and again, civil rights activists in Louisiana found the black middle class and clergy to be significant obstacles to organizing. One activist in East Felicana Parish reported that the lack of interest in voter registration in 1964 could be attributed to, among other things, the "general fear-inducing activity of the very active community of Toms. Every move we make is broadcast by them to the whole town."[12]

Indeed, the "mass meeting" technique represented a rudimentary form of working-class control over the black middle class and redefined the political decision-making process in the black community. Prior to the civil rights movement, racial conflicts and issues were normally negotiated by intermediaries: middle-class power brokers, the NAACP, or the Voters Leagues.

During the civil rights movement direct democracy mass meetings assembled the black community to make decisions by consensus, a process that functioned not only to build community support for the leaders' decisions, but also to prevent middle-class leaders from making secret agreements and compromises with the white power structure. Plebiscitary democracy guaranteed that all agreements had to pass muster with the black rank and file: the working class, the poor, and the youth.[13]

There were good reasons for the suspicions exhibited by the rank and file. Black leadership was more complex and divided than the undifferentiated, united image reflected in the popular historical myth of the civil rights movement. The movement did not march in unison and speak with one voice. The black community had its share of traitors, rascals, and ordinary fools. In general, though, the leaders of the Voters League in Jonesboro were honorable men who had the community's interests at heart. Nonetheless, it was difficult for the league to generate enthusiasm for voting rights when the ballot benefited only a handful of elite blacks. For most black voters in Jonesboro, elections offered little more than a Hobson's choice between racism and more racism.

Deep divisions existed between the black clergy and the movement in Jonesboro. Only one church, Pleasant Grove Baptist Church, initially supported the movement. Pleasant Grove had a highly active and concerned membership, led by Henry and Ruth Amos who operated a gas station and Percy Lee Bradford, a cab driver and mill worker. The dearth of civil rights church leaders in Jonesboro was no anomaly. In both large cities and small towns in the South, the attitude of black clergy toward the movement generally ranged from indifference to outright hostility. Medgar Evers, the martyred Mississippi NAACP leader, once grumbled that the ministers "won't give us 50 cents for fear of losing face with the white man." Martin Luther King did not mince words about the complacency of his brothers of the collar in Birmingham: "I'm tired of preachers riding around in big cars, living in fine homes, but not willing to fight their part," said King. "If you can't stand up with your own people, you are not fit to be a leader."[14]

The conservative character of rural black clergy was owing to several factors. Church buildings were vulnerable to arson in retaliation for civil rights activities (black churches in the South were frequently located outside of town in remote, unguarded areas). It was common for insurance companies to cancel insurance on churches that had been active in the movement. Moreover, black ministers depended on good relationships with whites to obtain loans for the all-important brick-and-mortar building projects.

But the clergy's conservatism was also emblematic of the contradictory character of the black church. On the one hand, the church was a force for change. It provided a safe and nurturing sanctuary in a hostile, oppressive world. In the midst of despair, it forged a new community, nourished racial solidarity, defined community values, and provided pride and hope. And when it adopted the twentieth-century "social gospel" theology, as practiced by Martin Luther King, the black church could even be a powerful vehicle for social justice and national redemption.

In contrast to this uplifting role, though, the black church could also lapse into a fatalistic outlook that bred passivity and political cynicism. Fatalism is a rational and effective adaptation in reactionary times when people live on hope alone. Some of the black clergy preached the gospel of resignation— extolling the glories of heaven and eschewing social and political reform— and, worse yet, honored the color line and its attendant traditions of deference. During the Montgomery Bus Boycott, black leader E. D. Nixon gave voice to the frustration that many felt with the black clergy. "Let me tell you gentlemen one thing," Nixon told a group of ministers he had gathered to organize the boycott. "You ministers have lived off of these wash-women for the last hundred years and ain't never done nothing for them." Nixon scolded that it was shameful that women were leading the boycott while the ministers were afraid to even have their names published as supporters. "We've worn aprons all our lives. It's time to take the aprons off . . . if we're gonna be mens, now's the time to be mens."[15]

In contrast to the spotty record of the black church in the rural movement, the black fraternal orders were frequently the backbone of resistance. Fraternal orders such as the black Masons (e.g., Prince Hall) and Elks were woven into the fabric of rural southern black life in the early 1950s and 1960s. Fraternal halls frequently served as meeting spaces for civil rights activities and self-organized fraternal institutions—free of the constraints of Christian pacifism promulgated by the church—were one of the primary cultural mechanisms for sustaining black masculine ideals of honor, physical courage, and protection of family and community. Nearly all of the male civil rights activists in Jonesboro belonged to one or more of these orders.[16]

There were exceptions to the conservative churches, and the Pleasant Grove Baptist Church in Jonesboro was one of them. The church had attracted several firm civil rights advocates and in late 1963 members of Pleasant Grove, along with the Voters League, invited the Congress of Racial Equality (CORE) to initiate voter registration activities in Jonesboro and Jackson Parish. Well known in the Louisiana movement, CORE was preparing a major summer project in 1964. Part of the new breed of national civil rights organizations, it was young, energetic, and committed to nonviolent direct action. At the height of the modern civil rights movement in 1960–65, four national organizations led organizing efforts in the South. The two largest and best financed were the venerable NAACP, working primarily through its local chapters and state offices, and the smaller but higher-profile Southern Christian Leadership Conference (SCLC), organized by Martin Luther King. The Student Nonviolent Coordinating Committee (SNCC), which grew out of the 1960s sit-in movement, was also initiated by King's organization, but it soon took on a life of its own and became the dominant national organization in Mississippi. CORE worked throughout the South but Louisiana was one of its strongholds; the group had been active in the state since the 1960 sit-ins.[17]

Formed in 1942, CORE originated as a predominantly white pacifist organization, emerging out of the Fellowship of Reconciliation, a Christian pacifist group that had been active since World War I. The early leaders of CORE were profoundly influenced by the nonviolent teachings of Mohandas Gandhi. At the center of their strategy was the concept of nonviolent direct action: moral conversion through nonviolent protest. CORE advocated direct action and militant protest without violence or hatred against the opponent. Its principles prohibited members from retaliating against violence inflicted on them. Nonviolence would convert their enemies through "love and suffering." The organization had pragmatic as well as philosophical reasons for advocating nonviolence in the South: CORE's black leaders, such as James Farmer and Bayard Rustin, feared a brutal white backlash if blacks engaged in retaliatory violence.[18]

Despite its strong commitment to racial justice and community activism, CORE had made only modest progress in the black community in the 1940s and 1950s. Its greatest achievement was the 1947 Journey of Reconciliation, a desegregation test of a Supreme Court decision that banned segregated seating in interstate travel. Interracial testing teams attempted to integrate buses in the upper South but encountered strong opposition and failed to galvanize a broader movement. But in 1961 CORE catapulted into the ranks of national civil rights organizations through its role in the electrifying Freedom Rides. Courageous CORE activists led integrated groups on bus rides through the South in a campaign to integrate interstate travel facilities. They braved mobs, beatings, firebombs, and jails. By 1962 they had triumphed in integrating most bus travel and terminal accommodations.[19]

In the early years of the movement the membership of both CORE and SNCC took their pacifism seriously. CORE's roots were in ecumenical religious pacifism, whereas SNCC's drew on philosophy and modern religion—finding its moorings in Gandhi, the reform-minded social gospel, and existentialism.

Nonviolence and its faith in moral suasion were embedded in the genetic material of SNCC at its founding Raleigh Conference, in 1960, where King proclaimed that the "philosophy of nonviolence" was a central theme of the conference and the idea of "reconciliation" with one's enemies—in this case, he meant white southerners—was paramount. "Our ultimate end must be the creation of the beloved community," declared King. "The tactics of nonviolence without the spirit of nonviolence may indeed become a new kind of violence." Later, when the organizers were drafting SNCC's goals, Nashville sit-in leader James Lawson opposed making "integration" the first and foremost goal; instead, he insisted that it should be nonviolence. He won the day.[20]

SNCC activists attempted to apply their Gandhian strategy in Greenwood, Mississippi, the first major SNCC project launched in 1961. Bob Moses, SNCC's most influential leader, initially attempted to persuade local blacks not to take up weapons in self-defense. As time went on and the hope for federal protection waned, for many SNCC and CORE activists nonviolence became more a political tactic than a universal imperative. By 1963 and the Birmingham campaign, even Martin Luther King had abandoned hope of winning the hearts of white southerners; he opted for a strategy of confrontation with the white South to gain sympathy from the white North. Some SNCC activists turned a blind eye to local armed self-defense, and by 1964 many SNCC staffers carried weapons themselves. But whatever misgivings SNCC activists had about pious nonviolence, they kept their concerns to themselves. From 1960 to 1965 SNCC consistently and assiduously cultivated a public image as a devoutly nonviolent organization. As late as the spring of 1964, when many black intellectuals and activists were questioning the effectiveness of nonviolence, SNCC leader John Lewis told *Dialogue Magazine* that although SNCC was reexamining its pacifist doctrine, "The shedding of blood is not part of our framework; it's not a part of our philosophy," and he personally accepted "the philosophy of nonviolence." When asked if this doctrinaire commitment to pacifism was at odds with the mass movement's growing dissatisfaction with nonviolence, Lewis admitted that SNCC had a problem. "I'm not sure whether SNCC as an organization is ready and prepared to catch up with the masses," he said.[21]

Indeed, the debate on armed self-defense did not make its way onto SNCC's national agenda until near the end of the movement, when the organization finally supported the right of local people to defend themselves—something black Mississippians had been doing all along. At a national staff meeting in Atlanta on 10 June 1964, the issue emerged when the SNCC leadership learned that Greenwood SNCC staff were arming themselves. Reports during the meeting left little doubt that guns in the SNCC Freedom Houses were the least of their concerns; local people everywhere in Mississippi were arming themselves and encouraging SNCC to arm as well—much to the consternation of many SNCC staff members. Hollis Watkins noted that although local people had always kept guns in their homes for protection, the mood had changed. "There was a nonviolent attitude then," said Watkins. Charles McLaurin reported that members of the Revolutionary Action Movement (RAM), a black Marxist nationalist group, were successfully promoting armed self-defense among black farmers in the Mississippi Delta, despite the best efforts of SNCC staffer James Jones to "stamp out the ideas brought in by outside groups" that were "killing formerly workable ways." Some staff wondered aloud if armed self-defense might lead to a bloody pogrom against blacks. The dangers posed by the upcoming Freedom Summer were undeniable, but black staff member Prathia Hall reminded the group of its nonviolent faith in redemptive suffering and how, as Martin Luther King had argued in the early days of the movement, white violence that met no resistance would eventually shame the federal government into intervening. "We must bring the reality of our situation to the nation," said Hall. "Bring the blood onto the white house door. If we die here it's the whole society that has pulled the trigger by its silence." Hall's comments reflected the prevailing attitude among the devotees of nonviolence: the blood of the persecuted, not the persecutor, was the only blood of salvation. Still, many staff members were reluctant to not accept the protection proffered by local people. After intense debate, SNCC passed a resolution that local people had the right to defend themselves and SNCC would not discipline staffers who local people happened to protect. SNCC then reaffirmed its policy that no weapons were allowed in the Freedom Houses or in any SNCC office or project; nor would SNCC staff or volunteers be allowed to carry weapons; if volunteers were caught with guns, they would be expelled from the organization. Moses dispatched Stokely Carmichael to Greenwood to squelch the armed self-defense project. SNCC continued to proselytize for nonviolence during the 1964 Freedom Summer, and its training programs flooded the South with hundreds of new idealistic adherents of nonviolence. At the Freedom Summer volunteer training center in Oxford, Ohio, more than nine hundred volunteers went through nonviolent training led by devout pacifist ideologues like James Lawson. And in most projects, local African Americans drawn into the movement were required to undergo nonviolence training in preparation for attacks by police or vigilantes. So even as SNCC activists became disillusioned with nonviolence and the black/liberal coalition, particularly after the disappointing 1964 Democratic National Convention, the public image of SNCC and the national civil rights movement, for friends and foes alike, remained a nonviolent one.[22]

CORE in Louisiana began with the same kind of commitment to nonviolent idealism as SNCC. Dave Dennis, who later became a major movement leader, recalled that members of the New Orleans CORE chapter engaged in fasts and vows of silence to prepare themselves for the discipline of nonviolence. CORE volunteers were required to take an oath that they would "meet the anger of any individual or group in the spirit of good will" and "submit to assault and will not retaliate in kind by act or word." The young white CORE workers tended to be the more devout pacifists, according to CORE leader Ronnie Moore, a black native-born Louisianan, and there was always a division between the national CORE leadership based in New York and the chapters in the South. Moore's introduction to the movement occurred when he attended a workshop on nonviolence in the fall of 1961 while a student at Southern University in Baton Rouge. But after two years in the trenches—including fifty-seven days in solitary confinement for a charge of "criminal anarchy" (attempting to overthrow the government of Louisiana)—Moore regarded nonviolence as more of a tactic than a philosophical precept. Civil rights workers had varying levels of commitment to the principle of nonviolence: some were "philosophical" Gandhians who believed that nonviolence was a universal moral imperative; that it was the only path to lasting peace; that redemptive suffering could indeed transform enemies. Other activists fell within the "strategic nonviolence" category: they felt that there were occasions when defensive violence was necessary and acceptable, but that by refraining from violence, the movement could assert moral superiority over racists and win sympathy from liberals and the world community. Still to others, nonviolence was merely "tactical"; they held no illusions about converting enemies. For them, nonviolence was an expedient protest method, valued because it won sympathy for the movement; more important, it deprived racists of an excuse to escalate their violence during an encounter. Movement people were constantly cautioning community members that defensive violence would invite a "bloodbath." One young black volunteer from Tallulah, Louisiana, told an interviewer that, although he was not a pacifist, he accepted the doctrine because CORE had told him that "all the southern white man wants is for the Negro to hit him so he can kill him." The volunteers streaming into the South for the 1964 summer projects reflected all these viewpoints, often with overlaps, but most agreed on one thing: nonviolence was the most effective way to appeal to the conscience of northerners and encourage federal intervention.[23]

Ronnie Moore clearly fit into the tactical nonviolence category. In 1963 he caused a minor controversy when he publicly suggested that armed self-defense was justified in CORE's campaign in St. Francisville, Louisiana. But, as in the case of SNCC, Moore remained discreet about the armed self-defense activities around CORE projects, primarily to assuage the national office's fear of losing white liberal support. Moore kept his silence on armed activities even during the rise of the Deacons. "So I guess the deepest prayer in the [national office] was that whatever comments that we make in support of the Deacons, that they would never hit the *New York Times*," recalled Moore with a laugh. "And so we didn't make too many public statements." Local blacks also guarded several CORE Freedom Houses in the Deep South as early as 1962, according to movement veteran Michael Flug, but even the black defenders "were not interested in publicly advocating armed self-defense." The movement was "playing to the media," recalled Flug, and publicizing armed self-defense "tactically . . . wasn't a good idea."[24]

In 1964 CORE planned an ambitious "Louisiana Summer 1964" project, CORE's counterpart of the Mississippi Freedom Summer. The Louisiana project was to focus on voter registration and desegregation of public facilities and public accommodations. CORE had already established several local projects in the state, including a beachhead in North Louisiana in Monroe, about sixty miles east of Jonesboro. Monroe's moderate NAACP leadership had invited CORE to organize the community, but CORE had little success until it linked up with more militant working-class union leaders at the Olin-Mathieson paper plant. Police harassment and an uncooperative registrar of voters seriously hampered CORE's efforts. From the outset, the civil rights group's presence rankled the Ku Klux Klan, and it was not long before the Klan burned crosses on the lawn of the house where two CORE workers were staying.[25]

The first CORE organizers to visit Jonesboro were representative of the social mix of CORE's field staff. Mike Lesser was a white northerner with no experience in organizing in the South; in contrast, his black colleague Ronnie Moore was a seasoned organizer with eighteen arrests. Beginning in January 1964, Lesser and Moore made several trips to Jonesboro to assist the Voters League and local high school students in launching a voter registration campaign. Their initial success prompted CORE to assign several task force workers to Jonesboro in the late spring of 1964 in preparation for the summer project.[26]

One of the first arrivals for the summer project was Catherine (Cathy) Patterson, a young African American from Birmingham. Patterson had been deeply moved by an experience at the George Washington Carver High

School, in Birmingham, where she was a classmate of Fred Shuttlesworth Jr., the son of Birmingham's firebrand civil rights leader, the Reverend Fred Shuttlesworth. One day young Shuttlesworth arrived at school with his face badly bruised and swollen. A racist mob had mercilessly beaten him and his father during a demonstration. "When I heard about that, it just moved me to action," recalled Patterson. "I guess I was outraged. It's one thing to hear about it, and it's another thing to see it on television. But to see someone that you are sitting next to in class severely beaten . . . he was a child, just like I was."[27]

The incident inspired Patterson to plunge into political activism, first leading demonstrations in Birmingham and later joining CORE after graduating from high school in January 1963. She was first sent to Gadsden, Alabama, for nine months of organizing and then on to Atlanta for nonviolence training. At the training session, Patterson met most of the team that would be assigned to the summer project in Jonesboro. Among them was Ruthie Wells, a young black from Baton Rouge, and the two white activists: William "Bill" Yates, a Cornell University English professor, and Mike Weaver.[28]

After completing her training, Patterson was dispatched to Jonesboro in the spring of 1964, joining Danny Mitchell, a Syracuse University graduate student. Eventually the Jonesboro summer project contingent comprised half a dozen activists; four blacks and two whites. Fear in the black community was so acute in Jonesboro that no local black family offered to house the CORE activists. The task force workers had to settle for a small house on Cedar Street in the black community, lent to them by a sympathetic black woman who had moved to California. The CORE workers christened the small home "Freedom House" and set about organizing voter registration.

The young Jonesboro activists took seriously the idea that their enemies could be converted by the moral strength of nonviolence. As one CORE volunteer in Bogalusa put it, they felt that if there was violence against the movement, "the good people, who have a good conscience, will recognize the brutalities, and it will work on their conscience." In this sense, they were more idealistic than most of the Freedom Summer volunteers, the majority of whom probably regarded nonviolence as a path to hearts in the North—not the South. Nonetheless, Cathy Patterson had been schooled in nonviolence by devoted Gandhians like James Bevel, and when she arrived in Jonesboro she immediately began earnestly searching for sympathetic white supporters among town locals. It was a short search. Virtually all the town's leaders were segregationists, including Sheriff Newt T. Loe (a "rabid segregationist," noted Danny Mitchell) and Police Chief Adrian Peevy. CORE discovered only one sympathetic white person, the town pharmacist, but this lone convert preferred to keep his conscience to himself.[29]

The new CORE activists were undeterred by these failures, remaining confident in their nonviolent faith and secure in the knowledge that history was on their side. For the young crusaders, nonviolence seemed to be sweeping the world, drawing sustenance from Gandhi's success in India—one of the first fruitful anticolonial revolutions following World War II.

But theirs was a misplaced confidence, rooted in a limited—if not naive—understanding of southern history. Gandhi's strategy would be difficult to transfer to the United States: "Bombingham" was not Bombay. There were critical differences between India's anticolonial struggle and the black liberation struggle unfolding in the Deep South. East Indians were the vast majority in their homeland, far outnumbering their oppressors, who constituted little more than a tiny occupying army. Support for colonialism by the British people was waning in the postwar years. In general, British workers did not believe that their social and economic status depended on the continued exploitation of Indians. Cold War rhetoric exalting democracy and freedom made it difficult for the British to use force to suppress the rebellion. Thus, Gandhi had the advantage of engaging a distant enemy that was constrained from using violence by domestic indifference and international opinion.

The United States was a different matter. In contrast to East Indians, blacks were a tiny minority surrounded by a white majority. And unlike the British working class, white southerners were invested in domination. Slavery protected whites from the most degrading forms of labor and provided them with relative economic security, status, and privilege. The slave system had transformed poor whites into gendarmes for white supremacy. Time and again, whites demonstrated that they were willing and eager to defend their caste position at the expense of black life and freedom. Moreover, the geographic proximity of whites facilitated their use of terror as a political tool. And use it they did. Emancipation made little difference. Whites resorted to wholesale violence to overthrow the biracial Reconstruction governments. In the years of de jure segregation that followed, white social and economic status continued to be predicated on black subjugation. The benefits of segregation constantly reinforced white loyalty to racism and violence. While international opinion may have influenced the British peerage, it meant nothing to planters in the Mississippi Delta, let alone "corn and 'tater" whites in the piney woods.

It was these underlying material and social interests that made segregation resistant to moral appeal. Few in the United Kingdom believed that Indian independence betokened the end of British economic security or culture. But southern society rested on white supremacy. The death of segregation meant the death of the old social order. Segregationists were not far from the truth when they charged that integration was revolution. The new abolitionists were asking southern whites for more than their hearts and minds: they were demanding their caste status and the privileges pertaining thereto. It is little mystery, then, why nonviolence failed to evoke love and compassion in the hearts of southern whites.[30]

The old social order was not going to relent without battle in Jonesboro, and the reality of violence soon became a concern for the CORE task force. Police harassment had always been troublesome for civil rights activists in the South, and the Jonesboro police did occasionally tail activists during their voter registration visits in the countryside. But by southern standards, Jonesboro's police department treated CORE reasonably well. Danny Mitchell described the police chief's policy toward CORE as "I'm here to protect you . . . but we don't want any demonstrations."[31]

The Klan and other racist vigilantes posed a graver danger. From the outset, menacing carloads of young whites targeted the Freedom House as they cruised through the black community and shouted obscenities and threats. This type of harassment was not new. For years, whites, acting with impunity, would drive through the black "quarters" verbally harassing and physically assaulting residents. The practice, referred to as "nigger knocking," was a time-honored tradition among whites in the rural South. But the presence of black and white civil rights activists in the community added a frenzied intensity to the ritual. It was not long before verbal assaults turned to violence. In one foreboding incident, a gang of young whites broke several windows at the Freedom House. The black community responded to the attacks with a mix of concern and uncertainty. They had never been confronted with the challenge of defending strangers in their midst. Caution was the order of the day. A reckless display of armed self-defense might provoke whites to retaliate with deadly force.

The unwritten racial code of conduct in the South forbade blacks from using collective forms of self-defense, a prohibition that stemmed from ancient fears of bloody slave rebellions. The black community in Jonesboro anxiously searched for a way to defend their charges without violating the racial code, but the imminent threat of violence left few alternatives. Within a few days, a small number of local black men began to quietly guard the CORE activists. Slowly they appeared, unarmed sentinels, silent and watchful. At first they did nothing more than sit on the porch of the Freedom

House or follow the activists like quiet shadows as they went about their organizing work.[32]

Among this initial group of guards was Earnest Thomas. The short, powerfully built twenty-nine-year-old supported his five children as a paper mill worker, mason, and handyman. His life centered on the institutions and amusements of small-town African American life: he was an occasional churchgoer, a member of the black Scottish Rite Masons, and a devotee of barroom dice games. Held at arms length by the "respectable" black middle class, Thomas nonetheless commanded community respect for his courage and martial skills. His street savvy and cool, intimidating demeanor earned him the nickname "Chilly Willy." "Chilly was very firm," recalled Annie Purnell Johnson, a local CORE volunteer. "He didn't care. Whatever he said he was going to do, he did it." His determination was accented by his penchant for force. "He was violent too," said Johnson. "He could be very violent if he wanted to be. If you pushed his button, he *would* deliver."[33]

Thomas attended high school in Jonesboro through the eleventh grade, then dropped out and served a stint in the air force during the Korean War. Like many young blacks in the South, military service dramatically changed his attitude toward Jim Crow. Three years and eight months as an airborne radio operator had afforded him brief and seductive glimpses of a world free of segregation. He met northern blacks who, with a better education and more opportunities, were increasingly impatient with the slow pace of change. Thomas absorbed their restless craving for freedom. The military also provided him, and thousands of other southern blacks, with the tools to realize this dream of freedom: leadership skills and an appreciation of the power of disciplined collective action. Discharged from the service, Thomas spurned the South and journeyed northward to Chicago. He worked for one year at International Harvester but soon returned to Jonesboro to raise a family.

Thomas was eager to work with CORE, but he had serious reservations about the nonviolent terms imposed by the young activists. He admired their devotion and energy, but the college students seemed dangerously naive about the potential for terrorist violence. CORE made it clear to Thomas that it was unwilling to compromise its stand on nonviolence. It had a long-standing policy that activists should not accept armed protection from local people. In Gulfport, Mississippi, one Freedom Summer participant recounted how the volunteers had rebuffed offers of protection, much to the dismay of local residents. "We had a problem with a man . . . who took it upon himself to protect us from the white men who visited us yesterday," the volunteer wrote. "He came over at night with his friends and brought along a machine gun and ammunition and told us not to worry. But he finally got ticked off at us, because we got ticked off at him. That machine gun had us edgy."[34]

If the CORE activists sounded like missionaries, there was a good reason. Theirs was a religious style of organizing, characterized by an evangelical faith in doctrine and an unswerving belief in a bipolar world of good and evil. Religious doctrine, as immutable truth, could not be compromised to suit the sinner. One either accepted or rejected the divinely inspired word. One was either saint or sinner.[35]

Like most black men in the South, however, Earnest Thomas thought it better to be damned than dead. He and the other men in the defense group politely resisted CORE's attempt to dictate the terms of the local movement. Indeed, there was little support for the nonviolence that CORE was advocating among black southerners. Even James Lawson, the movement's foremost spokesperson for Gandhian nonviolence, admitted later that there "never has been an acceptance of the nonviolent approach" in the South and the idea that blacks had initially accepted nonviolence and then became disillusioned was "nonsense."[36]

Thomas quickly emerged as the leader of the defense group. No doubt his military training had accustomed him to organization. While other men would come and go, Thomas made it his responsibility to elevate the level of organization and instill discipline and order. During the day, the guards simply watched and kept their weapons concealed. But at night the veil of darkness provided cover for hooded terrorists. The guards knew that a show of weapons would discourage Klan violence. So the night brought the moon, the stars, and the guns.

Guns posed a dilemma for CORE from the very beginning. The defense group had no difficulty in accepting CORE's right to determine its own nonviolent strategy and, on the whole, thought it an effective one. But its members were not prepared to abdicate their responsibility to defend their community. They were unwilling to extend nonviolence to all aspects of the black freedom movement, particularly in the center of a Klan stronghold. That would be suicide. They were outnumbered two-to-one, and the police offered no protection.

Underlying the conflict over nonviolence was a deeper issue of autonomy. Who would determine the local organizing strategy for the black movement? Should it be the national organizations, with their imported strategy, dominated by a coalition of middle-class blacks, organized labor, and white pacifists and liberals? Or would the local community, with its own strategy determined by local experience, prevail? CORE initially won the philosophical argument, overcoming locals with superior debating skills and the force of a coherent worldview and strategy. But slowly "Chilly Willy" and his working-class colleagues began to find words for their thoughts and gain confidence in their own judgments and opinions.

Thomas's quest for autonomy was not self-conscious and deliberate. But instinctively he and the defense group began to assert their authority over local matters. They wanted the right to defend their community with force if necessary. CORE had balked at these terms and suggested a compromise in which the guards concealed their weapons during the day. The debate found its way into many late-night discussions around the kitchen table in the Freedom House. Cathy Patterson remembered the activists admonishing Thomas, "Chilly, if you guys are going to be out there with guns, you have to hide them." Thomas would ask why. "Because you're going to invoke violence," replied the activists. "If you have a gun, you have to be prepared to use it. And we don't want people to get hurt." Thomas patiently listened to their arguments and then answered firmly, "You're stepping on *my* toes. *We're* doing this. We know this town. We know these people. Just let us do it."[37]

CORE relented. "What happened was that Chilly Willy and them started going out with us," recalled Ronnie Moore, "and their position was, 'O.K., you guys can be nonviolent if you want to . . . and we appreciate you being nonviolent. But we are not going to stand by and let these guys kill you.'"[38]

The defense group's objection to the nonviolent code went beyond the issue of guard duty. Many of the men, including Thomas, declined to participate in any nonviolent direct action, including pickets and marches, because of the rules of engagement set by CORE. "If you were attacked, if you were spat upon, if you were kicked or jeered, we were very clear that we were not to respond to that," noted Cathy Patterson. CORE quickly discovered that the black men of Jonesboro were unwilling to endure the humiliation attending these restrictions. "There was too much pride to do that," said Patterson. Nonviolence required black men to passively endure humiliation and physical abuse—a bitter elixir for a group struggling to overcome the southern white stereotype of black men as servile and cowardly. For the black men of Jonesboro, nonviolence appeared to ask them to sacrifice their manhood and honor in order to acquire it.[39]

Nonviolence also demanded that black men forego their right to defend family members who joined nonviolent protests. This tested the limits of their forbearance. The institution of white supremacy was a complex web of social and political customs, proscribed behaviors, government policies, and laws. Some aspects of racism were more endurable than others. At its most innocuous, segregation was little more than demeaning symbolism. For the most part, blacks and whites drank the same water, ate the same foods, and rode the same buses. But some racist practices were intolerable insults to black manhood. Compromising the sanctity of family was one of those transgressions. "The things that go with racial segregation . . . you lived with that," said Cathy Patterson of separate seating and other peculiarities of physical segregation. "They were things you just had to accept." But violence against family and home violated the ancient right to a safe hearth and home. "When they saw their own children get hit or beaten," the men "reacted very differently." Nonviolence obliged black men to stand idly by as their children and wives were savagely beaten, a debasement that most black men would not tolerate. They clung tenaciously to their claims to manhood and honor. Ultimately, nonviolence discouraged black men from participating in civil rights protests in the South and turned the movement into a campaign of women and children.[40]

The precepts of nonviolence clashed with black men's notions of self-respect and honor. At times this conflict placed black men in painful quandaries, as when women activists called men to task, questioning their manhood if they refused to walk the picket line. In nearby Natchez, Mississippi, where another Deacons chapter would soon emerge, Jesse Bernard, a young NAACP worker, stood before a mass meeting and challenged black men to rise to the occasion. "If the children walk the line, you can protect them," Bernard admonished the men. "All I want to say is every man in here with idle time, if you can't walk the picket line from tomorrow on, won't you come by and sit on the side somewhere and see what's happening, so that if some of those people come up to hurt some of your children, your heart will be right. . . . I want to see every man who stood up and said he was a man be out on that picket line."[41]

Things were not that simple. African American men stayed off the picket lines for good reason: the physical and emotional risks that black men assumed when they joined a nonviolent protest far outweighed what black women and children suffered. In the moving short documentary *Panola* by Ed Pincus, the film's subject, an African American man named Panola from Natchez, ends the film with a stunning soliloquy in his one-room shack. As he delivers his angst-filled words, Panola constantly returns to the theme of "kill or be killed." For Panola, the choice on the picket line was "kill or be killed." Bound by notions of masculine honor, black men had much more to lose than women and children: what was at stake was their pride, manhood, and, very likely, their life. Not only were men more likely to be attacked—witness that black men were virtually the only victims of lynching—but if attacked, many believed that upholding their dignity left but two choices:

kill or be killed. Nor would their sense of honor allow them to sit idly and watch their families be brutalized. From the perspective of most African American men, walking the picket line meant making a choice between life and death. James Jackson, a Deacons leader from Natchez, summed up the dilemma: "When I grab that sign and get on the picket line, I couldn't say that I'm not afraid, man . . . I still have fear, you know, but I'd stay right there and die before I turned around."[42]

The CORE activists in Jonesboro began to slowly grasp the predicament they had created for black men. The compromise with armed self-defense provoked "intense philosophical discussion and debates" within the CORE summer task force. The controversy eventually led some activists, like Mike Lesser, to leave CORE. But for most activists, the palpable fear in Jonesboro gradually eroded their faith in the grand intellectual theories. There was a conflict over the issue of nonviolence, observed Cathy Patterson, but "there also was enough fear that the conflict was more intellectual than it was real." Patterson herself arrived at what she considered a principled compromise: "During the day I thought it was inappropriate to have anyone with us bearing weapons. But when it got dark, we were in a great deal of danger. I had no objections to their presence at night. We were defenseless at night."[43]

Self-defense became an immediate concern as the movement shifted from voter registration to direct action desegregation demonstrations. CORE's initial voter registration drive provoked some harassment—generally limited to white teenagers driving through the community and shouting taunts. Most whites regarded CORE's presence as a nuisance more than a menace. Voter registration organizing confined CORE activists to the black community, so the organizers seldom crossed paths with local whites. The subdued response by whites was understandable. Despite its symbolism, black voter registration posed little threat to white supremacy and the segregated caste system. Even if all blacks in Jonesboro were registered, they would comprise only one-third of the vote. At best, the black vote could be bartered for influence, but it would not fundamentally alter social relationships. White businesses would continue to thrive on segregated labor, white jobs would remain secure, and life would amble along as usual in the little mill town.[44]

But desegregation was another matter. Segregation was the foundation of the social and labor systems of the South. Desegregation challenged the system of privilege that ensured whites the best jobs, housing, education, and government services. If the segregation barriers fell, white workers lost substantially more than a separate toilet. The conflict over segregation was ultimately a deadly contest for power—as Jonesboro blacks would soon discover.

The Deacons Are Born

ONE SWELTERING EVENING in late July, only a few weeks after CORE had arrived in Jonesboro, electricity to the black quarters was suddenly cut off, plunging the community into an eerie darkness. In the dim shadows, Earnest Thomas joined a few friends in front of a hotel, assuming that the local power company was conducting line repairs. The men talked and joked in the pitch-black street, the glowing tips of their cigarettes bobbing in the dark. Suddenly Thomas noticed a flashing red light in the distance. As it grew nearer, it became apparent that a police car was leading a caravan of more than fifty vehicles into the black community. Children ran yelling with excitement to greet the parade. But as the convoy grew nearer, Thomas caught his first glimpse of the hooded men who filled each car, tossing leaflets into the street. Thomas was dumbstruck: the assistant chief of police was in the lead car escorting the Klan. As each car passed, Thomas noticed that the license tags had been covered to conceal the identity of the Klansmen. But it was a small town, and Thomas and others easily recognized many of the cars as belonging to Jonesboro residents, including several upstanding white businessmen and even the owner of a grocery store in the black community. The sight of the hooded convoy sent a shudder of fear through many older blacks. But the children, oblivious to the danger, grabbed the swirling leaflets and brought them to their anxious parents. The leaflets warned blacks to stay away from CORE and the civil rights movement. Though the Klan convoy frightened the old, the invasion only further incensed Thomas and his friends. Little did the Klansmen realize that their act of provocation would, in a matter of weeks, give rise to a well-organized and public black militia dedicated to ending Klan terror, and that the armed self-defense group would spread through the Deep South to more than twenty-one cities and recruit hundreds of members—and become the bane of the Ku Klux Klan.[1]

The Klan caravan was a direct response to the desegregation campaign initiated by CORE in June. While in Mississippi, Freedom Summer volunteers were explicitly instructed to restrict their activities to voter registration and avoid direct action desegregation protests, CORE had given the local chapters in Louisiana more latitude to test the new civil rights bill that would become effective in July. The prospect of a militant desegregation campaign similar to Birmingham provoked considerable anxiety in the black community. Many blacks feared that Jonesboro's tiny six-man police department would prove unwilling or incapable of protecting the activists. Moreover, it was becoming increasingly clear that Earnest Thomas's informal defense group formed in the spring of 1964 was an insufficient substitute for police protection.

Taking the initiative to avert a disaster was a newcomer to the black community, Frederick Douglas Kirkpatrick. At six feet four inches, Kirkpatrick was an imposing figure. He had been a Grambling University standout athlete and briefly played professional football. A stern visage and stentorian basso voice gave him a commanding presence and natural leadership qualities. Kirkpatrick arrived in Jonesboro in 1963, an ambitious young high school athletics coach from nearby Homer in Claiborne Parish. In Homer, Kirkpatrick had led his teams to two state championships. Now he had advanced his career as the new physical education teacher and athletics coach at Jackson High School, the black high school in Jonesboro. Though he had no formal religious training, Kirkpatrick had assumed the title of "Reverend," a common practice in his day. His father had provided him with a religious upbringing, and the elder Kirkpatrick himself was a staunch Church of God in Christ preacher who had built an impressive ministry of three churches in Claiborne Parish.[2]

Kirkpatrick's optimism about his new position quickly gave way to disappointment. The conditions at Jackson High were abominable. The school offered no foreign languages. A new library was filled with empty shelves. Textbooks were tattered hand-me-downs from the white schools. Students were routinely dispatched as gardeners to maintain the superintendent's personal lawn. The only vocational offerings were home economics and agriculture, a curriculum that condemned blacks to live as maids and sharecroppers.[3]

With CORE coming to Jonesboro, Kirkpatrick and other black leaders began discussing the idea of a black volunteer auxiliary police squad that would assist the established police force in monitoring Klan harassment in the black community. Unlike Thomas's informal self-defense group, the auxiliary police unit would be officially sanctioned, providing legitimacy and respect. Kirkpatrick approached Chief of Police Adrian Peevy with the request for a volunteer black patrol, and much to everyone's surprise, Peevy accepted the proposal and promptly deputized Kirkpatrick and several other blacks, including Henry Amos, Percy Lee Bradford, Ceola Quals, and Eland Harris.

Peevy issued the squad an old police car with radio, guns, clubs, and handcuffs, and local white merchants donated money to outfit the men in crisp new uniforms. The police chief assured them that their police powers extended to whites as well as blacks and that they could arrest whites if necessary. Peevy's decision to form the squad appeared uncharacteristically enlightened for a white lawman in North Louisiana, and many in the black community questioned his motives. Some, like Earnest Thomas, suspected that he planned to use the squad as a convenient and politic way to discipline and control the civil rights movement: "They were looking for some black policemen to do their dirty work," scoffed Thomas.[4]

Kirkpatrick understood the dilemma confronting him. He knew that Peevy expected the black squad to discourage demonstrations and arrest civil rights workers. But he thought that, despite these limitations, the squad could provide a modicum of protection for the black community and CORE. It was not his only concern. Though a respected community leader, he also occupied jobs that obligated him to the white power structure. Kirkpatrick was employed by the public schools as a teacher-coach and by the town as a part-time manager of the public swimming pool. His position as de facto chief of the black police placed him in a potentially compromising position. Local laws and courts mandated segregation and gave police the power to disrupt civil rights protests. In his new role, Kirkpatrick would be thrust in the embarrassing position of enforcing segregation laws and thwarting lawful protests. Many agreed with Thomas's observation that Kirkpatrick was wearing "too many hats."[5]

Among the members of the new police squad were several men who had already worked with Thomas in the informal defense group. They were mature and respected community leaders, like Bradford and Amos, who had been active in the Voters League. All of the volunteers were relatively independent of the white power structure. Amos owned a gas station, Harris was a barber, and Bradford owned a cab service and also worked at the mill. The black squad began patrolling the community at night in June 1964, assuming many of the duties of the informal defense group. The patrol appeared to deter harassment, and aside from a few incidents, June was relatively quiet.

At the beginning of the summer, Cathy Patterson and Danny Mitchell were joined by two more black CORE task force organizers, Fred Brooks, a black college student from Tennessee, and Willie Mellion, a young black recruit from Plaquemine, Louisiana. The expanded task force continued its work with the Voters League, concentrating on voter registration. But the implementation of the Civil Rights Act's public accommodations provisions in July 1964 radically changed the strategy of the civil rights movement. Previously CORE's summer project had centered on voter registration, which liberal contributors and foundations had supported financially. Liberals viewed the vote as key to transforming the South; they also hoped that new black voters would strengthen the Democratic Party in the upcoming fall presidential race. But for most blacks in Jonesboro, voter registration seemed more like vacant symbolism. Archie Hunter, an African American CORE volunteer from New York, summed up how many poor blacks felt about voting: "It's only a ballot he's putting in the box, and he wants food. He wants a ballot put in his stomach." It was difficult for civil rights workers to tell someone who had "12 children, living in a shack, working for, say, $12 a week. . . . 'You should get out and vote. This will make your condition better.' "[6]

It made even less sense for teenagers who were years from voting age. As July drew near, young people in particular grew impatient with the racial barriers to education, public accommodations, and employment. They importuned the CORE activists with demands for direct action protest to test the public accommodations provisions of the Civil Rights Act. In Mississippi, the Student Nonviolent Coordinating Committee (SNCC, pronounced "Snick") was encountering the same community restlessness to test the desegregation laws, as the Freedom Summer activists continued to focus on voter registration.[7]

Local people were not the only impatient ones. On 22 June Fred Brooks, the irrepressible young CORE organizer from Tennessee, daringly flaunted segregation laws by drinking from the "whites only" water fountain in the Jackson Parish Court House. Deputy W. D. McBride hustled Brooks into Sheriff Newt T. Loe's office and ordered him not to repeat the offense. Brooks spun on his heels, headed toward the fountain, and defiantly drank from it again.[8]

Deputy McBride, flustered and seething, ordered Brooks back into his office and hastily summoned Kirkpatrick in his capacity as a police deputy. It was the first test of the black police. When Kirkpatrick arrived, a furious Sheriff Loe cornered Kirkpatrick. "You'd better tell this boy something about drinking from these white water fountains," steamed the sheriff. "I'm not gonna have this. I'm gonna peel his damn head." The incident ended without an arrest.[9]

Relations with law enforcement continued to deteriorate as CORE stepped up its desegregation protests. On 4 July, a sheriff's deputy detained Robert Weaver, a CORE task force worker, and took him to the police station for interrogation and fingerprinting. Sheriff Loe lectured Weaver that blacks did not need CORE since they could register to vote in Jackson Parish. The sheriff warned Weaver to leave town by morning, and one deputy threatened to "bust his head" if he saw Weaver again.[10]

Ronnie Moore and Mike Lesser became the next victims of the terror campaign. On 8 July the two CORE organizers left Jonesboro for the one-hour trip to Monroe. As they drove out of town, they noticed three carloads of whites abruptly pull onto the highway behind them. Lesser nervously watched in the rearview mirror as the cars trailed behind. He and Moore were seasoned activists who understood the danger posed by the stalking caravan. The two tensely discussed their predicament. With rugged terrain skirting both sides of the road, their only option was to stay on the blacktop. Lesser pushed the accelerator in an effort to outrun the pursuers, but one car in the caravan suddenly passed them, blocking their escape. Moore and Lesser frantically debated whether to ram the car from behind. As the seconds ticked away the two continued to speed deeper into the pine forest and farther away from the relative security of Jonesboro. Moore decided that they had to turn around. He ordered Lesser to execute a quick U-turn in the middle of the road.[11]

Lesser slammed the breaks and wheeled the car around, placing the vehicle on a collision course with the two remaining pursuers who were blocking both lanes. Moore recalled their fatalistic mood. "We decided at that moment that we were going back to the freedom house, either in one piece or with one of those cars." Lesser dropped the accelerator to the floor and streaked toward the oncoming cars. At the last moment one of the cars veered to the side and was sideswiped as Lesser and Moore sped by. "That was the first game of chicken that I probably ever played," remembered Moore.[12]

The two organizers raced back to Jonesboro, reaching speeds of one hundred miles an hour. From the safety of the Freedom House, they called the sheriff's office to file a complaint. Within minutes, Loe and members of the black police squad arrived. Loe had already received a complaint from the whites Moore and Lesser had eluded. To their amazement, Loe ordered the black deputy to arrest them for reckless driving and leaving the scene of an accident. The deputy refused and Loe eventually departed. Fearing another attack on Lesser and Moore, the black squad provided them with an armed escort to Monroe that evening. The black deputy's refusal to arrest the activists was the first time that the black police failed to perform according to

Loe's expectations. It was clear that the squad was not going to be willing accomplices in repression.

The campaign of harassment against CORE increased in the days following the implementation of the Civil Rights Act. On 11 July, six CORE task force members including Brooks, Weaver, Yates, and Patterson were stopped by Jackson and Lincoln Parish law enforcement officials along with the Louisiana State Police. Under the pretext of investigating a robbery, police photographed and physically threatened the CORE workers and searched and impounded their car.[13]

Emboldened by the conduct of police officials, racist vigilantes also escalated their attacks on the movement. On 13 July, three whites in a car confronted CORE workers in the front yard of the Freedom House. Harassing the pacifists had become routine for the young hooligans, but on this occasion they were startled by their reception. In a matter of minutes, three black policemen—Kirkpatrick, Eland Harris, and Henry Amos—arrived and ordered the whites to leave. The young men bristled at the command coming from the black officers but eventually retreated, punctuating their departure with a threat to return with 125 whites to "make trouble." As word of the threat spread in the black community, dozens of volunteers with guns flooded into the streets. The show of force deterred additional attacks for the day.[14]

The spontaneous show of armed support for the black policemen reassured them that they could rely on a substantial body of men to complement their ranks when necessary. Ironically, by refusing to protect the black community, the white establishment had inadvertently forced the black community to arm itself and assume responsibility for its own defense. If the harassment was intended to dissuade CORE and the community from demonstrating, the strategy failed woefully. Young blacks were even more determined to test the Civil Rights Act through direct action. The shift from voter registration was reflected in Jonesboro CORE's decision to reorganize into two sections: a direct action program, coordinated by Fred Brooks, and a voter registration section, supervised by Cathy Patterson. Two principal targets for desegregation were selected in July: the public library and the town swimming pool.[15]

The segregation practices at the public library particularly vexed young blacks. Although their tax dollars supported the library, blacks were prohibited from using the library building and obtaining library loan cards. Their only access to books was the periodic visit by the bookmobile. The library test began with a letter to the head librarian from the Voters League requesting access to library cards. When there was no response, a group of young protesters led by CORE entered the library and attempted to obtain cards on 22 July. Within minutes, Sheriff Loe arrived and ordered the protesters out of the library and the doors locked. The protesters left peaceably but renewed their efforts the next day, this time picketing outside the library. Once again law enforcement officials were summoned and promptly arrested twenty-four people for parading without a permit.[16]

Police told the protesters that they were being arrested in response to a complaint lodged by a mortuary business located across the street from the library. The proprietor had claimed that the chanting protesters were "offending" his deceased clients. The protesters would later muse that it was the first time in history that someone had been arrested for "disturbing the dead."[17]

The direct action demonstrations increasingly posed problems for Kirkpatrick's black police squad. Town authorities were determined to use the squad to enforce the illegal segregation laws. The situation came to a head on 29 July. As part of the first concerted public accommodations tests, a group of young protesters converged on the M & D Restaurant and Cafeteria in downtown Jonesboro. The restaurant owner, Margaret Temple, refused service to the testers at the front entrance, ordering them to purchase their food at the back door, as was the custom. When the testers refused, Temple angrily shouted, "Y'all damn niggers ought to be out trying to find work to do, because ain't no damn nigger coming through my front door as long as I'm running this place."[18]

The protesters and cafe owner were at a standoff until Kirkpatrick and another black officer arrived. Temple demanded that Kirkpatrick "come get these damn niggers," but he ignored her order and, instead, turned to the protesters and asked if they were disturbing the peace. The group responded in unison with a resounding "No!" The commotion quickly attracted a crowd of whites, including an angry elderly man wielding a stick. Kirkpatrick confronted the white man and stood his ground. The standoff lasted several minutes until a second black officer intervened and abruptly ordered the protesters to "move out."[19]

Within a few hours, the black police faced another test. CORE moved to its next target of the day, the "whites-only" municipal swimming pool. Testers arrived at 2:00 P.M. and found the pool locked and several parish deputies and town police officers waiting beside the street. When the pool opened shortly thereafter, the testers attempted to enter but were turned away. Several police officers gathered at the pool entrance, including Kirkpatrick. Police Chief Peevy commanded him to order the protesters to leave. Kirkpatrick complied, twice asking the protesters to disperse. The protesters refused to budge. Peevy grew irritated and, as Kirkpatrick watched helplessly, ordered the white police to arrest fifteen protesters, ten of whom were juveniles. Peevy also had two mothers of the juveniles arrested on charges of "contributing to the delinquency of a minor" by allowing their children to participate in the protest. The "contributing" charge was subsequently used to arrest virtually the entire CORE staff in the days that followed. During the next three days of protest police arrested a total of thirty-nine protesters.[20]

The black police had not fared well in their first outing. They had been forced to disband a lawful protest at the M & D Restaurant and then to assist Sheriff Loe in breaking up the swimming pool demonstration. The protests underscored the squad's contradictory and untenable position in the community. Some blacks in Jonesboro began to wonder if they had merely traded vigilante repression for black police repression.

The wave of protests and arrests quickly brought the Ku Klux Klan into the fray. It was on the evening of protests that the Jonesboro assistant police chief had led the Klan caravan of fifty cars through the black community. As soon as the caravan passed, Thomas joined a delegation of black men, including some of the black police, and drove directly to Police Chief Peevy's house to await his return. When Peevy arrived, the delegation demanded to know why the police department had escorted the Klan through the black community. Peevy responded stiffly that his department routinely escorted funerals and he considered the Klan parade the same thing. The black men were not persuaded. Thomas recalled that they bluntly informed Peevy that it would not happen again, "because *we* won't allow that to happen again. We told him straight up that there would not ever be a passing through the community like that." If it did happen again, "there was going to be some killing going on." The police chief listened stoically in his yard. If he did not respond in word, he did in action; Peevy never again provided an escort for the Klan.[21]

The Klan's convoy was only the beginning of its well-planned night of terror. The night riders spread across Jackson Parish and dotted the landscape with a score of blazing crosses. A frightening situation was also unfolding at the courthouse. Under the cloak of darkness, approximately one hundred armed whites with rifles had converged on the parish jail and were threatening the civil rights protesters held there as prisoners.[22]

Local CORE activists hastily called Marvin Rich, CORE's attorney in New York, and apprised him of the dangerous mob scene at the jail. Rich immediately called Lee White, a presidential assistant, and roused him from his slumber. White, in turn, contacted the Justice Department and arranged for the FBI to intervene. The mob was soon dispersed, and several armed black men surreptitiously stood guard for the rest of the night from adjacent rooftops.

The Klan convoy and the mob scene at the parish jail were the last straw. Whatever trust the Jonesboro black community once had for local law enforcement had been extinguished by the recent police harassment and collusion with the Klan. These were dark days for the civil rights movement across the South. In nearby Philadelphia, Mississippi, the National Guard was combing the woods for James Chaney, Andrew Goodman, and Michael Schwerner, the civil rights workers murdered by the Klan with police complicity. John Doar of the Justice Department had told the Freedom Summer volunteers that because of the doctrine of federalism and states' rights, FBI agents could only observe and investigate incidents of police or vigilante harassment and violence; they could not make an arrest unless a federal law was violated. If the local police and federal government would not protect the Bill of Rights, who was left? The black police squad had been helpless against the mob action and the Klan caravan. Despite their efforts to the contrary, the squad had become the unwitting tool of the white power structure in neutralizing the protest movement. Kirkpatrick had managed to finesse several encounters, but he could not overcome problems posed by the contradictory role of the squad: in the final analysis, the white establishment was the squad's source of authority, and the custodians of white supremacy were not about to arm their own grave diggers. The only reliable means of defense would be an independent self-defense organization, exclusively accountable to the black community. Power had to be seized, not bequeathed.

The arrogant and insulting intrusion of the Klan in the black community had left many black men angry and eager for action. The practical issue of protecting the community was paramount, but the Klansmen's caravan was more symbol than substance. For most of the black men, the issue was honor, not safety.

Within a few days, a determined group of approximately twenty black men met at the union hall to discuss forming a self-defense group. The meeting brought together the two groups that had been active in armed defense: Kirkpatrick's black police squad and Thomas's informal defense group. The two groups had overlapping membership and essentially the same goals of community protection.[23]

The black police had not been a complete failure. They had kept night riders out of the black community and had probably deterred police brutality during arrests that they witnessed. The community understood Kirkpatrick's dilemma. Annie Johnson remembered Kirkpatrick as an activist who "could get something started if you listened to him," but also someone who had conflicting roles that placed him between the community and the white elite. "But he still took care of his people."[24]

Forming the squad had raised community expectations about its rights. That Jonesboro had acceded to the request for black police appeared to validate the black community's claim for the right of self-defense. Once conceded, a right is difficult to revoke. Whatever its limitations, the black police squad had consolidated a group of leaders committed to self-defense, and in effect, the town had inadvertently provided blacks with an opportunity for training in leadership and self-defense. In its effort to subordinate the black community, the white power structure had helped sow the seeds of independence.

At the meeting following the Klan caravan, chaired by Kirkpatrick, the most pressing item on the agenda was arranging for increased patrols and coordinating assignments and communications. The Klan parade had caught the black community unprepared. Protecting the Freedom House and the community would no longer be left to an informal decision-making process. The primary outcome of the meeting was an organized self-defense group to complement the black police. Unlike the black police, this group would be free to operate as it pleased and beholden to no government agency. Several developments would have to transpire before the organization crystallized, and it would be another six months before the group agreed on a name, the Deacons for Defense and Justice, and adopted a formal leadership structure.[25]

By the beginning of August, Jonesboro's black community had two security units working closely together: the black police squad and the new self-defense group. The police squad continued to patrol the community as the new defense group tightened security measures, organizing sentries at the Freedom House, escorting CORE workers as they registered voters, and patrolling the community as well. Volunteers had conducted similar activities in the past, but now security was better organized and more diligently attended to. The defense group posted guards at key community entrances and used CB radios to coordinate security. Earnest Thomas made regular guard duty assignments, recruiting from the shift workers at the paper mill.

Armed with the new defense group and a renewed sense of determination, the community launched a second desegregation offensive in early August. Fred Brooks led a group of five protesters in an assault on the Jonesboro Public Library. The testers were nervous given that the previous library protest had resulted in twenty-four arrests. Within minutes sheriff's deputy James Van Beasley and another deputy arrived on the scene, demanding that the group "move out." When the protesters stood their ground, Van Beasley returned with a menacing police dog and forced the group to hastily retreat across the street, where they stood quietly. Van Beasley followed the protesters and ordered them to "scatter." Kirkpatrick and Eland Harris arrived shortly and began negotiating with Brooks and Van Beasley. They were soon joined by Danny Mitchell. Unable to reach an agreement, the protesters, many of them children, returned to the library with the deputies in pursuit with snarling police dogs. Kirkpatrick stopped the deputies and warned them not to use the dogs on the children. The deputies hesitated. Finally, Van Beasley retreated with the dogs, but he later arrested several protesters for disturbing the peace. Unlike in previous encounters, at the library protest Kirkpatrick and the black police stood firm against the white deputies.[26]

The formation of the defense group reflected a profound change in the thinking of African Americans in Jackson Parish. A new sense of entitlement and a new combativeness were emerging in the black consciousness. These changes were evident in men and women alike. Shortly after the defense unit formed, the Klan attempted to light a cross at the home of the Reverend Y. D. Jackson in rural Jackson Parish. As soon as the torch touched the cross, shots rang out. Jackson's wife had unloaded her gun at the startled Klansmen. The frightened night riders beat a hasty retreat. The white robe and hood were losing their mystique in Jonesboro.[27]

At the end of August CORE's summer project closed and the Jonesboro task force disbanded. Danny Mitchell left for his graduate studies at Syracuse University. Cathy Patterson headed for Florida A&M; she eventually transferred to Syracuse, where she and Mitchell were married in 1965. Those who decided to stay with CORE, like Bill Yates and Ruthie Wells, were dispersed around the state. The only organizer who remained in Jonesboro was the energetic young Fred Brooks. Brooks was a bright and eager organizer, but sustaining the Jonesboro campaign was a daunting task for the inexperienced teenager.

By most standards, the summer project had been a failure. Though voter registration had increased, the task force had been unable to desegregate the library, swimming pool, and almost all public accommodations. Neither had it built a community organization that could survive CORE's departure. Thirty years later Cathy Patterson Mitchell expressed her disappointment tersely: "I think we left Jonesboro a worse place."[28]

Her verdict was probably too harsh. Thrust into the heart of Klan country, the young activists were forced to overcome the formidable organizing barriers of fear and terror—with little support or protection from the federal government. By the summer's end, CORE had filed more than fifty complaints with the FBI regarding intimidations, threats, and denial of service, with virtually no response from Washington.[29] Despite their failures in Jonesboro, the CORE volunteers had inadvertently made one significant accomplishment: they had helped bring about an armed self-defense organization that would soon capture national attention.[30]

As Fred Brooks took the leadership reins in September, his biggest problem was that CORE's national leadership had backed away from desegregation and once again made voter registration a priority, hoping to gain more Democratic Party voters for the upcoming presidential election. Brooks was left with a program that had little appeal in Jonesboro. Then he received orders to set up a kindergarten and freedom school, but the community displayed even less interest in these self-help projects. In truth, segregation and discrimination remained the paramount issue for local blacks. In Jonesboro, as in thousands of other small southern towns, the Civil Rights Act had done little to end Jim Crow.

Why did CORE continue to pursue voter registration and self-help projects despite local indifference? In part, it did so because both CORE and SNCC had emphasized voter registration ever since they had accepted funding in 1961 from the Voter Education Project (VEP)—created by the Kennedy administration explicitly to divert civil rights groups from direct action organizing.[31] Moreover, in 1964 the eyes of the nation were focused on the heated presidential race between liberal Democrat Lyndon Johnson and conservative Republican Barry Goldwater. Goldwater had opposed the Civil Rights Act, and many black leaders believed that the presidential contest was critical to the future of the black movement. There was also widespread fear of a white backlash against the civil rights protests, a development that could only benefit the Republicans. With these problems weighing heavily on their minds, the national civil rights organizations subordinated local struggles to the new national agenda. Black salvation would now be found in the Oval Office—not in the streets.[32]

But resistance to desegregation in the South created a different strategic imperative for local movements, and Jonesboro was no exception. On 9 October 1964 Chief Peevy announced that the town of Jonesboro was dismantling the black police squad. Peevy explained that since CORE had departed and the demonstrations had subsided, the black deputies were no longer needed. The black community responded to the announcement with a sense of betrayal and anger.

Many blacks believed that Peevy had capitulated to pressure from the white community. They knew that most whites disapproved of black men armed with guns and badges. The black police had not proved to be dependable minions of the police chief either, having refused to arrest and intimidate black protesters. Whites were also incensed when Kirkpatrick had used his police powers to defy white racists and chastise white officers for using racist language on their radios.[33]

The black community responded quickly to Chief Peevy's announcement, circulating a petition and organizing a march demanding that the black police squad be reinstated. But their protests were to no avail. Kirkpatrick and his fellow deputies found themselves without an organization. With the squad disbanded, the community turned to the defense group for protection. An informant would later tell the FBI that the primary catalyst for the Deacons for Defense and Justice was the town government's decision to disband the black police.[34]

Yet the Deacons did not take form overnight. There were formidable obstacles to converting the defense group into a viable organization. Foremost were complacency and individualism. Creating a new organization required effort. It upset old routines, disturbed the comfortable anonymity of everyday life, and called on individuals to subordinate personal needs to community interests. Any new organization could upset the social and political arrangements in the community. Leaders had to be chosen, inspiring jealousy and factionalizing.

There were also vexing political concerns. An armed self-defense organization was clearly at odds with the orthodox creed of nonviolence. There was a hint of blasphemy in elevating self-defense to an organizational form. Like sin, armed self-defense was practiced more than it was confessed. Through an unspoken agreement, black leaders had protected the movement's nonviolent image by downplaying armed self-defense activities. Better that protection be left to silent men in the shadows of the movement.

But it was primarily the lack of organizing skills that prevented the defense group from becoming a viable enterprise. Most of the group's members were in the habit of joining organizations, not forming them. The group had met throughout the summer but had failed to develop an organizational and funding structure that could sustain it through the inevitable hardships of the movement—a structure that would also provide the wherewithal to expand to other communities. The men were understandably wary of collecting dues, electing officers, and taking responsibility for a new organization. They had the will but not the way. The solution to their dilemma would shortly arrive from Nyack, New York.

Charlie Fenton was a twenty-three-year-old white activist who had descended from two generations of policemen in Nyack. An authoritarian upbringing only succeeded in exciting a rebellious spirit in the young Fenton. Iconoclastic, even as a teenager, Fenton had converted to pacifism by the time he was sixteen—for no particular religious or philosophical reasons—and dropped out of high school. To escape from home, Fenton joined the navy on his seventeenth birthday in 1958. He volunteered for the Hospital Corp, assuming that he would be armed with nothing more dangerous than a bedpan. He had not anticipated that even corpsmen were required to complete boot camp. When handed a rifle and ordered to fire, Fenton balked. His protest cost him fourteen days in the brig.[35]

After four years of service as a medical corpsman, the navy discharged Fenton and he decided to live in San Francisco. The bay area was a CORE stronghold, and Fenton soon joined the organization and volunteered for CORE's 1964 summer project. The nonviolence training and the Bay City's contagious political ferment had transformed him, in his own words, into a "a real gung-ho revolutionary."[36]

Fenton completed a month of training at the CORE center in Plaquemine, Louisiana, in May 1964 and then was assigned to the Monroe project in the northern part of the state. He was arrested and spent most of the summer in the Monroe city jail, where white inmates tortured him mercilessly; they beat him so severely that he had to be hospitalized. They forced him to eat soap and to take scalding showers that blistered his skin. When he was released from jail, Fenton returned to San Francisco to recuperate, but testifying to his remarkable courage and determination, he soon returned to Louisiana to help revive the Jonesboro project. By the first week of November 1964 he had joined Mike Lesser in Monroe. With the Philadelphia, Mississippi, murders fresh in their minds, Lesser and Fenton waited for nightfall to make the journey to Jonesboro. They wove through back roads and soon pulled into the backyard of CORE's little Freedom House on Cedar Street.[37]

Fenton was both startled and distressed by what he saw. "I got out of the car and realized that I was surrounded, *absolutely surrounded* in an armed camp. They were on top of the roofs, they were under the building . . . they were all around the buildings." The defense group had turned out in full force to welcome Fenton. He perused the scene and slowly walked around the front of the building and onto the porch. The men warmly greeted him with shotguns and rifles in tow. Inside the door Fenton spied several additional rifles leaning against the wall. The effervescent Fred Brooks explained that the men had heard that Fenton was arriving and wanted to honor him by organizing the best protection that they could offer. "I was impressed," said Fenton, "but I was not very happy."[38]

Fenton wasted little time expressing his dissatisfaction. "Well, the very first night I was there I told them that I didn't like the guns in the house," he recalled. Somewhat bewildered and dismayed, the men honored his request and slowly left the house. Some never returned. Fenton wondered if he had made the right decision. Years later he acknowledged the impertinence of his edict to the townspeople. "Here was this snotty nose white boy," Fenton recalled wistfully, "coming to the middle of their war and telling them that I didn't like their weapon of choice."[39]

Within a few days Fenton realized that his strict adherence to pacifism was hindering his organizational efforts. The men were not going to subject themselves to humiliation and physical abuse simply to conform to his philosophy. And without the men, Fenton's frontline protest troops would be women and children. The use of children on marches, some as young as six years old, had stirred controversy during the Birmingham campaign of 1963, but the practice had become widely accepted in the movement by 1965. Fenton deeply opposed the tactic. He was unwilling to use children as shock troops against the police and Klan.

Fenton's change of heart was also spurred on by local black leaders. During his first days in Jonesboro, several black leaders had pulled him aside and implored him to be more flexible on the issue of weapons. The men felt naked without their guns and helpless to assist him "the way they want to be able to do." Fenton was discovering that the black community had its own strategy, inchoate and expressed in action more than in word, but nevertheless a strategy. Local African Americans wanted the right to control their movement, even if it contradicted CORE's precepts.

During the civil rights movement, two strategies invariably competed for the loyalty of the community: an explicit nonviolent strategy imported by national organizations and an implicit unarticulated strategy revealed in the attitudes and behaviors of the community itself. With the Deacons the community had found a voice for its own feelings about armed self-defense. Fenton found himself in the dilemma of choosing between democracy and principle: he quickly chose democracy.

Fenton did not abandon his initial goal to form a nonviolent civic group in Jonesboro. Instead, he opted for a two-phased plan. In the first phase, he would assist in forming a formal self-defense organization. This involved helping the local defense group structure its organization and clarify its goals and program. Once he had gained the confidence of the group, Fenton planned a second phase in which he would gently move the group toward nonviolent community organizing. He hoped that the members would "figure out things they could do for me that didn't have to have a gun." In the

interim, Fenton would maintain the appearance of nonviolence by requesting that the men not carry their weapons inside the Freedom House.[40]

Fenton eagerly set out to organize a "protective association" that combined activism with self-defense. He arranged a meeting at the Masonic
Hall, where the men would "feel comfortable with their guns." They gathered on a crisp Tuesday night in November 1964.[41]

The meeting proved chaotic and tense. The gathering brought together
a broad range of people with conflicting strategies and political temperaments. There was, as always, the element of fear. Some participants worried
that their names might be leaked to the police or the Klan. Others questioned
whether the community really needed another organization: Weren't things
fine as they were? Some objected that "as soon as we call ourselves something, then somebody will say that we'll have to have dues." And so it went.
But there were strong advocates for action, like Thomas and Kirkpatrick.
After vacillation and substantial quibbling, the meeting finally turned the
corner. "All of a sudden they were saying 'well let's meet here again next
week,'" recalled Fenton. The enthusiasm for the self-defense group was
infectious. There was no turning back.[42]

The meeting at the Masonic Hall represented a watershed in the history of
the Deacons. On that night the Deacons were born as a *political organization*. Previously the defense group had only been a patrol, a secret auxiliary
to the nonviolent movement. Now it was on its way to becoming its own
movement.

Within the next few weeks the Deacons for Defense and Justice quickly
took form through a series of Tuesday night meetings at the Masonic Hall.
The Deacons successfully coalesced the defense group and the veterans of
the black police squad, combining into one organization all the men committed to armed self-defense.

The role of women in the new organization was problematic. Traditionally, women were excluded from organized self-defense activities in the
black community, although they defended themselves and their community
when necessary. Throughout the movement, large numbers of women refused to participate in nonviolent activities for some of the same reasons as
men, among them the belief that self-respect depended on the ability to
defend oneself and the notion that nonviolence was ineffective against white
supremacy. Gender divisions also reflected the fact that the Deacons had
borrowed many of its practices from black fraternal orders, including male
exclusiveness. Typically, if women participated in fraternal orders, they did
so in separate "auxiliaries."[43]

No women had taken part in the Jonesboro patrols during the summer of 1964, but now the defense group was becoming a community organization, and the same gender roles that had encouraged male participation were limiting the role of women. Several women, including Ruth Amos, did attend meetings and play an active role in the Deacons. It was difficult to exclude activist women like Amos because, although self-defense was the male prerogative, civil rights activities were not considered the sole province of men. There were rumors of women in other Deacons chapters organizing target practice. At one point the Deacons attempted to reconcile the gender conflict by forming a women's auxiliary entitled the "Deaconesses," but the effort apparently never took root.[44]

It was several weeks before the group formally adopted the name "Deacons for Defense and Justice," and the origins of the name remain enigmatic. Initially the group referred to itself as the "Jonesboro Legal and Defense Association" and later, the "Justice and Defense Club" or "J & D Club." In memorandums to the regional office, Fenton euphemistically described the new group as a "home owners protective association." Several years after the Deacons disbanded, Kirkpatrick published and recorded a song, "Deacons for Defense and Justice," that offered one explanation for the name:[45]

Then what shall we call ourselves
And still keep our right to be a man
For the time has surely come for us
To take our stand

The man that asked the question threw out an idea:
Let's call ourselves the Deacons and never have no fear,
They will think we are from the church
Which has never done much
And gee, to our surprise it really worked.[46]

Kirkpatrick's lyrics suggest that the term "deacons" was selected to beguile local whites by portraying the organization as an innocent church group, an account he proffered in at least one interview as well. But there are other more convincing explanations. Harvey Johnson said that the group chose the name because the role of the self-defense group was comparable to church deacons "who took care of business in the church." Cathy Patterson recalled that in the summer of 1964 the CORE staff began referring to their guards as the "deacons," because CORE had first worked with them in their capacity as church deacons. When a CORE staff person needed an escort, he or she would summon "the deacons," and the name stuck. The most plausible explanation is that the name was a portmanteau that evolved over a period of time, combining the CORE staff's first appellation of "deacons" with the tentative name chosen in November 1964: "Justice and Defense Club." By January 1965 the group had arrived at its permanent name, "Deacons for Defense and Justice."[47]

The name reflected the group's desire to identify with traditionally respected symbols of authority, peace, and moral order in the black community. By combining the terms "Deacons" and "Defense," the name also embodied a political paradox that bedeviled the Deacons throughout their organizational life. The Deacons were attempting to wed two contradictory symbols: Christian pacifism and violence. They hoped to identify with Christianity while defying its pacifist teachings. For the time being, the Deacons turned their attention to more practical matters.

One of the group's first challenges was raising funds. It was difficult for an organization like the Deacons to survive without adequate funds to free up members for organizational duties. The defense group had been limited by lack of funds in the past; the men used their own money to purchase weapons, ammunition, gasoline, and communication equipment. Chief Peevy had reclaimed the black police squad's radios in October, so the black community lacked even rudimentary communication equipment to monitor Klan and police activities. The Deacons took to fund-raising with remarkable enthusiasm and success, taking in $437 in the first two meetings—a substantial sum for a poor community. They used it to purchase two citizen band radios and four walkie-talkies.[48]

The presence of the militant organization infused the movement with a new spirit. In contrast to the moribund voter registration campaign, CORE had discovered in the Deacons a strategy that captured the imagination and support of the community and, for the first time, attracted men to the movement. Fenton was ecstatic, reporting back to CORE's regional office in New Orleans that the new organization was responsible for the increase in "community morale, programming, [and] fund raising." Fenton believed that he had stumbled on an organizing strategy that could revitalize CORE: create hybrid organizations that combined self-defense with community organizing. He boasted that "the community of Jonesboro is probably the best organized Negro community" in Louisiana and recommended that CORE organize similar "home owners protective associations" around the state. The defense group was already energetically recruiting other Jackson Parish communities. "We have arranged for the Jonesboro association to invite a few leaders from the towns of Chatham, Eros, Hodge, North Hodge, [and] Quitman, to attend the meetings of the Jonesboro association," reported

Fenton and Willie Green, "to first, show these invited guests how a community operates when they get organized and secondly, try to establish a home owners protective association, incorporating the entire parish."[49]

Jonesboro was pioneering a new strategy for the movement; but why was this remote mill town the birthplace for the first public armed self-defense organization in the Deep South? Informal and clandestine defense groups had sprung up intermittently over the years, but the Deacons for Defense and Justice quickly acquired the hallmarks of a *political* organization—a public presence in the political debate and a desire to expand organizationally. Several factors came together to give birth to the new group. First was the unique character of the Jonesboro community: a large, working class relatively insulated from economic reprisals. There was also the exceptional and charismatic leadership of Frederick Kirkpatrick and Earnest Thomas. Then there was Ronnie Moore, an early convert to clandestine self-defense, having publicly supported self-defense in 1963 long before any other leader in CORE or SNCC, who oversaw Fenton's work. Moore could have squelched Fenton's self-defense project—a fate that Fenton would have encountered in most other national civil rights organizations—but he did not. It may have been inevitable that the dynamics of the movement would have pushed CORE in the Deacons' direction. The working class in the Deep South was beginning to realize its own political agenda, and no civil rights organization could oppose that agenda and maintain credibility at the grass roots.

One crucial factor contributing to the Deacons' birth was CORE's strategic shift to community organizing. CORE played a key role in garnering publicity for the Deacons and helping them organize, but it would have never lent its support had CORE adhered to its earlier strategy emphasizing preconceived programs like voter registration. CORE and SNCC had both wrestled with the tension between voter registration, which fulfilled a national agenda, and community organizing, which was intended to promote grassroots "participatory democracy" and develop the capacity of local communities to lead their own movements. By the end of the 1964 Freedom Summer, many activists had concluded that the voter registration strategy came at the expense of addressing the felt needs and interests of southern blacks or, at worse, was simply another case of patronizing outsiders telling blacks what was best for them. The Congress of Federated Organizations (COFO), the umbrella organization in Mississippi, had prohibited demonstrations and desegregation tests during the Freedom Summer project, instead concentrating on voter registration, freedom schools, and enrollment in the Freedom Democratic Party (to challenge the white Mississippi delegation at the Democratic National Convention). But voter registration was meeting with less enthusiasm day by day in Mississippi as in Louisiana. Young people in Greenwood "were quite unmoved by the idea of registering to vote," said Sally Belfrage, a Freedom Summer volunteer. One young girl spoke out at a meeting against the embargo on desegregation tests. "You say that we have to wait until we get the vote. But you know, by the time that happens the younger people are going to be too old to enjoy the bowling alley and the swimming pool."[50]

Both CORE and SNCC were sensitive to the problem and following the 1964 presidential election had deemphasized voter registration and rallied around the slogan "Let the People Decide." CORE had moved more decisively in the direction of community control.[51] Dave Dennis, a major figure in CORE and COFO, succinctly summarized CORE's evolution in a 1965 interview. "We found last summer that, when the volunteers left, a lot of things collapsed, because volunteers were doing all the work and the local people themselves had nothing to do," said Dennis. "There wasn't any real basic attempt to get them involved, beyond just participants, that is, as an audience." In the past the movement had believed that there was a "federal intervention and central solution to the problem. Now we find out that it is not the solution to the problem, because those things are not really speaking to those problems . . . that people are having." The challenge of participatory democracy was compounded by the white northern volunteers who invaded Louisiana and Mississippi in 1964. Mike Lesser, a veteran activist and CORE's Louisiana state program director, thought that most volunteers paid little heed to the wishes of local blacks. When asked if he thought that the volunteers came to "work on what they want rather than what the communities need," Lesser's response was to the point: "I really say that out of the whites that come to work in the South, maybe 10% of those people really are sensitive to what their role is and really contribute something—the others don't."[52]

By the time Charlie Fenton arrived in Jonesboro in the fall of 1964, he was already inclined to let democracy have its way. When the community pushed for an armed self-defense organization that combined defense with community organizing, Fenton facilitated the process. Only one year before, it would have been movement sacrilege to suggest that a Gandhian organization should help build an armed self-defense group. As the Deacons were first taking form in Jonesboro, across the state line in Mississippi SNCC had moved quickly to prevent a group of teenagers from defending themselves against shooting attacks in Greenwood. A SNCC staffer told a hastily called meeting of teenagers, "We don't have the strength, even if we wanted to, to carry guns and fight back." One young girl asked, "Yeah, and do you mean we jus' s'pose to let the Man beat in our head?"[53]

Fenton had taken a different tack in Jonesboro. He could be proud of the Deacons, for he had played a role in forming the group. A middle-class, self-educated activist, Fenton had contributed skills that helped transform the defense group into a formal organization. In the new spirit of community organizing, he had placed his talent in the service of the community, allowing the community to settle on its own strategy and goals rather than imposing a predetermined program. Still, Fenton never abandoned his commitment to nonviolence while he worked with the Deacons. He continued to have faith that the Deacons would eventually gravitate toward nonviolent community organizing. A few months later Fenton told reporters that he hoped the Deacons would "become a civic organization bettering the community and eventually making the defense part of it obsolete." In the final analysis, an organization like the Deacons would have eventually developed somewhere in the South, if not in Jonesboro. The Ku Klux Klan drew its strength from its regionalism, and it was inevitable, given the lack of police and federal protection, that a regional black militia like the Deacons would emerge to oppose it.[54]

The Deacons set about creating a formal command structure of elected officers. Percy Lee Bradford, a mill worker and cab owner, was elected the first president of the Deacons. One of the community's most respected leaders, Bradford was a longtime member of the Voters League and had served on the black police squad. Henry Amos, another veteran of the civil rights movement and member of the police squad, was elected vice president. Bradford and Amos were representative of the social milieu that comprised the Deacons: mature, sober and industrious men, deeply religious and well respected in the community.

Though the Deacons never adopted formal membership rules, they did adhere to strict recruiting standards. Members had to be u.s. citizens, at least twenty-one years old, preferably registered voters, and of good moral character. In contrast to the Black Panthers, who recruited from the unemployed and the margins of society, the Deacons screened prospective members to exclude people with "criminal tendencies" and quick tempers. Individuals of poor reputation and troublemakers were unacceptable.[55]

The Deacons continued to meet regularly on Tuesdays at the Masonic Hall. Attendance varied from twenty to more than seventy-five people, depending on the level of activity. The membership fee was ten dollars, and monthly dues were two dollars; only dues-paying members could vote. The group adopted a standard meeting format using parliamentary procedure, with the reading of minutes and committee reports. All major decisions were made democratically, while day-to-day patrolling and monitoring duties were mainly directed by Earnest Thomas.

Meetings primarily focused on defense logistics. The daily routine of guarding CORE workers and the community required decisions on assignments, patrol schedules, and equipment purchases. Although their mission was principally defense, the Deacons soon found that they were also the leading civil rights group in Jonesboro, and their meetings expanded to address political questions regarding the ongoing desegregation campaign.

In addition to planning defense, the Deacons' meetings provided moral support for new recruits. The gatherings became a pulpit for the new creed of manhood, a crusade against passivity and fear. The Deacons implored, bullied, and shamed potential recruits into accepting their role as defenders of the black community. Charlie White, a young mill worker who had patrolled with the black police squad, recalled that the meetings were intended to instill pride and confidence in a new recruit, and "to get the man to stand up" for the community.[56]

Like many of his fellow Deacons, White believed that the mere presence of black men in the movement deterred Klan and police terrorism. According to White, women and children alone on the protest lines actually encouraged Klan harassment. When black men joined the line, the Klan and police acted with restraint. "You had some people who respect you for being nonviolent," said White. "Then on the other side, you had your people that were trying to run over you because they could. That's where the Deacons come in. When the radicals from the other side came up, we had somebody to take care of them."[57]

Taking a name for their organization broke with the tradition of self-defense groups remaining anonymous and informal. The next step—the one that other groups had balked at in the past—was going public. The *New York Times* would make quick work of this task.

CHAPTER

3

In the *New York Times*

BY THE END of November 1964 the Jonesboro Deacons, equipped with their new walkie-talkies and citizen band (CB) radios, were patrolling regularly. The movement drew inspiration from the new organization: during the previous summer the Jonesboro CORE would have been fortunate to attract twenty people to a desegregation protest—yet on 16 December a massive display of 236 protesters arrived at the Jonesboro library to integrate it. Overwhelmed, town officials quickly conceded and opened the library to blacks, but not before removing all tables and chairs to prevent "race mixing." The furniture embargo did not last long. The black movement in Jonesboro had scored its first major victory.[1]

Buoyed by the successful library campaign, activists ushered in the new year by renewing the campaign to desegregate public accommodations. On New Year's Day 1965 Deacons leader Earnest Thomas boldly led three other blacks into the M & D Restaurant. In June 1964 the black police squad had been forced to scuttle the first integration attempt at the M & D. This time the outcome was quite different. With the Deacons leading the protest, the owner grudgingly served the testers. More restaurant tests occurred on 2 and 4 January, meeting with mixed success. One restaurant resisted integration by closing its doors and firing its black employees. A few restaurants would later circumvent desegregation laws by becoming nominally "private clubs."[2]

The desegregation protests spread to nearby Hodge, where Fenton and the Deacons led another mass meeting. The increased pace of desegregation activities was lifting morale, and on 4 January 1965 Jonesboro community leaders assembled to plan an expanded desegregation campaign. The presence of the Deacons was clearly helping to overcome fear and passivity: In contrast to their past timorousness, three ministers came forward and offered their churches for voter registration.

Local police monitoring CB radio communications soon learned of the existence of the Deacons but apparently made no effort to harass or intimidate them at this stage. The FBI first took notice of the group in early January 1965. On 6 January the New Orleans FBI field office sent a coded radio message and letterhead memorandum to J. Edgar Hoover concerning the "Deacons for Defense and Justice." An unidentified source—probably local or state law enforcement officials—informed the FBI that a self-defense unit had been formed in Jonesboro. The memorandum noted that, although the Deacons' aims were "much the same as those of the Congress of Racial Equality (CORE)," the new organization was "more militant than CORE and . . . would be more inclined to use violence in dealing with any violent opposition encountered in civil rights matters."[3]

The FBI had little difficulty obtaining detailed information on the new group. In the years to follow, the bureau produced more than 1,500 pages of comprehensive and relatively accurate records on the Deacons' activities, largely through numerous informants close to or even inside the organization. It does not appear that any of the informants were exchanging information for money or personal benefit. An overall reading of the FBI documents suggests that most people on the inside provided information to the FBI in an effort to assuage fears that the Deacons were a violent or revolutionary organization.

Percy Lee Bradford, the Deacons' president, was one of those who cooperated with law enforcement officials in the belief that he was protecting the group. In an interview with an unidentified agent on 5 January 1965, Bradford went to great lengths to emphasize that the Deacons were strictly defensive in nature and would use violence only if attacked. Bradford volunteered that they had CB radios and walkie-talkies and that they routinely patrolled the black community. He went so far as to provide names of officers and leaders in the new group and estimated the Jonesboro group's size at 250–300 members.[4]

It is doubtful that there were three hundred dues-paying members in the Jonesboro organization. Bradford was using a tactic with the FBI that became standard practice for the Deacons: exaggerating the group's size to deter Klan and police harassment. The Deacons' leadership in other chapters continued this practice throughout the life of the organization. The only exception was when, in an effort to reduce pressure and attention from law enforcement, informants occasionally downplayed membership figures.

Still, the figure of three hundred members was not altogether inaccurate. The definition of the term "membership" may vary depending on one's race, culture, and class. The Deacons employed a criterion for membership far different from that used by white middle-class civic groups. In black political organizations like the Deacons, a person might be regarded as a member for simply expressing support for their goals and activities. In the fluid world of social movements, an organization may have a small formal membership but be capable of commanding a large number of supporters.[5]

The Deacons were evolving from a secret society into a political movement for self-defense. As they grew, the terms of membership became more flexible and inclusive. Membership was not restricted to those who paid dues and carried a membership card. The term "Deacon" began to denote a new militant political outlook. At a certain point in the organization's evolution, simple agreement with its principles was sufficient to be considered a member.[6]

There were, in effect, four tiers of membership in the Jonesboro Deacons—a structure that would be reproduced in other chapters. The first tier, the "activist core," comprised approximately 20 members who paid dues and regularly attended meetings and participated in patrols. The second tier, "active members," consisted of about 100 men who occasionally paid dues and attended meetings but usually took part in activities only when necessary. The third tier, the "reinforcements," comprised roughly 100–200 men who did not pay dues or attend meetings but agreed with the Deacons' strategy and could be depended on to volunteer if needed. The fourth, and most amorphous, tier contained the "self-proclaimed" Deacons: those individuals who, without official sanction, declared themselves to be Deacons. Though lacking formal ties to the organization, this fourth tier helped popularize the Deacons and their self-defense strategy. In Jonesboro, total dues-paying members never exceeded 150, but an additional 100 "reinforcements" could be counted on to support and defend the organization. So Bradford's figure of 300 "members" was not far off the mark.[7]

Bradford's 5 January interview with the FBI was the first time the Deacons were forced to explain their philosophy to the outside world. After two months of life, they still had no written statement of purpose expressing their goals and strategy. The Deacons had been called into existence by the exigencies of survival: the Ku Klux Klan had left little time to contemplate organizational philosophy. Born out of the nonviolent movement, the Deacons now found themselves in the awkward position of challenging the movement orthodoxy on nonviolence. Their initial efforts were halting, confused, and frequently contradictory.

In the FBI interview, Bradford attempted to allay the bureau's concerns by emphasizing that the new group was loyal to the precepts of nonviolence. He stressed that the Deacons were a peaceful organization whose goals were similar to those of CORE. This was certainly true with regard to CORE's civil rights objectives, but there was, of course, a crucial difference between the two organizations: unlike CORE, the Deacons were armed and prepared to kill in self-defense. Bradford tried to distinguish the Deacons from vigilante organizations by stressing that the Deacons were committed to self-defense, as opposed to retaliatory violence. The challenge for Bradford was to reconcile self-defense with nonviolence. It was a difficult, if not impossible, task.

The FBI found Bradford's characterization of the Deacons as a peaceful group unconvincing. The New Orleans field office promptly reported to J. Edgar Hoover that the group was "more militant than CORE and that it would be more inclined to use violence in dealing with any violent opposition encountered in civil rights matters." If Hoover was alarmed by this new armed organization, he showed no sign of it. The New Orleans memo to Washington went unanswered for the time being.[8]

But the growing movement in Jonesboro did not escape the attention of the Klan. Under the cloak of darkness on Sunday morning, 17 January 1965, arsonists struck at two Jackson Parish churches that had been active in the movement. Pleasant Grove Baptist Church, whose members included Deacons leader Henry Amos, was burned to the ground. Bethany Baptist Church also went up in black smoke. Both churches were located in remote rural areas that were difficult for the Deacons to protect. The churches continued to be a target of Klan terror after they were rebuilt. Arsonists returned and burned down Bethany Baptist a second time in November 1965, and both churches remained frequent targets of gunfire.[9]

In addition to Klan assaults, law enforcement agencies launched a harassment campaign against the Deacons. On 30 January Percy Lee Bradford and Earnest Thomas had been patrolling during the day and guarding a group of college students who were in town to help rebuild the burned churches. The two Deacons stopped around midnight at the Minute Spot Cafe. Bradford and Thomas stood in front of the cafe talking, with Bradford cradling a twelve-gauge shotgun. Police stopped and arrested Bradford, charging him with displaying a dangerous weapon in a public place while under the influence of an intoxicant.[10]

The white community was growing alarmed by this new organization. After living in fear for generations, black community morale was buoyed by the sight of defiant black men, armed and ready to die for their community. Much to the consternation of whites, the Deacons were everywhere: standing guard on the rooftops of the Freedom House, patrolling the streets with guns at their sides, marching into segregated cafes. They had reclaimed their community and whites could no longer ignore their existence. The tables had turned. "I know the whites, they were kind of afraid, those that had [black] women working for them back then," remembered Annie Johnson. "A lot of them were afraid to come and get their day workers." Some whites demanded that their domestic workers find their own way to work. Also inspired by the the new militancy, many domestics refused to endure the racial insults that went with the job. "Then a lot of the women quit because of different things that was said in the homes while they was there. Remarks and things," said Johnson. "They quit."[11]

The Deacons did not hesitate to play on white fears. The group produced a leaflet threatening to kill anyone caught burning a cross in the black community and then arranged to have black domestic workers leave the leaflets at the homes of their white employers. The Deacons "weren't violent people," maintained Johnson, "but I think the whites knew that whatever they said they were going to do, they did it."[12]

Until February 1965 the Deacons had remained a clandestine organization. People in the community and law enforcement officials were aware of their presence, as were the handful of CORE staffers around the state, but the Deacons had been content with relative anonymity. They still regarded themselves as merely the defense arm of public civil rights organizations. They had no reason to go public. Secrecy was the best way to protect their membership.

On 21 February 1965, however, the Deacons made the irreversible leap into public life. It was inevitable that they would attract national media attention. Violence *against* the movement had been a mainstay of reporting in the South. Now the story was violence *by* the movement. Veteran reporters were familiar with informal self-defense groups, but the Deacons were different. They were willing to openly extol the virtues of armed self-defense. By combining self-defense with political organizing, they represented an intriguing new direction for the movement.

The Deacons' story broke prominently in the 21 February Sunday edition of the prestigious *New York Times*: the headline read "Armed Negroes Make Jonesboro Unusual Town." The article, penned by Fred Powledge, described Jonesboro as an ordinary southern community, relatively untouched by civil rights legislation. He noted that "Whites Only" signs were still posted, several restaurants continued to segregate, and blacks "edge toward the curb when they pass a white man, and their heads bow ever so slightly." But there was one thing different about this secluded redoubt of segregation: "Here the Negroes . . . have organized themselves into a mutual protection association," reported Powledge, "employing guns and shortwave radios."[13]

The story painted a sympathetic portrait of the Deacons, focusing on their defensive philosophy and characterizing them as a stabilizing influence against white terror and police violence. There was no smell of gunpowder and blood here. Indeed, the portrayal of the Deacons as a "mutual protection association," a term Fenton favored, suggested something closer to a genteel civic club. Powledge highlighted the group's strong religious convictions, citing Bradford's description of its philosophy: "We pray a lot, but we stay alert too."[14]

Powledge let the story unfold through the voices of the members themselves. The Deacons told him that they deterred, rather than provoked, violence. Their presence had already "kept Jonesboro from developing into a civil rights battleground" and had discouraged police from brutalizing activists. They had even rescued a young black man from a possible lynching after he was accused of kissing a white girl. Powledge estimated the organization's size "between 45 and 150 active members." Sheriff Newt Loe declined to comment, telling the *New York Times* reporter that if he had anything to say, he would "give it to my newspaper boys around here." "We got boys in Shreveport and Monroe who see things the way we do," said the sheriff.[15]

The article quoted Charlie Fenton at length attempting to justify CORE's cooperation with a group that advocated armed self-defense. Powledge observed that Fenton was accompanied by his personal bodyguard, Elmo Jacobs, a former platoon army sergeant and Deacons member. Fenton defended CORE's policy by pointing out that the Deacons were not allowed to bring guns to the Freedom House. They represented the kind of "indigenous organization" that CORE desired to work with. Fenton wanted to cut back his leadership role and become more of a "liaison and helper." "Hopefully I will be able to help them translate their power into political terms as this thing progresses," he said. He also hoped that the Deacons would "become a civic organization bettering the community and eventually making the defense part of it obsolete." Powledge expanded on this theme, noting that the Deacons wanted to extend "their efforts to include other things—negotiating with downtown, becoming more active in Jonesboro politics."[16]

Despite Fenton's openness to the new group, the Deacons would eventually pose problems for CORE. "Now you have to deal with the non-violent movement and the self-defense movement," observed Ronnie Moore years later. "And it's more than what you have to say to the press. You really have to monitor so that one movement would not undercut the other movement and wouldn't get out of hand. I mean, what stops self-defense from turning into a violent movement against an act of aggression?"[17]

The *Times* article was an auspicious debut for the Deacons. Powledge had not suggested that they might escalate violence, nor had he highlighted the obvious strategic differences between the Deacons and CORE. Future media coverage would not be as charitable. In the *Times* article, the Deacons had convincingly portrayed themselves as moderates adapting to the realities of white terrorism. They posed no threat to the established organizations. They downplayed strategic differences with the rest of the movement, claiming that they had the same objectives: equality and justice. But underneath the carefully crafted image was a profound difference. The national civil rights organizations sought equality by shaming the nation with nonviolence. The Deacons sought equality through force and self-reliance.

The *Times* story accelerated the Deacons' transformation from a vigilance group into a political challenge to nonviolence. For the most part, the earlier self-defense groups viewed themselves as apolitical auxiliaries to political organizations. They advanced no strategic vision distinct from the existing civil rights organizations. Moreover, they avoided publicity to protect themselves—and to preserve the myth of a nonviolent movement.[18]

The Deacons broke from this tradition in two important ways. First, they fused self-defense with politics, thrusting themselves into the public arena to compete for political legitimacy, resources, and the loyalty of movement activists. They had transformed self-defense from the movement's "family secret" into a principled challenge to nonviolence. They gave explicit politics to what had been implicit in the actions of working-class men and women for years.

Second, the Deacons developed an autonomous, locally controlled organization that could survive without external leadership and funding from white liberals and national pacifist organizations. The Deacons' staff, funding, and political legitimacy flowed from the local community. They flourished or foundered depending on the level of local support. In contrast, projects sponsored and funded by national civil rights organizations could continue to operate regardless of community support—or even despite local opposition.

In truth, CORE, along with the Student Nonviolent Coordinating Committee (SNCC) and most other national civil rights groups, had great difficulty creating community organizations that could survive the departure of the national organization's staff. The 1961 McComb, Mississippi, project, which became SNCC's template for organizing in the Deep South, managed to register only six voters during a six-month campaign. When SNCC left in December 1961, its local structure collapsed. Most local projects sponsored by national civil rights organizations employed strategies that depended on the skills and resources of the educated and middle-class staff and volunteers. Although this led to short-term successes, it also left local communities dependent on external resources. Public relations, fund-raising, paid staffs, and legal strategies all required skills and resources that normally did not exist among poor, less-educated blacks in the rural South. Indeed, the SNCC staff members who opposed the Freedom Summer project were primarily concerned that local organizations would become dependent on the young white volunteers—as they had seen occur in other projects in Mississippi.[19]

In contrast, the Deacons adopted an organizational model that built on existing skills and resources. Most local men were comfortable with the Deacons' structure, based on familiar organizational forms (e.g., the military, fraternal orders, and social and benevolent clubs). Nor were the group's goals and strategies an exotic import; black men had been defending themselves and their communities for decades, albeit clandestinely. The Deacons had created an organization that comported with the community's political goals and resources. It did not require members to write press releases, develop legal strategies, and negotiate with the Justice Department.

More significantly, the Deacons' program of self-defensive violence ensured their independence from mainstream civil rights groups and the black middle class in general. Since liberals and pacifists opposed armed self-defense, the command of self-defense organizations fell to indigenous black leaders. This organizational distance from middle-class groups permitted the Deacons to develop an independent political strategy that more accurately expressed the interests of the black working class. Indeed, the Deacons constituted the *only* regional civil rights organization in the South that was completely controlled by black workers.[20]

The 21 February *New York Times* article had overlooked these unique features of the Deacons, although subsequent coverage did recognize their significance. The twenty-first of February emerged as a watershed date for the Deacons by ushering in three simultaneous events, each event connected to the other like three heavenly bodies aligning to cast a portentous shadow. First, 21 February was the day that the *Times* article made the Deacons a political reality by thrusting them into the national arena. It was, for political purposes, the Deacons' birth date. Second, it was the day that the Jonesboro Deacons established a chapter in Bogalusa, Louisiana, taking the first step toward converting the Deacons from a local group to a regional organization. And third, 21 February was the day Malcolm X was gunned down in Harlem. The foremost critic of nonviolence had fallen victim to enemies willing to silence him "by any means necessary." On the day that Malcolm X perished, the Deacons were born. Violence had been both executioner and midwife.

Malcolm X's death also led to the Deacons' first contact with the revolutionary wing of the black movement. Earnest Thomas was troubled by the news that rival Black Muslims had murdered Malcolm, and he persuaded the Deacons to underwrite an investigative trip to New York. Thomas arrived a few days after the assassination and immediately plunged into the heady world of New York's black nationalist community. Unlike in Jonesboro, the black activists in New York were heavily influenced by revolutionary nationalist ideologies and Marxist-Leninist doctrine. Black nationalism in New York comprised many currents. There were the Black Muslims, who represented a mixture of black separatism and religious fundamentalism. There were Garveyites, the ideological heirs of black nationalist Marcus Garvey, who electrified the black community in the 1920s. There were community and labor activists who identified with the pro-Soviet Communist Party USA (CPUSA) and dissident communists who had left the CPUSA for the revolutionary Maoist sects. And there were young veterans of the civil rights movement who had been radicalized by their experience in the South and deeply impressed by the revolutionary nationalism of the emerging Third World African nations.[21]

Thomas drank in this exciting underworld, which, for the most part, viewed the Deacons as brethren in the armed revolution. One introduction led to another, and Thomas was quickly exposed to a wide variety of critics of nonviolence and reformism. He met with Malcolm X's colleagues and later with Leroi Jones (Amiri Baraka), the nationalist writer and playwright. The New York trip set a leftward political course for Thomas, though he was still far from a Marxist convert.

Thomas also made contact with members of the Revolutionary Action Movement (RAM). Headed by Max Stanford, RAM was a small national network of Marxist-Leninist black revolutionaries. RAM had been a stalwart supporter of Robert F. Williams, the NAACP leader who had fled to Cuba to avoid criminal charges arising from his armed self-defense organizing in Monroe, North Carolina. In the coming months, the connection between the Deacons and RAM would spark considerable attention from the FBI.[22]

Thomas returned to Jonesboro and within a few weeks the Deacons had consolidated their organizational strength by legally incorporating the group. On 8 March James Sharp, a black attorney from Monroe, filed incorporation papers with the Louisiana secretary of state. To incorporate an armed black organization in Louisiana during the height of the civil rights movement required a good measure of subterfuge. The Articles of Incorporation buried the Deacons' true objectives beneath several paragraphs of platitudes about good citizenship and democracy. Their stated purpose was to "instruct, train, teach and educate Citizens of the United States and especially minority groups in the fundamental principles of the republican form of government and our democratic way of life."[23] In addition, the Deacons would educate persons about voting rights, citizenship, economic security, and the "effective use of their spending power." Not until the end of the purpose section does the document mention defense: "This corporation has for its further purpose, and is dedicated to, the defense of the civil rights, property rights and personal rights of said people and will defend said rights by any and all honorable and legal means to the end that justice may be obtained."[24] The charter conveniently omitted mention of weapons and armed self-defense.[25]

The charter did not change the attitude of law enforcement toward the Deacons, but it did carry a special significance for the group's members. Many blacks in the South in the early 1960s believed that while they could possess a weapon in their home, they could not legally carry weapons on their person or in their vehicle. "We weren't allowed to carry 'em," one Deacon told an interviewer. "Not even in our cars, loaded. Most of us only had 'em loaded since we joined the Deacons." There was good reason for this misunderstanding of the law. There had been a long history of white attempts to limit the availability of weapons to blacks. Most nineteenth-century firearm statutes in the South were intended to prevent free blacks from obtaining firearms. Louisiana slaves were denied firearms unless they had written permission to hunt within the plantation boundaries, and antebellum laws in both Louisiana and Mississippi banned freedmen and free people of color from carrying a pistol. Most concealed weapon laws in the South originated as attempts to limit black access. The discriminatory nature of these laws was so flagrant that a Florida Supreme Court judge was moved to comment that the 1893 Florida act that prohibited carrying a gun on one's person was "never intended to be applied to the white population." Similar concealed weapons laws in Alabama, Arkansas, Georgia, and Kentucky were primarily designed to disarm blacks. Because of these laws and their discriminatory applications, many African Americans understandably thought that they could not carry a weapon. This put them at a distinct disadvantage with the Klan, since whites carried weapons with impunity. If blacks could not transport weapons, they were limited to defending their homes; they could not defend civil rights activists as they escorted them in the community, nor could they effectively guard protest marches and other civil rights events. The Deacons were convinced that their charter gave official sanction to their right to bear arms in defense of their community, and that it prohibited law enforcement officials from interfering with the exercise of this right. "In the charter, we had to protect people's property and churches and so forth," recalled James Stokes, a Deacons leader in Natchez. "And therefore couldn't no one take our weapons from us. So we could carry our weapons just like the local law enforcement officers carry theirs." If a policeman stopped Stokes and objected to his weapon, Stokes would simply produce the charter and insist that it entitled him to carry a weapon.[26]

Rather than legitimate their claim on the Fourth Amendment, the Deacons invoked a higher authority: the ancient natural right of a man to defend hearth and home against attack. This was a right that whites found more difficult to dispute—even under segregation laws. On one occasion when the Jonesboro Town Council chastised the Deacons for turning to weapons, the Deacons argued that they were living by the same customs as white men. "We weren't trying to do nothing out of order," remembered Harvey Johnson, a Deacons leader. "But we told them: 'It's just like if someone is going to come over and run us out of our house. We not going to put up with that.'"[27]

By asserting their natural right to self-defense, the Deacons seized their rights by force rather than have them conferred by a beneficent elite. Rights conferred from above—as if a reward for good behavior—are fragile liberties. More a privilege than a right, they depend on the continuing goodwill of the dominant group. In contrast, inalienable and natural rights, seized from below by force, are as strong as the subordinate group's will to defend them. Nonviolence had made blacks dependent on the sympathy of a fickle white conscience in the North. Civil rights were awarded on the condition that blacks complied with white expectations of appropriate behavior: that is, refrain from using the same methods of force that whites had employed to gain their own rights. If black behavior ceased to meet with white approbation, then whites could withdraw the right.

In the coming months, as the Deacons confronted the Klan and police violence, it would become clear that they were not afraid of offending white sensibilities. The national civil rights organizations had been waiting for years for a mythical guardian angel to descend from Washington and vanquish their tormentors. The Deacons waited no more.

Not Selma

REAL VICTORIES FOR the civil rights movement at the local level were scarce in the Deep South and virtually nonexistent in Louisiana up through 1964. Severe repression by local authorities and the Klan, combined with economic pressure by white business elites, made it difficult to end segregation and discrimination even after the passage of the Civil Rights Act. But at the beginning of 1965 the Deacons and the Jonesboro movement stood poised to accomplish something that no other local or national organization had done before in the Deep South: force a segregationist governor to directly intervene to the benefit of the civil rights movement.

Although the February *New York Times* article sparked some national interest in the Deacons and the Jonesboro campaign, the nation's attention was still riveted on the unfolding drama in Selma, Alabama, where Martin Luther King had launched a voting rights campaign. While the Jonesboro movement, like most local movements in the South, was attempting to win freedom by coercing change in local power relations, King was explicit about his strategy of relying on the federal government for relief. King exhorted blacks to "fill the jails and 'arouse the federal government' to assure the ballot." The Deacons took a different tact. Emboldened by their successes, the Deacons and the local movement began to define equal rights as more than civil rights: they wanted equality as consumers and beneficiaries of government services. Their focus would soon shift from desegregation to education and city services, and as it did, they would lock horns with middle-class members of the black community who propped up the status quo system.[1]

Frederick Kirkpatrick was not only a leader in the Deacons, but also a popular physical education teacher at Jackson High School. Kirkpatrick carried his activism into the school by quietly discussing school conditions with students and encouraging them to participate in the desegregation protests. Some of his teaching colleagues rebuked him for his actions, and he soon received a visit by the black principal of Jackson High. Was it true that he had encouraged students to join in the protests? asked the principal. Kirkpatrick admitted that he had. The principal ended the inquiry without taking action against Kirkpatrick, but news of the confrontation soon spread though the school, fueling rumors that he might be fired.

Kirkpatrick's problem with his black colleagues at Jackson High was not unusual. In small southern communities, many black teachers and school administrators were indifferent, if not hostile, to the civil rights movement. This varied within regions and was more pronounced in rural areas. There were many causes of this conservatism, including economic dependency and fear. Black teachers and school administrators served at the pleasure of white school boards—boards that did not hesitate to fire teachers whom they suspected of supporting the civil rights movement. The few teachers who did openly support the movement were often pressured to moderate their activities by colleagues who feared that activism would bring reprisals against the entire faculty. Black administrators were not above discharging an activist teacher to preserve their standing in the white community or simply save their own careers.[2]

Fear and economic insecurity were not the only obstacles to teacher activism. Many teachers thought that civil rights protests undermined self-reliance and violated the creed of self-help. These educators were the political heirs of Booker T. Washington, the nineteenth-century African American reformer who popularized a strategy of black uplift that subordinated social protest to self-help. Teachers who subscribed to Washington's views often disdained protest as vulgar and déclassé. Their high status and relative affluence had bred elitism, individualism, and complacency.[3]

It is understandable that black professionals who had overcome the constraints of Jim Crow would have little sympathy for a movement that represented segregation as an insurmountable barrier to personal progress. Success fostered an individualistic mentality among teachers that was occasionally mixed with a genteel condescension toward the working-class "rabble" and street element that comprised the protest front lines. The class divisions within the black community were clear to the activists who felt the sting of condescension. "I think they [teachers] feel that they've gone through too much to get the job . . . to throw it away behind a movement," said David Whatley, a militant from Ferriday, La. "If they would get fired or something, then they would come. But as long as things were going well for them, they made no waves. They would sit in their fine homes, and they would drive their new cars. They didn't feel that they could dirty their reputations."[4]

School boards expected black principals to maintain discipline and prevent civil rights protests in the schools, a task that grew increasingly difficult as students became more active in the movement outside the classroom. At Jackson High, students were coming to resent the servile way that some administrators accommodated segregationist forces. They were impatient with the slow pace of change and were primed for battle. The opportunity soon presented itself.

On Sunday, 7 March 1965, hundreds of families in Jonesboro sat in stunned silence as they watched news accounts of the "Bloody Sunday" police attack on marchers on the Edmund Pettus Bridge in Selma, Alabama. With the images of the Selma attack still swimming in their heads, students returned to Jackson High the next morning. As the day progressed, the rumor spread that administrators planned to fire Kirkpatrick. He added momentum to the rumor by discussing his possible termination with students in his physical education class. "Kirk kind of just put a little icing on it and stirred it up a little bit," recalled Annie Johnson, a Jackson High student at the time. The rumored firing infuriated the students. "The kids went nuts over it," said Johnson.[5]

As the rumor swept through the school, the students abandoned their classrooms and flooded into the halls. Local authorities would later, with characteristic hyperbole, describe the walkout as a "riot." In truth, it never reached the fever pitch of a full-scale revolt, but students did enjoy a few unsupervised hours of protest flavored by juvenile mischief.

Commandeering the halls, the students vented their anger on symbols of white authority and black collaboration. At one point some of them broke the glass frames of wall photographs of the black principal, J. R. Washington, and the white Jackson Parish School superintendent, J. D. Koonce. Another group hurled bottles and smashed the glass on the school trophy case. By noon, school authorities realized that they had lost control of the situation and decided to cancel classes for the balance of the day.[6]

The reason for the walkout quickly expanded beyond the issue of Kirkpatrick's rumored discharge. Within days, the protest developed into a full-fledged school boycott, with students demanding parity with whites and black control of the schools. The Kirkpatrick incident became a catalyst for all the grievances of a lifetime. With assistance from Charlie Fenton and other adults, the students drew up a list of demands to present to the school board. Most of the demands centered on long-standing grievances of unequal distribution of resources. The students called for improvements at the school, including rebuilding the gymnasium, adding an auditorium, and expanding the "woefully inadequate" library that consisted of a handful of books. A demand to integrate the schools was added—almost as an afterthought.[7]

Control of the curriculum was an issue as well. Jackson High offered black students only two vocational tracks: agriculture or domestic service. The students insisted that the administration expand the curriculum to include training in auto mechanics and clerical skills; they also wanted "Negro history courses."[8]

The students organized the boycott with imagination and verve. The Deacons' direct link to the protest was through Glenn Johnson, student body president and leader of the student protest. Glenn was the son of Harvey Johnson, a founding member of the Deacons. Every day, hundreds of students would rise before dawn, prepare for school, and rush to catch the school bus. But instead of attending class, they armed themselves with picket signs and freedom songs and jubilantly protested outside the school throughout the day. When they were not picketing, they organized spirited marches through the community to the school board offices. They frequently directed their ire at "Uncle Toms" in the black community, marching on black churches that refused to host civil rights activities. At the end of the day, tired but in high spirits, the students filed back into the buses and returned home. The picket line had become their school.[9]

By the third day of the boycott the halls of Jackson High were virtually deserted. Police, the sheriff's department, and segregationists joined forces in a futile attempt to destroy the boycott. They harassed students and arrested several picketers, including Charlie Fenton. But the students had the momentum. On Wednesday, 11 March, the school board closed Jackson High in an effort to deter further protests. They announced that the school would reopen the following Monday, at which time all students would be expected to return.[10]

The school closure was a stunning setback for Jonesboro's white community. They watched in humiliation as power slipped into the hands of defiant black children. Desperate and angry, the white power elite quickly decided to take drastic action to suppress the rebellion.

On Thursday, 12 March, the students returned to picket and march. As they paraded around the school singing and chanting boisterously, an ominous drama was unfolding beyond their vision. Several carloads of police quietly converged on the perimeter of the black community. The police quickly set up roadblocks at all the principal arteries into the "black quarters," effectively cordoning off the students from the rest of the community. They were assisted by an odd group of volunteers, identified only as the

"Citizens Highway Patrol." The motley group was little more than a deputized posse of white segregationists and Klan members recruited especially for the blockades. The sentries refused to explain the reason for the barricades, saying only that they were containing a "disturbance" at the high school.[11]

The cordon caught the Deacons by surprise. They had not expected the city to resort to such extreme measures. Thomas and a small group of Deacons immediately began to drive from street to street, frantically searching for an unguarded entry point. They feared that the police and Klan were planning violent reprisals against the children at the school, and their apprehension intensified when they learned that the deputies had even refused entry to white journalists and officials of the Justice Department.

The Deacons' fears were justified. Inside the cordon, the police and posse were acting with impunity. Deacon Olin "Satch" Satcher was already inside the black quarters when the roadblocks were erected. Satcher stepped out of his car and coolly began to walk toward his house, a .22 caliber rifle cradled in his arm. Within seconds a squad of police and posse members descended on him. One of the posse, a member of the Jackson Parish School Board, violently assaulted Satcher, clubbing him on the head. After the beating, police arrested Satcher and shuttled him off to the parish jail.

Sealed off from the students and the black community, Thomas vainly searched for an opening in the cordon. He tried a back road but was stopped by a deputy and two posse members. Thomas recognized one of the posse as a Klansman who had participated in the Klan parade through the black community the previous summer.

One of the posse members commanded Thomas to leave, punctuating his order by cocking his gun in Thomas's face. Thomas reluctantly retreated but soon renewed his efforts, this time accompanied by two Deacons, Henry Amos and Charles White. The group probed the perimeter but still found all entries guarded. They decided to return to the barricade where Thomas had been turned back and threatened earlier. The Deacons stopped their car fifty feet from the barricade.

As White watched, Thomas and Amos left the car and marched toward the makeshift sentinels. Thomas was mad. He was unaccustomed to having a gun shoved in his face, and he was determined to set things straight with the sheriff's deputy who had watched the incident. Thomas confronted the deputy and demanded to know what they were doing: "You got the road blocked," he protested bitterly, "you can't get in and out of town." The deputy ignored him. Thomas then asked the deputy for his name. Why did he want to know? asked the deputy testily. Because he intended to file a complaint, replied Thomas, to find out who deputized the posse member who had cocked a gun in his face at the roadblock earlier in the day.[12]

Thomas's audacity sent the deputy into a fit of rage. "Who in the god damn hell do you think you are?" bellowed the deputy. Thomas sensed the situation was reeling out of control, so he turned away and began to calmly walk back to the car with Amos. He had taken only a few steps when he heard the click of a shotgun cocking. "Get them up," growled the voice from behind.[13]

The deputies handcuffed Thomas so tightly that the steel cut into his flesh. As one deputy twisted the cuffs, the other two slapped Thomas and jabbed at his ribs and kidneys with a shotgun and nightstick. One deputy stuck a pistol in Thomas's nose and taunted him. "Smell out of this, you black son-of-a-bitch," barked the deputy. "You better not move or I'll have hair flying everywhere."[14]

Thomas knew that his life hung in the balance. Glancing up, he spied a knot of black bystanders atop a nearby hill who were watching the scene unfold. Thomas pointed out the witnesses to the deputy. The deputy surveyed the situation, then holstered his gun and loosened the painful handcuffs. The deputies searched the Deacons' car and found two pistols and a shotgun. Thomas was arrested for threatening a police officer and resisting arrest. One officer claimed that Thomas had threatened him with a pen knife, which was seized as evidence. Later that night Deputy James Van Beasley came by Thomas's cell. "God damn it," gloated Van Beasley, "you won't be at that meeting tonight to raise hell." Thomas was held incommunicado for twenty-four hours, refused water, and finally released on bond the next day. The charges were eventually dropped, but one small injustice still bothered Thomas thirty years later. "I never did get that pen knife back," he said wistfully.[15]

By the end of the day, police had jailed several Deacons who had attempted to reach the students inside the cordon. But the Deacons' sacrifices had been rewarded; by acting quickly and resolutely, they had averted major bloodshed like the movement had experienced in Selma. Their presence, armed and willing to challenge the authorities, had deterred police officers and vigilantes from attacking the defenseless students. The day's events must have confounded the police and the Klan, accustomed to black men deferring to authority. The police could ignore the Civil Rights Act and all the blustering threats of enforcement from the North, but the Deacons were something very different. New laws changed nothing in Jonesboro, but new men were changing everything. Just how dramatically life had altered was borne out by a harrowing confrontation that occurred a few days later. On a bracingly cold March morning the students had gathered for their daily picket at the high school. As soon as they arrived, the police on the scene summoned a fire truck. When the fire truck arrived, the police ordered the firemen to prepare to open their hoses on the children in the wintry cold. Fred Brooks, the young CORE activist, had accompanied the children to the picket line and now watched helplessly as the crisis deepened. Suddenly a car pulled in front of the school. The doors swung open and four Deacons, led by Thomas, stepped out and began calmly loading their shotguns in plain view of the police. Brooks and the students watched the Deacons in stunned silence.[16]

The firemen walked toward the students with their hoses in tow. Then Brooks heard one of the Deacons say, "Here he comes. O.K., get ready." Brooks was speechless. "I was scared as shit. It looked like all hell was going to break loose." He remembered one of the Deacons giving the order: "When you see the first water, we gonna open up on them. We gonna open up on all of them." The Deacons then turned to the police and issued a deadly serious ultimatum. "If you turn that water hose on those kids, there's going to be some blood out here today."[17]

The police officers warily eyed the four Deacons standing before them, shotguns loaded and readied, faces grim and determined. Prudence prevailed. The law enforcers retreated and ordered the fire trucks to roll up the hoses and depart.

Although it never found its way into the history of the civil rights movement, the Jonesboro showdown was a historical marker in the emergence of the new black political consciousness in the South. For the first time in the twentieth century, an armed black organization had successfully used weapons to defend a lawful protest against an attack by law enforcement. Previously, the Deacons had claimed only the right to self-defense against racist terror. Now they asserted their right to defend themselves against government violence as well.

In Selma, march leaders were regrouping after the brutal Bloody Sunday attack. Organizers failed a second attempt to cross the Pettus Bridge on 9 March, the same day white vigilantes attacked and viciously bludgeoned one of the marchers, Boston minister James Reeb. Reeb died two days later. As the confrontation escalated in Selma, suddenly the Jackson High School boycott came to national attention. On Sunday, 14 March—one week after Bloody Sunday—CORE director James Farmer appeared on ABC's *Issues and Answers* news program. Farmer unexpectedly announced that the civil rights campaigns in Jonesboro and Bogalusa would be the focus of CORE's next "major project." He recited a litany of crimes committed against the black movement in the two Louisiana mill towns: church burnings, police brutality, and unbridled Klan violence. He expressed frustration with the mounting problem of local police brutality against the movement as it sought enforcement of the Civil Rights Act. Farmer's comments reflected the growing consensus among national civil rights organizations that new federal legislation was needed to enforce the act. Calling for a "federal presence" in Jonesboro and Bogalusa, Farmer demanded that federal marshals and FBI agents make "on-the-spot" arrests of local police engaged in brutality or rights violations.[18]

Despite the national attention, Jonesboro's establishment continued to harass the Deacons. On Monday, 15 March, the school board abruptly fired Olin Satcher, the Deacon who had been arrested and brutalized by police during the 11 March siege. The same day police arrested another Deacon, Cossetta Jackson, for possessing two concealed weapons. Police also confiscated Jackson's CB radio in an effort to disrupt the Deacons' communication system.[19]

The police harassment began to concern federal authorities as they observed from the sidelines. They speculated that the arrests and intimidation might provoke the Deacons to retaliate violently. On 15 March a federal government official who had visited Jonesboro warned the FBI that the Deacons were planning some "drastic action" in the next two or three days. On 19 March FBI headquarters, acting on the tip, instructed the New Orleans FBI field office to interview members of the Deacons. Headquarters characterized the Deacons as "allegedly formed to provide assistance to Negroes being arrested" and cautioned the New Orleans office that the Deacons were "alleged to be arming." J. Edgar Hoover's hostility to civil rights organizations was well known, and in this context the New Orleans field officers no doubt understood the "interview" order as instructions to harass the Deacons and discourage participation in the group.[20]

The FBI commenced a series of interviews in Jonesboro and Bogalusa clearly intended to intimidate the Deacons by suggesting that the FBI was investigating the group for illegal weapons. Typical of these interviews was the night Harvey Johnson was accosted by two FBI agents in front of his house as he returned from a protest march. The agents asked little about the purpose of the Deacons, nor did they raise questions about Klan violence or police harassment. Instead, Johnson recalled, they grilled him about illegal weapons. One agent told him, "They tell me you fellows got all kinds of machine guns and hand grenades." Puzzled, Johnson asked where the FBI got its information. The answer was, from a "Chicago magazine." Johnson waxed indignant, telling the agent, "Where you got that from is just a whole lot of junk."[21]

Police and FBI harassment of the Deacons had little effect on the student boycott. By the second week the resolve of the town fathers was beginning to weaken as they grew anxious that CORE would make Jonesboro another Selma. For all their fervid segregationist talk, the town leaders were businessmen—and segregation was becoming bad for business. The white establishment was confronting a new brand of black leadership in the Deacons. The older Voters League community leaders, for the most part small business owners, had been supplanted by more militant and unyielding working-class leaders such as Earnest Thomas, Percy Bradford, Henry Amos, and Charlie White.[22]

Superintendent Koonce began to search for avenues of compromise. He offered to arrange a meeting at the school board office between the board and fifteen parent representatives. But because his proposal excluded students from the negotiation process, parents and students rejected the request. They countered with a proposal that the board meet with all the parents and students at Jackson High on 22 March. The board, desperate but still prideful, agreed to meet with both parents and students but now demanded that the boycott be canceled and the children return to school before they would negotiate.

A mass meeting was called to consider the proposal to end the boycott, and hundreds from Jonesboro's black community spilled into Johnson's Skating Rink to debate the issue. Some favored the compromise, but the Deacons aggressively opposed it. Thomas and Bradford argued that the boycott was the black community's only bargaining chip. If the boycott was canceled, the school board would have no reason to agree to the demands. In the end, the Deacons prevailed and the community voted to continue the boycott.[23]

The events in Selma continued on a parallel path with the Jonesboro campaign, though diverging in one important way: the Selma campaign was dominated by appeals for federal protection, whereas the Jonesboro campaign chose to rely on local community resources. Federal intervention in Selma was soon to come. By 21 March President Lyndon B. Johnson had federalized the Alabama National Guard and deployed hundreds of federal law enforcement officials and military personnel to protect the second attempt at a Selma-Montgomery March.

On 22 March James Farmer arrived in Jonesboro amid great excitement and addressed an audience of six hundred people. Farmer reaffirmed CORE's plan to make Jonesboro a major project in the summer, likening the campaign to another "Selma." Farmer was "shocked by the fact that in Jonesboro there is practically no compliance with the public accommodations section of the Civil Rights Act nearly a year after passage." He pointed out that four restaurants and the library were still segregated, and blacks were still denied the simple dignity of home mail delivery. Farmer promised to increase staff for the summer project (voter registration and public accommodation tests) and finished his oration to thunderous applause.[24]

Farmer departed for New York, and the Deacons returned to expanding their political role in the community. On 24 March Earnest Thomas audaciously led a delegation of Deacons into the mayor's office and presented the city with a list of demands for community improvements. The demands centered on an equitable distribution of government services and resources. The Deacons called for a cleanup drive to rid the black community of trash and refuse; they wanted the city to erect street signs and provide house numbers throughout the black section; and, echoing Farmer's complaint, they demanded postal service for the black community.[25]

The lack of postal service was particularly irksome. For years blacks had endured the indignity and inconvenience of receiving their mail at the post office, rather than via the home delivery provided to whites. To send or receive a letter, blacks had to travel to the post office, often incurring the added expense of cab fare. Thomas was fed up with the practice and made his resolve clear to the mayor. "I told him that he was going to have mail delivery in thirty days. If not, we were going to file in federal court." The mayor demurred, claiming that there could be no mail service until the streets and houses were properly named and numbered. "He said it will take longer than thirty days because we got to get street signs and we got to order those." Thomas offered a solution: the Deacons would provide makeshift street signs and house numbers. The mayor agreed and mail delivery started promptly.[26]

In Alabama the Selma-Montgomery March was proceeding with few incidents, some 25,000 marchers now enjoying the full protection of the federal government. Despite the show of force, President Johnson still avoided a showdown with white terrorists, and he declined to bring his full powers to bear to compel local authorities to uphold law and order. Segregationists remained firmly in control of the police, the jails, and the terror apparatus.

If Johnson had forgotten this last point, he soon received a tragic reminder. On 25 March, the last day of the Selma-Montgomery March, a carload of Klansmen pulled alongside the car of Viola Liuzzo, a white Detroit housewife and mother of five, as she ferried marchers from Montgomery to Selma. She was accompanied by Leroy Moton, a young black activist. As the car came flush with Liuzzo's, the Klansmen unleashed a volley of gunfire. Liuzzo was killed instantly.[27]

The murder deeply stunned and moved the nation. The Klan had picked the wrong target. In the past its victims had been strangers to most white northerners: Michael Schwerner and Andrew Goodman were "beatnik" Jewish kids from New York; James Chaney was a young black man from Mississippi. But Viola Liuzzo was one of their own. Her photograph featured on television news programs across the nation showed a beautiful young woman with a kind, innocent smile. She was a teacher, a housewife, and a loving mother—in short, the idealized image of white femininity. That the Civil Rights Act was now the law of the land made the attack appear even more senseless and barbaric. The next day President Johnson, with J. Edgar Hoover at his side, appeared on television to angrily declare war on the Ku Klux Klan. The president called for new legislation to curb the Klan and a special congressional investigation into the terrorist organization. Liuzzo's murder also propelled forward the FBI's secret Counter Intelligence Program (COINTELPRO) to disrupt the Klan.[28]

The Klan had always harbored a special hatred for white Yankee civil rights activists. Black activists were a target as well, but the presence of white northerners, particularly white women, in the company of black men enraged the hooded night riders. In Jonesboro, the Klan had also singled out white activists for threats and brutal treatment. In the summer of 1964 Klansmen had appeared at the Freedom House and demanded the "two white guys." On another occasion a black man reported to CORE that Police Chief Adrian Peevy had asked him to "beat those white fellows to the point of death" in an attempt to drive them out of the community.[29]

In the wake of the Selma tragedy, news arrived that Cathy Patterson and Danny Mitchell had organized a group of white Syracuse University student volunteers to travel to Jonesboro during spring break. The students planned to help rebuild the two churches destroyed by arson in January. The Deacons were justifiably anxious for their safety. But undeterred by the Selma violence, the black community forged ahead toward a militant confrontation with the school board. The day after Liuzzo's murder, an impressive phalanx of 375 students and parents marched to the school board office in the brisk cold of early dawn. In a daring maneuver, the protesters surrounded the office and blocked all entrances. The tactic succeeded in closing the school board office; even Superintendent Koonce did not bother to report to work.[30]

Governor John McKeithen sensed a disaster in the making in Jonesboro. With the violence on the Selma march, the Liuzzo murder, and now the Deacons and the militant Jonesboro campaign, McKeithen hastened to preempt a bloody battle in Louisiana. On Friday, 26 March, as black students and parents surrounded the Jackson Parish School Board office, the governor announced that he would travel to Jonesboro the following day to attempt to negotiate an end to the two-week-old boycott of Jackson High School.

McKeithen's announcement marked a turning point in southern history. No governor before him had intervened to negotiate a settlement in a civil rights protest in the Deep South. Most southern governors either neglected or openly obstructed enforcement of the new civil rights laws. It was politically advantageous for them to allow a crisis to escalate out of control, forcing the federal government to intervene. The tactic relieved them from enforcing the desegregation laws while increasing the governors' popularity as stalwart defenders of southern honor. McKeithen departed from this script. "I've been told that I couldn't win re-election if I came here," said McKeithen in Jonesboro during the negotiations. "But I'm here today. The only person who stands to get hurt here today is your governor."[31]

We can only speculate as to McKeithen's motives for assuming the role of racial moderate. He would later say that his actions reflected the growing moderation of his own white constituents. It was true that throughout the South white moderates were increasingly voicing their support for détente with the civil rights movement. The causes for this change in attitude were complex. Some whites were sincerely troubled by the moral dimension of segregation; others were simply embarrassed by the unflattering media attention focused on the South. Still others feared that southern intransigence and violence were damaging the South's economy by hindering its ability to attract new industry.

Politicians like John McKeithen also understood that the civil rights movement was radically changing the face of southern politics. As black voting power grew, zealous segregationists found themselves at a disadvantage. It was politically expedient for some politicians to cultivate a moderate image by currying favor with black voters. Even before the Voting Rights Act, Louisiana had a substantial percentage of registered black voters—more than 16 percent, and the impending voting rights legislation promised to increase this percentage to well over 25 percent. McKeithen's moderate stance in Jonesboro thus stood to gain him more votes than he might lose.[32]

In Jonesboro McKeithen had both the Deacons and the Klan to reckon with. He took steps to undermine both groups, though he would ultimately target the Deacons for his severest measures. In early March he had considered instructing Louisiana attorney general Jack Gremillion to investigate existing laws that could be used to break up the Deacons through arrests. McKeithen had also discussed a plan to discredit the Klan through embarrassing congressional hearings on the group—but he took no steps to use his considerable state power to disarm or destroy the Klan.[33]

Regardless of his motives, McKeithen's actions in Jonesboro won him the instant enmity of the Ku Klux Klan. In response to the Jonesboro negotiations, the Klan lit up the night sky in the Baton Rouge area with nearly two dozen blazing crosses, including one brazenly ignited near the state capitol.[34]

The momentous negotiations with the governor occurred over the weekend of 27–28 March. Local attorney William "Billy" Baker, appointed a special liaison for McKeithen, arranged an integrated meeting with about forty persons at Jackson High, including a "school committee" led by Fred Kirkpatrick and several other Deacons.

The negotiations on Saturday, 27 March, were a sterling victory for the black community. Faced with the steely determination of the Deacons and the students, McKeithen had conceded virtually all of the boycotters' demands. He agreed to additional textbooks and water fountains, library improvements, and new landscaping and playgrounds. Although he could not promise funds to rebuild the gym, in the aftermath of the boycott voters approved an $800,000 bond issue for a new gymnasium.[35]

In return for the concessions, the students agreed to temporarily suspend the boycott and return to school. They left open the option to protest unresolved grievances in the future and even issued a statement declaring that they would continue to protest in school through the "observance of prayer and studying of Negro history."[36] A biracial committee was formed to negotiate future issues. The Deacons had made history: Their willingness to use public armed force had brought a segregationist governor to his knees, compelling him to negotiate with African Americans as equal citizens.

The marches and pickets would continue for several months, targeting both school and desegregation issues. But something had changed in the mill town. The change was apparent to Cathy Patterson, the young CORE activist, when she returned to Jonesboro with a group of fellow Syracuse University students after the boycott. Only seven months had passed since her departure, but Patterson immediately sensed the difference. When she had first arrived in Jonesboro in the spring of 1964, not a single family offered their homes for lodging, for fear of Klan retaliation. CORE activists had to find separate quarters in a house owned by an absentee landlord. But now, in the spring of 1965, black families without hesitation invited the civil rights activists into their homes. Patterson observed a new determination and courage in the average citizen. "I think it had a lot to do with the Deacons," she reflected. "And I think it had a lot to do with members of the community sensing their own capacity to protect themselves."[37]

"Example is not the main thing in influencing others," said Albert Schweitzer. "It is the only thing."[38] The Deacons were exemplars for the "New Negro" in the South. Their militance and combativeness had been absorbed into the political consciousness of the New Negro. When, in Cathy Patterson's words, blacks sensed "their own capacity to defend themselves," when they accepted that they were entitled to the same rights, respect, and honor as whites, the Deacons became unnecessary. In a reciprocal process, ordinary people became Deacons, and the Deacons became ordinary people.

Honor was a hallowed value for the Deacons. Honor had, in many cultures, historically functioned as a mechanism to deter physical attacks and banditry. In the masculine code of the South, an "honorable man" was someone who was willing to retaliate swiftly and violently to avenge any insults or affronts to himself or his family. He was willing to risk his life to defend his family and property. Potential predators would think twice about attacking an honor-bound man—or assaulting his kinfolk or community in his absence. The Deacons' deterrent power depended on the Klan believing that the Deacons would retaliate against any affront with deadly force. And Klansmen, as Ronnie Moore observed, "didn't want to die. They didn't mind killing; they just didn't want to die."[39]

Moore's insight was borne out in one episode in Jonesboro in the spring of 1965. In early April the movement had shifted its focus back to desegregating public accommodations, including several restaurants that remained segregated. The campaign expanded to demand an end to occupational discrimination and to protest police brutality. Student volunteers flooded in from the University of Kansas, Louisiana State University, and Southern University at Baton Rouge.[40]

The influx of white student volunteers caused considerable anguish for the Deacons. They did not want another killing like the Liuzzo murder in the Selma campaign. But the Yankee invasion was bound to inflame the Klan, and on 9 April the racists made their move. During the day a Kansas University student ran out of gas, and Elmo Jacobs, a Deacons leader, offered to help the student retrieve his car. Jacobs loaded four white students and a friend into his station wagon. As he drove down the highway, suddenly a brown Chevrolet station wagon pulled in front of Jacobs and brought his car to a halt. Startled, Jacobs looked through the windshield and saw a single-barrel shotgun emerge from the car blocking his path. The gun let out a deafening blast that left fourteen pellets in Jacobs's door.[41]

Elmo Jacobs never flinched. "Well, that made me went to shooting," said Jacobs. He quickly grabbed his gun and returned a volley of fire as the students watched in horror. His terrified assailants panicked and fled in a hail of gunfire.[42] It was the first and last armed attack on a civil rights worker in Jonesboro. Jonesboro was not Selma.

CHAPTER

5

On to Bogalusa

WASHINGTON PARISH ALWAYS had a dark and violent side. Located in the southeastern corner of Louisiana, the vast forested parish was bordered on two sides by Mississippi; local folklore held that desperados and rascals from Mississippi sought refuge by slipping across the border and blending into the countryside of Washington Parish. Its frontier character and fiercely independent farmers and loggers—both black and white—made for an explosive mixture, as evidenced in the "Balltown Riot" that erupted in 1901. The violence began when a rumor circulated that local blacks were preparing to massacre whites. A mob of white men surrounded a black church and started shooting the worshippers. Blacks returned fire, resulting in the death of fifteen blacks and three whites, according to official accounts. Local blacks, in keeping with their tradition of pride and defiance, claimed that many more whites were killed than authorities were willing to admit. "Old Man Creole killed about six," recalled John Wilson, a black farmer, who was interviewed by Horace Mann Bond in the 1930s. Eighteen years later, in 1919, the Great Southern Lumber Company of Bogalusa, the largest industrial town in the parish, became a target for a militant campaign engineered by the anarcho-syndicalist International Workers of the World (IWW). The IWW's interracial organizing drive culminated in the mill police murdering four white unionists who were defending a black union organizer. Although Great Southern had defeated the union threat, management lived in perpetual fear of a worker uprising; at one point the mill manager built a secret escape tunnel in the basement of his home. It was on this bloody terrain that the Deacons would take root and lead one of the most remarkable and successful local campaigns of the civil rights movement.[1]

The Great Southern Lumber Company was at the heart of the social conflicts that bedeviled Bogalusa in the twentieth century. In 1905 two Pennsylvania businessmen, brothers Charles and Frank Goodyear, scouted the

Bogue Lusa Creek area in Washington Parish for the site for a new lumber mill. The Goodyear brothers had made a fortune in coal and lumber in Pennsylvania, and they were now determined to harvest the bounty of Louisiana's expansive longleaf yellow pine stands. The Bogue Lusa Creek site was a barren clearing buried in a vast forest of millions of acres of virgin pine. For centuries the area had been home to a few bands of seminomadic American Indians. In the nineteenth century a handful of white homesteaders settled the region and took up farming and small commercial logging operations.[2]

The Goodyear brothers decided on the Bogue Lusa site for their business and quickly raised $15 million to erect an enormous sawmill. In 1906 the Great Southern Lumber Company was born and with it the city that the Goodyears named Bogalusa—later dubbed the "Magic City" by city boosters.[3] By 1907 the mill buildings and workers' housing were completed using 14 million feet of timber. The sawmill began operations on 1 September 1908, and an adjoining paper mill was established in 1917.

Bogalusa was a classic company town. Great Southern owned virtually every board and nail in the place: more than 750 homes, the town hospital, the utility services, and the company stores. The lumber company even trademarked the town's name. The only thing not owned by Great Southern were the people who labored in the mill. Nonetheless, the company ruled the institutions that ruled the people: city government, the judiciary, and the police.

Great Southern's workers were hewn from the independent stock of yeomen who peopled the pine country in nearby Mississippi. They were a coarse lot, hardened by the toil and misery of logging and subsistence farming. They knew nothing of time clocks, shift work, supervisors, and the discipline of modern industry. They had been masters of their few simple tools: the saw, the logging chain, and the mule. The Goodyears were confronted with the daunting task of transforming this headstrong and proud peasantry into a modern, regimented, compliant workforce.

Like most northern concerns conducting business in the South, Great Southern honored local segregation customs and reproduced them throughout the town and mill. Workers' housing was strictly segregated by race. In later years this extended to separate housing for Italians and Jews. Schools, parks, public facilities, rest rooms, parish fairs, parades, and water fountains were all segregated. Even hospital services were segregated. A black mother could have a baby at the local hospital, but, as a matter of policy, white nurses refused to bathe the child.

Great Southern also segregated jobs and cafeterias, break rooms and bathroom facilities in the mill. Approximately 15 percent of the workforce was comprised of black men. White women worked in the mill, but no black women did. Black men were largely excluded from operating machinery and relegated to the arduous "yard" occupations involved in moving and stacking timber.

The black community, which numbered eight thousand by 1965, emerged over the years in several distinct neighborhoods. The community neighboring the business district was dubbed "Jewtown" because of its proximity to Jewish stores in the downtown district. Other districts included "Poplas Quarters" (named in the tradition of "slave quarters"), Moden Quarters, Mitch Quarters, and East Side and South Side.[4]

Swept up in the tidal wave of unionization during the late 1930s, the mill was finally organized into segregated union locals in 1938. But by 1938 the leviathan sawmill, the largest in the world, had consumed all the timber within its grasp. Poor planning forced the mill to switch to processing pulpwood used primarily in paper production. Pulpwood could be processed from young pine trees that took only fifteen years to grow.[5]

Between 1938 and 1965 the mill and city underwent a radical transformation. Mill operations were increasingly automated and Great Southern was sold and resold, eventually coming under control of the Crown-Zellerbach Corporation based in San Francisco in 1960. As the mill changed hands, its new owners decided to withdraw from managing workers' housing and city services. Beginning in 1947, the mill owners systematically divested, radically transforming the city's political and social structure. In 1947 the mill closed the last of its company stores. In 1950 the company sold more than five hundred company homes to their occupants and donated the company-owned hospital to a nonprofit corporation. In the years that followed the company continued to divest all of its city services and withdrew behind the mill's gates. The denizens of Bogalusa, comprised almost exclusively of workers and hardly any middle class, were left to their own devices to run the city.[6]

The company's gift to the citizens of Bogalusa was a ticking bomb. Between 1961 and 1965 Crown-Zellerbach poured $35 million into modernizing the sawmill and box factory. The mechanization drive resulted in the layoff of five hundred workers and intensified competition between blacks and whites for the dwindling number of jobs. Crown-Zellerbach did little to assist the city in mitigating the social problems posed by the drastic layoffs. It offered no programs to retrain displaced workers or to attract new industry. While the city's civic and government institutions foundered in the face of these problems, the unions did attempt to fight back. A futile nine-month strike lasted from August 1961 to April 1962. In the end it cost Crown-Zellerbach $15 million and added to the class and racial tensions in the city.[7]

Though Crown-Zellerbach was the source of virtually all of the economic suffering visited upon Bogalusa, race became the scapegoat. At the same time that the corporation was throwing hundreds of workers into the street, the federal government was pressuring Crown-Zellerbach to end discriminatory practices in hiring and promotions. In March 1961 President John F. Kennedy signed Executive Order 10925, which mandated a "fair employment policy" to end racial discrimination by companies that conducted business with the federal government. Crown-Zellerbach's government contracts brought it under the provisions of the order, but rather than quickly implement and support these changes, the paper company evaded the new regulations. It fed the fires of racial hatred in Bogalusa by dragging out the divisive negotiations for several years. To add to the growing tensions, the white union local vigorously opposed the antidiscrimination reforms in an effort to protect the privileged position of whites in the mill.[8]

In May 1964 Crown-Zellerbach finally agreed to implement one fair employment reform: integrating the process by which temporary workers were selected—the "extra board." For the first time in Bogalusa's history, unemployed and desperate whites found themselves competing with blacks as equals. The predicament enraged white workers but left them with few remedies. They had lost their last battle with the company in the strike of 1962. The only protection they enjoyed was their white skin, and now the federal government, along with the company and blacks, was threatening to deprive them of this remaining privilege. White frustration and anger with the company and government were soon diverted into hatred for a more vulnerable enemy: black labor.

Given the simmering racial and class conflicts, it should come as no surprise that Bogalusa became the site of the most virulent and disciplined Klan offensives in modern history. Unlike most of Louisiana's nonunion cities, white workers in Bogalusa were well organized as a result of decades of trade union experience. In the 1960s new technology, the drive for profits, and the emerging black freedom movement conspired to deprive them of their perceived birthright. The civil rights movement became the stage for the last battle of organized white labor in Bogalusa. Unable to defeat the company, whites attempted to secure their caste privilege at the expense of black rights. Every concession to integration became a symbolic attack on the status and security of white labor.

This was the boiling cauldron Crown-Zellerbach handed city leaders in

1964. Bogalusa's political and business elites were confronted with two intractable forces: on one side, a well-organized white population, wracked by economic problems and consumed with racial hatred; on the other side, an increasingly militant black working class, equally well organized and resolute. For fifty years the mill's owners had successfully managed the conflict between these groups through authoritarian social control mechanisms. Now the owners left a power vacuum—one that the Klan would soon fill.[9]

The militance and independence of Bogalusa blacks were rooted, in part, in their unique origins as independent farmers and loggers in a racially mixed society. Horace Mann Bond's study of Washington Parish, conducted in 1934, reveals a remarkable degree of social interconnection and miscegenation between blacks and whites in the nineteenth century. According to Bond, following the Civil War a large number of white men entered into informal unions with black women and in many cases these family loyalties survived for generations. White men frequently provided for their mixed-race daughters by giving dowries of land and arranging for marriages to respectable and ambitious young Creole men. They also helped their mixed-race sons establish themselves economically through loans, land, employment, and interceding with local authorities on their behalf. "Cheap land and miscegenation in Washington Parish," wrote Bond, "made possible the development of segregated Negro farm-owning communities under the patronage of white relatives, who, in the nature of things, were usually members of the old white families in the community." By the 1930s four thousand blacks farmed more than fifteen thousand acres. Blacks in Washington Parish had been treated as social equals in ways that would have astounded blacks in the plantation delta. This special treatment, as limited as it was, had disappeared by the 1930s, but its legacy was an abiding feeling of equality and elevated expectations among the parish's blacks that kindled the militancy in the movement in the 1960s.[10]

The path to Bogalusa for the Jonesboro-based Deacons for Defense and Justice began in the spring of 1964. A weak and largely ineffective National Association for the Advancement of Colored People (NAACP) had existed in Bogalusa since 1950, headed by William Baily Jr., a retired railroad worker. The chapter had managed to open up registration rolls to blacks in 1950 and file a successful voting rights suit in 1959, when local segregationists attempted to purge 1,377 blacks from the voter rolls.

The leading civil rights organization in the early 1960s was the Bogalusa Civic and Voters League, headed by Andrew Moses. Bogalusa, like Jonesboro, had a significant number of registered black voters who could tip the balance in city elections. The Voters League concentrated on voter registration and often used its influence to bargain for political favors. League leaders told one visiting activist that the league was "significant in swinging elections, and for this reason, also, the power structure is willing to listen to them."[11]

By 1964 young members of the Voters League were pressuring Moses to increase the pace of change. Moses and several other respected black leaders began meeting with city officials as part of the Bogalusa Community Relations Commission, a biracial organization created by the white power structure to address civil rights issues. The black bargaining team sought desegregation concessions from the city through quiet negotiations. But the commission accomplished little in 1964 other than the hiring of two black deputies and the first all-black garbage truck crew.[12]

In May 1964 CORE created a stir when its New Orleans office announced that it intended to conduct a voter registration drive in Bogalusa. CORE was active in several communities close to Bogalusa and conducted highly publicized campaigns in Hammond and Clinton. Andrew Moses, though, was not eager to see CORE in Bogalusa. He had always moved slowly and cautiously, and his Voters League risked losing credibility with the white power structure if protests erupted.[13]

White leaders in Bogalusa were also concerned about CORE. One CORE report observed that "the white community, evidently noting the demonstrations in Hammond and the recently established [CORE] Regional Office in nearby New Orleans, is scared to death of CORE. The Power structure, anxious to attract industry and people to Bogalusa, will do almost anything to keep CORE out." The report added that because the power structure feared disruptive protests, it appeared "to be willing to give in to at least certain demands."[14]

To avert CORE's planned intervention, the mayor and the Bogalusa Commission Council asked the Voters League to persuade CORE to postpone its planned campaign. On 10 July 1964 Moses led a delegation of three Voters League leaders, all members of the Community Relations Commission, to meet with CORE's Ronnie Moore. Some militant members of the Bogalusa movement questioned Moses' motives. Gayle Jenkins, a member of the Voters League, claimed that the black delegation was working at the behest of the city government, and that the town fathers "paid them to go and talk to CORE and ask them not to come in."[15]

Indeed, the meeting had an air of official negotiations about it, with Moses presenting Ronnie Moore with a letter of representation from Bogalusa mayor Jesse Cutrer. Moses asked CORE to delay any organizing plans to provide time for the Community Relations Commission to resolve problems in an orderly manner. Moore agreed and informed Mayor Cutrer that the group had decided that it "must remain patient in order to bring about social adjustments." CORE and the league would give the mayor "six months to make certain progressive steps toward implementing the provisions of the 1964 Civil Rights Act" during which time CORE pledged to stay neutral to allow the Voters League to resolve the problem.[16]

CORE had scouted Bogalusa in the summer of 1964 and thought that the city had great organizing potential and was "ripe for CORE's type of program." Discontent with white intransigence ran high. The Civil Rights Act and other federal civil rights mandates had changed nothing in Bogalusa. Although segregation signs were down at the Crown-Zellerbach paper mill, the company left intact separate water fountains and toilets. Blacks were not allowed in the unemployment office during morning hours, and when they were admitted in the afternoon, whites were allowed to cut in front of them. The Washington Parish Charity Hospital refused black patients except on Thursdays. Lunch counters, restaurants, and nearly all public accommodations remained segregated. Blacks were limited to "broom and mop" occupations at downtown stores, and black neighborhoods lacked street lights, paved streets, and a sewerage system.[17]

Bogalusa's black community certainly had its share of challenges, but it also had the leadership sufficient for the task at hand. Along with the Voters League, there was a well-organized black farmers' cooperative and the black local of the Pulp and Sulphite Workers Union had developed several young charismatic leaders. The union had a political education committee that had implemented a program for voter education. CORE considered the black community a "well organized and reasonably informed community. . . . In short, we feel that Bogalusa can easily be one of the most exciting and challenging places this summer and for a long time to come."[18]

But CORE's optimistic assessment of the paper mill town seriously underestimated the organizational strength of the white working class and the Klan. With the decline of the White Citizens Council, several new and violent Klan organizations began aggressively organizing in the Bogalusa area. The Original Knights of the Ku Klux Klan (OKKKK), founded in Jonesboro as an offshoot of the United Klans of America, started recruiting in Washington Parish in 1963. It publicly announced its presence by burning crosses throughout the area on 18 January 1964. In response, Lou Major, editor of the *Bogalusa Daily News,* attacked the Klan in an editorial three days later. The Klan retaliated by burning a cross in front of Major's house. In May 1964 the Klan conducted its first rally in Bogalusa, no doubt in response to rumors that CORE was planning an organizing drive there.[19]

The first public accommodations civil rights protest took place on 3 July 1964, when two 12-year-old black girls spontaneously integrated the Woolworth lunch counter, sparking an ugly confrontation with a white mob. The girls' courageous act was the first and last direct action protest in Bogalusa in 1964. Black and white leaders returned to the strategy of negotiations with CORE as the Klan watched from the wings.[20]

In October 1964 the federal Community Relations Service (CRS), the agency responsible for assisting communities in implementing the Civil Rights Act, convinced Bogalusa businessman Bascom Talley to form a group of white business and civic leaders to oversee orderly desegregation in the mill town. Talley, an attorney and publisher of the *Bogalusa Daily News*, and CRS representatives were concerned that young blacks were growing restless with the snail's pace of change. They hoped that the business and civic leaders could preempt disruptive protests. Talley was something of a liberal anomaly on the race question. He had recently been appointed to the CRS, although discreetly omitting the news story from his own paper. A respected member of Bogalusa's business elite, Talley quickly called together a group comprising a few liberal businessmen and several religious leaders, most of them not natives of Bogalusa. The first meeting at Talley's home was attended by Reverend Jerry M. Chance, minister of the Main Street Baptist Church; Ralph Blumberg, operator of a local radio station; Reverend Paul Gillespie, minister of the Memorial Baptist Church; Lou Major, editor of the *Daily News*; Reverend Bruce Shepherd, rector of St. Matthews Episcopal Church; and two CRS representatives.

Talley's group decided on a modest and relatively harmless event to launch their integration efforts. They would sponsor a testimonial dinner for Vertrees Young, the former mayor of Bogalusa and the city's most venerated leader. The dinner would feature Brooks Hays, a former Arkansas congressman, now a Rutgers professor and CRS consultant. Hays had served as president of the Southern Baptist Convention and as a special assistant to Presidents Kennedy and Johnson. Despite his decidedly liberal credentials, Hays's Arkansas roots provided an acceptable southern pedigree. The plan called for Hays to discuss how other communities had successfully integrated public accommodations under the Civil Rights Act. The Hays Committee, as it came to be known, hoped to exclude potential disrupters from the event by making it by invitation only. The committee invited a select group of one hundred white businessmen and professionals and eight black leaders. In early December it formally invited Hays to speak at the Episcopal Church House on 7 January 1965.[21]

The Klan responded to the news with a well-coordinated and vicious terror campaign against the Hays Committee. Klansmen burned crosses at the homes of committee members. They assailed the members and their families with relentless death threats. They tampered with their telephones, causing them to make bizarre noises (it was later revealed that some Klansmen worked for the phone company). Night riders silently cruised by committee members' homes at all hours. The Klan distributed more than six thousand handbills door-to-door, carrying the ominous warning that "those who do attend this meeting will be tagged as integrationist and will be dealt with accordingly by the Knights of the Ku Klux Klan." Pressure also increased on the vestrymen of the Episcopal church, the planned site of the Hays speech. After the Klan burned a cross on the church lawn, the vestrymen quickly withdrew their invitation to the Hays Committee.[22]

As the intimidation increased, it became clear that local officials were allowing the Klan to terrorize openly. In the fall of 1964 Bogalusa's OKKKK chapter had at least 150 paid members and several hundred additional supporters at their beck and call (in late 1964 the OKKKK changed its name to the Anti-Communist Christian Association to protect itself from federal legal actions, but it remained known publicly as a Klan organization). At the height of the OKKKK's power, it was estimated that Bogalusa contained 800 Klansmen, more Klan members per capita than any other American city. The liberal press appropriately dubbed the mill town, "Klantown USA."[23]

The Louisiana Klan offensive was much more than a knee-jerk reaction by a few misfits. From the standpoint of most white people in the Deep South, the Klan campaign *was* the motive force of history. More than a battle against the new status of African Americans, the Klan's mobilization was, in the end, a defense of three centuries of caste privilege. Between 1964 and 1965 the Klan conducted a highly sophisticated campaign of terror, mobilizing thousands of men into a paramilitary militia. It combined terror with boycotts, mass demonstrations, and lobbying. In Louisiana and Mississippi, the Klan seized control of local governments and carved out a territory where civil rights activity was virtually impossible. Joseph Sullivan, who led the FBI's investigations in Mississippi in 1964, put it succinctly: "They owned the place. In spirit, everyone belonged to the Klan."[24]

In Bogalusa the Klan set up headquarters at the fire station directly across from City Hall. It organized a special terrorist squad to conduct well-planned assaults and cross burnings. For months the Klan had been arming its members for guerrilla warfare. Howard M. Lee, an auto repair shop owner and an Exalted Cyclops OKKKK unit leader in Bogalusa, obtained a federal firearms license and began equipping a small army of Klansmen in Louisiana and Mississippi in 1964. During the period of May–August 1964 alone, Lee bought

651 weapons and 21,192 rounds of ammunition, then illegally passed along the weapons and bulk ammunition to other Klansmen for resale without recording the sales or true names of purchasers. In one transaction he provided James M. Ellis, another OKKKK unit leader, with 65 Italian rifles. Local officials ignored Lee's activities; it would take a federal court eighty miles away in New Orleans to finally bring Lee to justice.[25]

The terror quickly isolated the Hays Committee from the rest of the community, its few supporters silenced by fear and official complicity. "We were just six guys bucking the whole darn town," said the Reverend Bruce Shepherd. City officials were appeasing the Klan, said another community leader, who asked for anonymity when interviewed by *Nation* magazine. "The Klan cannot survive here unless it has official sanction," he said. City and law enforcement officials had indeed turned a blind eye to the criminal violence, emboldening the Klan to even more flagrant transgressions. The police department was riddled with Klansmen: eighteen Bogalusa auxiliary police officers swore out of the Klan in April 1965 so they could remain on the force and deny Klan membership. At one Klan meeting members openly debated a proposal to bomb the church where the Hays Committee had scheduled its event.[26]

Mayor Jesse Cutrer and Police Commissioner Arnold Spiers attempted to conciliate Klansmen by appearing at a Klan meeting at the Disabled American Veterans Hall on 18 December 1964. But it was too late to reverse the momentum the Klan had gained as a result of the leadership vacuum. All Cutrer could do was ascend the podium and nervously survey the 150 hooded Klansmen glaring at him through slitted sheets. The Klan castigated the Hays Committee as integrationist, though none of its members had ever advocated integration. An OKKKK leaflet attacked Talley's *Daily News* as "amalgamationist" and reviled him for concealing his membership on the CRS. Talley was also the Klan's favorite target for class-based attacks on the wealthy. In one leaflet the Klan resorted to doggerel to reproach Talley: "This man would love the nigger / In order to grow financially bigger."[27]

Moderates like *Daily News* editor Lou Major were confounded by the bitter response. "I'm neither an integrationist nor a segregationist," Major protested. "We didn't want Bogalusa to become another McComb with bombings and burnings. Now for the first time in my life, I have a loaded pistol in the house." Talley laid the blame for the Klan's success on the failure of white businesses and government leaders to support the Hays Committee. "There has been a leadership vacuum here and that's what the Klan thrives on," offered Talley. "That and stupidity."[28]

Talley and his besieged colleagues frantically searched for an alternative site for the Hays event after the Episcopal church withdrew its facility. In the last week of December crosses blazed across town as the Klan intensified its intimidation campaign. On Monday, 4 January 1965, with only three days left before the scheduled speaking event, the Hays Committee requested the use of City Hall. But the Klan had already gotten to the mayor and the Bogalusa Commission Council. Cutrer promptly turned down the committee on the pretense that the event would be a private meeting in a public place. In addition, he rebuked the Hays Committee for interfering with the "quiet progress" that he was making on race relations through the Community Relations Committee.[29] The mayor's capitulation to the Klan signaled the end of any semblance of freedom and democracy in Bogalusa. The OKKKK now reigned supreme.

The mayor and the council's appeasement of the Klan set a pattern for the coming months. Writing to Vice President Hubert Humphrey, Leroy Collins of the Community Relations Service lamented that the mayor and council "have not furnished the sort of enlightened leadership that tends to mobilize strong business and civic support" and "appear more interested in conciliating the Ku Klux Klan than in enforcing the Civil Rights Act." With CRS representatives on the ground in other southern communities, Collins knew that there were other paths available to Bogalusa's white leaders. Only a few miles away in Hammond, the town fathers had weathered a similar crisis in the heart of Klan country. In 1963 black high school students in Hammond independently organized a protest march against segregation and forced city leaders to form a biracial committee to negotiate their demands. Infamous racist leader Judge Leander Perez of Plaquemines Parish soon caught wind of the integration plans and launched a campaign to reverse the gains blacks had made. But the mayor of Hammond took a hard line against Perez and the Citizens Council—in contrast to the Bogalusa experience. The mayor refused to allow the judge to use Hammond's parks for protest rallies and made it clear that Perez and his followers were unwelcome in the city. Perez retreated, and Hammond managed a relatively peaceful transition to integration.[30]

How little it took to counter mob politics speaks volumes about what could have been another path toward equality. Southern business and government leaders shared a large responsibility for why the South was consumed for ten years—between the *Brown* decision and the Voting Rights Act—by a horribly destructive and futile conflict. In the 1950s southern racial liberals discouraged aggressive enforcement of civil and voting rights by telling northern whites that federal intervention would drive moderates into the arms of segregationists and cause a second civil war. In truth, it was the absence—not the presence—of federal intervention that encouraged racist extremism and violence. Segregationists confused silence with consent, and appeasement only made them redouble their war to maintain white supremacy. The Hammond episode clearly demonstrated that decisive southern leaders could neutralize the Klan. But these exemplary acts of leadership were precious few, and we can only speculate about the outcome had more leaders taken this path. Alabama governor Jim Folsom had his opportunity early in the civil rights movement. The first showdown between state and federal authorities over segregation occurred in March 1956, when white mobs prevented Autherine Lucy, a black woman, from entering the University of Alabama in Tuscaloosa. Years later one noted Alabama journalist opined that Folsom could have changed the entire course of the subsequent civil rights movement had he only stood up to the mob; instead, Folsom disappeared on a three-day fishing and drinking trip.[31]

Bogalusa leaders' acquiescence to the Klan mystified many outsiders. Brooks Hays was astonished by the controversy that his planned appearance had created. The protests were the product of "a bunch of dunderheads," Hays told one CRS official. In all his experience in the South, he had never seen anything like Bogalusa: "That is the goddamnest place I've ever been."[32]

That the Klan had forced out Brooks Hays, President Johnson's top troubleshooter for racial problems, was bound to attract national attention. Local media had kept silent about the Klan attacks, but the story went public on 5 January 1965, when the Hays Committee courageously published a signed editorial in the *Bogalusa Daily News*. The editorial recounted the Klan's terror campaign and condemned the Klan and the cowering performance of the city government. "It is a shame," wrote the six Hays Committee members, "and we are ashamed, that fear should so engulf our community that it strangles free speech and the right of peaceful assembly, and makes a mockery of democracy."[33]

The sting of national publicity caused the town fathers to reconsider their ill-fated policy of appeasement. In response to the Klan terrorism, Police Chief Claxton Knight and Safety Commissioner Speirs announced a $500 reward for information concerning the cross burnings. And on 6 January, Mayor Cutrer went on television to denounce violence and call for "full and complete law enforcement at all times regardless of race, creed, or color." The announcements and official protests against the Klan were empty gestures; Bogalusa city police never made a single arrest for the harassment of the Hays Committee or the scores of cross burnings.[34]

Crown-Zellerbach also contributed to the Hays fiasco. There was a growing consensus among business and civic elites in southern manufacturing centers that integration was inevitable and had to be achieved in an orderly fashion to ensure economic health. Company towns like Bogalusa that sold products nationally could ill afford the negative publicity that Birmingham had experienced; Crown-Zellerbach's paper products were vulnerable to a national boycott. Yet Crown-Zellerbach relinquished leadership to a weak, ineffective group of leaders who were no match for a well-organized, working-class–based Klan insurgency. Had Crown-Zellerbach intervened in behalf of the Hays Committee, the Klan would have faced a formidable foe. But by the time the paper company realized the consequences of its silence, the opportunity for a peaceful desegregation had passed.

In contrast, Bascom Talley represented the new southern businessman guided by enlightened self-interest. Talley was a segregationist, yet he believed that the South would suffer if it held to its old ways. Early on, his *Bogalusa Daily News* set a course that reflected this perspective. In a trenchant editorial on 6 January, the paper argued that Brooks Hays would have served to reduce racial tensions, smooth the transition toward integration, and avoid racial demonstrations and violence. The *Daily News* feared another Little Rock in Bogalusa, pointing out that racial conflict "wrecks a town's economy" and "spreads fear and unrest and smears a community's image statewide and nationally."[35]

Governor John McKeithen was also slow to learn the lessons of Birmingham. Following the Bogalusa incident, McKeithen castigated Brook Hays for meddling in Louisiana's affairs. "If I were Brook Hays," he said, "I would stay in Arkansas. They have twice as much trouble as we have." The governor declined to visit Bogalusa, claiming that his presence would only inflame the local problems. The cross burnings were not a matter of concern either, since they did not intimidate anyone, including blacks, said McKeithen. "The more we talk about Bogalusa, the more trouble we have," he complained. "We have had no church burnings here, no bodies pulled from the river, no one shot on the highway as in other states."[36]

Mayor Cutrer joined McKeithen in chastising the Hays Committee and attempting to avert a crisis by declaring it resolved. "We have been through a very trying period which has put each one of us to the test," asserted Cutrer. "And we have come through with flying colors."[37]

Cutrer was dead wrong. The Hays incident was the beginning, not the end, of Bogalusa's problems. Young blacks were already upset that the Voters League had kept CORE out of Bogalusa. The league's quiet negotiations had accomplished nothing more than delivering the city into the hands of the Klan. The young militants in the league began to pressure Andrew Moses to start testing public accommodations. Simultaneously, Crown-Zellerbach officials were growing nervous about the negative national publicity that the Hays incident had generated. In early January company officials told Cutrer to arrange for an orderly staged testing of public accommodations. The plan was to test facilities, declare Bogalusa in compliance with the Civil Rights Act, and quickly return to normalcy.[38]

With national attention focused on Bogalusa, Cutrer knew that the Community Relations Committee would have to make rapid progress. He had already notified restaurant and motel owners that they must face the facts regarding the Civil Rights Act. Federal officials were pressuring the mayor to comply with the act or lose federal funds. Cutrer contacted Andrew Moses and other black members of the Community Relations Commission and arranged for a symbolic choreographed day of testing public accommodations. Cutrer promised that the testers would have adequate protection and that he would ask the Klan not to interfere. Moses agreed to the plan and reluctantly acceded to the young militants' demand that CORE participate in the tests. Moses and city officials were adamantly opposed to CORE intervening in Bogalusa, but they failed to persuade the young militants. Moses and three other Voters League members—L. C. Dawson, Robert S. "Bob" Hicks, and Gayle Jenkins—met with Ronnie Moore at CORE headquarters in New Orleans. CORE agreed to assist in the tests and dispatched two white representatives to Bogalusa: staff member William "Bill" Yates, a former English professor at Cornell, and volunteer Steve Miller, an Antioch student.[39]

Yates and Miller planned on four days of tests; they were not told that the Voters League had agreed to only one day. Prior to the test, scheduled for Friday, 28 January, Yates and Miller worked with the league to prepare for the actions. CORE trained the volunteer testers, most of them teenagers, in nonviolent protest techniques. The league arranged for the public schools to be closed so that the students could participate. The city grew tense as the day of testing drew near. State and city officials took precautions to guarantee an orderly, well-orchestrated desegregation test. Governor McKeithen arranged to have State Highway Patrol troops present to augment Bogalusa's small police force. On the eve of the event, Mayor Cutrer delivered a radio speech urging citizens to avoid the test area and to remain calm.[40]

The day of testing went surprisingly well. The Negro Union Hall served as headquarters for the operation, and the testers were shuttled between the hall and the testing sites. Andrew Moses led groups of four in testing sixteen eating establishments, two movie theaters, and the Austin Street Branch of the Washington Parish Library. Seven businesses refused to serve the testers, including Capos Restaurant and the Dairy Queen. The Klan stayed out of sight for most of the day. There were only a few incidents of harassment, and those were directed at CORE's representatives. While Bill Yates was waiting outside Plaza Restaurant, a group of white men jeered him, calling him a "Hebrew" (Yates was not Jewish) and menacingly drawing their fingers across their throats. Police stopped a large group of white men when they threatened to attack Steve Miller and a group of blacks who had just successfully tested the food counter at the Acme Drug Store. Miller had been shuttling the teenagers in his new red Barracuda, a sports car that his parents had recently purchased for him. Other than these few incidents, the testing went as planned. The Klan had honored its pledge not to intervene. The crisis appeared to be over.[41]

But there was still the matter of the seven establishments that had refused to comply with the desegregation law. At the end of the day the testers assembled for an informal meeting. The mood was exuberant, and the testers were feeling exhilarated and confident after a day of daring escapades. One of the teenagers suggested that they continue with more tests. Moses was not pleased with this development, since he had promised the town fathers that there would be only one day of tests. "Everybody was feeling good," recalled Steve Miller, "so the kids especially, as young people will do, they said 'O.K., let's do some more!' So at the end of the meeting, I just yelled, 'O.K. we'll be back Monday!'" It was an impulsive move that added to the tension between Moses and CORE. "I didn't have any sense of what I was doing, but it put Moses on the spot," said Miller. "And he had to call a meeting for 4:00 P.M. that day." But when they arrived for the meeting, the Union Hall was locked. Moses had canceled the meeting.[42]

The schism between CORE and the Voters League found its way into news reports. Earlier in the day, Moses had told the media that no further tests were scheduled and that injunctions might be sought against the establishments that refused service, but that decision would await a planned evaluation of the day's activities. But CORE was sending a different message. Bill Yates told a reporter that he planned to remain in Bogalusa for some time and that there would be more tests at the seven establishments that had failed to comply. Moses and CORE were apparently at loggerheads.[43]

The showdown between Moses and CORE occurred the following Monday, 1 February. Yates and Miller returned to attend an evaluation and victory meeting of the Voters League. Over the weekend the conflict festered between old and young members of the league. Blacks on the Community Relations Committee had been operating with no accountability to the black community. They were older moderates, hand-picked by the white power structure. Militants like A. Z. Young and Bob Hicks had been purposefully excluded. The militants had reached the limits of their patience with negotiation and compromise. Hadn't Moses and his colleagues capitulated to the Klan on the Hays Committee event? Hadn't "quiet negotiations" meant diversions and preservation of the status quo? Hadn't the old leaders acquiesced to the city's demand that the tests be limited to one day of empty symbolism that allowed half a dozen businesses to flaunt the law? To the young militants, nothing had changed.[44]

The mass meeting on 1 February exploded into a sharp debate when Yates and Miller suggested more tests and protests. Andrew Moses held firm. But by the end of the meeting it was apparent that Moses had lost control of the Voters League to the younger members. It had been a tense and exhausting exchange, but Yates and Miller were hopeful. The black community had sided with CORE, and the two representatives were excited at the prospect of organizing a campaign in Bogalusa. As darkness fell, the Voters League activists grew concerned about the safety of the two CORE workers. CORE had ignored Mayor Cutrer's agreement with the Klan that CORE would visit Bogalusa for only one day of testing. Now Yates and Miller were back in Bogalusa planning additional protests. Moreover, Bob Hicks and his wife Valeria (Jackie) were preparing to violate a strict racial taboo. They had offered to let Yates and Miller to stay at their home that night. No white person had ever spent the night in the "colored quarters" in Bogalusa.

Bob and Jackie Hicks sat down for dinner that night with their five children, Bill Yates, and Steve Miller. When they finished eating, they retired to the living room to watch television and talk over the day's events. Suddenly there was a knock at the door. Bob Hicks opened it and found Police Chief Knight and a deputy standing in the doorway looking grim. Claxton Knight was the archetypal southern lawman: a tall, lanky man who always sported a Stetson cowboy hat. He had bad news. A surly mob of whites had gathered on Columbia Street and were threatening to come after Yates and Miller. The CORE organizers would have to leave immediately. There was little that could be done to protect them. It might not be a bad idea if Hicks and his family left as well.[45]

Bill Yates did not respond well to ultimatums. The former college professor had an arrogant streak that even tried the patience of his friends. "Bill Yates was a hot head," recalled Bob Hicks. "He had a bad temper, a real bad temper." Yates's temper flared with Chief Knight. The two exchanged heated words, with Yates barking to Knight that he did not "like the goddamn idea of you trying to run me out of town." Yates paused, then turned to Hicks and asked if he and Miller could stay the night. "Hell yeah," said Hicks defiantly, "you're a guest in my house."[46]

The two police officers left in a huff. As they walked back to their car,

Yates asked if they planned to protect the house in light of the threats. Hicks remembered Knight's blunt response: "He wasn't going to play no nursemaid to some niggers and people down here in the house." The police chief returned to his patrol car and for a few minutes sat quietly in the dark with two deputies.[47]

The frightening prospect of a lynch mob arriving at the door in the next few minutes sent the Hicks household into a panic. The family was armed with a rifle, a shotgun, and two white pacifists who refused to touch either weapon. It was a woefully inadequate arsenal. But Bob and Jackie Hicks were levelheaded activists and they mobilized quickly; Jackie promptly called several friends for assistance. Within minutes, word of the Klan mob swept through the black community. One couple arrived to escort the children to safety; the woman was so nervous that she panicked and drove off, leaving her husband stranded at the house.[48]

When it became known that the Hicks family needed protection, the black men of Bogalusa responded swiftly. "A lot of black men in the community started coming down," recalled Hicks, and they were talking about how they were "going to kill us some Klan tonight." Chief Knight and his deputies watched in silent disbelief from their patrol car as a line of black men—armed with shotguns and rifles—rapidly filed into the Hicks house. After a few minutes Knight left. Moses arrived soon afterward but then left to make calls and never returned.[49]

Yates was busy on the phone trying to secure police protection so that he and Miller could return to New Orleans. Using a standard CORE technique, Yates placed calls to CORE contacts around the country, as well as local and national media. In the next few hours hundreds of telephone calls inundated local, state, and federal officials demanding that Bogalusa police provide protection for the CORE workers.

Within an hour of Knight's visit, the Hicks house was reinforced with more than twenty-five fully armed black men. The men sat for hours in tense silence, watching the streets for any sign of danger. Occasionally a police car drove by slowly and shined a spotlight on the house. Finally, Chief Knight returned to the house at about 4:00 A.M. The phone calls to CORE contacts around the nation had had their intended effect, and Knight now assured Hicks that the CORE workers would be safe.

The truth was that there never was a Klan mob on Columbia Street. Knight concocted the story to bluff Yates and Miller into leaving Bogalusa. Charles Christmas and Saxon Farmer, the leaders of the OKKKK, had demanded that city officials remove Yates and Miller, and Knight, lacking the nerve to sum-marily arrest and deport the two CORE workers, had resorted to a clumsy ruse.[50]

Knight's ploy to expel CORE had backfired and converted the civil rights struggle into a contest of honor for blacks in Bogalusa. The phony Klan threats against CORE and the Hicks family had only increased the stakes for the black community. In the past, the Bogalusa Klan had limited its harassment to white accommodationists; now it was threatening the sanctity of the home and the right to free expression in the black community. Defending CORE became a test of manhood and a point of honor for Bogalusa blacks. And honor was everything to the tough, proud mill workers—white or black. "You had what you would call diehards on both sides," explained Bob Hicks. "Whites in Bogalusa have been diehards for conviction. Bogalusa blacks have been diehards for conviction." Beyond defending their principles, blacks in Bogalusa simply did not like to lose. "They were sore losers," mused Hicks. "In whatever they got involved in, whatever they committed themselves to, they didn't want to lose. They wanted to win. They wanted to come out on top."[51]

The Klan mob incident had started—rather than stopped—the Bogalusa civil rights movement. "Had it not been for that . . . I don't think there would have ever been a movement in Bogalusa," Hicks stated. The mob incident was Bob Hicks's personal Rubicon as well: "I took whites into my home. No one else in the Bogalusa Voters League would do that . . . but when I brought them into my home, I was locked in." Hicks was not the only one locked in. The men who gathered that night to defend the Hicks family and CORE had irreversibly taken their first steps toward becoming the largest and most famous Deacons chapter in the movement.[52]

The Bogalusa Chapter

6

THE FOLLOWING MORNING Bill Yates and Steve Miller safely departed Bogalusa with a police escort. Their visit had left the city in an uproar. Embarrassed officials issued a denial that a white lynch mob had threatened the two representatives of CORE. The growing rift between Voters League moderates and militants resurfaced publicly when Andrew Moses told the media that there would be no further CORE activity in Bogalusa without the league's approval. CORE's second visit had also enraged the Klan, furious that city officials had not expelled the CORE organizers as it had demanded.[1]

But CORE was not through with Bogalusa. The intrepid Miller and Yates returned the next day, Wednesday, 3 February. They had been invited by local black union officials to discuss the developments. The CORE workers also hoped to meet again with city officials. Late that afternoon Yates and Miller left the Negro Union Hall in Miller's car to drive to New Orleans. They soon realized that a strange car containing five white men was following them. The car carried five segregationists, including Delos Williams and James Hollingsworth, members of the Original Knights of the Ku Klux Klan (OKKKK). Miller and Yates nervously drove around the black quarters for several minutes, the Klan car in close pursuit. The pair balked at leaving town by the single highway between Bogalusa and New Orleans. It was too risky—a narrow highway with few turnoffs for escape: "We just knew that we weren't going to go out that way," recalled Miller. Finally, Yates decided to attempt to telephone for help from Andrey's Cafe, a small restaurant in the black quarters. He yelled for Miller to stop the car. Miller hesitated but deferred to the judgment of the older Yates. Yates quickly jumped out of the car and headed to the restaurant phone.[2]

Suddenly the Klan car pulled in front of Miller's car, blocking his path. Shots rang out and one of the Klansmen tossed a brick at Miller's car. The

Klansmen leaped from their vehicle and caught Yates. They threw him to the ground and violently beat and kicked him, leaving him with severe internal injuries and a broken hand.

Yates finally escaped his attackers and stumbled into Andrey's Cafe. Miller parked his car behind the cafe and joined Yates. Inside were four or five older men. The eatery was a tiny matchbox of a building, little more than a single room 15 by 15 feet. The two CORE activists watched anxiously as at least four more carloads of Klansmen quickly joined the first car and began to slowly circle their prey.

A tense quiet descended on the room as Miller and Yates nervously considered their options. Their first line of defense was visibility. Miller quickly began to feed nickels into the pay phone, making a series of frantic calls. First, he called his mother in San Francisco, an activist in her own right, and told her to start a chain of phone calls to alert authorities and the media to their plight. Calls soon flooded into the offices of the Louisiana attorney general, the state police—anyone who could bring pressure to bear on local authorities. Miller also contacted CORE's New Orleans and Baton Rouge offices as well as the wire services. It was a frightening yet exhilarating situation for the nineteen-year-old Miller. "Remember Goodman, Schwerner and Chaney?" Miller asked a UPI reporter on the phone. "Well you're talking to the next ones right here. We're about to get it."[3]

Within minutes after the attack on Yates, several black men armed with rifles quietly slipped into Andrey's through the back door. Among them were the same men who had guarded the Hicks home a few days before. They took up their positions with an efficiency of motion. "I'm sure many of these men were combat veterans," recalled Miller. "They certainly deployed themselves as such." The armed men were a comfort to the two pacifists and a stabilizing presence as the crisis unfolded. At one point Miller panicked when the pay phone would not work. "They cut off the phones. They cut off the phones!" Miller shouted to the men in the room. One of the black men who had been watching Miller calmly diagnosed the problem. "Son, you got to put a nickel in there first."[4]

Even when Miller managed to put the nickel in the slot he still had problems, for local white telephone operators, as in the March 1965 siege in Jonesboro, refused to put through calls to the black community. Phone company employees outside of Bogalusa were drawn into the unfolding drama. One indignant Boston operator refused to get off the line until she succeeded in connecting her long-distance caller to Bogalusa. As they waited for word from the outside, Miller surveyed the dimly lit garrison and the stern militia standing guard over him. It was a philosophical epiphany for

Miller. "Up to that point, I embraced the concept of nonviolence," said Miller. Now necessity made him an apostate. "At that point I guess I said, 'Oh, I guess I'm not nonviolent anymore.'"[5]

Eventually FBI special agent Frank Sass in New Orleans reached Miller on the pay phone in Andrey's. The Klan caravan circling the block had melted away at sunset, but it was still unsafe for Miller and Yates to leave the cafe. Agent Sass told Miller not to leave until Sass could come to Bogalusa and talk to local authorities. Miller retorted that the agent should not delay calling the Bogalusa officials; he and Yates needed protection immediately, and they had already notified the media. "The world is watching," Miller warned.[6]

As the resident agent for Bogalusa, Sass was familiar with the recent civil rights activities there. He soon arrived at Andrey's but balked at entering the building. "Steven Miller, come on out," yelled the agent in his distinctive southern drawl. One of the black guards cautioned Miller that the cafe door was illuminated by a light, making Miller a clear target if he ventured outside. "Don't you go out there and silhouette yourself, boy," warned the man. So Miller told Sass to come in if he wanted to talk. The FBI agent opened the door and took a few steps inside. He was not prepared for the scene confronting him: the tiny restaurant was packed with black men armed with rifles and shotguns. "His mouth dropped a foot," remembered Miller with some amusement. "He literally couldn't talk for four or five minutes. He just stood there stunned."[7]

When Sass regained his composure, he took affidavits from Miller and Yates, surrounded by their armed defenders. By this time the CORE organizers were growing cocky about their bargaining position—bolstered by the small army at their command. They told Sass that they were not leaving Bogalusa. They demanded medical treatment for Yates, and they lectured the FBI agent about how "things were getting out of hand" in Bogalusa. Sass did not enjoy the scolding and he left without making any promises, saying only that he would speak with the state police. The black guards waited a few hours for him to arrange protection, but when the agent failed to return they decided to move the CORE men to the home of Bob and Jackie Hicks. They concealed them in the back seat of a car and transported them in an armed convoy to the Hicks house. When they arrived, Yates and Miller were greeted by a second defense force, scattered in trees, behind bushes, and inside the house.[8]

It was imperative to get Yates to a hospital so his injuries could be treated, but the local hospital was out of the question. By 10:30 P.M. CORE's regional office had arranged for a state police escort for Yates and Miller. Four patrol cars soon arrived at the Hicks home. The ranking patrolman walked to the door. "He came in, took about four steps into the room, and saw all these guys with guns and his mouth fell open and he was rooted to the spot," said Miller. "He was just dumfounded." The armed guards relished the moment. "I definitely remember these guys were getting a kick out of this, because at that point they were basically holding the upper hand."[9]

Miller and Yates said their good-byes and thanked their newfound Samurai. As they were leaving the house, they passed Jackie Hicks sitting quietly in a chair with a forlorn look. Miller bent down and kissed her on the cheek, much to the horror of the onlooking white patrolman. It was a small gesture of gratitude, but one that boldly flouted the color line. "I was always very proud of that," said Miller thirty years later.[10]

City police escorted Miller and Yates to the edge of town, where state police formed a convoy for the trip to the Lake Pontchartrain bridge. The pair eventually arrived safely in New Orleans. True to form, Mayor Cutrer and other city officials later denied that the attack on Yates had occurred, attributing it to the "vivid and unrestrained imaginations" of Yates and Miller. Governor McKeithen rebuked the two at a press conference in Baton Rouge, labeling them "professional troublemakers" and speculating that Yates's shattered bones and internal injuries were "self-inflicted." Adopting the same appeasement policy toward the Klan that had brought Bogalusa to the brink of chaos, McKeithen repeated his claim to the media that Louisiana had no racist violence problem. Nevertheless, the governor announced that state police would provide twenty-four-hour protection for core—no doubt to safeguard Yates and Miller from their "vivid and unrestrained imaginations."[11]

The second attack on Yates and Miller sealed Andrew Moses's fate. Moses realized that core was in Bogalusa to stay and that the testing and other forms of direct action protest would continue, regardless of his promises to the town fathers. Moreover, most of the league's younger leaders had demonstrated that they would support and defend core. Moses had lost the confidence of blacks and whites alike. His resignation from the Voters League within a few days marked the end of the naacp strategy of accommodation and negotiation in Bogalusa. The man who would ultimately replace Moses symbolized the new strategy of militant confrontation, coercion, and force. His name was A. Z. Young.[12]

At forty-two years old, A. Z. Young bridged the older and younger generations, combining mature judgment with a youthful passion for justice. The 6-foot 4-inch goliath was a strong-willed charismatic working-class leader with a flair for the dramatic. He was blessed with considerable oratorical skills and a gregarious personality and had provided militant leadership for the black local of the Pulp and Sulphite Workers Union for several years. A stint in the army during World War II imparted a military demeanor to Young. He had seen combat, serving as a tank commander in the 761st Tank Battalion under General George Patton. Young's military experience and union activism had schooled him in leadership and the art of negotiating from a position of power.[13]

Two other emerging leaders joined Young in the Voters League: Bob Hicks and Gayle Jenkins. Hicks brought a quiet determination and luminous intelligence to the league. A man of great personal integrity and determination, Hicks had already assumed leadership in organizing self-defense in the community. His cousin, Gayle Jenkins, had the best organizational instincts of the triumvirate. As secretary-treasurer, Jenkins managed the league's finances. Her quiet, thoughtful manner counterbalanced Young's penchant for showmanship and hyperbole.

All three were solidly working class in their backgrounds and political instincts. Contrasting sharply with their middle-class predecessors, the new leaders were passionately independent and militant, and not wedded to the political tenets of nonviolence. Whereas the league's previous leaders had gained concessions through brokering power, electoral bargaining, and quiet negotiations—all predicated on accommodating white interests—the new leaders cared little about courting the favor of whites. They eschewed negotiations and deal making from a position of weakness. They preferred direct action that forced a crisis and coerced concessions. They had few qualms about using force as a political tool, even if it alienated whites.

Nor were the new leaders constrained, as were their forebears, by aspirations to white bourgeois propriety. Whereas the old Voters League had been mired in an uninspired voter registration campaign, the new Voters League favored a direct challenge to civil and economic inequality. Their legitimacy rested on community consent, not the blessing of City Hall or national civil rights organizations. Locally led and locally funded, the new league was impervious to the pacifist agenda imposed by the national organizations and liberal funders.[14]

As the Voters League regrouped in February 1965, the OKKKK, encouraged by official appeasement and virtual immunity from prosecution, was planning an offensive. Its strategy was to silence all opposition, black and white. It would force businesses that had desegregated to resegregate, and it would coerce elected officials to defy the Civil Rights Act. To accomplish these ends, it would employ a variety of tactics, including boycotts, mass mobilizations, mob violence, and terrorist attacks.

In the months that followed the OKKKK mobilized thousands of whites to disrupt picketing, marches, and other forms of desegregation protest. Although the violent attacks on protesters often appeared to be spontaneous, they were actually the work of small, highly organized terrorist squads called "wrecking crews." An elaborate communication network of Klan members and supporters linked by phone and citizen band (CB) radios allowed the Klan to swiftly dispatch wrecking crews to impromptu civil rights protests.[15]

The Klan campaign of intimidation escalated on 14 February 1965, when Bob Hicks received a bomb threat by telephone. The next day Sam Barnes, a tough ex-convict and Voters League supporter, went to Landry's Restaurant with six black women. Within minutes the Klan wrecking crew, led by Virgil Cockern, descended on Landry's. The crew consisted of nearly thirty men, including Sidney August Warner, Delos Williams, James M. Ellis, Charles Ray Williams, and Albert Applewhite. Cockern and another accomplice brandished clubs and threatened to kill Barnes and the black women if they did not leave the restaurant. Barnes decided to retreat and returned to the black quarters as two Klansmen followed closely behind.[16]

Shortly afterward, Cockern took his crew to a gas station in the white part of town where four unfortunate black teenagers had stopped to purchase gas. One of the Klansmen placed a gun to the head of one of the boys and ordered the teenagers to leave the station. Three days later, on 17 February, Cockern and crew struck again. This time they stopped the Reverend Jerry Chance, a Hays Committee member, and threatened to harm him for his role on the committee.[17]

The Bogalusa City Police made no attempt to stop the attacks and in fact took pains to arrest blacks who had armed themselves in self-defense. On 19 February police stopped black activist Joshua Mondy for a traffic violation and arrested him for possession of a weapon. In addition to the Klan wrecking crew's violence, racist sympathizers at the telephone company continued to disrupt the phone service of civil rights activists such as Bob Hicks. Their telephones frequently failed to work or made odd noises, and operators refused to help them make long-distance calls. A subsequent investigation revealed that one of the principal Klan leaders in Bogalusa worked as a supervisor at the telephone company.[18]

The Klan campaign of terror culminated in thirty-three incidents in the month following the January desegregation tests. Throughout January and February local and state law enforcement officials failed to arrest a single Klansman, although CORE faithfully reported every incident. By the third week of February the Klan had silenced most white moderates and had forced nearly all of the businesses that had desegregated to resegregate. No example better demonstrated the Klan's power to ruthlessly crush white dissent than the case of Ralph Blumberg.[19]

Blumberg was one of the seven original Hays Committee members. In 1961 he purchased WBOX, the local radio station that broadcast news and country and western music. A World War II veteran and a member of Bogalusa's small Jewish community, Blumberg quickly became a successful businessman and respected civic leader. But his participation on the Hays Committee produced a sudden reversal of fortune.

The Klan singled out Ralph Blumberg for special persecution because he had broadcast the Hays Committee's editorial against the Klan in January 1965. The campaign against Blumberg was relentless. Night riders drove nails into the tires of his car and smashed the windshield. An anonymous caller threatened to kill his wife and children, forcing him to first send them to St. Louis and later to shuttle them around to Jewish homes in Bogalusa and New Orleans.[20]

The Klan accompanied the personal threats and violence with a campaign to destroy Blumberg's radio station by intimidating sponsors into withdrawing their advertisements. It threatened businesses with a boycott if they continued to advertise on WBOX. One advertiser received thirty-seven threatening calls. By March 1965 Blumberg had lost all but six of his original seventy advertisers. Financial ruin was imminent. At first Blumberg endured the harassment in silence. He even met with Klan leaders, who denied that they were coordinating the harassment campaign. But on 18 March, Blumberg struck back with an editorial calling on Bogalusa citizens to speak out against "the few who intimidate and attempt to control and infect the community like a plague."[21]

Racist terrorists swiftly responded to the editorial. That night, under cover of darkness, an assailant fired six shots from a high-powered rifle into the WBOX transmitter. The next day Blumberg's engineer hastily resigned. Blumberg's editorial against the Klan and his appeal for public support predictably failed. Both Governor McKeithen and Mayor Cutrer offered little sympathy and instead reproved Blumberg for sensationalism. McKeithen insisted that the Klan had little influence in Bogalusa and that Blumberg had "done the city of Bogalusa a great disservice" by claiming to be a victim of Klan terror. McKeithen also intimated that Blumberg had an ulterior motive for bringing negative publicity to the city—that he would soon win a lucrative job from an eastern newspaper or radio station. The mayor dismissed Blumberg's editorial as an example of Blumberg's habit of bringing national shame to the community. Cutrer blamed the station owner for his own predicament, observing that, as a result of his broadcast of the Hays Committee editorial, CORE had targeted the community. The mayor also questioned Blumberg's claims of Klan harassment, noting that none of WBOX's sponsors had complained of intimidation to local law enforcement officials.[22]

By August 1965 the Klan had frightened away all of WBOX's local advertisers, save for Bill Lott, the owner of a local Honda dealership. The radio station limped along with financial assistance primarily from Jewish supporters in New Orleans and New York. More than $8,000 in contributions was raised, mostly in New Orleans. A New York merchants' group bought one hundred public service commercials featuring the preamble of the Constitution. The national organization of the Presbyterian Church funded a series of half-minute commercials narrated by comedian Stan Frieberg. The advertisements implored Bogalusans to live by the Bible and love one another: most white Bogalusans had demonstrated that they were willing to do neither. In November 1965 Blumberg was forced to sell his station and leave Bogalusa. With his departure, the Klan had succeeded in driving out the last voice of white dissent in Bogalusa.[23]

As the events intensified in Bogalusa, civil rights lawyers filed a series of federal suits that placed increasing pressure on government bodies statewide. On 15 February a suit filed in Federal District Court in Baton Rouge requested the desegregation of state vocational-technical schools, including two located in Bogalusa: the Sullivan Memorial Trade School and the Sidney James Owen School. Judge E. Gordon West took only four days to issue a permanent injunction barring discrimination. The action coincided with another suit filed by the NAACP the same week in Judge West's court seeking to end segregation in all Louisiana public schools.[24]

The escalating Klan attacks forced Bogalusa's black leaders to seek protection. In early February Steve Miller and Bill Yates traveled to Jonesboro on CORE business. During the visit they discussed the Klan problem in Bogalusa with Earnest Thomas, Frederick Kirkpatrick, and other members of the Jonesboro Deacons. The Deacons suggested that Yates arrange a meeting with Bogalusa leaders to consider starting a Deacons chapter. Yates agreed, and the meeting was scheduled for 21 February.[25]

On the morning of the twenty-first, Charlie Fenton with his dog Duffy picked up Thomas and Kirkpatrick for the six-hour journey to Bogalusa. Fenton was driving a CORE station wagon with an ominous history. The vehicle was one of two donated in 1964 for the Freedom Summer campaign in Mississippi. The other station wagon had been driven by Schwerner, Goodman, and Chaney on the night they were murdered in Philadelphia, Mississippi.

The delegation of Jonesboro Deacons and Duffy headed south to Baton

Rouge, where they stopped for Bill Yates and Steve Miller. The integrated group was apprehensive about driving to Bogalusa through the Klan-infested Florida parishes. Ronnie Moore, who had secured cooperation from the state police in the past, arranged for a police escort for part of the trip.

As the journey continued, the conversation turned to unpleasant speculations about an ambush. The group knew that the Klan was connected through a network of CB radios. Kirkpatrick dismissed the nervous chatter, tapping his Bible: "Don't worry, I got the Good Book." A few miles down the road Kirkpatrick told Miller, who was now behind the wheel, to pull over so that he could answer nature's call. Miller kept driving, reluctant to stop in a remote rural area. Kirkpatrick repeated his request but Miller continued to ignore him. Finally, Kirkpatrick demanded that Miller stop. Miller relented, and Kirkpatrick left the car still clutching his Bible. When he returned, Kirkpatrick held up the Bible to reassure Miller. "Don't worry," he repeated with a large smile, "we got the Good Book." Kirkpatrick then opened the Bible to reveal a small derringer in a hollowed-out compartment carved in the "Good Book."[26]

The group arrived at the Negro Union Hall in Bogalusa at approximately 8:00 P.M. Fourteen men were assembled, including Bob Hicks, who had taken the lead in organizing the meeting. Most of those attending were men like Charles R. "Charlie" Sims and Alcie Taylor, who had been instrumental in the informal defense group that had guarded Hicks and other activists.

Kirkpatrick and Thomas entered the hall with guns in their waistbands. As the meeting began, they drew their pistols and placed them on the table. All the other participants followed suit, and the table was soon heaped with guns. The proceedings were tense. "We were all very scared," said Fenton.[27]

Fenton, the devout pacifist, had been assigned to guard the door with his dog Duffy and ordered not to speak or call attention to himself. He was not to allow anyone in or out. It was, according to Fenton, all very "cloak and dagger" and "high drama stuff"—and he loved it.[28]

While the Deacons portrayed themselves as strictly a self-defense group whenever they spoke to the media—courting public opinion and favorable publicity—their clandestine organizing meetings allowed them to sound a different theme. Here their goal was to shock black men out of the lethargy of fear and convince them that the Deacons had the requisite courage and martial expertise to counter the Klan. And so they did.

Kirkpatrick and Thomas plunged into their presentation with "fiery rhetoric" and "stern admonitions to secrecy and loyalty and discipline," recalled Fenton. Kirkpatrick lambasted the accommodationist leadership in the black community. "You been led by the tap-dancing Negro, and the head-tapping Negro—in other words, the plain old Uncle Tom," Kirkpatrick crowed to the Bogalusa group. The nonviolent movement's preoccupation with "rights" was diverting black men from a more important calling. "You got to forget about *right*, because *right* ain't gonna get you justice." If black men wanted justice, they would have to pick up the gun. "Wherever you're at, you be ready," Kirkpatrick warned. "Keep plenty of stuff in your car and at home. I carry with me almost all the time a hundred rounds. . . . Now in my town we have groups patrolling each street. We guarding intersections and every time a white man comes in[,] an automatic radio call is dispatched to a car to stop him and ask him his business. When the policeman come around we right on him too—we patrol him. You got to let him know that as taxpayers, you are the ones who send him to the commode, you the ones that buy his air conditioners, and those big cigars he smokes, and the dirty hat he wears."[29]

"Chilly Willy" Thomas elaborated on how the Deacons used two-way radios in Jonesboro and detailed plans to develop a statewide network of Deacons linked together by radios and the use of a secret code. Kirkpatrick touted the benefits of such a network statewide: "If they [white police] get to raising sand in Bogalusa . . . they'll see us coming down every road all over the state. When you come in with 300 or 400 cars, string out those automobiles up and down. The man gonna think twice before he moves, 'cause he knows he done moved on the devil."[30]

The presentation was a mix of exhortation, exaggeration, and martial posturing—all to good effect. If some black men in the South were paralyzed by fear, then these Jonesboro men were the antidote. Thomas's military training showed through. He chastised blacks for buying cheap small-caliber weapons, like .22 caliber pistols, and urged them instead to purchase larger weapons, like shotguns and .306 rifles. Kirkpatrick added that if they did buy pistols, they should standardize their purchases with larger-caliber .38 pistols, which would allow them to buy ammunition at a bulk discount.[31]

The Jonesboro Deacons challenged the Bogalusa men to prepare for major warfare. "We have contacts in Chicago and Houston for automatic weapons—for .50-caliber and .30-caliber," Thomas boasted. A man in the audience asked if those were machine guns. "Yeah," Thomas replied, "and we got grenades too. We want to be ready if they want to be violent."[32]

Thomas also discussed how to handle the inevitable problem of local black opposition to a Deacons chapter in Bogalusa. He encouraged the Bogalusa men to meet with local black leaders and influential groups such as ministers and teachers to persuade them to support the new organization. If they refused, then they did not deserve to be leaders. Thomas offered the services of the Jonesboro Deacons to help convince black middle-class leaders if the local chapter failed to do so.[33]

Thomas explained how Bogalusa could affiliate with Jonesboro. The local chapter would assess initiation fees of ten dollars and then monthly dues of two dollars. These funds would be used to purchase radio equipment, walkie-talkies, ammunition, and literature. Ten percent of the monthly dues would be forwarded to the Jonesboro office—now officially the Deacons' state headquarters.

Although Thomas and Kirkpatrick emphasized the defensive role of the Deacons, behind closed doors they proposed an additional tactic: using armed groups to stop police harassment. Thomas suggested that armed patrols could intervene to stop illegal or violent arrests. The mere presence of armed black men could deter illegal arrests, he argued.[34]

The meeting lasted until nearly midnight. Deciding to form a Deacons chapter, the Bogalusa men immediately elected officers and scheduled their first organizational meeting for one week later, on 28 February. The Jonesboro and Baton Rouge visitors prepared to depart but first drove to Bob Hicks's house. Soon after they arrived, they noticed a strange car circling the block. Suddenly, shots rang out and everyone fell to the floor. Within a few minutes reinforcements arrived, and word spread that a large caravan of cars had been spotted nearby. It looked like it would be trial by fire for the Bogalusa Deacons.[35]

The Deacons developed a plan to have several cars leave the house as decoys. Despite the clear danger, Fenton felt reassured by the cool, professional demeanor of the Bogalusa Deacons. They were "in control . . . acting more like an organized unit than it would have been under another circumstance," he recalled. "They knew what they were doing."[36]

Several cars departed, and when no one appeared to follow, the CORE station wagon left accompanied by several cars of armed men from the Bogalusa chapter. After they had driven what they thought was a safe distance from Bogalusa, the armed escort broke away and returned to the city. But within a few minutes the Jonesboro group realized that they were being followed again. Thomas was at the wheel and sped up, sending Duffy sliding around in the back of the station wagon. The car accelerated to more than one hundred miles an hour down the two-lane highway. Despite the speed, their pursuers were gaining on them. At the height of the chase Fenton turned around and saw Kirkpatrick sitting ramrod straight in the back seat, his eyes closed tight. He had laid his gun on the seat and was clutching his

Bible to his chest. Fenton knew they were in trouble. "It scared the hell out of me," he said."[37]

A few miles ahead loomed a major obstacle: the traffic light in the town of Sun. If they stopped for the light, the men would be a sitting target for their Klan pursuers. They hastily discussed their options as they raced into the pitch-black night. "All three of us committed that we would rather go through it and die in fire than get stopped," said Fenton. Thomas, exhibiting his gritty nerve, successfully executed a daring turn in Sun and headed back toward New Orleans. He soon lost the Klansmen. When the trio arrived in New Orleans, Fenton called CORE leader Dick Haley to report the incident. Haley listened sympathetically but reprimanded Fenton for getting involved with the Deacons. The station wagon proceeded back to Jonesboro in the late hours of the night, and the three exhausted men finally arrived home at daybreak.[38]

The Jonesboro Deacons' first effort to expand had met with success in Bogalusa. Indeed, the Bogalusa chapter would eventually overshadow the Jonesboro group in organizing strength and publicity. The men in Bogalusa were eager for an alternative to nonviolence. Their motives for affiliating with the Deacons were not much different from the motives of their counterparts in Jonesboro: they wanted security, honor, and dignity. The immediate impetus for joining was simply that law enforcement officials had refused to uphold the law and defend black rights. "What these people had in Jonesboro," said Bob Hicks, "is that since we can't get the local officials to protect us in our community, our neighborhood, let's back up on the constitution of the United States and say that we can bear arms. We have a right to defend ourselves since the legally designated authorities won't do it. So this is all we done. That's all."[39]

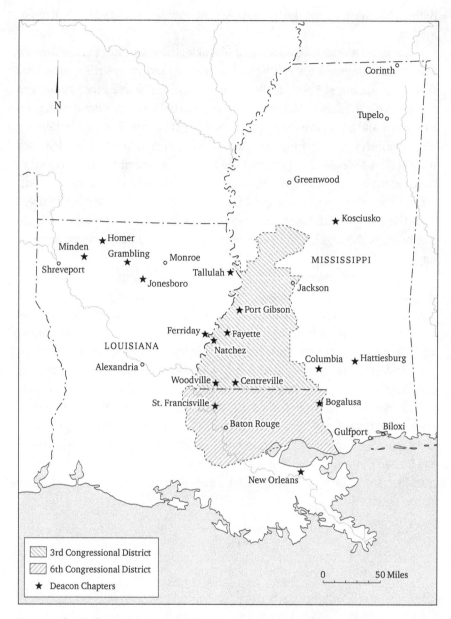

Deacons for Defense chapters in Mississippi and Louisiana. The shaded area represents a virtual "Klan nation" that operated outside of the Constitution—comprised of Ku Klux Klan strongholds in the Mississippi Third Congressional District and the Louisiana Sixth Congressional District.

CORE volunteer Steve Miller standing next to a cross burned in rural Jackson Parish, Louisiana, in 1965. (Courtesy Ed Hollander)

CORE volunteers, staff, and local activists in Jonesboro, Louisiana, assemble to re-build the Pleasant Grove Baptist Church, destroyed by arsonists in 1965. The Deacons for Defense provided protection for Syracuse University student volunteers. *Front row, left to right*: Alvin Culpepper (CORE), unidentified volunteer, Charlie Fenton (CORE), and the Reverend E. H. Houston, church pastor. *Second row, fifth from left*: Cathy Patterson (CORE). *Top row, fourth from left*: Ronnie Moore (CORE). *In the doorway, left to right*: Mike Lesser (CORE) and Jonesboro residents Eddie Scott, Lee Gilbert, and Freeman Knox. The remaining people are unidentified. (Courtesy Ronnie Moore Collection, Amistad Research Center, Tulane University, New Orleans)

Boycotting Jackson High School students protest at a black Jonesboro church that refused to allow civil rights activities. (Courtesy Ronnie Moore Collection, Amistad Research Center, Tulane University, New Orleans)

Earnest "Chilly Willy" Thomas, one of the principal founders of the militant Deacons for Defense in 1964 and vice president of the Jonesboro chapter. Thomas also served as a key national organizer and established the Chicago Deacons chapter in 1965. (Courtesy Chicago Historical Society)

Earnest Thomas (with two-way radio) guarding a civil rights meeting in Jonesboro in 1965. (Courtesy Ed Hollander)

Frederick Douglas Kirkpatrick, a key founder of the Deacons for Defense. This 1965 photograph was taken during the Jackson High School black student boycott, a protest triggered by a rumor that school officials planned to dismiss Kirkpatrick from his position as physical education teacher. (Courtesy Ed Hollander)

After the civil rights movement, Fred "Brother Kirk" Kirkpatrick became a well-known folksinger and activist in New York City. (Courtesy of Brunella Kirkpatrick)

Jonesboro Deacons for Defense leaders Cosetta Jackson and Elmo Jacobs. Jacobs had a shoot-out with white vigilantes who attacked a group of college student volunteers on 9 April 1965. (Courtesy Annie Purnell Johnson)

Ceola Qualls and Percy Lee Bradford. Qualls served on the volunteer black police unit in Jonesboro in 1964. Bradford was president of the Jonesboro Deacons. (Courtesy Annie Purnell Johnson)

Cossetta Jackson in 1965. Jackson was treasurer of the Jonesboro Deacons chapter. He was arrested for possession of a concealed weapon while guarding protesting students at Jackson High School. (Courtesy Ed Hollander)

Charlie Fenton, the CORE activist who helped develop the Jonesboro self-defense organization that later evolved into the Deacons for Defense. In the background is a small Klan cross that was burned at the local black high school on 2 January 1965. (Courtesy Ed Hollander)

CORE's Jonesboro Freedom House. Local black activists taunted the Klan by placing a mock coffin in front of the house. The coffin carried the inscription (with misspellings and partly obscured by a poster): "Here Lies the Grand Dragon, May He Rest in Peace." (Courtesy Ed Hollander)

James Jackson, president of the Natchez, Mississippi, Deacons. Jackson ran a local barbershop. (Courtesy Janet Herbert)

James Jackson (at right) at a rally in September 1965. Frame taken from the documentary film, *Black Natchez*. (Courtesy Ed Pincus Collection, Amistad Research Center, Tulane University, New Orleans)

MEMBERSHIP CARD

THIS IS TO CERTIFY THAT

NAME *Rev James Stoker*

ADDRESS *NATCHEZ MISS*

Is a member in good standing with the
DEACONS FOR DEFENSE AND JUSTICE
For The State of Mississippi

Registered Date *19/2* 196*5* Expires

Pre

Original membership card for Mississippi Deacons for Defense dated 2 September 1965. The Reverend James Stokes has carried the card in his wallet throughout his life. (Courtesy Rev. James Stokes)

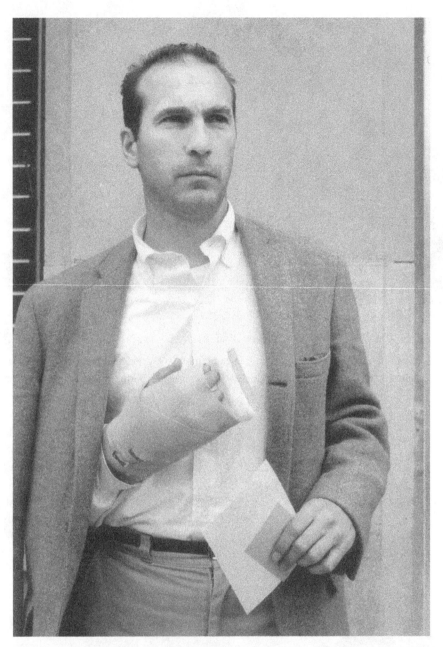

CORE volunteer Bill Yates with his hand in a cast after an attack by white vigilantes in Bogalusa. The attack motivated local blacks to form a Deacons chapter. (Courtesy Ed Hollander)

Charles Sims, president of the Bogalusa Deacons and a key national organizer. (Courtesy Corbis)

Left to right: Joe Sartin (Deacon), Charlie Sims (Deacon), unidentified person, Robert Hicks (Bogalusa Civic and Voters League), and Reese Perkins (Deacon). (Courtesy Ronnie Moore Collection, Amistad Research Center, Tulane University, New Orleans)

Robert Hicks, leader of the Bogalusa Civic and Voters League. Though never formally a member of the Deacons, Hicks arranged the meeting with the Jonesboro Deacons that led to the founding of the Bogalusa Deacons chapter. (Courtesy Ronnie Moore Collection, Amistad Research Center, Tulane University, New Orleans)

Ronnie Moore, CORE field secretary. In 1963 Moore became the first CORE leader to publicly support armed self-defense. (Courtesy Ronnie Moore Collection, Amistad Research Center, Tulane University, New Orleans)

Whites line the streets to taunt and assault civil rights protesters in Bogalusa in 1965. (Courtesy Ronnie Moore Collection, Amistad Research Center, Tulane University, New Orleans)

CORE national director James Farmer (center, in suit) leads the 1965 march in Bogalusa, with Ronnie Moore (left of Farmer, in suit) and A. Z. Young (left of Moore, in white shirt). Members of the Deacons joined the march to protect protesters. (Courtesy Ronnie Moore Collection, Amistad Research Center, Tulane University, New Orleans)

Local whites attempt to break through a police line to assault marchers in Bogalusa. A. Z. Young, militant president of the Bogalusa Civic and Voters League, is at left. (Courtesy Ronnie Moore Collection, Amistad Research Center, Tulane University, New Orleans)

Labor leader Victor Bussie (foreground, left) and Bogalusa mayor Jesse Cutrer during negotiations with the Bogalusa Civic and Voters League. Two Deacons accompany them: Charles Sims (in white shirt and cap) and Royan Burris (in white shirt). Burris became chapter president in 1967. (Courtesy Ronnie Moore Collection, Amistad Research Center, Tulane University, New Orleans)

CORE director James Farmer speaks at a premarch rally in Bogalusa. The movement in Bogalusa, like the movement in most communities in the Deep South, was comprised of teenagers. CORE's Louisiana program director, Mike Lesser, is in the upper lefthand corner. (Courtesy Ronnie Moore Collection, Amistad Research Center, Tulane University, New Orleans)

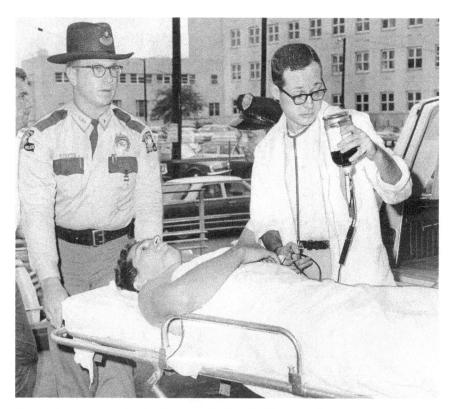

On 8 July 1965, a mob of whites attacked civil rights marchers in Bogalusa. In an attempt to fend off the attack, Deacon member Henry Austin fired three shots, wounding Alton Crowe of Pearl River, Louisiana. Crowe, seen here being wheeled into a New Orleans hospital, survived the attack, but the shooting had a profound impact on federal civil rights policy. (Courtesy Ronnie Moore Collection, Amistad Research Center, Tulane University, New Orleans)

DEACONS
FOR DEFENSE & JUSTICE

TIME:

THURS., OCT. 21
8:30 P. M.

PLACE:

I. L. A. HALL
2700 S. CLAIBORNE AVE.

ERNEST THOMAS
Why Deacons Were Organized

CHARLES SIMS
Why Bogalusa Joined The Deacons

AUBREY WOODS
What Role Deacons Will Play
In New Orleans

Flyer publicizing a meeting of the Deacons in New Orleans in the fall of 1965. (Courtesy Special Collections, Tulane University Library)

National Guard troops and state police face off with civil rights protesters along the 105-mile Bogalusa–Baton Rouge march in 1967. (Courtesy Secretary of State W. Fox McKeithen, Louisiana State Historical Archives)

Charles Sims, president of the Bogalusa chapter of the Deacons for Defense, taunts the Ku Klux Klan by displaying replicas of Klan robes at a rally in Bogalusa in January 1966. The militant Deacons had planned to defy the Klan by wearing the robes in a march but cancelled the maneuver in response to pleas from city officials. (Courtesy Corbis)

7

The Spring Campaign

BOGALUSA'S BLACK COMMUNITY first learned of the local Deacons chapter the day after it formed. On Monday night, 22 February 1965, Bob Hicks gave a report on the Deacons to a Voters League meeting comprising mostly teenagers as the new chapter patrolled the Negro Union Hall grounds in full force. Hicks discussed his initial organizing meeting with the Jonesboro group and explained how the chapter operated. "They set up a patrol system for the Negro community. They got radios, walkie-talkies, grenades, gas bombs, M-1 rifles." Hicks promised that marauding whites would now be kept out of Bogalusa's black community, and the meeting erupted in thunderous applause. "No white person will be allowed in a Negro area at night—salesman or anybody," Hicks assured the cheering crowd. "It takes violent blacks to combat these violent whites. We're gonna be ready for 'em. We're gonna have to be ready to survive."[1]

The first meeting of the Bogalusa Deacons took place on 28 February at the Negro Union Hall. Approximately fourteen men attended. Law enforcement agencies were prepared, and an informant reported back to the FBI the names of ten men who were present.[2]

Although Bob Hicks led the effort to bring the Deacons to Bogalusa, he did not serve as an officer of the new chapter. Attorneys for CORE had advised the Voters League to maintain some organizational distance from the Deacons. Hicks occasionally served as spokesperson for the Deacons, especially to the national media, but he continued to work primarily through the league, of which he was vice president. The organizational distinction between the Voters League and the Deacons was carefully maintained to protect the nonviolent image of the league and CORE. "CORE had represented the pacifist thing," said Hicks. "In order for people to try to support this type of thing, we couldn't bring them [CORE and the Deacons] in together. So we just separated the two." In fact, the two organizations were separate in name only. Hicks and A. Z. Young, though identifying themselves as officers of the league, were deeply involved in the Deacons' activities and consistently supported the group's self-defense philosophy. The two organizations were further intertwined by having the president of the Deacons, Charles Sims, also serve as treasurer of the Voters League.[3]

At first glance Sims appears to have been a strange choice to head an organization named after church leaders. Charlie Sims was about as rough as they came. His arrest record carried twenty-one entries dating back to 1957. He prided himself on his rap sheet and bragged that he had frequently been arrested for whipping "white boys on the biggest street they have in the city . . . I wasn't afraid of the law or nobody else." He had a reputation as a barroom brawler who strolled about town with a black jack in one pocket and a loaded pistol in the other.[4]

The years of hard living had taken their toll on Sims's scarred frame. His balding head was sprinkled with gray. A few teeth were missing, and his penetrating eyes were frequently bloodshot. Like Earnest Thomas, Sims was a veteran, having served with the army in Europe during World War II. He attended NCO (noncommissioned officer) school and attained the rank of sergeant as a shooting instructor. He boasted that now, at age forty-one, he could still "strike a match at 50 feet" with his rifle.[5]

Sims's travels in the military had profoundly affected him. "I moved around," he said. "I saw things I never thought about in Bogalusa. I went to the library and I studied." As in the case of many black GIs, the freedom Sims experienced in Europe made him more determined to overcome segregation in his homeland. "One day in the Army I see a corporal who was a policeman in Bogalusa," recalled Sims. "He see me in integrated places and all that. He got out of the service first. He sees me back in Bogalusa—me still in uniform. First thing he says, 'Remember, you're not in the Army now.' I made up my mind then not to be pushed around."[6]

The Deacons leader had been tested under fire in civilian life as well as in military combat, albeit in circumstances less impressive. On 6 December 1959 his girlfriend, Beatrice Harry, shot and wounded him during a fight. Beatrice was jailed as Sims fought for his life in the hospital. Sims summoned his mother and told her not to allow authorities to prosecute his girlfriend in the event that he died. Beatrice was innocent of wrongdoing, he said; she was only defending herself from a potential beating at his hands. Sims lay in the hospital for forty days, staring at the ceiling. "You live your life over like that," he observed several years later. "I never took the time out before to sit down and listen to my own thoughts." When he recovered, Sims refused to cooperate with the prosecutors of Beatrice Harry. He even told the district attorney that he could not read or write so he could not sign a statement against her. Sims and his would-be murderer eventually reconciled, and the two were still living together when Sims joined the Deacons in 1965.[7]

As a young man, Sims never had much interest in politics. But one day on television he saw a policeman dragging a woman "like she was a piece of wood" during a civil rights protest. The scene stuck in his mind, and soon afterward he joined the Voters League. His military background and pugnacious temperament made him a logical choice for Deacons president. Crude and lacking formal education, he was nevertheless an articulate and disarming spokesperson for the organization. Moreover, like other Deacons leaders, Sims was economically independent of the white power structure. Indeed, no one was quite sure how he made a living. He was an inveterate hustler who inhabited the twilight between casual labor and banditry. He listed his occupations as insurance salesman and cab driver, but mainly he lived, as one friend politely phrased it, "by his wits." He gambled. He hustled. He was beholden to no man. "He was free," said his friend Bob Hicks.[8]

For vice president the chapter selected Sam Barnes, a fifty-five-year-old ex-convict with twelve arrests. Barnes possessed all of Sims's courage and none of his bravado. He had already been on the front line, having been assaulted by the Klan during the February tests. In the months that followed he seemed to be wherever trouble erupted. Alcie Taylor and Royan Burris completed the list of chapter officers. Unlike Sims and Barnes, Taylor and Burris were reputable figures in the black community. Taylor worked in the paper mill and eventually served as an officer in the Pulp and Sulphite Workers Union. Burris was the youngest chapter officer. A small, wiry man, he ran the local barbershop, the center of communication for the black community. His size was no obstacle to his role as guard. The indomitable Burris was assigned as picketing coordinator for the Voters League, placing the Deacons at the center of all of the league's public protests.

There was an obvious difference between the leadership of the Bogalusa and Jonesboro Deacons chapters. Whereas Jonesboro's leadership was primarily law-abiding and comprised religious community leaders such as Percy Lee Bradford, Henry Amos, and Frederick Kirkpatrick, the Bogalusa group was dominated by less-than-respectable figures like Sims and Barnes, men who defied the law and social conventions. Every black community in the South had at least one man like Sims or Barnes—the legendary "bad nigger" feared by whites and blacks alike. Their reputation for violence served them well in their confrontations with the Ku Klux Klan.[9]

The difference in leadership between the two chapters owed to the fact that in Jonesboro the Deacons played two roles: civil rights organization and paramilitary defense group. In Bogalusa, the Voters League predated the Deacons. This allowed a leadership overlap between the two organizations. It was natural that the Deacons would attract the more combative men, warriors hardened by the military, the streets, or the prisons. Their chief prerequisite was reckless courage—a quality found more frequently in the hustler and street thug than in the preacher.

The Bogalusa Deacons plunged into their work. Approximately fifteen men comprised the chapter's core. Typical of this inner sanctum were steadfast loyalists like Burtrand Wyre. Wyre was a neighbor of the Hicks family and had come to its aid the first night it was under siege by the Klan. He maintained his vigil over the family for several years. "And the only time that he would go home was to change clothes," remembered Bob Hicks. "He stayed in my house, slept in my house, sometimes wake up in the morning with just me and him and my wife, all three of us laying down across the bed, asleep in our clothes. And he would take me to work, when he wasn't working or even when I got ready to get off he would be there in a car with somebody to pick me up. He stayed in my house for four years."[10]

In addition to the core group, the Bogalusa chapter had scores of men called "well wishers." These, perhaps numbering nearly two hundred, were mostly paper mill employees who were willing to help with security as needed.

The Bogalusa chapter began meeting every week at the Negro Union Hall. Unlike the Jonesboro Deacons, leadership was concentrated in the hands of one man: Charlie Sims. Sims ran the chapter like the army sergeant he had been. He managed the money, made the assignments, and barked out orders to his subordinates. Even Earnest Thomas, a proud veteran, found Sims's style a touch heavy-handed. "In the meetings, he was like a General; he shouted commands," remembered Thomas. But Thomas respected Sims's effectiveness. "Well, I was impressed that he was militant and that he wasn't going to stand for them running rough shod in the community. So I was impressed with him. He seemed to have a pretty good group together."[11]

The Bogalusa Deacons set up patrols and guarded meetings and homes. As Thomas had predicted, not everyone in the black community welcomed them. FBI records indicate that at least one black leader provided law enforcement organizations with extensive information on the Deacons. The informant, most likely a moderate black leader hostile to the new group, attended the first chapter meeting on 28 February. An FBI report noted that the informant intimated that the Deacons would not be successful "as he was of the impression that his Negro community were not desirous of becoming affiliated in any way with an organization which had as its purpose a defiance of law and order."[12]

Governor McKeithen, who had been deeply involved in the unfolding Bogalusa crisis, learned about the Bogalusa chapter within days after it was formed. Whereas McKeithen had appeased the Klan in Bogalusa during the Hays incident, he would not tolerate a black organization that protected the community from Klan terror. McKeithen immediately took steps to destroy the Deacons, asking Louisiana's attorney general, Jack Gremillion, to research legal methods for terminating the new organization.[13]

The Deacons were, even from McKeithen's perspective, only half the problem in Bogalusa. Despite his efforts to publicly deny the power of the Ku Klux Klan, law enforcement officials had apprised him that the Klan in Bogalusa was "without question the better organized unit of all the units in Louisiana." With his conciliatory policy toward the Klan failing, McKeithen now contemplated plans to undermine the Klansmen in Bogalusa. He considered asking Louisiana's congressional delegation to request hearings with subpoena power to investigate the Klan. According to the FBI, the governor felt that "if such an inquiry were held into the structure, purpose, and potential for violence, that this public exposure would cause it to dissolve." It is unclear whether or not McKeithen followed through on his plan. The matter became moot when, in the wake of the Viola Liuzzo murder, President Johnson called for congressional hearings on the Klan which commenced in the fall of 1965.[14]

Governor McKeithen was not the only official monitoring the Deacons. Leroy Collins, the former governor of Florida and a noted racial moderate, was the director of the Community Relations Service (CRS), the government organization created to assist in the orderly implementation of the Civil Rights Act. On 15 March 1965 Collins called on U.S. Attorney General Nicholas Katzenbach to express his concern about the Deacons, whom he likened to the right-wing Minute Men. Collins requested background information on the Deacons and any information regarding the FBI's investigation.[15]

When the *New York Times* broke the story on the Jonesboro Deacons on 21 February, FBI director J. Edgar Hoover ordered the New Orleans field office to commence an immediate investigation. In his memo to New Orleans, Hoover focused on Earnest Thomas's claim that the Deacons could obtain automatic weapons—and his advice that armed patrols should intervene to stop police arrests. "Because of the potential for violence indicated, you are instructed to immediately initiate an investigation of the DDJ [Deacons for Defense and Justice]," Hoover wrote. He cautioned the field office to "be alert" for the spread of the organization and "for any indications of subversive and/or outside influence." Hoover was especially concerned about illegal weapons and ordered New Orleans to follow up on "Chicago and Houston contacts for automatic weapons." He also instructed the New Orleans office to increase the number of informants within the Deacons and to conduct "interviews" to discourage "illegal arming and illegal action by the group."[16]

Hoover's instructions to conduct "interviews" to "discourage illegal arming and illegal action" was bureau code for disrupting the Deacons in general. The use of intimidating interviews was the first of several steps Hoover took to undermine the Deacons. Before the year was out, he added the organization to his "security index," a list of people the FBI planned to detain in the event of a national emergency. He also targeted the Deacons for further disruption through the bureau's covert Counter Intelligence Program (COINTELPRO), a "dirty tricks" project to destroy domestic radical political organizations, including black militant groups.

The New Orleans field office zealously followed Hoover's orders and commenced a series of interviews intended to intimidate Deacons so they would terminate their membership. Indeed, the office had already begun a campaign to disrupt the Deacons before the director's memo arrived. On 25 February Frank Sass and another FBI agent visited Bob Hicks at his home and warned him not to get involved with the Deacons. Sass hinted that if any black shot a white in self-defense, the black person would be charged with murder. Hicks calmly told Sass that self-defense was a constitutional right. Sass angrily stormed out of Hicks's house. Charlie Sims received similar treatment from the FBI.[17]

The Deacons had their work cut out for them. The Klan, equipped with approximately fifty CB radios, constantly monitored police calls, which allowed it to coordinate attacks on protesters. In late February 1965 the Voters League initiated a new series of tests at public establishments, frequently led by Deacons. A pattern of Klan response to the tests quickly emerged. As soon as testers arrived, the business manager would tell the testers that he could not serve or protect them. The proprietor would then make a phone call and within minutes a mob of whites would converge on the business.

On 28 February Royan Burris and Bob and Jackie Hicks tested the Redwood Hotel. They were refused service and decided to leave—not a minute too soon. Within three minutes after they departed, approximately thirty Klansmen came into the hotel looking for them. Law enforcement officials offered no protection for the testers; indeed, they regarded the actions as a needless intrusion on their time. FBI agent Sass told one Deacon to stop calling him every time someone was arrested. On another occasion Police

Chief Claxton Knight told Burris that the testing was "raising hell" with his fishing time.[18]

The Klan attacks intensified in March. On 4 March Klansmen stopped the Reverend Bruce Shepherd, a member of the Hays Committee, as he drove down the highway. The Klansmen ordered Shepherd to leave town or face being killed. A carload of blacks happened upon the scene and rescued the minister.[19] On 17 March Deacons leader Royan Burris was stopped by a Washington Parish K-9 unit and three Bogalusa policemen and arrested on a theft charge. The policemen handcuffed the Deacon and slapped and stripped him outside the police station. Inside the station they formed a circle around him and pushed him around. One officer, Vertrees Adams, brutalized Burris to the extent that he needed medical attention. When released from custody, Burris went to the Community Medical Center for treatment but was turned away.[20]

The harassment continued unabated throughout March and April. The Deacons were simply outnumbered and outorganized by a Klan that was exempt from the law. The Voters League and the Deacons were in a quandary over how to move forward. The intermittent tests were achieving little, other than demonstrating the Klan's strength. The black movement in Bogalusa needed a bold strategic measure that would bring national attention and reinforcements. Their prayers were answered on Sunday, 14 March 1965, when CORE director James Farmer announced on national television that Bogalusa and Jonesboro had been selected as the sites of the national organization's next major project.[21]

CORE's announcement guaranteed that Bogalusa—and the Deacons—would become a focus of national attention. The news bolstered the spirits of the Voters League and the Deacons while it sent local officials into a panic. Mayor Cutrer reacted swiftly to Farmer's embarrassing charges against the Bogalusa police. In a brief statement, Cutrer denied the charges of police brutality and intimidation and added that, contrary to Farmer's claims, no churches had been burned in Bogalusa (he was right—the church burnings had been in Jonesboro).[22]

The national publicity about the campaign of terror in Bogalusa was bound to embarrass city officials into taking some symbolic action against the Klan. Later that week Cutrer issued a tepid public statement calling for restraint and lawfulness in response to Farmer's announcement and hinting that the city would take a firmer stand against the Klan's rampant violence and intimidation. Cutrer read a timorous statement by city and parish law enforcement officials acknowledging that Bogalusa had experienced some cases of what they euphemistically called "malicious mischief," including "throwing of tacks in driveways, breaking of glass, and so forth." The Klan could only sneer at the mayor's idle threats.[23]

On 28 March the Voters League organized a successful "Freedom Rally" at the Negro Union Hall. The rally itself was without incident, but the Klan conducted a series of assaults that tested the Deacons' organization and mettle. A carload of whites chased CORE activists Ronnie Moore, Bill Yates, and Kimme Johnson in their car as they tried to leave the rally. They were subsequently rescued by two carloads of armed Deacons who escorted them from the city. Four Klansmen attacked and beat Jones Radcliffe from Bogalusa as he left the rally. Radcliffe managed to strike one of his attackers, so the Deacons provided him around-the-clock protection. The same night a carload of whites forced L. C. Magee off the road and into a ditch as he was returning home from the Freedom Rally. The following day whites lobbed a can of tear gas into the Negro Union Hall after the Voters League had finished a meeting.[24]

By the end of March Governor McKeithen was beginning to feel the pressure posed by civil rights conflicts in the Bayou State. On 26 March he announced plans to negotiate an end to the black student boycott of Jackson High School in Jonesboro. But McKeithen continued to insist that the Klan did not dominate a single community in Louisiana and that Louisiana's racial violence paled by comparison to that in other southern states. The only shooting incident that McKeithen could recall involved the shots fired into Ralph Blumberg's radio station transmitter. "As long as we can keep the thing down to a few bullets in an empty building at night, instead of rape, mayhem, and murder, I feel we have done all right," said the governor confidently.[25]

Events in Bogalusa quickened as the community prepared for the CORE invasion. City leaders had formed a Community Affairs Committee (CAC) the previous February, comprising the heads of civic, labor, and religious organizations. The CAC was created to address civil rights issues by exchanging information with the city administration, serving as a sounding board for proposals, and advising the mayor and the Bogalusa Commission Council. Attorney John N. Gallaspy chaired the group, banker Gardner S. Adams served as vice chair, and ultimately six Crown-Zellerbach officials joined the committee. By March the CAC had made little progress. It had tried unsuccessfully to persuade restaurants to comply with the Civil Rights Act and had failed to secure improvements in the black community such as street lighting.[26]

Most of the Deacons' early work had, as in Jonesboro, centered on guarding homes and civil rights workers, providing security for rallies, and patrolling streets. April brought increased responsibilities as the first of several groups of student volunteers descended on Bogalusa during spring break. Sixteen CORE volunteers from the University of Kansas arrived in the first week of April and began work on voter registration. The recent Liuzzo murder heightened the Deacons' concern for the safety of the young volunteers, particularly the women.

The northern students plunged into what must have seemed a surreal world of danger and violence. They had no qualms about accepting armed self-defense in the climate of fear that gripped the mill town. The Deacons taught the volunteers basic security precautions and escorted them around town twenty-four hours a day. Many young students were so frightened that they could not sleep the first few nights in Bogalusa—jumping nervously at every noise. The Deacons' nonchalant attitude toward guns alarmed more than one Yankee neophyte. On one occasion the Deacons had to leave a female volunteer alone in an isolated house. They issued her a gun and left the stunned young woman on her own.[27] Twenty-three-year-old Anita Levine, a student at the University of California in Berkeley, arrived in Bogalusa with nine other civil rights workers on 14 April. The volunteers stayed at ten different homes, where the Deacons constantly stood guard at the windows at night. On Easter Sunday Levine and another white volunteer joined her host and two other women to attend a sunrise service at the Methodist church. "The Deacons had given us instructions to tell them whenever we were going to drive," recalled Levine. The church was only four blocks from the house, so the Deacons told Levine to go ahead and they would follow in a few minutes. The women pulled out of the driveway and soon noticed a car tailing them along with two police cars behind it. The trailing car sported a Confederate flag license plate, which identified it as a Klan car. The Klansmen began to menace the women, passing them and then pulling alongside. Levine pulled in front of the Methodist church and left her engine running. The five women waited anxiously in the deserted street as the Klan car kept driving up and down in front of the church, brandishing guns out the windows. The police remained in their patrol cars. Finally, the Deacons arrived on the scene and the Klan and police cars immediately sped away. It was a frightening experience but one that allowed Levine to see the changing face of southern blacks as well. "It's so great to see a Negro family in the South that knows its rights and is not afraid," she told a reporter.[28]

Forbidding characters like Charlie Sims, outfitted with pistols and blackjacks, were disarming figures to the students. But the young volunteers were no less a novelty to their hosts. Working-class blacks like Sims and Hicks had never seen privilege and wealth of this magnitude. "Some of the kids were from nice homes," noted Hicks. "Lot of their parents were wealthy." Hicks remembered how money was no object for them:

You go get gas, take them somewhere, they'd say "I'll pay for it. Here it is." Drop out a credit card there on them. Yeah. And you'd get ready to make a telephone call, and "No, here, here, take my telephone card." They had telephone card, credit card. And when they got ready to leave, you pick them up and maybe take them to New Orleans, and they would give you some money to take your car to New Orleans. And they get down there and they'd get on the airplane, hit that airplane, and hit the air, and gone. And go flying all over the country.[29]

Hicks became good friends with Steve Miller's wealthy family in San Francisco. The Millers assisted in fund-raising when Hicks traveled to San Francisco. The rich and famous were a heady experience for the paper mill worker born in Pachutta, Mississippi. "They [the Millers] had a home sitting way back up there in them hills up there," said Hicks. "Filthy rich. He a big time lawyer in San Francisco. When we came into dinner . . . I was sitting there with judges. Big judge. And wife with five or six rings."[30]

But middle-class whites brought more than money and sweat to the movement: they often brought a missionary's arrogant presumptions about their own superior judgment and little respect for the political wisdom of local people. Hicks encountered this problem with Bill Yates. "When he said something or done something, he wanted you to do what he wanted. If you had an idea or different thing, he didn't want to go by your idea, he wanted to do exactly what he said." The imperious attitude was not well received by the determinedly independent black Bogalusans. "Bogalusa was not a part of CORE, wasn't a part of nothing . . . Bogalusa was a town that ran its own movement," explained Hicks. "Bill Yates and I fell out about the same thing. That they wanted to come in and tell us what to do, how to do, and when to do."[31]

With volunteers flooding into Bogalusa, tension grew as the Voters League announced that it would organize its first civil rights march on Friday, 9 April. James Farmer would be flying in as the guest speaker. The announcement that the league was going to march in the middle of the Klan's stronghold sent city leaders into a spin. To head off the protest, the Commission Council quickly passed an emergency ordinance—of dubious constitutionality—prohibiting mass picketing and protests. The "disturbing the peace" ordinance limited pickets to three and required people to leave business premises on demand of an employee or the owner. The ordinance also contained provisions aimed at Klan attacks, including a prohibition against disrupting a lawful assembly. But by this point city government had little control over either the black movement or the Klan, and the ordinance was never enforced.[32]

A pall of fear fell over the city as the day of the momentous march approached. Two days before the demonstration, on 7 April, the Klan launched a series of preemptive attacks that singled out student volunteers. Klansmen harassed the University of Kansas students as they canvassed with local blacks. One Klansman waved a pistol at Linda Cook, a student volunteer, and shouted, "Now's a good time to kill a white nigger." Earlier in the morning Bill Yates left the Hicks house and noticed a green pickup truck with three men circling the block. As Yates got into his car, the truck abruptly blocked his path and one of the men leaped from it with a blackjack. Yates recognized the man as one of the Klansmen who had attacked him and broken his hand in February. He rolled up his window and started the car as the man tried to break his window. Yates put the car in reverse and escaped down the street with the truck in pursuit. He circled the block and returned to the Hicks house. Standing on the front porch to greet the Klansmen was Jackie Hicks—with pistol in hand. The pursuers wisely retreated.[33]

That night the Klan struck twice more. In the first incident, Klansmen gathered under cover of darkness on the edge of the black community near the Negro Union Hall. They erected two coffins: one coffin bore Bill Yates's name, the other Bob Hicks's. A sign on the coffins read, "Here lies CORE." The Klansmen illuminated the ghoulish scene with flares and a spotlight and burned a ten-foot cross.

Later that night Yates and several University of Kansas students were staying with the Hicks. There were at least seven Deacons posted at the home, some outside concealed behind bushes and trees. Among them was Henry Austin, a young insurance salesman and air force veteran from Baton Rouge. At approximately 1:00 A.M. a car drove slowly by the Hicks house. Suddenly it stopped and a white man emerged and threw a piece of brick through the rear window of a Volkswagen bus owned by one of the Kansas students. Bob Hicks rushed out of the house, and a shot rang out from the car as the white man was pulled back in. Hicks grabbed his pistol and fired two shots at the fleeing vehicle, setting off a volley of fifteen shots from the Deacons. Austin emptied his gun into the Klan car and watched sparks fly off it as the Klansmen sporadically returned the fire.

It was the Deacons' first shoot-out with the Klan, and the fledgling group had proved itself disciplined and able. None of the Deacons was injured; their attackers may not have fared quite as well. Though never confirmed, rumors circulated that one Klansman was shot and another killed in the exchange. Black hospital workers reported that the injured Klansmen were secretly shuttled to an Alabama hospital, ostensibly to protect their identity and police complicity in covering up the attack. As in the past, Governor McKeithen and local authorities downplayed the incident; some went so far as to deny that the gun battle ever took place.[34]

But CORE's sophisticated public relations operation, centered in New York City, guaranteed extraordinary publicity for the Deacons. The shoot-out at the Hicks house made the front page of the *New York Post* under the headline: "Klansmen and CORE in Louisiana Gun Battle." Apparently based on an interview with CORE staffer Bill Yates, the story featured a photograph of Bob Hicks brandishing a rifle as he examined the shattered window of a student's van. The article did not mention the Deacons by name, referring to CORE's armed defenders as "Negroes guarding the house." The piece dubbed Bogalusa the "Klan Capital" of America, an unflattering though fitting moniker that soon gained popularity with the media.[35]

It had been a long night for the Deacons, and now they faced the challenge of shepherding the upcoming march. Law enforcement officials braced for the protest with additional state police, auxiliary police, and deputized firemen. Black teenagers could not contain their excitement in anticipation of the historic event. On 8 April, the day before the march, the teenagers staged a spontaneous walkout and march from Bogalusa's black Central Memorial High School. At 10:25 A.M. two hundred students assembled outside the school and began advancing to the downtown area. Within a few minutes police halted the march on the grounds that the students did not have a parade permit. The demonstration ended in a standoff between the students and local police reinforced with snarling dogs in K-9 squad cars.[36]

Later that day Voters League president A. Z. Young led a delegation of blacks into City Hall to protest the decision to halt the students' march and to discuss a list of demands issued by the league two days earlier. From the outset, the Bogalusa movement gravitated toward bread-and-butter issues; the downtown boycott was intended to win jobs, not lunch counter stools. The league's demands for reform bore the distinct imprint of its working-class leadership, placing less emphasis on civil equality and voting rights and more emphasis on economic power and parity. The seven demands were for equal economic opportunity in public and private employment and municipal licensing; equal educational opportunities and desegregated educational facilities; desegregation of all public accommodations and facilities; sewers, paved roads, and adequate street lighting in the black community; enforced housing codes; inclusion of black leaders at a decision-making level on city, parish, and industrial and development planning boards; removal from city ordinances of all unconstitutional discriminatory laws; and employment of black city policemen.[37]

Mayor Cutrer was not about to negotiate these or any other demands with the militant new leadership of the Voters League. He told the media that he and the Commission Council had been meeting with a "very fine Negro committee" since July 1963, but the leadership of the league had changed. In effect, the city was refusing to negotiate with the black community's largest civil rights organization. Moreover, the mayor argued, several demands had already been met: streets in the black community were all paved, and street lighting conversion was proceeding. Cutrer added that six blacks had taken the civil service exam for police officer in 1963 but all had failed it.[38]

The night before the civil rights march the Voters League staged a large, enthusiastic rally at Central Memorial High. James Farmer arrived from New York to serve as the keynote speaker. The Deacons accompanied Farmer from the New Orleans airport and stationed guards inside the school. Their presence outside was hardly needed. With the eyes of the nation on the small mill town, local authorities had decided not to invite further Klan attacks by their absence. An impressive phalanx of more than one hundred law enforcement officials ringed the school, including all of Bogalusa's thirty-four-member police force, two dozen deputized firemen and sheriffs' deputies, and fifty state police and FBI agents.[39]

The police cordon around the rally site kept the Klan at bay, forcing it to conduct a simultaneous rally of more than two hundred people across town. At one point Klansmen attempted to take a caravan of thirty-two cars into the black quarters but were stopped by city and state police. The Klan would have to wait to exact its revenge.[40]

The high school auditorium was packed with spirited young people. Ronnie Moore soon took the stage to encourage the students to boycott classes the next day in order to attend the march. He said that the march would protest police brutality and economic injustice in Bogalusa. Following Moore on the dais, James Farmer reiterated the Voters League's demands for fair employment; Crown-Zellerbach needed to hire black women and eliminate its segregated promotion system. Farmer also chastised the older generation of blacks, telling the audience of teenagers that "if our parents had been willing to go to jail and die, we wouldn't have to go through this." The rally went without incident, and the Deacons and the Voters League sent the children home for a night's rest before the big event.[41]

The morning of the march tension hung over Bogalusa like an ominous cloud. The Deacons took their places among the demonstrators. An impressive column of four hundred marchers departed the Negro Union Hall at 9:07 A.M. It was only four short blocks to their destination: City Hall. Word came that huge crowds of Klansmen and their white sympathizers were already gathering along the parade route in the main business district. The angry mob of white hecklers far outnumbered the police. The marchers proceeded nervously into the business district led by the indomitable James Farmer. The scene they encountered was horrific. The protesters were forced to march through a gauntlet of hundreds of shrieking whites, with threats and screams of "niggers" reverberating through the streets. As the marchers approached the corner of Third Street and Columbia, a rabid group of whites bolted into the street and violently attacked them with fists and picket signs. A young Klansman, Randle C. Pounds, raced toward Farmer and lunged violently at him with a blackjack. Police caught Pounds just before he struck Farmer. The violence was contagious. As the melee spread, white gangs beat bystanders, including a *Life* magazine photographer. In the chaos a white man, Jimmy Dane Burke, attacked an FBI agent who was photographing incidents.[42]

Ordered by police officials to turn back, the besieged marchers quickly returned to the Negro Union Hall to regroup. Within a few minutes three hundred whites led by the Klan assembled at City Hall and confronted a line of state policemen guarding the entrance. A delegation of four white men, one identified as the Grand Wizard of the Louisiana Knights of the Ku Klux Klan, conferred with Mayor Cutrer as the restless mob milled around the building. Within an hour the Klan leader emerged from the meeting. He told the crowd that the mayor had informed him that the civil rights demonstrators were going to march again later that day with police protection. The Klan leader instructed the mob to disperse and not attempt to prevent the march since it "could not win against either local police or federal officials."[43]

Soon after the mob retreated, James Farmer and members of the Voters League met with Cutrer and Commissioner Arnold Spiers. The meeting was a victory for the league, as Cutrer had previously refused to negotiate with the group and Farmer. Not only was the mayor now meeting with them, but he also reassured the black delegation that he would continue to confer with the Voters League. Further, Cutrer promised that the Klan would not be allowed to congregate in the business district during the second march later in the afternoon. The mayor kept his word. Vehicular traffic was blocked and the demonstration occurred without disruption.

When the marchers arrived at City Hall, Farmer, Moore, and other speakers addressed the crowd with high spirits. Cutrer's conciliatory attitude at the earlier meeting was an encouraging sign. Farmer told the crowd that the mayor had agreed to further talks with the Voters League. Then, to the marchers' amazement, Cutrer emerged from City Hall to address the group. He surprised the audience by calling for negotiations rather than demonstrations. The day's events had forced the mayor to move the debate from the streets to the negotiating table.[44]

The marchers were not the only ones shaken by the Klan attack. In the midst of the confusion, Assistant Police Chief L. C. Terrell had wheeled his police car into Louis Applewhite, a Klansman and nephew of Albert Applewhite, a Klan "wrecking crew" leader. Applewhite was taken to the hospital. Terrell panicked when he realized that he had nearly killed the relative of a major Klansman. The highly distraught officer returned to City Hall and, armed with a shotgun, ensconced himself in the mayor's office. Terrell was convinced that the Klan was going to retaliate by killing him. The dazed policeman rocked back and forth in his chair mumbling to himself, "They're not going to kill me. They're not going to kill me." CRS representative Jerry Heilbron, who was in the room with Terrell, watched nervously as the officer continued to mutter to himself, cradling the shotgun in his arms. In Heilbron's words, the officer was "really off his rocker." A local minister arrived and suggested that the group pray for guidance. Heilbron, the minister, and Terrell got on their knees and prayed. But they were unwilling to leave Terrell's situation to divine intervention. Someone summoned Terrell's doctor, who soon arrived and administered a sedative to the troubled officer.[45]

Cutrer stayed true to his promise to negotiate with the Voters League, and within days he organized a team that included approximately sixty white merchants. The business group, with the assistance of three representatives of the federal Community Relations Service, scheduled its first meeting with black community representatives on 13 April. But the talks collapsed before they even started when the white businessmen refused to meet exclusively with the Voters League. Instead, they demanded that the black negotiating team include representatives of two other moderate black groups. The league responded to the ultimatum by refusing to meet with the business group. To increase the pressure for negotiations, the league announced that it would begin a picketing campaign at downtown stores to compel black employment at the businesses.[46]

With negotiations stalled, the Voters League commenced picketing six stores on 14 April. The new city ordinance restricted the protesters to only two picketers per store. The situation was particularly difficult for the Deacons, who stood guard. The league picketers were shadowed by Klan picketers who walked alongside carrying signs saying, "White Man give this merchant your business." The following day the Klan threw a firebomb at a house on the edge of the black community where CORE volunteers had stayed. The local fire department refused to respond to the call for help.[47]

If there were ever any doubts that the Bogalusa police and the Klan were collaborating, the events of 15 April would dispel them. Earlier that day the police arrested and detained Charles Williams, a local black man. As Williams was being booked, a door opened to an adjacent room and Williams saw six men dressed in Klan robes—one of them wearing a law enforcement uniform under his robe. The hooded officer entered the booking room and cursed Williams. "You black son of a bitch," barked the officer, "pull off the damn cap."[48]

Government officials scrambled to head off a major clash. In a presentation to the Bogalusa Chamber of Commerce, Governor McKeithen sounded a new theme of reconciliation and patience. He told the business leaders that their "generation in Louisiana has the responsibility to keep the peace" and to keep their "heads while those about us lose theirs."[49]

As the Easter holiday was rapidly approaching, Mayor Cutrer appealed to the Voters League to halt the picketing for the Easter weekend. The league refused to call a moratorium on picketing until the city agreed to negotiate its demands. But the situation on the picket line was becoming more tense and creating insurmountable problems for the Deacons. Klansmen marched side by side with the black picketers as mobs of whites waved rebel flags and jeered from the sidelines while law enforcement officials stood idly by; some policemen even joined in the heckling. By Good Friday it was clear that the Deacons and the Voters League could not guarantee the safety of the demonstrators, so they decided to temporarily withdraw the pickets and file a complaint with city officials.[50]

Police abuse was becoming a paramount issue of the Voters League. On Good Friday the league presented Mayor Cutrer with additional requirements, calling for an "end of unequal enforcement of law in Bogalusa" and "the end of abuses and harassment of Negro picketers." It also demanded that the city fire officers involved in harassment. The league underscored its new conditions by announcing that it had invited James Farmer to lead another march to City Hall, this time protesting police abuse.[51]

Farmer returned to Bogalusa on 22 April to address an evening rally at the Ebenezer Baptist Church. The sanctuary was filled with nearly five hundred people, almost all of them school children. An army of state police guarded all intersections leading to the church, part of a massive influx of 375 state troopers earlier in the day. The growing generational schism between young and old was apparent at the rally. Youth leader Don Lambert rose to give a speech chastising adults for not assisting in the civil rights drive. The issue had come to light earlier in the week when CORE spokesperson Wilfred T. Ussery told the media that a militant teenage element in the league was pushing for bigger demonstrations than the leadership wanted. Ironically, the militant leaders of the Voters League and the Deacons were finding themselves cast as moderates in the rapidly radicalizing movement.[52]

The rally at Ebenezer Baptist Church was not the only civil rights event where sharp generational conflicts were manifest. A few weeks later comedian Dick Gregory spoke at another Voters League rally, offering a humorous respite from the grim business of political protest. Gregory delighted his young audience of more than five hundred by excoriating old folks as "too lazy or scared" to participate in the civil rights movement: "When you die, Lord knows I hope it's soon, then the civil rights movement can move forward."[53]

As time progressed, the Deacons became more explicit in their view that the black freedom movement required a revolution against both the old leadership and the worldview produced by the economic reality of the past. Accommodation had been an effective strategy of resistance for the powerless. But times had changed. Deacons member R. T. Young advised young Voters League members that "the young Negro must erase the image of the older Negroes—we must turn their young minds to education, one of the biggest weapons." Young counseled the youngsters that "automation is here to stay and the Negro of the cotton field is gone forever . . . abide by the Constitution of the United States and seek what your government has promised you and mankind."[54]

Farmer played down the generational divisions in his rally speech, though he reserved criticism for faint-hearted black ministers who had refused to support the movement or allow their churches to be used for organizing activities. The charges of accommodation peeved many of the black clergy. The Reverend W. J. Nelson protested to the *Bogalusa Daily News* that he had been unfairly labeled an "uncle tom."[55]

The black movement's resolve and the potential for mass civil violence were forcing the federal and state governments to intervene in the crisis. On 20 April 1965 the U.S. Department of Justice filed the first of several legal actions to enforce the Civil Rights Act in Bogalusa. Attorney General Nicholas Katzenbach signed the suit filed in federal district court in New Orleans asking that six restaurants be enjoined from refusing service to blacks. Meanwhile, Governor McKeithen was working diligently to restart the stalled negotiations in the city. McKeithen was particularly worried that another major march would ignite open warfare between the Deacons and the Klan. Gun sales had increased dramatically in Bogalusa, which was already an armed camp.[56]

On 22 April McKeithen arranged for three state leaders to publicly offer to mediate the crisis: Senator Michael O'Keefe, AFL-CIO state leader Victor Bussie, and Democratic Party leader Camille Gravel. The next day he met with city officials and the Community Affairs Committee and persuaded them to sit down with the "Bussie Committee" mediators on Friday, 24 April. Simultaneously, the governor was working to persuade the Voters League to suspend its rallies and picketing in exchange for new negotiations. For this task he turned to Vice President Hubert Humphrey. Humphrey had been in Louisiana two weeks earlier and had been following the situation in Bogalusa. He contacted CORE's James Farmer and convinced him to help ease tensions by leaving Bogalusa on the twenty-third. Farmer also agreed to cancel a planned rally that was to feature Dick Gregory. On Good Friday, as the Klan taunted black protesters on the picket line downtown, the Bussie Committee began intense meetings with the Voters League and city officials and the CAC. By the end of the day the Bussie Committee had scored a major breakthrough. The city and the Community Affairs Committee agreed to begin new negotiations with the Voters League the following week. In exchange, the league agreed to suspended picketing. The Voters League and the Deacons had forced the city back to the bargaining table.[57]

McKeithen, feeling that the crisis had been surmounted, withdrew the army of 335 state police from Bogalusa over the Easter weekend. But segregationists and the Klan were not to be denied. The Original Knights of the Ku Klux Klan (OKKKK) distributed several hundred leaflets announcing a boycott of merchants who complied with integration, as well as the *Bogalusa Daily News* and the WBOX radio station. On 27 April George L. Singleman, executive secretary of the New Orleans Citizens Council, joined Paul Farmer of the Washington Parish Citizens Council (and brother of Klan leader Saxon Farmer) to announce plans for a major march and rally on 7 May to protest the compromise. Singleman denounced the Bussie Committee and claimed that Bogalusa had been targeted by communists since 1956.[58]

Now McKeithen and Cutrer were forced to take measures to undermine the Klan march and rally. Rally organizers had invited Sheriff Jim Clark of Selma, Alabama, a hero to white supremacists. McKeithen personally contacted Clark and convinced him to withdraw from the rally. McKeithen had always been a staunch segregationist, but his new conciliatory approach to civil rights groups made him the Citizens Council's new bête noire. One Council spokesperson labeled him an "integrationist" sympathizer and castigated the Bussie Committee members as "all out integrationists." Compounding the Council's problems were rumors that the rally was actually being organized by the Klan and that two hundred black Southern University students planned to attend and disrupt the rally.[59]

Despite the machinations of elected officials, the segregationists managed to stage an impressive march and rally on 7 May. Approximately three thousand people participated in the march, which ended at Goodyear Park. Marchers listened to George Singleman of New Orleans and Judge John Rarick berate Governor McKeithen and other officials for interfering in Bogalusa's affairs (that both Singleman and Rarick were "outsiders" escaped attention). The rumor that the Klan had actually organized the rally seemed to be confirmed by the speaker list, which included Saxon Farmer, Grand Wizard of the OKKKK, and Jack Helm, Louisiana state leader of the United Klans of America (UKA).[60]

The Klan counteroffensive did not stop the negotiations, which got under way on 16 May at the office of Jack Martzell, attorney for the city of Bogalusa. Attending were Martzell; Lolis Elie, a black New Orleans attorney with ties to CORE, representing the Voters League; Mayor Cutrer; and members of the Commission Council and the Bussie Committee. The talks were cordial but tense, with Klansmen circling City Hall in trucks. The initial meeting was productive. Attorneys announced that a joint statement on racial progress in Bogalusa would be issued at some point and that further conferences were planned.[61]

With the negotiations in progress and the picketing halted, an eerie calm began to envelop the city. There had been virtually no incidents of Klan violence since local officials had announced negotiations with the Voters League three weeks earlier. The league decided to take advantage of the decreased tensions and quietly integrate Bogalusa's Cassidy Park. Bob Hicks secured permission from Mayor Cutrer in advance and notified city police and the FBI of the test plans for 19 May. On the afternoon of the nineteenth, Hicks, his wife Jackie, and their son Gregory, approximately twenty other blacks (mostly teenagers), and one white volunteer arrived at the park to integrate it. Sam Barnes, the Deacons' vice president, went along to guard the group, equipped with his pearl-handled .38 revolver. The adults stood by their cars watching the children playing on the swings and merry-go-rounds. Two policemen observed at a distance.

Soon the adults noticed a group of twenty-five white men approaching the park. The white men stopped and spoke briefly to the two policemen. The men then walked toward the children brandishing guns and clubs. The leader of the mob took off his belt and wrapped it around his fist. He asked the children on the merry-go-round if they were having fun, then suddenly struck a seven-year-old girl. Mayhem broke out as the white mob charged through the playground ruthlessly attacking the children and women. Bob Hicks and Sam Barnes rushed to their defense as the city policemen waded into the melee indiscriminately clubbing blacks and unleashing their K-9 dogs. One policeman pulled his gun as he approached the children. Jackie Hicks drew a pistol to fend off the attackers. Barnes also pulled his .38 revolver. Police restrained Bob Hicks as he watched a police dog viciously bite his son Gregory.[62] Hicks could barely contain his rage. He wished that he had brought a weapon. "I guess that's about the only time that if I had something, I probably would have done something," said Hicks years later.[63]

During the brutal attack several blacks were injured, including a seventy-five-year-old woman who was knocked unconscious. Sam Barnes was arrested and charged with assault for pulling his revolver to protect the children. As the dust settled, Bob Hicks took the elderly woman and his son to the Bogalusa Community Medical Center, where they were both refused emergency room assistance. Eventually Hicks had to drive ninety miles to find treatment for the two at a New Orleans hospital.

The following day more than five hundred whites gathered to prevent a second attempt to integrate the park. When no blacks showed up, a gang of thirty whites brutally attacked Terry Friedman, a white *New Orleans Times-Picayune* photographer, as he walked toward the park. The group kicked and beat Friedman and threw parts of his camera equipment into a nearby creek as police stood by.[64]

Despite the climate of fear and violence, the work of the Bussie Committee continued; on 23 May the committee made a major breakthrough. A. Z. Young and Cutrer signed a six-point agreement in which the city met almost all of the Voters League's demands. Cutrer took to the airwaves that night to announce the agreement in a radio speech. He stated that the Commission Council, with the full support of the Community Affairs Committee, planned a series of sweeping desegregation reforms. The city had agreed to repeal all segregation ordinances, open all public facilities and parks to all races, guarantee impartial law enforcement by city police and equal protection of citizens exercising their rights, and hire blacks as policemen and in other city positions. The mayor also promised to promptly investigate any violation of these strictures by police and enact necessary ordinances regarding sewerage and water distribution to allow indoor plumbing in the black community and paved streets and improved lighting. In exchange, the Voters League would cancel its picketing, pending negotiations with the store owners, and defer further attempts to integrate the parks. Cutrer argued that the reforms were necessary to bring city laws in line with federal laws, and to restore calm and end the harm to the city's industrial and business growth. The mayor's message was one of achieving social peace and economic progress through unity.[65]

It was a stunning victory for the Voters League. Later that night James Farmer addressed a jubilant victory rally, declaring that the Klan had become "a laughing matter." Farmer promised full cooperation with Cutrer and praised him for having gone further "than any other Southern Mayor." Optimism had to be tempered with caution, though. "Now we must see to it that deeds follow these words," said Farmer.[66]

Not all CORE officials were as sanguine as Farmer. "Mike [Jones] reports that the Negroes' morale is quite low and that a number of whites seem angry at the mayor's conciliatory statement last night," noted a CORE report filed on 24 May. "He fears that this is just the beginning of [the] expression of white frustration and anger at the mayor's betrayal of them." As it turned out, Mike Jones was right. The Klan had lost the first battle by relying on Cutrer. Within hours of the mayor's announcement, the Klan would regroup to mount its own lethal counteroffensive.[67]

With a Single Bullet

8

ON 11 JANUARY 1935 a white mob dragged Jerome Wilson from the Washington Parish jail and lynched him. Wilson had won a new trial for a shooting on his father's farm in 1934 that had left his brother and a parish deputy dead. The incident had occurred, according to an older member of the black community, "cause them boys cussed that white man." No African American attempted to save Wilson or avenge his murder; fear of attack so overwhelmed the black community that some people even refused to leave the "colored quarters." The Wilson family, prosperous and respected landowners, was economically ruined and fled the parish. Three decades later something had changed in the spirit of black people in Washington Parish and Bogalusa; they would respond in a radically different way to murderous assaults by vigilantes. Before the summer of 1965 ended, a white segregationist would lie on the streets of Bogalusa with three Deacons bullets in his chest.[1]

The morning after Mayor Jesse Cutrer's momentous speech announcing desegregation concessions, Bogalusans awakened to find utility poles plastered with scores of a new Klan poster: "Welcome to the Jungle, J. H. Cutrer, Chief; Victor Bussie, Ambassador; A. Z. Young, Witch Doctor." Later that day a group of whites festooned the City Hall entrance with a sign reading, "Nigger Town, U.S.A." As darkness fell, several hundred whites assembled at Cassidy Park and tore down the gates and signs announcing the park closed by order of the Commission Council. Members of the group raucously paraded around the park, honking their horns in celebration of their victory. An intimidating mob of one hundred whites invaded a Community Affairs Committee (CAC) meeting and denounced the Bussie Committee, calling for an end to "meddling in the affairs of Bogalusa." The CAC, badly shaken by the confrontation, quickly began to distance itself from the Bussie Committee and the compromise. It was the first of a series of reversals in the face of the Klan's renewed terror campaign.[2]

The Klan also flexed its muscles in its first open confrontation with the Deacons. On 26 May 1965 a crowd of students had congregated the evening of Graduation Class Night at Central Memorial High School. During the ceremony, approximately seventy-five whites gathered outside the school, including Saxon Farmer, leader of the Original Knights of the Ku Klux Klan (OKKKK), and a group of Klansmen. Minutes later, A. Z. Young and the Deacons arrived to confront the Klansmen, supported by an equal number of blacks. After an edgy standoff, city and state police descended on the scene and dispersed both groups. A few hours later another Deacon, twenty-seven-year-old Fletcher Anderson, was sitting in his car in front of a restaurant when Deputy Sheriff Vertrees Adams approached. Adams ordered Anderson to start the car and race the engine; when Anderson complied, the deputy arrested him for driving with a faulty muffler. While making the arrest, Adams discovered a weapon in Anderson's car and added a concealed weapons charge. At the police station, Adams and other police officers lined Anderson up against a wall and punched and kicked him.[3]

The Klan increased its pressure on local businesses as well. It had been over a month since the Voters League had suspended picketing on Columbia Street, yet none of the merchants had agreed to negotiate the league's demands for jobs. Its patience exhausted, the league decided to renew picketing. On Saturday, 29 May, young black picketers appeared in front of stores in the downtown area. The situation soon deteriorated into chaos as Klansmen ran amuck in the business district, brutally attacking the picketers. Police officers did little to stop them; when law enforcers did act, they were more likely to arrest the black picketers than the offending Klansmen. Seventeen people were arrested that Saturday, eleven of whom were black—among them, Jackie Hicks.[4]

Though the day had been a setback for the Bogalusa Voters League, the violent attacks and arrest of black children did shake many African Americans out of their lethargy. That night hundreds of angry adults attended a huge league meeting at the Negro Union Hall to discuss the day's events. The scene outside the hall was a surreal carnival of hate, as hundreds of whites waited menacingly. Smaller groups of whites stalked the downtown area late into the night. A convoy of ten cars drove past the house where CORE leader Ronnie Moore was staying that night as the Deacons stood guard. Once again the Klan reigned supreme in Bogalusa.[5]

For the next few days the Klan escalated its well-coordinated attacks on the picketers. The wrecking crews staged diversionary strikes to draw police off the picket line, then sent flying wedges of Klansmen to assault the picketers with clubs and lead pipes. The Klan became so bold that on 31 May it drove a New Orleans television crew from the city. The same day Governor Mc-Keithen traveled to Bogalusa and met secretly with Klan leader Saxon Farmer and fourteen other white supremacists. That a standing governor would enter into negotiations with an extremist organization engaged in systematic terrorism raised serious questions about the state of moral leadership in Louisiana. In a prescient memo to Vice President Humphrey, John Stewart, a Humphrey aide, pointed out that McKeithen's "principal weakness" was his constant efforts to accommodate the white supremacists. McKeithen "has attempted to please both the moderates and the extremists," Stewart told the vice president, "and this approach cannot, in the end, provide the leadership and direction to avoid violence and bloodshed." McKeithen's conclave with the Klan proved fruitless: the attacks on picketers continued, and by the end of the first week of June McKeithen had redeployed 212 troopers in Bogalusa. At the same time Mayor Cutrer had retreated from his détente with the Voters League, informing the media that the league was responsible for increased tensions. In the end, only the Voters League and the Deacons refused to be intimidated by the Klan counteroffensive.[6]

The Klan campaign reached a bloody crescendo in early June. In 1964 Sheriff Dorman Crowe had hired two black deputies, honoring a campaign promise he had made in return for black votes during his unsuccessful re-election bid. The two deputies, O'Neal Moore and Creed Rogers, were limited to patrolling the black community. On the night of 2 June 1965, Moore and Rogers were patrolling as usual when they noticed a pickup truck following them. Suddenly the truck pulled alongside the deputies and several shots from a high-powered rifle rang out. Moore was killed instantly. His partner suffered facial wounds but survived. Within an hour Ray McElveen, a paper mill worker at Crown-Zellerbach, was arrested in nearby Tylertown, Mississippi. McElveen was driving a truck that matched the description of the vehicle involved in the attack. When apprehended, he was carrying membership cards for the Citizens Council of Greater New Orleans and the National States Rights Party, an extremist white supremacist group. Mc-Elveen also carried a "special agent" card for the Louisiana Department of Public Safety, signed by state police director Thomas Burbank. Saxon Farmer eventually posted bail for McElveen, who was later identified as an OKKKK member. In the subsequent inquiry even white police investigators became targets of the terrorists. On 4 June unknown assailants fired six shots into the home of Deputy Doyle Holliday, who was leading the investigation for the sheriff's department. Within minutes of the shooting an anonymous caller phoned Holliday's house and asked, "Did we get anyone?"[7]

McKeithen condemned the Moore murder and offered a $25,000 reward for the killers, but he continued to deny that the Klan was active in Bogalusa—despite the fact that he was secretly negotiating with Klan leaders. At a press conference McKeithen said he was confident that justice would be served and predicted that Louisiana would be vindicated by guilty verdicts against the assassins. "We're going to catch them. We're going to catch them all," he promised. History would prove otherwise. No one was ever convicted of the murder of O'Neal Moore.[8]

Moore's death produced a flood of national publicity for the Bogalusa movement and the Deacons. On 6 June 1965 *New York Times* readers opened the Sunday paper to a front-page story on the Deacons, carrying the portentous headline, "Armed Negro Unit Spreads in South." Only a few months earlier the *Times* had characterized the Deacons as merely a local phenomenon and a movement anomaly. Now it was taking a second look at the Deacons, acknowledging their growing popularity and the challenge they posed to entrenched civil rights leadership.[9]

The *Times* article contributed greatly to the image of the Deacons as an expanding political organization that had to be reckoned with. It highlighted the defense group's rapid growth, quoting Earnest Thomas and other sources as saying that the Deacons had "50 to 55 chapters" in Louisiana, Mississippi, and Alabama and as many as 15,000 members—though the paper cautioned that the figures were unreliable and that the Deacons were primarily concentrated in Louisiana.[10]

The story described the Deacons' activities, including guarding civil rights workers with weapons and their running gun battles with the Klan. The *Times* reporter noted that the Deacons characterized their organization as law-abiding and, according to Earnest Thomas, "strictly for defense" and "highly disciplined."[11]

The article also marked Thomas's first appearance as a national spokesperson for the Deacons and his first opportunity to publicly defend the group's self-defense policy within the existing framework of nonviolence. Yes, civil rights workers willingly took risks on the picket line, Thomas conceded. But hearth and home were another matter. Everyone had the right to defend the sanctity of the home, even the civil rights worker. An activist might forego his right of self-defense on the picket line, "but when he goes to bed at night he is entitled to rest without worry," said Thomas. "That's where the Deacons come in."[12]

The *Times* article was skeptical that nonviolence could be so easily reconciled with self-defense. The Deacons, it maintained, raised hard questions for advocates of nonviolence. "Should a civil rights organization committed to nonviolence align itself with the Deacons, and accept their services?" CORE leader Richard Haley answered the question with the same ambivalence toward the Deacons that characterized the other national civil rights organizations. Though they appreciated the protection, the Deacons violated the movement's nonviolent principles and imperiled liberal support. Haley had chastised Charlie Fenton for working with the Deacons back in February and when the group formed. A few months later Farmer told the media that CORE tolerated the Deacons but hoped to convert them: "Even in the church you have your sinners: we feel we can demonstrate to these people with our philosophy of love and nonviolence that there is another way."[13]

The *Times* reporter pointed out that CORE had a close relationship with the Deacons and seemingly approved of them. Haley admitted the close relationship but suggested that it was, in part, based on self-interest. "The deacons made the difference between safety and bad health last summer for CORE workers in Jonesboro," he observed. They had "the effect of lowering the minimum potential for danger now, which can only encourage people to participate in protests." For Haley, there was no contradiction between the Deacons and nonviolence; the Deacons were practicing "protective nonviolence." And though he worked with the Deacons, Haley remained faithful to his first principles. "But I still have to believe in my own mind that nonviolence is more effective than even the Deacons."[14]

Still, glimpses of Haley's own growing disenchantment with nonviolence came through in his comments to the *Times* reporter. The CORE leader noted that the nature of the attacks on civil rights workers had changed dramatically in recent months. During the lunch counter sit-ins, white violence was usually limited to dousing protesters with catsup or shoving them off a stool. Now the attacks were frequently deadly. "The nonviolence theory holds that there is an innate goodness in a man," he explained, "and that this works on his conscience while he is battering you on the head." This nonviolent strategy had been effective in focusing national attention on the South and winning "sympathetic public opinion" in the North, but northern sympathy was slow to translate into protection—something the Deacons provided.[15]

The June 1965 *Times* story redefined the Deacons as an alternative to the nonviolent movement and correctly recognized that they were more than a defense group—they also played a role in changing black political consciousness. "One aim of the deacons," the article asserted, "is to dispel an old-

Southern white notion that the Negro is docile and will not fight back."[16] It was a stubborn stereotype, and there was solid research supporting the writer's claim. A study conducted at the Army War College between the two world wars showed that the majority of student officers believed that "the negro is docile, tractable, lighthearted, carefree, and good-natured. If treated unfairly, he is like to become surly and stubborn, though this is usually a temporary phase."[17]

Shortly after the *New York Times* article appeared the Deacons landed on the front page of the *Los Angeles Times*. In the second week of June, while Bogalusa reeled from the O'Neal Moore killing, Charlie Sims traveled to Los Angeles for the Deacons' first serious foray into national fund-raising. There he found a sympathetic ear in the black community but received a chilly reception from the local media. Two developments contributed to this turn of events. First, once the Deacons began to significantly expand and recruit in new areas, they could no longer be dismissed as a marginal phenomenon. Their rapid growth and increasing media exposure threatened the hegemony of traditional civil rights organizations, such as the Southern Christian Leadership Conference (SCLC), which enjoyed liberal media support. Segments of the media felt compelled to neutralize the upstart Deacons, who promised to escalate the violence. Second, there were widespread and well-justified fears that the summer of 1965 would be wracked by explosive race riots. The previous summer had witnessed several small race riots in northern cities, including New York and Chicago. Sitting on the powder keg of racial turmoil in major urban areas, some media organizations sought to discredit any group that legitimated violence as a political tool, fearing that self-defensive violence might ignite a major riot.

Los Angeles was a smoldering fire of racial discontent in June 1965, when Charlie Sims arrived in the city for the first leg of his California fund-raising trip. The *Los Angeles Times* published two articles on the Deacons during Sims's visit. The front page of the 13 June Sunday paper carried the sensational headline, "Negro 'Deacons' Claim They Have Machine Guns, Grenades for 'War.'" The lead paragraph reported on a secret meeting in which the Deacons claimed to have "machine guns and grenades for use in racial warfare," and the Deacons made little effort to deny the allegation. "You don't tell your opponents what you are doing in any kind of conflict," Bob Hicks told the *Los Angeles Times*.[18]

The 13 June story relied heavily on a highly negative FBI report on the first two Deacons meetings conducted in Bogalusa in February. Apparently an informant had surreptitiously tape-recorded the meetings and the resulting information was widely disseminated to the media in FBI memorandums. In one meeting, Earnest Thomas and Frederick Kirkpatrick claimed to have access to grenades and automatic firearms. At a second meeting, Bob Hicks allegedly urged participants to forcibly obstruct police from making illegal arrests. "No white person will be allowed in a Negro area at night—salesman or anybody," Hicks was quoted as saying in the meeting.[19]

The talk about grenades and automatic weapon arsenals had been nothing more than boasts and exaggerations. The Deacons were not preparing for an apocalyptic race war, as the *Los Angeles Times* piece insinuated. But the hyperbole was grist for the mill. The damaging FBI allegations found their way not only into that particular article, but they also became a mainstay for negative media coverage in the months that followed. Despite their efforts to portray themselves as part of the nonviolent movement, the Deacons were depicted by the *Los Angeles Times* as a potentially violent organization masquerading as a self-defense group. "The Deacons insist their purpose is only defensive," huffed the newspaper, "however at both February meetings they talked of preventing whites from going into Negro residential areas at night" and encouraged "armed confrontation with policemen when negroes are arrested."[20]

The paper also highlighted Kirkpatrick's comments quoted in the FBI memorandum urging blacks to buy high-powered rifles and ammunition and claiming that he carried more than one hundred rounds of ammunition. "It takes violent blacks to combat these violent whites," Kirkpatrick reportedly said. "We're gonna be ready for 'em. We're gonna have to be ready to survive."[21]

The story was so critical of the Deacons that readers might have reasonably concluded that the Deacons were more of a threat to peace than the Ku Klux Klan. Indeed, it failed to mention the Klan carnage visited upon blacks in Bogalusa, ranging from beatings to the recent murder of Deputy O'Neal Moore. The Klan had all but disappeared from the pages of the *Los Angeles Times*. But if readers were lulled into believing that the Deacons, not the segregationists, were the source of violence in the South, at least one quotation may have brought them to their senses. "My men are watching them closely," growled Bogalusa Police Chief Claxton Knight. "If one of them makes the wrong move he's gonna get his head blown off."[22]

The *Los Angeles Times* resisted the Deacons' efforts to portray themselves as an auxiliary to the nonviolent movement and instead defined them as part of an emerging "militant" movement. Like the *New York Times*, the Los Angeles paper recognized that the Deacons' philosophy was inherently counterposed to nonviolence, and that the paramilitary group was part of a growing revolt against the established civil rights leadership. "The rising militancy of the Deacons," noted the *Los Angeles Times*, "and the expansion of the movement is a new element in the civil rights movement which federal and state officials view with concern."[23]

This harsh treatment of the Deacons may have been, in part, a reaction to Sims's hint that they might organize a chapter in Los Angeles. Since the Deacons' primary focus had been on the Klan, what conceivable role could they play in California? asked the *Times*. "Man, there's police brutality and people with that white supremacy stuff everywhere," replied Sims.[24]

Sims's comments on police brutality would certainly resonate with northern blacks. But were the Deacons prepared to change their emphasis from Klan violence to police violence? Sims was probably thinking aloud in the interview and had not given serious thought to the implications of such a strategic shift. Clearly the Deacons' leadership was not of one mind. Interviewed by telephone in Bogalusa, Bob Hicks demurred on the prospect of a Los Angeles chapter. "They got problems out there just like everywhere else," admitted Hicks, "but nobody's shooting at anybody in Los Angeles."[25]

The following day the *Los Angeles Times* followed up with a second critical article entitled "Deacons Chief Defends Aims on Visit to L.A.: Use of Arms Necessary Because of Lack of Justice for Negro in South, He Says." The Deacons had "amassed machine guns and grenades and rifles for any eventuality," reported Paul Weeks in the unflattering profile. Sims argued that the Deacons resorted to weapons only because law enforcement refused to protect blacks in the South. The reporter was not convinced. "But federal and state authorities are worried," he warned. "The Deacons, they say, are playing with matches in a powder magazine. Regardless of his words, how can Sims or his associate leaders ward off an explosion when mob passions flare?"[26]

There was some justification for the media's skepticism about the Deacons' commitment to purely defensive violence. Sims was tailoring his message to his audience, and the following day he struck a far more militant pose when he appeared on black journalist Louis Lomax's television show in Los Angeles. Now speaking to a sympathetic black studio audience, Sims dropped all pretense of Gandhian nonviolence. In the event of future trouble in Bogalusa, he declared, "blood would be flowing down the streets like water." The threat received wild applause.[27]

The scathing rebuke of the *Los Angeles Times* set the pattern for future media attacks on the Deacons. The Deacons' detractors would argue that the self-defense group was taking the law into its own hands—that the Deacons were the black counterpart of the Klan. Evoking images of irresponsible vigilantes and disruptive provocateurs, the *Times* coverage was the beginning of media efforts to discredit the Deacons as an extremist "Negro KKK."

Although there was an obvious moral chasm between the actions of the Klan and the Deacons, many white journalists in 1965 made no ethical distinction between offensive and defensive violence. They feared that black retaliation against the Klan or the police would only escalate the violence and lead to bloody civil disorder. Anxious about any efforts to arm blacks, large segments of the white media, particularly local news outlets, turned a deaf ear to arguments in support of self-defense.

Sims's media coverage in Los Angeles began to snowball. He caught the attention of *Life* magazine columnist Shana Alexander, who later arranged interviews with Sims and a young white civil rights worker who had been organizing in Bogalusa in the spring. The liberal columnist approached the Deacons with a mixture of trepidation and grudging admiration. Had nonviolence run its course? asked Alexander. Was it a luxury reserved for liberals observing the movement at a safe distance? "Both interviews strengthened my conviction that nonviolence must be the moral keystone of the civil rights movement," wrote Alexander. But the terrifying accounts of Klan violence in Bogalusa made her realize "that one's feeling about nonviolence are influenced more by geography and circumstance than by moral principle."[28]

Alexander's article underscored the martial spirit of the Deacons, characterizing them as "armed Negro vigilantes" led by a "warlike Deacon chieftain. . . . The Deacons say they have grenades and machine guns . . . and that they will not hesitate to use their entire arsenal if necessary," noted Alexander—converting the FBI's allegation into a fact. "Such militancy on the part of southern Negroes is so utterly without precedent that many people don't know what to make of the Deacons." Were they truly "freedom fighters" or, as had been rumored, "protection racketeers" or "Mao-inspired terrorist conspirators."[29]

Sims, with characteristic savvy, cast himself as a reluctant apostate of nonviolence. "I don't approve of the Deacons myself," Sims mockingly confessed, "but we have no choice." And if Alexander lived in Bogalusa, she would not have a choice either. "Visit Bogalusa, and *you* will look for *me*," chastened Sims.[30]

Sims punctuated his argument with his trademark bluntness. He suggested that the three civil rights workers murdered in Philadelphia, Mississippi, in 1964 were victims of nonviolence as well as of the Klan. "If we'd had the Deacons there, three more men would be alive in Mississippi today," Sims told Alexander. "Or else a lot more would be dead."[31]

The Sims interview left the columnist convinced of the necessity of armed self-defense in the South. "If I ever have to go to Bogalusa," she concluded, "I should be very glad to have his [Sims] protection, despite the fact that where brave men like Sims really belong is not in the Deacons but in the ranks of the Bogalusa police department."[32]

Jet magazine covered the Los Angeles visit as well, bringing the story to millions of African Americans. Black media like *Jet* played a crucial role in the movement. In many rural areas blacks did not have television and even radio signals were weak. Local white media generally ignored the movement; some local blacks did not even know about civil rights protests in their own region. For many blacks, the well-worn copies of *Jet* that were passed around in African American shops and businesses were the only source of information about the movement. The *Jet* story on Sims highlighted the conflict between the Deacons and the nonviolent movement. *Jet* had a difficult time finding civil rights leaders in Los Angeles—far removed from the Klan—who would speak favorably of the Deacons. Don Smith, president of the Los Angeles chapter of CORE, said that "this may be a necessary part of the Negro revolution, but philosophically I am opposed to all forms of violence, no matter who preaches it." H. Hartford Brookins, president of the United Civil Rights Committee was equally brusque: "I'm unconditionally opposed to their methods and what must be the end of their methods." The Reverend Thomas Kilgore, chairman of the Western Christian Leadership Conference, joined in condemning the Deacons: "I disapprove of keeping civil rights workers alive with guns. The non-violent approach has brought pressure to bear on those elements which discriminate. The Bogalusa movement, under the Deacons—a misnomer—represents a danger to 20 million Negroes." Sims had little patience with his critics comfortably ensconced in California: "I wonder if those men think that I risk losing my life for kicks?" he asked contemptuously.[33]

Sims's trip to Los Angeles had helped generate tremendous national publicity for the Deacons throughout June, but soon the exigencies of organizing on the front lines brought him back to Bogalusa. There the Voters League was opening a new front with a legal strategy designed to force local authorities to uphold the law. On 25 June CORE attorney Nils Douglas filed *Hicks v. Knight* in federal court in an attempt to compel law enforcement officials to protect the First Amendment rights of civil rights activists. The suit requested $425,000 in damages from Police Chief Knight and other law enforcement officials for brutality and harassment of civil rights protesters. In addition, it called for a restraining order to force local and state officials to end their attacks, harassment, and arrests of black demonstrators—and to protect the demonstrators from Klan and civilian attacks as well. Filed on behalf of eleven Bogalusa civil rights activists, including Deacons vice president Sam Barnes and several other Deacons, the suit also asked the court to end racial discrimination and segregation in the Washington Parish Jail and to reopen city parks without discrimination. The legal action listed thirty allegations of brutality, harassment, interference, and failure of officers to protect civil rights workers.[34]

Testimony on the suit began the following Monday, 28 June, in Judge Herbert W. Christenberry's court in New Orleans. It was the first thorough public airing of police abuse and misconduct in Bogalusa. Activists and Deacon members testified in vivid detail about the wild mob attacks at Cassidy Park, the police beatings of Deacons like Barnes and Fletcher Anderson, and the reports of hooded deputies at City Hall. The defendants countered with testimony from a series of law enforcement officials who claimed to have seen no abuse. FBI agent Frank Sass took the stand and swore that he had never seen any armed men on Columbia Street, nor had he seen anyone, police or otherwise, harass or beat picketers. Major Tom Bradley of the state police claimed that in his months in Bogalusa he never saw any harassment of demonstrators; indeed, he had never seen a white person even curse a demonstrator. The normally staid Judge Christenberry struggled to contain his skepticism. "You can hear all right?" Christenberry asked the officer.[35]

The hearings had sent the Deacons into a flurry of activity. Anonymous telephone calls were made to the home of Bob Hicks threatening to kill him and anyone else who testified at the hearing. The Deacons tightened security measures and escorted witnesses for the plaintiffs to and from court. On the evening of 28 June, Fletcher Anderson returned home after spending the day testifying. Around midnight six white men approached his house and pounded on the door, identifying themselves as policemen. Anderson refused to open the door. Suddenly six shots were fired from outside the house. When Anderson called the police department to report the shooting, he was told that "this is what happens to you when you go up against the police department."[36]

During the Christenberry hearings startling news leaked out that, after a two-month moratorium on mass marches, the Voters League and CORE planned to step up their campaign with a bold series of seven marches in seven days. Beginning on 7 July each march would be led by a major civil rights leader, including James Farmer, Dick Gregory, Harry Belafonte, Elton Cox, and James Bevel. Rumors swept Bogalusa that CORE was calling in hundreds of volunteers from around the country to participate. It appeared that Bogalusa would become the Selma of Louisiana. Adding to the anticipation were the events that transpired at CORE's national convention in Durham, North Carolina, held the weekend of 4 July. At that conference CORE openly debated its policy on nonviolence—a measure of the changes that the Deacons were forcing in the movement. While remaining true to its pacifist principles and declining to alter its policy on nonviolence for its own members and activities, CORE passed a resolution to accept Deacon protection wherever offered. Earnest Thomas, representing the Deacons at the conference, declared that the era of nonviolence was over. "We stopped the whippings," he told the cheering delegates. He added a blunt warning to the Ku Klux Klan: "All that hell you raising is going to come to a screeching halt."[37]

In the days preceding the planned marches, segregationists staged another rally in Bogalusa, this time attracting a crowd of 4,500. The rally featured arch-racist General Edwin Walker, who, in another ironic link to Louisiana, had narrowly escaped being assassinated by Lee Harvey Oswald the previous year in Dallas. During the rally, a gang of whites attacked and beat two East Indian students visiting Bogalusa when they were mistaken for African Americans. Governor McKeithen later brushed off the attack on the students. "You're going to have some there who are going to want to hurt somebody," said McKeithen. "I'm just happy that something worse did not occur."[38]

Tension grew as the first march in the series drew near. It would be the first march since the murder of O'Neal Moore and the filing of *Hicks v. Knight*. The Deacons prepared feverishly despite police harassment. A few days before the demonstration, state police arrested Sims for speeding following a harrowing high-speed chase in which the Deacons leader tried to elude Deputy Vertrees Adams. On 7 July approximately 350 protesters, mostly teenagers, began the march to City Hall in a drenching thundershower. CORE organizers were disappointed that adults failed to attend, and their frustration began to show. "CORE is just wasting money here," complained Isaac Reynolds, a CORE field secretary. White bystanders honked their horns to drown out the freedom songs, but otherwise the march made it without serious incident to City Hall. There Voters League leaders presented a new list of demands, including that Crown-Zellerbach hire black women, make promotions based on seniority, and dismiss employees that committed violence. The league also asked the city to dismiss outstanding charges against demonstrators, require public establishments to desegregate, and compel merchants to initiate fair hiring policies.[39]

The Deacons then prepared for the second march of the series scheduled for the next day, 8 July. Henry Austin and Milton Johnson were assigned to guard the rear of the march in A. Z. Young's car. The pair—Austin at twenty-one and Johnson at twenty-six—were younger than most Deacons. Austin was unquestionably one of the brightest and best-educated Deacons. Originally from New Orleans, he had served in the air force, where he took a few college classes. Articulate and personable, Austin made a good living selling small burial insurance policies. He wore a suit and tie when he made his rounds on Friday night to collect the modest weekly premiums—before the paychecks disappeared. Austin had been O'Neal Moore's insurance man and knew Moore well. The two had frequently watched football games together. Manhood and self-respect were the center of Austin's attraction for the Deacons. "The Negro in the South has been stripped of his manhood," Austin told an interviewer in 1965. "No respect for him as a man when he's picked up by the police force. The white man down the street doesn't respect him." But with the Deacons, the black man has "found a way at last to protect himself, to make himself feel like a man. And this is only human nature. To want to be a man if you're a man."[40]

Austin's talents, however, were marred by a volatile temper. Bob Hicks liked the bright young man but considered him a "hot head" who "couldn't control his emotions." While in the air force, Austin had stabbed a white soldier during an altercation in which the white man had called him a "nigger." Austin spent two years in prison for the crime. It may have been Austin's temper combined with his youth that led Charlie Sims to initially reject his application to the Deacons. Eventually Sims succumbed to Austin's persistent requests.[41]

The 8 July march wound its way to City Hall without any significant problems. But as the marchers began the return route, it became evident to Austin that the police were losing control of the white hecklers who lined the streets. The white mob was throwing rocks at Austin and Johnson and jumping on their car. Austin told Johnson to roll up the windows and lock the doors. Suddenly a piece of brick soared from the crowd and struck Hattie Mae Hill, a black teenager. Some volunteers from the Medical Rights Committee rushed to her aid and attempted to move her into a station wagon. The white mob surrounded the frightened girl and began hitting her and tearing her clothes. Austin told Johnson to get out and bring her back to their car. Johnson leaped from the vehicle and managed to rescue the girl and throw her into the back seat. Now the mob turned on Johnson, pinning him against the driver's side door and preventing his escape. Austin grabbed his .38 caliber pistol, shoved open the driver's door and stepped in front of Johnson to face the angry mob. "I have a gun!" he shouted, but his voice could barely be heard over the din of the crowd. When he fired a warning shot into the air, the mob continued to advance. Austin took aim and fired three shots into the chest of one of the white attackers, Alton Crowe. The tormenters recoiled in shock. They stared speechless at the black man holding the pistol.[42]

Austin knew that the police would be there in seconds. He calmly threw the gun on the car seat and placed his hands above his head to show that he was unarmed. The police arrived and handcuffed Austin and placed him across the trunk of the car as the white mob began to howl. As Austin stood handcuffed, a wiry old white woman sprang from the onlookers and began shrieking, "They killed a white man. Kill the niggers!"[43]

Austin was in imminent peril of being lynched. Governor McKeithen arranged for him to be transferred to a jail in nearby Slidell, but the Bogalusa police panicked at the thought of moving the prisoner. The detective assigned to escort him demanded a machine gun for his car, and the police deployed several decoy patrol cars from the Bogalusa jail to mislead the angry mob. An officer tossed Austin into a patrol car and shouted, "Nigger, lay down in the back seat."[44]

Austin made it safely to the Slidell jail. In New Orleans Alton Crowe, the young white man Austin had shot, lay on an operating table fighting for his life. One bullet had missed his heart by inches. Austin had not intended to kill Crowe; he had aimed for his midriff, but the pistol jerked upward at the last moment. But his intentions were irrelevant given the circumstances. "If that man dies," Austin told himself while sitting in jail, "they're damn sure going to electrocute your ass."[45]

Austin knew that he had violated the time-honored racial code of conduct that prohibited black men from collectively defending others from violence. Since the days of slavery, only plantation masters—or their modern-day counterparts, the police—had that prerogative. Henry Austin had shattered the code with the flash of a muzzle. The Alton Crowe shooting marked an unheralded but significant turning point in the black freedom movement. It was the first time in the modern civil rights struggle that a black organization had used lethal force to protect civil rights marchers. The incident ultimately helped convince the federal government to change its civil rights legal strategy in the South. The shooting signaled that blacks were prepared to use deadly force if Washington failed to protect their constitutional right of free speech: "It was no longer a situation where they could take advantage of black people with impunity," said Austin thirty years later.[46]

Initially, A. Z. Young and Charlie Sims denied that Austin and Johnson were Deacons, hoping to distance the Voters League and the Deacons from the shooting. But their denials did not last long. It soon became clear that most of the black community regarded Austin as a hero. After Sims bailed out the young Deacon (Alton Crowe survived the shooting), Austin returned to a warm welcome in Bogalusa. Men shook his hand and bought him drinks. Elderly women greeted him affectionately on the street and pressed a few dollar bills into his hand. The Crowe shooting did no damage to the Deacons' standing in the black community. The *New York Times* reported that at a mass rally the day after the shooting, Young introduced Sims and four hundred young black people "leaped to their feet in a delirious ovation." The night before, Sims had received wild applause at a rally when—going well beyond defensive violence—he issued a bold warning to racist vigilantes who had threatened to kill Young. "This I say to you: If someone is lucky enough to get past me to get to Mr. Young, then you will have four or five hundred funerals to go to."[47]

The talk of white funerals infuriated the governor. In the wake of the Crowe shooting, McKeithen pursued a "plague on both your houses" strategy toward the Deacons and the Klan. He condemned both the violent racists and the civil rights groups as equally responsible for the Bogalusa crisis. But McKeithen reserved his harshest criticism for the Deacons and failed to even mention the Klan by name. The governor castigated Young and Sims as "cowards" and "trash" and declared that "no decent negroes" were participating in the civil rights marches.[48] McKeithen's appeasement of the Klan was the rule rather than the exception for white Louisiana politicians. A subsequent investigation of the Klan conducted by the Louisiana Joint Legislative Committee on Un-American Activities issued a final report that likened Klan secrecy and intrigue to the "Halloween spirit that is common to most Americans."[49]

In the days to follow, the Klan reacted to the Crowe shooting by denying the obvious. For a black man to shoot a white man in broad daylight and live to tell about it was simply inconceivable to the robed terrorists. So they pretended that nothing had changed. One Klan leader, speaking to the *New York Times*, dismissed the Deacons as cowards, invoking the servile stereotype that they were struggling against: "I don't care how many guns that bunch of black Mau Maus has," said the Klansman, "they don't have the prerequisite—guts."[50]

But it was manifest that the Deacons haunted the Klansmen's thoughts. At a huge rally in Crossroads, Louisiana, on 18 July, United Klans of America leader L. C. McDaniel promised more violence against the Deacons. "I have never advocated violence," McDaniel told his audience, "but where such trash as the Deacons for Defense are on the scene, I don't think protecting our rights could be termed violence."[51]

Professional racists Connie Lynch and J. B. Stoner whipped up a crowd of thousands at a Bogalusa segregation rally following the Crowe shooting. Lynch, a California-based extremist, threatened genocidal warfare in Boga-lusa: "We're gonna clean the niggers out of these streets . . . that means bashing heads or anything else it takes. There's lots of trees around here and we don't mind hangin 'em." J. B. Stoner, erstwhile Imperial Wizard of the Christian Knights of the Ku Klux Klan, did his best to tap the economic anxiety of the white paper mill workers. "Every time a nigger gets a job," Stoner asserted at a rally, "that's just one more job that you can't have."[52]

Behind the bombast and threats was a profoundly distressed Klan. "Most whites do not admit it," wrote the *New York Times* after the Crowe shooting, "but the Deacons send a chill down their spines." The truth of this was borne out in subsequent marches. In the days following the shooting the huge mobs of whites disappeared. The Crowe shooting—and an increased police presence—discouraged ordinary whites from attending the Klan's counter-demonstrations. The Klan could no longer organize mass attacks on black demonstrations in Bogalusa. This inability to organize mass direct action protests reduced the Klan to isolated terror tactics and diminished its influ-ence over nonaffiliated segregationists in the mill town.[53]

The Crowe shooting also marked a political watershed for the Deacons. It would be difficult, if not impossible, for the Deacons to continue to reconcile the group's armed self-defense with Martin Luther King's nonviolent strategy. It was unmistakable that the Deacons were no longer simply exercising the right to defend hearth and home. Their actions now implied the right to defend black people exercising their constitutional right to free speech any-where, even in public spaces. Dr. King moved quickly to dissociate himself from the Deacons. "We can't win our struggle with nonviolence and . . . cloak it under the name of defensive violence," he said in the wake of the shooting. "The line of demarcation between aggressive and defensive violence is very slim." For King, a key issue was that armed self-defense jeopardized white support. "The Negro must have allies to win his struggle for equality," he warned. "And our allies will not surround a violent movement. What protects us from the Klan is to expose its brutality. We can't outshoot the Klan. We would only alienate our allies and lose sympathy for our cause."[54]

The Crowe shooting posed problems for CORE as well. CORE depended on white liberals for funding, and it was precisely this kind of armed self-defense that endangered the organization's political legitimacy and financial support. CORE was already $250,000 in debt and having difficulty raising money to underwrite its fifteen projects in Louisiana. Writing only days after the Crowe shooting, nationally syndicated columnist Nicholas Hoffman pointed out that CORE's collaboration with the Deacons could cause them to lose "the financial support of Northern liberal whites who are strongly moved by the idea of a nonviolent social revolution." But repudiating armed groups like the Deacons carried a price for national groups as well. "If they have nothing to do with local Negroes who arm themselves, the locals will have nothing to do with them, and the big groups will lose their position of leadership."[55]

Richard Haley had wrestled with CORE's relationship to the Deacons in a memorandum to CORE staff in the South. Haley began by noting that it was "a generally accepted belief among our La. CORE workers that some of our people might have been assaulted or even killed had the Deacons not taken over the job of protection." But the Deacons raised some thorny questions. Some members of the media were questioning whether CORE had remained faithful to its nonviolent principles. They wanted to know if CORE supported the Deacons and worked jointly with them. In addition, the Deacons had asked to use CORE automobiles and radios and had inquired about securing loans. It was clear that CORE needed to establish a "definite policy" toward the Deacons to provide guidelines for staff to standardize its public relations response. Haley conceded that CORE workers were no longer united around nonviolence. He identified several "schools of thought" on nonviolence within CORE: absolutists, who rejected all forms of violence; those who regarded nonviolence as only a tactic; those who admired but did not practice the "judicious use of violence"; and proponents of violence.[56]

Haley thought that the Deacons' use of force was comparable to government force. The Deacons were merely acting in place of the police; thus CORE should "regard the protective measures of the Deacons on behalf of CORE as we would regard any other proper police action." Haley proposed a cooperative and reciprocal working relationship with the Deacons. "We look to them to help us in emergencies and in turn, offer to help them in times of crisis." But he wanted to limit the level of joint work. He cautioned against becoming "involved in the program of any local organization on a permanent basis" and warned against planning and recruiting for the Deacons or providing financial support that was "likely to tie together these two groups" and become damaging to both. "Thus I view it a necessary part of CORE policy that we cooperate with the Deacons as a civic group and, when necessary as a protective agency," concluded Haley. But CORE staff would still adhere to nonviolent principles. "We are not prepared to violate the basis [sic] principles of nonviolence in conflict situations."[57]

While CORE anguished over the problem posed by the Deacons, a new source of violence was the harbinger of a much more serious challenge to the movement. The example of the Deacons had stimulated a new combativeness throughout the African American community. In the days following the Crowe shooting, young blacks in Bogalusa began to independently retaliate against white harassment. When two white men jumped a lone black man near the edge of the black quarters, a group of six blacks attacked the whites and sent them to the hospital. On another occasion two young whites slowly drove by a black drive-in and found themselves dodging bullets. On 18 July four young black men were arrested for shooting at whites in two separate incidents near Bogalusa. It was a far cry from the summer before, when whites could invade the black community without fear of retaliation. So many young people had taken to arming themselves that at one rally James Farmer told the marchers to "leave your hardware at home."[58]

The Deacons were wary of the new fighting spirit. The media frequently identified the young culprits involved in these incidents as Deacons, forcing Charlie Sims to berate the young militants for endangering the movement. Sims had to issue explicit orders that only the Deacons could carry guns. At a rally in late July, he gave a stern warning to the "trigger happy" contingent. "Everything you do, whether you're a Deacon or not, they call you a Deacon. We've got enough trouble on our hands now without you going across town carrying guns and stirring up trouble," Sims told the teenagers. "We've got enough guns to go it without you people."[59]

Bogalusa's descent into chaos sparked a debate on nonviolence in the national media. "Race and Violence: More Dixie Negroes Buy Arms to Retaliate against White Attacks," was the headline on the front page of the *Wall Street Journal* on 12 July 1965, followed by the portentous subheading that posed the question: "Non-Violence Coming to End?" Fred Zimmerman, who wrote the article, warned that "fear is mounting that angry Negroes are ready to reject the biblical injunction to 'turn the other cheek' and embrace an older, harsher code—an eye for an eye." He noted that bands of "militant, heavily armed" blacks were forming in small sleepy southern towns and, unlike mainstream civil rights organizations, they "are locally led, and they share an open contempt for the doctrine of nonviolence."[60]

Armed groups, primarily the Deacons, had spread to six states, reported Zimmerman, and had alarmed law enforcement and moderates who feared a "major bloodletting." He detailed the Deacons' organizing efforts, repeating their claim of fifty active chapters centered in Louisiana and the Mississippi Delta, and stating that new chapters had recently been formed in northern Florida, South Carolina, North Carolina, and Alabama. "These groups are all over the state now," Mississippi activist Charles Evers, brother of slain civil rights leader Medgar Evers, told Zimmerman, "and I'm glad they're around."[61]

Zimmerman's source for most of this information was probably the Deacons themselves, although he apparently corroborated some of the claims through others. Even if the Deacons' growth was considerably overstated—and it was—the resulting media image enhanced their standing as important opponents of the mainstream civil rights movement. Within just a few months, the Deacons had evolved from an anonymous guard group into a symbol of the revolt against nonviolence.

The *Wall Street Journal* article touched on the quandary the Deacons posed to mainstream civil rights groups, speculating that some national organizations had refused to disavow the Deacons because they feared the loss of support from local black communities that favored the armed group. James Farmer of CORE was quoted as saying that, although CORE's demonstrations were nonviolent, "I don't feel that I have any right to tell a Negro community they don't have the right to defend the sanctity of their homes." Other civil rights groups interviewed for the story refused to concede any ground to the Deacons. Paul Anthony, field director of the Southern Regional Council (which had spearheaded efforts to steer the movement away from direct action), was deeply troubled by the Deacons. Anthony warned that if "the Deacons really catch hold, it could mean the end of nonviolence in some areas of the South . . . which could cause a wave of violence with national repercussions." The Deacons were growing increasingly confident in criticizing mainstream civil rights groups. "We're going to have a war, I honestly believe that," Bob Hicks declared. "But we're not going to double up like CORE people do when we're attacked."[62]

Charlie Sims attempted to assuage fears of rampant violence by emphasizing the Deacons' self-discipline and defensive goals. Members were to only use their weapons to defend themselves, Sims maintained. "We're constantly riding all the members all the time about this." Still, the *Journal* story indicated apprehension about the Deacons, fearing that defensive force would provoke more Klan violence. "It's true that much of their activity is, in effect, guard duty," wrote Zimmerman. "But to Southern law enforcement agencies and to many groups trying to promote integration without violence—these armed bands are essentially vigilantes posing an increasing threat of bloodshed."[63]

Newsweek reporters also descended on Bogalusa in the wake of the Crowe shooting and published a piece on the "highly disciplined group of Negro vigilantes" whose "swift rise" and "spread" presented "nonviolence civil rights groups with a quandary." The article reprised the stories of the Deacons' arsenal of automatic weapons and grenades and aptly characterized their rhetoric as a "violent repudiation of nonviolent leaders." Firmly lodged in the "militant" camp by the media and their own rhetoric, the Deacons now found themselves with some unwanted allies. When *Newsweek* questioned Charlie Sims about the similarities between the Black Muslims and the Deacons, the Deacons leader took pains to dissociate his group from the separatists. "I despise the Muslims just as much as I do the Ku Klux Klan," Sims protested. "I don't believe in either white or black supremacy. I believe in equality."[64]

By far, the greatest boost to the Deacons' popularity in the African American community came one week after the Crowe shooting with the publication of a major story on the Deacons in *Jet* magazine. *Jet* was the most widely read black weekly digest in America and the principal source of black news and opinions for much of the black working class. Standard reading fare in barbershops and beauty salons—the communication centers of the black community—*Jet* reached deep into the rural South.[65] Its youthful staff included reporters like Larry Still, who was highly sympathetic to militant groups that were counterposed to the NAACP and other mainstream organizations. In its 15 July issue *Jet* carried a major story based on interviews with Charlie Sims during his Los Angeles visit the previous month. Louie Robinson and Charles Brown wrote the story, featuring a front-cover headline that read: "Negro Most Feared by Whites in Louisiana." The story was a virtual paean to Sims, including his photograph with the glowing caption: "reflects determination; inward, unswerving courage."[66]

Sims was at his best in the interview: disarming, unpredictable, and charming. He had honed his new image as a tough-talking militant. Sporting bloodshot eyes and his ragged smile, Sims first apologized to the reporters for wearing a suit with a white shirt at the interview. "This white shirt makes a good target at night," he observed whimsically. In Bogalusa he wore overalls. "They have nice, big pockets," he added, "also you can carry your pipe [gun] and plenty of shells."[67]

Eschewing the white media's pejorative term of "vigilantes," *Jet* described the Deacons as a "determined band of heavily armed Negroes who have vowed to defend themselves with guns from marauding whites who have terrorized black communities in the South." Sims said that the Deacons were committed to protecting all leaders of civil rights organizations—even those who opposed the Deacon's tactics. "As long as his face is black and he is in Bogalusa, we feel his safety is our responsibility."[68]

Sims related a series of violent incidents, all enlivened with his characteristic embellishments. The Klan had a $1,000 reward on him, he told the young reporters—an unconfirmed claim. He recounted a questionable tale about capturing Klansmen during the February Klan attack on Steve Miller and Bill Yates. The Deacons leader also recalled an incident in which Claxton Knight had warned that "whites were massing nearby to break up the meeting" and there was nothing the police could do about it. Sims told Knight, "Since you brought a message you go back and carry one: Tell them to come on we're going to stack 'em up like cross ties."[69]

Sims was carefully constructing a new image for the Deacons, something far more complex than the simple bodyguards they had been only months before. His tales of daring and courage were intended to convey a picture of black men upholding black manhood and racial honor. "They can put me in jail but they have to let me out one day," Sims told the reporters. "They can't curse and harass me and frighten me. I'm fighting harder now than ever before because I've got something to fight for that the average white man doesn't. I've never been free before and I want a whole lot of freedom."[70]

Thousands of African Americans read the article in *Jet*. Calls flooded into Bogalusa from people offering support and requesting assistance from the organization. The article led to the formation of several new Deacons chapters, but more important it stimulated a debate on nonviolence in black communities across the nation—from barbershops to barrooms.[71]

The Deacons had become a symbol of a sea change in black consciousness. They were coming to understand that using force was more than just a tactic to defend the movement; it was a whole different approach to obtaining freedom. A month earlier *Jet* had cogently summed up how the Deacons had forever changed the movement dynamic: "With deadly guns and bullets and the nonviolent philosophy living side by side in tense Bogalusa, whites in that area—perhaps for the first time in any Deep South civil rights drive— have a clear choice of alternatives."[72] In the coming days events in Bogalusa would force that choice.

CHAPTER

9

Victory

THE ALTON CROWE shooting on 8 July 1965 put local and state authorities on full alert. Bogalusa city officials vainly sought a restraining order to prevent the Voters League from continuing to march. Governor McKeithen asked the league to stop the marches and sent an additional 125 state troopers to Bogalusa, raising the total to 325. Meanwhile, the National States Rights Party launched its own legal attack on the Deacons, delivering affidavits to Washington Parish charging that Charlie Sims and two other civil rights leaders were violating Louisiana's statute forbidding common-law marriages (Sims was not married to his companion Bernice Harry at the time). The federal courts also weighed in on the day following the shooting when Judge Herbert W. Christenberry made a favorable ruling for the Bogalusa Civic and Voters League in *Hicks v. Knight*. Christenberry issued a temporary restraining order that Bogalusa and state officials protect civil rights workers against assaults, harassment, and intimidation. The jurist ordered law enforcement to stop the use of unnecessary force and to cease unlawful arrests, threats of arrest, and prosecutions. He also demanded that police officers not conceal their identity by covering or removing their badges. There were doubts that the order would be enforced. Christenberry refused to put any meaningful power behind his injunction when he declined the Voters League request to appoint a special u.s. commissioner to monitor compliance. During the hearings he openly mused from the bench that any injunction he issued would probably not be enforced—nor would it provide "the physical and moral courage" needed by the police to remedy their behavior. The largely symbolic decision meant that the black movement in Bogalusa would have to up the political ante if it wanted the Bill of Rights made a reality for blacks in Louisiana. This was precisely what the Voters League was planning.[1]

Despite the governor's entreaties, the league refused to back off and instead announced another march for Sunday, 11 July—the same day that segregationists had planned to march in Bogalusa. The league promised additional protests in the future, including a motorcade to the parish seat of Franklinton. On Sunday, James Farmer led the demonstrators from the Negro Union Hall to the downtown area. An eerie silence descended as Farmer walked quietly with his eyes looking straight ahead. The large mobs of whites that normally lined the streets had disappeared, the memory of Alton Crowe fresh in their minds. The marchers entered the downtown shopping district and passed through a subdued crowd of whites. National Guard helicopters hovered menacingly above the white mob as an army of several hundred police stood guard armed with machine guns.[2]

McKeithen decided to make another attempt to mediate the conflict. On Monday, 12 July, he sent his official plane to fly Bob Hicks and A. Z. Young to Baton Rouge. At the Governor's Mansion McKeithen implored Hicks and Young to call a thirty-day moratorium on marches—a "cooling off" period to renew negotiations. He promised to bring the city back to the negotiating table and arrange for segregationists Connie Lynch and J. B. Stoner to leave Bogalusa. Swayed by the governor's amiable charm—and no doubt impressed by the VIP treatment—Hicks and Young accepted his moratorium and agreed to present the proposal to the Voters League Executive Board that night. Following the meeting with McKeithen the two activists issued a statement saying that they agreed with the governor that "the Bogalusa demonstrations are hurting the state and are increasing bitterness between the races."[3]

Hicks and Young may have succumbed to McKeithen's charm, but the league's membership was not so easily seduced. When the compromise was introduced at a mass meeting later that night at the Ebenezer Baptist Church, cries of "No, No" rang out and the members overwhelmingly shouted down the moratorium proposal. A somewhat shaken Hicks and Young adjourned the meeting and went into executive session, where the Executive Board formally rejected McKeithen's proposal. McKeithen later accused Louis Lomax, a black journalist from Los Angeles who had attended the rally, of turning the league against Hicks and Young by promising to raise $15,000 to continue the campaign. The governor claimed that the two league leaders were "lucky to get out of that hall alive."[4]

But Lomax knew only too well that the Voters League and the Deacons were no quislings. "The genius of Bogalusa is its spontaneity," he told reporters. "The civil rights people are indigenously motivated and indigenously led." Lomax later caused a stir when he ridiculed the "Christian Mothers of Bogalusa," a white segregationist women's group that had recently staged a protest at the Federal Building in New Orleans. These were the same "scrawny white women" who went into the black neighborhood "selling goat meat and string beans," joked Lomax. The barb provoked an indignant editorial in defense of southern womanhood by the *Bogalusa Daily News*, which referred to the segregationist women as "fine ladies."[5]

The next day a determined but frustrated McKeithen flew to Bogalusa for a second attempt to negotiate a truce, but not before he sought and received the blessing of what he called Bogalusa's "white conservatives"— no doubt the Citizens Council and the Ku Klux Klan. The meeting was held in a room at the Bogalusa airport, attended by the Voters League Executive Board, Louis Lomax, city officials, representatives of the Community Affairs Committee, and Deacons leader Charles Sims. At the table the governor found himself face-to-face with Sims. It was a distasteful experience for McKeithen, who now had the distinction of being the only governor forced to negotiate with a black armed self-defense organization. Charlie Sims, the man with twenty-seven arrests to his name, must have felt a sense of personal vindication and accomplishment: in a few short months the grisly brawler had risen from hustling in the streets to negotiating with the Louisiana governor.[6]

Little headway was made during the heated meeting. McKeithen turned down the league's demand that he hire black state police. Mayor Cutrer was similarly intractable on the issue of integrating the city police. The Deacons and the Voters League remained defiant and refused to halt the demonstrations. During one angry exchange McKeithen told Sims that he had planned to have him arrested "on general principle" at the league march on the prior Sunday. McKeithen told Sims: "I sent word if you were seen, to arrest you. You have been bragging you were going to kill people, you were going to have funerals," referring to Sims's threat that if A. Z. Young were killed, white people would have several hundred funerals to attend. McKeithen warned Sims that he would have him arrested if he made further threats. Sims was unfazed. The negotiations broke off after an hour and a half, and McKeithen sulked back to Baton Rouge. "I don't know any more that I can do at this time," asserted the governor at an airport press conference. "I came over here to meet with colored people to demonstrate to them that I was prepared to humble myself as their governor, to listen to their complaints." To his dismay, the Voters League had repaid his magnanimity by talking to him "kind of ugly."[7]

Later in Baton Rouge McKeithen publicly lashed out at the Deacons, announcing that he had ordered the state police to confiscate all weapons found in cars or on persons in Bogalusa. The confiscation order would apply to both blacks and whites, explained McKeithen, but he left little doubt about who his target was. "We're going to run the Deacons out of business and anybody else that's got pistols and rifles and shotguns," he declared. Charlie Sims had, in the past, made clear how he would respond to such an order. "I would rather be caught in Bogalusa with concealed weapons," he would snort, "than without them."[8]

On 14 July Mayor Cutrer announced that the city had drafted an ordinance to confiscate guns in the event of an emergency. The Voters League responded to the challenge by promptly organizing a march on Wednesday, 14 July, to protest the threatened confiscation. It was a protest that Martin Luther King or any other civil rights leader would have found unimaginable: a nonviolent march demanding the right to armed self-defense. The march ended with a spirited, defiant rally defending the Deacons. "If it weren't for the Deacons not many of us would be in this church tonight," A. Z. Young reminded his audience. "They would have run us all out of town. . . . We got the lowdowndest white people in Bogalusa than anywhere."[9]

Louis Lomax assailed McKeithen's duplicity in threatening to disarm the Deacons while the Klan used guns with impunity. "They talk about picking up guns," Lomax told the crowd. "They didn't talk about it 100 years ago. They only talk about it when Charlie Sims has guns. Why didn't they pick up guns when the two Negro deputies were shot?" Bob Hicks waxed indignant at the governor's charge that Lomax had swayed the Voters League to reject the moratorium. "We are in command. We run this campaign. This is our town. When the hard fight is over, we have to live in Bogalusa." Hicks charged that state leaders had created the conditions that called the Deacons into existence. "Guns are the only protection you have if laws are no good," he maintained. "I don't know if I'd be here today unless I had a gun." It was McKeithen and Cutrer who had created the crisis by abdicating leadership to the Klan, continued Hicks. "The Governor has no power, the mayor has no power and if no one has any power everyone should run around wild." Young summed up the tense, apocalyptic mood of the rally: "We are on the verge of civil war."[10]

The Voters League and the Deacons had pushed the state to the wall. They were inviting volunteers from around the country to flood into the Bayou State and make Bogalusa the Selma of Louisiana. McKeithen panicked at the thought of the Bogalusa crisis sparking a wildfire of protests throughout the state and frantically sought the assistance of moderate black leaders. He convened a special committee to assess the situation in Bogalusa and head off further crises. The committee consisted of Dr. Albert W. Dent, president of Dillard University, Dr. Felton Clark, president of Southern University, and

A. P. Tureaud, attorney for the NAACP—old-guard civil rights leaders who, for the most part, had been superseded by the new militant direct action groups like the Voters League and the Deacons. Eventually the committee was expanded into a permanent integrated commission, the Louisiana Commission on Race Relations. The Voters League looked askance at the committee. CORE's Richard Haley would later belittle the commission as a committee "of the well-fed to deal with the problem of the hungry."[11]

By Thursday, 15 July, the crisis had come to a head. Beginning with the Crowe shooting on 8 July, the league had conducted seven days of relentless marches. It had defied the Klan and threatened to plunge Bogalusa into a bloody civil war. People lined up fifteen deep in department stores to buy weapons. McKeithen had failed to negotiate a truce due to his unwillingness to concede any of the league's demands. Now the governor decided to abandon the city and turn the crisis over to the federal government. He announced that he was withdrawing 280 of the 370 state troopers—a dangerous move that in effect handed Bogalusa over to the Ku Klux Klan.

At the same time, McKeithen contacted Vice President Hubert Humphrey and asked him to intervene in Bogalusa. Initially Humphrey rebuffed the governor. In the days to follow, Mayor Cutrer and A. Z. Young also sent telegrams to Washington urgently requesting help, this time addressed to President Lyndon B. Johnson. Both sides were attempting to draw in the federal government by using the imminent threat of a civil war in the streets of Bogalusa—as promised by the Deacons. But the question was much greater than the resolution of a community race relations dispute. After months of dodging the issue of southern lawlessness and rule by terror, the challenge for the president had come to this: Would he reassert the supremacy of the federal government and restore the U.S. Constitution as the law of the land in the Deep South? Moreover, would he force local and state governments to implement the new civil rights laws, enforce the Bill of Rights, and dismantle the racist terrorist network—rather than rely on an ad hoc deployment of federalized troops and the U.S. military for enforcement?

The answer came on 15 July, when Johnson announced that he was dispatching John Doar, the head of the Justice Department's Civil Rights Division, to Bogalusa to negotiate a compromise to the crisis.[12] At Justice Doar had been the lead person on voting and civil rights in the South and had worked closely with civil rights organizations since the beginning of the movement. By 1965 he had worn out his welcome among many civil rights activists by maintaining a policy of federal nonintervention. Echoing his Justice Department's superiors and the Kennedy administration's line, Doar justified the failure of the federal government to offer protection in the

South by invoking the doctrine of federalism: preserving law and order was the responsibility of local authorities. Under the policy, the Justice Department could not intervene on behalf of activists because the federal government lacked jurisdiction to protect civil rights workers or enforce constitutional rights; unless a federal law was broken, Justice could do nothing.

Doar knew better. The Justice Department had at its disposal several laws enacted during Reconstruction specifically to protect the rights of citizens and to rein in Klan terrorists. In addition, the 1957 Civil Rights Act empowered the federal government to protect voting rights. Moreover, the Justice Department always had jurisdiction to protect the rights and liberties extended in the Bill of Rights—including the right of free expression and the Fourteenth Amendment's provisions for equal protection under the law. Doar had used these laws successfully as early as 1960 to end reprisals against blacks who had registered to vote in rural Tennessee. In the face of pervasive and horrific Klan violence during the Freedom Rides of 1962, Doar also relied on the statutes to obtain a restraining order against the Montgomery police and the Klan to end attacks on the Freedom Riders, though he did not file any complaints to enforce the injunction.[13]

As the Kennedy administration backed off most of its campaign promises on civil rights, Doar and the Justice Department became little more than passive observers to the terror visited upon the movement. It took little southern political pressure to frighten off Justice when it did gingerly attempt to assert its rightful authority. In 1963, during the highly publicized police attacks on Student Nonviolent Coordinating Committee (SNCC) civil rights activists in Greenwood, Mississippi, Doar filed a lawsuit to force Greenwood to permit blacks to "exercise their constitutional right to assemble for peaceful protest demonstrations and protect them from whites who might object." When Mississippi's delegation condemned the action on the Senate floor, the Kennedys ducked for cover and ordered Doar to withdraw the suit. The Kennedys could afford to ignore the injustices and suffering in Greenwood since the blood was flowing only one way—unlike in Bogalusa.[14]

Thelton Henderson, the only black Justice Department investigator in Mississippi, confirmed the Deacons' suspicion that only black retaliation would produce enforcement of the new laws. The department's concern "was not necessarily how will we go about enforcing the civil rights laws," said Henderson years later, "but how much are the blacks going to take before they strike back, and then we will have to do something."[15] From the Little Rock crisis forward, three presidential administrations avoided a confrontation with the South by relying exclusively on federalized troops and federal law enforcement agencies to enforce civil rights laws and judicial rulings, rather than compelling local and state agencies to uphold the law and the Bill of Rights. Without local law enforcement support for rudimentary civil liberties, local African Americans would always lack effective means to redress their grievances.[16]

Now the Deacons forced the confrontation so long avoided. In a memorandum to Governor McKeithen (which Vice President Humphrey also reviewed), the Community Relations Service (CRS) underscored the pivotal role of the Deacons in driving the crisis. It was possible for Louisiana to peacefully settle its racial conflicts, the CRS told McKeithen, "But there is one other unique factor which must be mentioned: no other state has had to deal with *two* armed and organized groups. Armed groups of organized whites are not new, but the Deacons are a first" and "the possibility of a clash between the two armed and determined groups in Louisiana grows each day."[17]

John Doar clearly had a presidential mandate to take a symbolic stand in Bogalusa. Doar decided on a two-prong strategy to restore order and enforce the Civil Rights Act. First, he would force local authorities to uphold civil liberties and the national law. Second, he would destroy the Klan. To carry out his plan, Doar first had to document violations of Christenberry's injunction issued in *Hicks v. Knight*. He immediately arranged for the Federal Bureau of Investigation (FBI) to collect the evidence. He did not have to wait long. In the four short days Doar was in Bogalusa, Klansmen staged a series of carefully orchestrated assaults against isolated pickets. The smaller guerrilla attacks were their only alternative: The white crowds that had spontaneously materialized along the march routes had now evaporated in a cloud of fear. Perhaps drawing a lesson from the Justice Department's retreat in Greenwood, the Deacons escalated their threats of retaliatory violence. "I do not advocate violence and we are going to do whatever we can to keep down the civil war in this area," A. Z. Young was quoted as saying in the *Bogalusa Daily News*. "But, if blood is going to be shed, we are going to let it rain down Columbia Street—all kinds, both black and white. We are not going to send Negro blood down Columbia Street by itself, that's for sure."[18]

Most whites heeded Young's warning. Only a small group of hard-core Klansmen remained bold enough to risk attacking the civil rights activists. The Deacons always had problems protecting picketers, and those difficulties were compounded when the demonstration spread to Pine Tree and La Plaza Shopping Centers located some distance from the Columbia Street stores. The pickets were also more vulnerable given the reduced state police presence, which made it easier for the Klan to stage diversionary attacks and quick guerrilla assaults. Within days the FBI documented and filmed numerous Klan attacks on pickets and instances of police brutality. Doar personally watched in horror as the Klan attacked ten pickets at the La Plaza Shopping Center, pounding them into the pavement as forty state police stood idly by. When local Bogalusa police finally arrived, they arrested the picketers instead of the Klan attackers.[19]

On 16 July the Justice Department began its lethal attack on white resistance in Bogalusa. Doar filed five federal suits, signed by Attorney General Nicholas Katzenbach, designed to cripple the segregationist movement and establish the federal government's authority. Using the attacks at La Plaza as evidence, Doar first intervened in *Hicks v. Knight*, asking that the court hold in criminal and civil contempt Sheriff Arnold Spiers and Police Chief Claxton Knight for failing to enforce Christenberry's order and allowing the Klan attacks to continue. Doar also filed a criminal bill of information against Officer Vertrees Adams, charging him with violating the *Hicks* order in four counts of brutality and harassment. By seeking both criminal and civil contempt judgments against the law enforcement officers, the Justice Department was giving Bogalusa lawmen an ultimatum: enforce the law or face fines and jail sentences. Taking aim at the remaining segregated businesses, Doar additionally filed a civil suit against four Bogalusa merchants to force them to desegregate and comply with the Civil Rights Act.[20]

But the most effective action was Doar's suit against the Original Knights of the Ku Klux Klan (OKKKK) asking the federal court to enjoin the Klan from depriving citizens of their constitutional rights through intimidating and threatening civil rights activists, Washington Parish officials, and businesses. The suit charged that the Klan's goal was to deprive individuals of their rights and preserve segregation and white supremacy in Washington Parish. The suit named thirty-five defendants, including twenty members of the Klan and fifteen individuals. Charles Christmas of Amite was identified as the OKKKK's principal leader, and Saxon Farmer and Russell Magee were named as Washington Parish leaders. The suit charged that the group operated out of the Disabled Veterans Hall near Bogalusa and had committed twenty specific acts of intimidation and harassment. The action marked the first time that the Justice Department had purposefully used a federal suit to destroy the Klan in the civil rights movement era. It would prove a potent weapon.[21]

Suddenly Mayor Cutrer was falling all over himself to begin negotiations with the Voters League. Cutrer hastily took to the airwaves to announce his support for the league's right to march and picket and to urge citizens to simply ignore the protests. Police Commissioner Spiers and Chief Knight ran large advertisements in the *Bogalusa Daily News* calling for people to obey the law or face arrest. Civic and religious leaders, at Cutrer's urging, went on the radio and echoed the call to ignore the protests and return order to the city. The *Daily News* mustered the courage to publish an editorial demanding that the city enforce the law. And the Crown-Zellerbach Corporation began negotiations with the Voters League to end segregation and discrimination in the box factory. Even some Klan leaders jumped on the retreating band-wagon. At a United Klans of America (UKA) rally outside of Bogalusa on 21 July, UKA leader Robert Shelton told some four hundred Klansmen to ignore the civil rights protests. "Violence is just ammunition for the opposition," he declared.[22]

Business establishments that had refused to integrate suddenly opened their doors to blacks. On 20 July Deacons officer Sam Barnes led successful tests at La Plaza Restaurant, Redwood Cafe, and Acme Cafe—this time the police cordially escorted the testers during the tests. In total, activists tested five restaurants, all of which complied with the law. By the end of the month nearly all public establishments were desegregated. Cutrer also arranged for two blacks to take the Civil Service exam for the police department. They passed, with the highest scores ever recorded, and promptly integrated the police force.[23]

After seven months of wanton attacks by the Klan, none of the forty segregationists arrested for crimes had been prosecuted. Now Bogalusa's judicial machinery went into motion. City attorney Robert Rester, himself a secret Klan member, stepped up prosecutions of the white attackers. Not everything had changed, though. After pleading guilty to assaulting James Farmer, Klansman Randle Pounds received a paltry $25 fine and a suspended sentence.[24]

The hearings on the Justice Department's suits began on 26 July, but the court proceedings were anticlimactic: The Deacons had already triumphed. They had forced the Yankee government to invade the South once again. Virtually all of their demands would be met in the coming days. The hearings did, for the first time, publicly expose the depth and pattern of official malfeasance and police abuse in Bogalusa. Judge Christenberry convicted Knight, Spiers, and one officer of civil contempt, and on 30 July he ordered Knight and Spiers to develop a specific plan to ensure the protection of civil rights workers. If they refused to comply, Christenberry promised to proceed with criminal charges.[25]

The effect of the federal offensive was swift and dramatic. Overnight, Washington had crushed the white supremacist coup in Bogalusa and forced local authorities to uphold the law—something that the Justice Department had never before attempted in the modern civil rights movement. In retrospect, what is remarkable was how *little* was required to destroy the Klan and force local authorities to protect citizens' rights and liberties. The federal government did nothing more than threaten city officials with modest fines and light jail sentences. In the past, the Justice Department had avoided a showdown with southern law enforcement, fearing that a confrontation would antagonize the white South and escalate out of control. In 1964 SNCC had suggested to Justice officials Burke Marshall and John Doar that they could stop police brutality if they simply arrested one abusive sheriff. Marshall responded in a nervous voice that the federal government was "not going to fight a guerrilla war in Mississippi, and if they arrested a sheriff, they would have to fight this type of war." As Bogalusa revealed, when the Justice Department finally made its move, the "guerrilla war" turned out to be a tempest in a teapot.[26]

With their terrorist wing effectively destroyed, segregationists were reduced to peaceful protests to make their case. During the federal court hearings, white women picketers showed up in front of Doar's temporary headquarters at the Bogalusa Post Office to protest the Justice Department's cooperation with the Deacons. Pickets carried signs demanding that the Deacons be prosecuted: "Mr. Doar, You Have Indicted the Ku Klux Klan, How about the Deacons for Defense?" Dorothy McNeese, a Varnado resident and organizer of the protest, called for an investigation of the Deacons and assailed Doar as a minion for the paramilitary group. "We feel that Mr. Doar came to Bogalusa for one purpose only," McNeese charged, "and that was to draw nationwide attention and criticism away from an organization called the Deacons for Defensive [*sic*] Justice."[27] In an ironic reversal of roles, McNeese formed a white "women's civilian patrol" of more than three hundred women bent on protecting whites from the Deacons and annoying picketers. She also announced plans to train members in the "art of self-defense."[28]

Nothing much came of McNeese's "White Deacons." By August, marches and pickets occurred only sporadically. The movement was spent, and neither civil rights activists nor segregationists could muster much enthusiasm in the enervating tropical heat of August. Driven underground, the Klan launched a series of bomb attacks in early August. Two motels in Baton Rouge were bombed with a single stick of dynamite, including the Lincoln

Motel where Ronnie Moore was staying and the International Motel where a Canadian civil rights medical team had registered. But even the bombings could not revive the white mass movement. The Voters League also showed signs of fatigue. Their marches were losing support, and in desperation the leadership began pushing for night marches to attract more adults. But the courts prohibited what would have been an extremely dangerous and unmanageable form of protest.[29]

Like most catalysts in a radical social movement, the Deacons and the Voters League were never content with their achievements—which were substantial. *States-Item* columnist Alan Katz wrote that Bogalusa had taught southern whites that racist violence only generated national sympathy and resulted in federal repression—at the expense of local control. The Bogalusa civil rights movement had clearly won, said Katz. The city had recognized the Voters League as the primary bargaining agent for the black community. The movement had forced the city to repeal its segregation laws, desegregate public accommodations, and concede neighborhood improvements—including blacktopping streets and installing mercury lights. In addition, the city was negotiating with the Federal Housing Administration for loans to construct one hundred low-cost housing units.[30]

But Katz recognized an even more significant accomplishment for the Voters League and the Deacons. He quoted a thirteen-year-old Bogalusa girl who had been harassed and arrested during the Bogalusa campaign. "My folk used to be scared of the Ku Klux Klan," said the girl. "I'm not scared of them. I'm not afraid of anybody."[31]

In the wake of the Deacons' stunning victory in Bogalusa, the nation's opinion makers struggled to understand this new phenomenon in the Deep South. Although there were discrepancies between the Deacons' media image and their organizational reality, myth is reality in politics. For liberals, that myth was shaped in large part by the *New York Times*. On 15 August 1965 Roy Reed, writing for the *New York Times Magazine*, produced one of the most extensive and thoughtful stories published on the Deacons. Entitled "The Deacons, Too, Ride by Night," the lengthy article featured several prominent photographs of armed Deacons and a steely eyed Charles Sims. Reed described the Deacons as an "armed, semisecret, loosely organized federation" that was widely supported and was "well on their way to community leadership."[32]

Reed saw a major strategic difference that underscored the division between the Deacons and the mainstream civil rights organizations. The division, according to Harvard scholar Dr. Thomas Pettigrew, stemmed from the fact that oppressed communities may choose several paths to liberation, including to move toward their oppressor to "seek equality"—as symbolized by the NAACP and CORE—or to "move against the oppressor and fight him." The Deacons had taken the second path. Reed alluded to the inflated membership claims but gave little credence to the figures or to the reports of a cache of illegal weapons. Size was unimportant for a symbolic organization like the Deacons. "The importance of the Deacons at the moment is not in their numbers but in their psychological impact on both whites and Negroes." And what was that impact? The Deacons were an intimidating symbol to whites. Their willingness to shoot back had frightened whites and reduced harassment in Jonesboro, although it had raised racial tension in Bogalusa. Reed recounted several armed skirmishes between the Deacons and the Klan, including the shooting of Alton Crowe by Henry Austin one month earlier. "Far from dampening the spirit of Bogalusa Negroes, this foolhardy shooting seemed to stir their passions higher."[33]

The psychological impact of the Deacons on blacks was equally significant. "Part of the Negro's task in his struggle for equality is to convince the nation, and particularly the white south, that he is competitive, that he has will and backbone," said Reed. To do this, blacks had to overcome the deeply embedded white stereotype of blacks as "docile, unaggressive and martially inferior." In the past blacks had used nonviolence to prove their mettle, to show that they were "tough enough to take it and big enough not to hit back." Now groups like the Deacons in the South and the Muslims in the North were choosing a new direction. "They are determined to prove to the white racists, and perhaps to themselves, that the Negro not only can take it but that he can also dish it out." The Deacons had inspired pride in the community and had "proved to be a natural instrument for building community feeling and nourishing the Negro identity." Their strategy demonstrating that they could "dish it out" had also contributed positively to the new Negro identity.

Reed, like many other journalists and intellectuals of his time, was trying to grasp what the Deacons symbolized in the new black male identity. Implicit in his analysis was a connection between physical courage, manhood, and the New Negro. Also like his counterparts, Reed did not give attention to how this call to manhood affected gender roles and African American women in the movement. Only in recent years have scholars begun to address this nexus of masculine identity and gender.[34]

The growing class tensions within the movement also emerged in the story. Reed described Charlie Sims as a "good example of the new non-middle class Negro leader in the Southern Civil Rights movement." His police record and streetwise demeanor were no obstacles to leadership. "In other times he would have been simply a tough; now he is a hero." Frederick Kirkpatrick also underscored the Deacons' resentment of middle-class black leaders, telling Reed that he was fighting "Uncle Tom" preachers and their fatalist religious belief that "all good things come to those who wait." Kirkpatrick, a minister himself, scoffed at passive religious doctrine, arguing that "every generation is put here for a purpose, not to lollygag and do nothing." He planned to enlist young men to dig sewer lines in the black community, and in turn, black residents would be expected to register to vote. "And if they don't?" asked Reed. "We might have to make 'em go," replied Kirkpatrick bluntly. "We might have to drag 'em down. You see, they're holding back the whole program."[35]

Reed touched on how CORE and SNCC had quietly cooperated with the Deacons but noted how Martin Luther King opposed the Deacons' version of self-defense. "The line between defensive violence and aggressive violence is very thin," King had said in July. "You get people to thinking in terms of violence when you have a movement that is built around defensive violence." King's criticism of the Deacons was beginning to force the group into an adversarial relationship with the movement leader. Sims made little effort to conceal his contempt for King. The Deacons had recently invited a host of civil rights leaders to Bogalusa, but not King. "I want everybody here except Martin Luther King," said Sims. "If he came and they gun him, I couldn't protect him, because he don't believe in me."[36]

By the end of the summer of 1965, the Deacons had pushed their way into the national debate on nonviolence, with major stories in not only the *New York Times*, but also the *Wall Street Journal*, the *Los Angeles Times*, *Life* magazine, *Newsweek*, and *Time*. While publications like the *New York Times* shaped the image of the Deacons and the controversy on nonviolence for the white middle class, most blacks learned about the Deacons through black media like *Jet* and *Ebony* (the *New Orleans Times-Picayune* carried only one brief story on the Deacons—a disparaging article reporting on the Deacons leaders' arrest records).[37] *Jet* was widely read by self-taught working-class intellectuals of the day who strongly influenced opinion in the African American community. Its coverage of the Deacons was extensive and favorable, including a cover story in the 15 July 1965 issue with the enticing heading, "Negro Feared Most by Whites in Louisiana." In September 1965 *Ebony*, the leading black monthly magazine, expanded on *Jet*'s coverage with a lengthy piece by Hamilton Bims entitled "Deacons for Defense: Negroes Are Fighting Back in Bogalusa, Other Towns." The five-page story captured the excitement generated by the Deacons, identifying them as "one of the fastest growing" organizations in the civil rights struggle.[38]

Bims acknowledged that the Deacons' success was accompanied by controversy and criticism from King and other civil rights leaders. "For all their effectiveness, however," he noted, "the Deacons have become perhaps the most criticized and feared Negro organization since the Black Muslims." The Deacons were not the black counterpart of the Klan, as some critics had suggested. "I'm glad the Deacons exist," said James Farmer when questioned about CORE's "strange relationship" with the Deacons. "I know some are comparing them to the Ku Klux Klan. But how many lynchings have they committed? The Deacons are not night riders and anyone who likens them to the Klan is just evading the issue." Not only did Bogalusa's blacks believe that the Deacons deterred Klan violence, but with the Watts riot in Los Angeles fresh in people's minds, the Deacons now appeared to be a moderate alternative to random violence. "By giving the job to mature and restrained men," Bims argued, "they discourage Negro hotheads, who otherwise might trigger a racial bloodbath in the tense city."[39]

By the end of the summer of 1965 the media had turned the Deacons into a symbol of a new approach to black freedom—a challenge to the nonviolent orthodoxy. The Deacons also came to represent a profound change in the political consciousness and identity of African American men in the South, one marked by a self-respect gained by the willingness to use force to secure one's rights. They embodied the realization that African American men would never gain equal status if they denied themselves the rights and prerogatives of white men; that they would be forever stigmatized as second-class citizens, regardless of their legal status. Laws change behaviors, not attitudes. As long as whites believed that African Americans were undeserving inferiors, they would regard every black advance as a temporary concession. Black social and economic progress would depend on the goodwill of the white majority. Real equality required that whites view blacks as intellectual and moral equals, and this change in attitude could only occur when blacks acted as equals. Malcolm X summed up this relationship between black self-image and white perception when he declared, "You will never get the American white man to accept the so-called Negro as an integrated part of society until the image of the Negro the white man has is changed, and until the image that the Negro has of himself has changed." Similar to Malcolm's approach, the Deacons' strategy was intended to establish black men as the equals of all men; to claim their rightful place in society as fully human, invested with the same rights, privileges, and prerogatives as whites, and deserving of the same honor, respect—and fear. "They finally found out that we really are men," said Deacon leader Royan Burris, "and that we would do what we said, and that we meant what we said. They found out that when they ride at night, we ride at night."[40]

"The Negro in the South is a brand new breed," Charlie Sims told *Ebony*. "He's not the same man he was ten years ago." Buoyed by their spectacular success in Bogalusa, the Deacons were now poised to take their gospel of self-defense to the remotest and most forbidding outposts of the Deep South.[41]

CHAPTER

10   Expanding in the Bayou State

MELDON ACHESON AND three other CORE workers, in-
cluding Archie Hunter, an African American volunteer from Brooklyn, were
leaning against a car when they saw the white man drive down the street,
stop his vehicle, and get out. The four CORE workers were in the middle of a
black residential neighborhood in Ferriday, Louisiana, one of the most dangerous towns during the civil rights movement. The white man walked directly over to Mel Acheson and, without warning, began to viciously beat
him. The attacker ignored Hunter, probably assuming that he was a local
black. Hunter stood by and watched helplessly as the man pummeled his
friend. Hunter and the other CORE workers had taken nonviolent oaths, and
their only choice was to peacefully submit to attack or run. What troubled
Hunter the most, though, was that the attack was taking place in plain view
of the residents. "And I got very disgusted because the community—we had
about 300 people standing in the streets—and they were just watching,
without doing a thing." Hunter had enough. "So I got disgusted, and I leaped
up on the car, and I started yelling at the people and . . . screaming at the
people." One of the white CORE volunteers remembered Hunter telling the
crowd that "he was proud to be a black man, and he was disgusted with
them, and how could they do that to themselves . . . think so lowly of
themselves as to let this happen in their own community." Finally a small
group of local blacks freed Acheson from his assailant.[1]

Recalling the incident a few weeks later, Hunter was still furious and
frustrated. "See, the people here, they need someone to shake them out of
their fear for about 10 minutes—and then they just rescind back into it the
level of fear all over again." But Hunter's exhortations from the car top that
day did not go unheeded. Within thirty minutes of the attack, more than
five hundred angry blacks gathered. Hunter sensed danger and tried to calm
the mob by leading them in freedom songs. The police soon arrived and—

predictably—arrested Hunter and let the white assailant escape. But the silence had been broken. "Suddenly several people offered to let us stay with them," said Acheson. The issue now became one of honor. "The negro community feels guilty about letting 2 beatings occur in their neighborhood," reported Acheson, "so I walk around with my black eye and people can't get involved fast enough." In addition, a self-defense group was born overnight in Ferriday when "several local guys got their guns and guarded us that night and plan to continue as long as we're here." Later that night electrical and telephone services were cut in the black community, and the Klan fire-bombed two homes and shot into the home of CORE sympathizer Martha Boyd. Boyd was prepared and fired back at the night riders, smashing their windshield. But the significance of the events earlier that day was not lost on the CORE staff. "This is really an index of how demoralized and afraid the Negro community is," said volunteer Mike Clurman. "Just one white guy came walking into the Negro community and started belting the four CORE workers."

Ferriday was precisely the kind of place that the Deacons for Defense and Justice were searching for. Word of the Deacons was spreading like wildfire though informal communication networks in the African American communities—churches, extended families, fraternal organizations—as well as through activists in CORE and the Student Nonviolent Coordinating Committee (SNCC) eager to facilitate self-defense measures in their organizing communities. Charles Sims and Earnest Thomas were soon besieged with calls for help. The two Deacons leaders began a concerted, full-time effort to build Deacons chapters throughout the South, with an initial focus on Louisiana and Mississippi.

The Deacons' popularity stemmed from two key factors that fundamentally distinguished them from various black defense groups that preceded them. First, the Deacons transformed self-defense from a clandestine and locally restricted activity into a public and wide-ranging organization capable of challenging the entrenched movement leadership and its creed of nonviolence. By the end of 1965 the Deacons had moved from merely protecting the movement—as secret, provincial bodyguards for nonviolent groups—to competing for political legitimacy and seeking the loyalty of the movement rank and file. The Deacons were to armed self-defense what the NAACP was to civil rights at its formation in 1908; they transformed individual acts of defiance into collective action for group rights. By moving into the open, the Deacons forced a national debate on nonviolence in ways that the ad hoc, clandestine self-defense groups never could have done. "With the Deacons and their organization," observed Roy Reed of the *New York Times*, "the advocates of armed defense have a symbol and a rallying point."[2]

Second, to win the hearts and minds of the mass movement, the Deacons became organizational expansionists. Unlike precursors who were content with secret local organizing, the Deacons aggressively sought to proliferate chapters across the South in order to create a powerful mutual defense network capable of standing up to the Klan. By building a regional alliance, they overcame the fear that blacks faced insurmountable odds.

"So, see, we're not going to be in this fight by ourselves," a Mississippi Deacon once told a group of new recruits. "You know, like the Klan has a chapter here, one in the next county, and the next county. And when things start getting too hot for the Klans around here, they call in more Klansmen." The Deacons offered the same security in regionalism. "If we get our backs to the wall, and we're battling, we will always have the reserves. And they'll come in and they'll battle with us—the same guys, the same Deacons in Bogalusa and those other places."[3]

From 1964 to 1966 the Deacons developed affiliates in twenty-one communities, seventeen in the South and four in the North. These affiliates ranged from formal chapters to loosely associated networks of members. Some affiliates lasted only a few months; others endured for several years. At the height of his organizing, Sims professed to have formed more than sixty chapters with several thousand members. This claim was an exaggeration if, by chapters, Sims meant fully operational and dues-paying affiliates. The total national membership was approximately 300—far less than the 10,000 number often bandied about by Sims and Earnest Thomas.[4]

Both Sims and Thomas traveled extensively between 1965 and 1966; they talked with hundreds of potential recruits and may well have established more chapters than documented. In addition to the twenty-one formal chapters, a thorough review of FBI records, news reports, and interviews with Deacons yields an additional forty-six cities in which the Deacons had reported affiliates, but none of these could be verified. Always quick to inflate the organization's size and power, Sims may have stretched the definition of a chapter to include any city with Deacon recruits.[5]

Counting heads tells us little about the significance and impact of any organization in the black freedom movement. CORE, SNCC, and the Southern Christian Leadership Conference (SCLC) had only a handful of organizers in the Deep South, yet they played a central role in uprooting the region's racial caste system. Changes in political consciousness and racial identity occur through a largely symbolic process—as Rosa Parks taught the world. The

Deacons had a large symbolic impact not only because they carried guns, but also because they were remarkably effective organizers and quickly developed an impressive network of self-defense groups in Louisiana and Mississippi—in the heart of Klan country.

The Deacons launched their expansion campaign in the summer of 1965, first targeting Louisiana cities where CORE had been active. The Pelican State became the site of nine formal chapters: Jonesboro, Bogalusa, New Orleans, St. Francisville, Minden, Homer, Tallulah, Ferriday, and Grambling (a rumored Varnado chapter was primarily an auxiliary to the Bogalusa chapter).

The Jonesboro chapter aggressively took the lead recruiting in the northern part of the state. In the fall of 1965 Frederick Kirkpatrick, one of the founders of the Jonesboro Deacons, accepted a position at Grambling University's physical education department and immediately established a Deacons chapter in the all-black town. There was no significant civil rights movement in Grambling, since it primarily served as home to the 350 university faculty and staff members. The Grambling Deacons centered their activities in nearby Ruston, where civil rights laws were still flouted and federal courts were forcibly integrating Louisiana Technical College. The Grambling chapter shuttled civil rights workers to Ruston and neighboring cities and provided protection for black students integrating schools and public facilities. Kirkpatrick also organized Grambling students and faculty into a community organization entitled the "Great Society Movement." The organization filed desegregation suits on public accommodations in Ruston, protested at the Lincoln Parish School Board, agitated for public improvements, picketed seventeen businesses that refused to hire blacks, and organized voter registration drives.[6]

In neighboring Webster Parish, the small town of Minden had garnered national attention in 1947, when a white mob lynched a local black man. An NAACP investigation led to a rare federal prosecution. Although the accused murderers were eventually acquitted by an all-white jury, the unprecedented Justice Department intervention, over the vociferous protests of J. Edgar Hoover, had an impact on vigilante terror. The Minden murder was the last lynching in Louisiana.[7]

CORE workers arrived in Webster Parish in 1964 full of optimism about developing a project, but it was not long before the parish's principal black organization, the Better Citizens and Voters League, frustrated their efforts. The league was directed by funeral director M. M. Coleman, a conservative middle-class leader who opposed CORE's emphasis on desegregation, antipoverty projects, and job discrimination. Coleman favored concentration on voter registration activities and came to regard CORE workers as needless intruders. "There is an extreme caste system in Webster Parish," complained one CORE staffer in a memorandum. "The middle class Negro wants nothing to do with the lower classes." CORE was not alone in its assessment of Coleman. "He wasn't moving," said James Harper, a local activist and Deacons leader. "He didn't want to test the lunch counters. He didn't want to try to integrate nothing. He just wanted somebody to sit and talk about it." Despite widespread dissatisfaction with Coleman's accommodationism, CORE staffers committed a tactical blunder when they attempted to oust him from leadership—and four hundred black people walked out of a CORE meeting. Eventually CORE and local militants split off into the Webster Parish United Christian Freedom Movement (WPUCFM) headed by J. D. Hamilton.[8]

In the summer of 1965 CORE workers informed Earnest Thomas in Jonesboro that a group of men in Minden wanted to form a Deacons chapter. With J. D. Hamilton at the helm of the insurgent WPUCFM, things were heating up in Minden. The planned marches and threatened boycott of downtown businesses critically increased the need for protection.[9] Hamilton and James Harper, a twenty-seven-year-old munitions plant worker, traveled to Jonesboro to meet with Thomas and establish a Minden chapter. Harper was the son of a lumber mill worker and had served in the National Guard. As a child, he endured the humiliation of white children who passed by in school buses throwing things and shrieking racial epithets. "I felt like things needed to change," said Harper. "For especially if I had kids, I didn't want then to go through this kind of flack."[10]

The Klan had little presence in Minden. Still, the lack of police protection concerned Harper and other activists. The Minden Police Department boasted two black officers, but they were seldom sent to investigate the harassment of civil rights activists. "When we called them when we was being harassed, they always sent a white anyway," said Harper. Nonviolence was not an option, either. Harper participated in some CORE demonstrations, but his notion of manhood conflicted with CORE's proscription against fighting back. "Most of the time, I didn't put myself in a position where it might come to that," said Harper of nonviolent demonstrations. "Because I was going to strike back, and they would blame CORE on it."[11]

Harper was impressed with Earnest Thomas at their first meeting. Cool, menacing, and to the point, Thomas told Harper that the lack of police protection in Minden was no anomaly; in most cities in the South "you wasn't going to receive much protection from the police," so the men in Minden "had to protect ourselves." After the meeting Thomas sent Harper membership cards and literature on the Deacons, and Harper officially established a chapter, with Fred Kirkpatrick as the liaison from Jonesboro.

Thomas instructed Harper that the Deacons were strictly for self-defense and that he should "notify the sheriff's department, police department, and FBI" in the event of a problem.[12]

The Minden chapter began weekly meetings at CORE's Freedom House and other homes, coordinating closely with J. D. Hamilton's group. There was no need for patrols in the black community, but the Deacons did guard homes and escort marches. In contrast to the chapters in Jonesboro and Bogalusa, the Minden chapter enjoyed a cooperative relationship with local police, even furnishing them the names and automobile license numbers of individuals who harassed civil rights workers. In the only shooting incident, the Deacons subsequently guarded the activist's home and pressured the police into arresting the three white assailants. Harper believed that the low level of vigilante terror and police violence could be attributed to Minden's relatively enlightened white business leaders who reined in the violent racist element.[13]

Comprising young men in their twenties and thirties, the Minden chapter attracted approximately fifteen members and a much larger group of willing supporters. Most were military veterans and, because of employment at the nearby munitions plant, economically independent of the local white elite. Among the applicants were a number of young zealots attracted to the romantic image and prestige that the Deacons offered. "They just wanted to have a pistol on," recalled Harper with a smile. "They just wanted to shoot somebody. Yeah, we had them old radicals." Harper screened out the young hotheads in preference to military veterans who could "take an order" and "wouldn't just fire at random."[14]

Although the Minden Deacons did not flaunt their weapons as did other chapters, they were armed just the same. On one occasion Harper was arrested for carrying a concealed gun while guarding Hamilton. The FBI also visited Harper at his job and peppered him with questions about illegal weapons and rumors of planned violent actions. Rather than feel intimidated, Harper found the FBI's attention encouraging. "It made me feel a little better, because it let me know that the word [about the Deacons] was getting around, that somebody else might be getting a little afraid—on the other side of town," remembered Harper. "They figured that we might be a little more powerful than we were."[15]

Indeed, like other chapters, the Minden Deacons played on white fears and enjoyed influence well beyond their numbers. In the eyes of whites, the Deacons chapter was synonymous with militant protest in Minden. They frequently attributed to the Deacons actions for which they had no responsibility. If there was a sit-in or other protest, Harper recalled with amusement, "you would hear local whites say: 'They ain't nothing but the Deacons.'"[16]

Sometimes the mere presence of the Deacons discouraged racist harassment. In one incident Harper received a report that whites were harassing blacks at a recently integrated public swimming pool. Harper summoned the Deacons, and, to his amazement, the word spread quickly; nearly two hundred men arrived on the scene. The men left their cars and began nonchalantly talking with the white adults around the pool. The show of force brought a quick end to the harassment. To be on the safe side, the Deacons sent for sandwiches and drinks and spent the rest of the day leaning against their cars, watching the children peacefully frolic in the pool.[17]

The Deacons also captured the attention of a group of seasoned activists in the town of Homer, just north of Minden, nestled in the pine hills of North Louisiana, approximately an hour's drive from Jonesboro. Named after the poet, Homer took pride in its imposing Greek revival courthouse in the center of the town square. A chapter of the NAACP had existed in the 1940s and reorganized as the Claiborne Parish Civic League (CPCL) during the repression of the 1950s. The CPCL was a weak and timid organization until January 1965, when a small group of men led by Frederick Lewis infused it with a new militancy. Lewis was elected president of the CPCL and would also become the president of the Homer Deacons chapter.[18]

Fred Lewis was a pugnacious, short-tempered man from Holsey Stop, a small settlement outside of Homer. For most of his adult life, he lived on disability benefits, which provided him with a measure of independence. He attributed his commitment to the civil rights struggle to a childhood incident. As a twelve-year-old he had overheard a white man tell his father that he would not be permitted to vote. Young Lewis adored his father and thought that there was nothing he could not do—including vote. The injustice was etched in his mind forever. "And at that age, it never did leave me," recalled Lewis. "And I vowed right then, at the age of twelve, that if I ever got a chance, I was going to hit this thing a blow."[19]

The black community in Claiborne Parish resembled the independent industrial working-class communities of Jonesboro and Bogalusa. The lumber industry and a nearby munitions plant provided employment for many of the rugged descendants of wood cutters and yeoman farmers. Yet segregation remained entrenched in the spring of 1965. Fear overwhelmed the community as racist forces torched four black churches and two other buildings where voter registration had been conducted. In May Fred Kirkpatrick began to organize in Homer, bringing in CORE task force members and a busload of students from Jonesboro as reinforcements. At the same time Pam Smith, a young white student from Massachusetts, arrived to head up a CORE summer project in Homer.[20]

By the end of May Kirkpatrick had organized a Homer chapter of the Deacons, with Fred Lewis serving as president. Since Lewis also was president of the Civic League, the Deacons and the league were virtually indistinguishable. The Deacons chapter had approximately twenty members and functioned as the armed auxiliary of the Civic League; the two groups often held joint meetings. Although Lewis was technically the leader of the Homer Deacons, George Dodd, a munitions worker, served as the principal coordinator for the chapter.[21]

The summer of 1965 brought intensified activity by CORE in Homer. Pam Smith worked with local activists to organize mass meetings, desegregation tests, and nonviolent workshops. The Claiborne Parish Civic League presented a list of demands to the mayor, school board, and parish jury calling for desegregation, administrative jobs, and black police. The CPCL also targeted the black middle class, organizing a student march and community protest that forced school officials to dismiss an unpopular black principal at Mayfield High School. In addition, Lewis's CPCL had plans to oust five other black principals.[22]

Initially, local law enforcement officials were hostile toward the Homer Deacons, as demonstrated in an incident with Harvey Malray. Malray, one of the first recruits to the Homer chapter, was a courageous but slightly eccentric young man who prided himself on being a member of an organization comprising, in his words, "classy people." On 26 June 1965 Malray had been guarding a fish-fry fund-raiser at the Masonic Hall. Around midnight he left and headed for the Freedom House to receive his new assignment. As he strolled down the dark road with his shotgun cradled in his arm, a Homer policeman driving by saw him and screeched to a halt. "Don't you know it's against the law to be walking up and down a road with a loaded shotgun?" asked the officer. Malray pulled out his wallet and proudly presented his Deacons' membership card—executing the gesture as if the card conferred obvious and indisputable rights. The flustered officer had to think for a moment, then, with a note of bewilderment, retorted, "Still, I don't see anything on here about walking up and down a road with a loaded shotgun!"[23]

Malray managed to avoid arrest that night, but three days later police arrested him as he stood guard with his shotgun on the porch of the Freedom House. While in jail Malray refused to cooperate with the FBI, and friends bailed him out after a few days. Malray persisted in his Deacons' activities, guarding marches in Homer and in Jonesboro, where local police brutalized him. Years later when asked why he joined the Deacons, Malray's explanation was simple: "I just wanted something to do for the colored man."[24]

Change came slowly in Homer, but eventually public accommodations opened their doors, the library was desegregated, and the school system began implementing curriculum reforms. Despite the shaky beginning, relations between the Deacons and the Homer police improved. One Deacons leader attributed the new attitude of law enforcement to the federal injunction in Bogalusa. "I think since they did that, in Bogalusa, they'll be more careful," he said of the police. "In the state of Louisiana, in the whole South."[25]

On 20 August 1965 the CPCL organized a march to the school board, and, amazingly, local officials asked the Deacons to provide five members to help police the march. Lewis did not mince words with city officials when he described what they could expect from the Deacons. "You know that it's nonviolent," Lewis told them, "but we can get violent."[26]

More meaningful was the change in black men in Homer. After only seven months of organizing, the Homer Deacons felt confident enough to stage a remarkable night rally. On New Year's Eve, 1965, approximately fifty Deacons from surrounding chapters in Jonesboro, Minden, and Grambling assembled with local men for a night of celebration in an empty lot owned by the Reverend T. L. Green, also a Deacon. As midnight drew near, the Deacons hoisted an effigy of a Klansman, marked with a crudely penned sign saying simply, "Whitey." The men lighted the Klan effigy and roared with hoots and laughter as it burned to ashes. The Klan was vanquished into the smoky night.[27]

The Homer chapter operated throughout 1965 but appears to have been fazed out after black officers joined the city police force. A fifth Deacons chapter was established in Tallulah, a tiny cotton town in the northeastern corner of the state. In May 1965 Gary Craven, a young CORE task force member, reported the "beginnings of a Deacons of Defense and Justice Chapter in Tallulah." But the chapter had little to do. Tallulah was a black-majority community with several black policemen who provided adequate protection. Moreover, the black community had a formidable and fearless leader, Zelma Wyche, who was eventually elected chief of police. One CORE volunteer found the town's level of armed defense startling. "The day before I arrived to Tallulah, the Ku Klux Klan marched in the city," wrote John L. Gee. "The Klan was told by the sheriff of Tallulah, that the Negroes were armed and they wouldn't be unarmed." Tallulah blacks "also marched with their guns."[28]

The Tallulah chapter soon headed south to Ferriday—where Mel Acheson and the other CORE workers had been attacked—to organize a Deacons group. In addition to being one of the most racially despotic towns in the Deep South, Ferriday was the birthplace of singer Jerry Lee Lewis and his cousin, television evangelist Jimmy Swaggart. The town's fame for pop icons was surpassed only by its notoriety for human rights violations. Racist repression was so severe that no church or fraternal organization would host civil rights activities. Young civil rights activists were reduced to driving through the black community with a bullhorn to announce makeshift rallies held in empty lots.[29]

Ferriday sits across the Mississippi River from Natchez. Although the town had a 63 percent black majority, whites ruled it; one activist characterized the sheriff's office as "Klan ridden." Klan and police violence besieged the black community. In February 1965 racists firebombed two white nightclubs, the "Farm House" and the "Silver Dollar Club," in retaliation for hiring black bands. On 14 December Frank Morris, a Ferriday civil rights leader, was burned to death at his home in an unsolved arson. One month later night riders firebombed a black grocery.[30]

"Nearly everyone seemed to be paralyzed by fear of the Ku Klux Klan," wrote Mel Acheson, the young CORE worker from Tucson. Unable to find lodging in Ferriday's black community, CORE workers had to commute from Alexandria in order to establish a summer project in July 1965. Economic intimidation was another major source of fear in Ferriday. "The older people were afraid, because they had jobs that placed them in white people's houses as domestic workers, they were afraid to lose their jobs," said David What-ley, a local eighteen-year-old activist. "If they found out that their children were involved, they gave them an ultimatum: 'You get them out or you forget the job.'"[31]

CORE suffered a bizarre reception when two black men beat the first white CORE staffer who visited Ferriday. Local civil rights leaders suspected that the two men were acting at the behest of town authorities. Finally, on 13 July a Ferriday black man offered CORE one of his rental properties. Three days later the Klan firebombed his home, and the man asked the CORE workers to move. The Klan then issued an ultimatum that the CORE task force had to leave by Saturday, 17 July.[32]

Instead of retreating, CORE forged ahead and organized its first meeting on the day of the Klan's deadline. CORE workers met with 30 high school students, who also expressed interest in forming a Deacons chapter. But by 20 July work came to a standstill because locals were afraid to attend meetings. Then came the beating of Mel Acheson that had so infuriated Archie Hunter. The incident galvanized the community and led to a spirited rally of 300 people on 21 July. Building on the momentum, CORE organized a mass meeting on 24 July, which attracted 250 participants, but, to the civil rights workers' dismay, almost all of them were children and teenagers. On the same day CORE met with 24 teenagers and formed a new mass-organizing vehicle, the Freedom Ferriday Movement (FFM). A group of high school students immediately began to circulate a petition door to door and obtained nearly 800 signatures calling for federal protection of "their rights, property, and persons." The petition was sent to Attorney General Nicholas Katzenbach, along with the warning that citizens would "take measures to protect themselves if the federal government did not intervene."[33]

At the mass meeting on 24 July, a small group of young people decided to form a Deacons chapter; they were assisted by several CORE staffers who had worked with the Deacons in Tallulah, including Artis Ray Dawson. The chapter initially attracted only a few members, who patrolled during rallies and protected activists' homes at night.[34]

The conditions were so perilous in Ferriday that CORE staffers welcomed the presence of the Deacons. "You should realize, I think, that most people in CORE are committed to nonviolence only as a tactic," wrote Mel Acheson. "For many, it stops at the end of a demonstration or when the day's work is thru. Most take self-defense at night for granted (protecting the home, and all that)." The armed guards made the night riders edgy as well. Acheson reported that Klansmen no longer lingered in the black neighborhoods. Their tactic was to speed by a house and toss "a badly-made molotov cocktail (usually a gallon jug of gasoline, burning rag on top)" out of the car, then hastily retreat into the night.[35]

The CORE workers enjoyed modest success through the rest of the summer, organizing additional marches (though still dominated by children), a voter registration drive, a boycott of the local movie theater, and several desegregation tests. Their achievements were remarkable given the age and inexperience of their front line. At a test of Walgreens lunch counter, one nervous young participant gulped down his coke and, looking around at his fellow testers, nervously exclaimed, "What's taking you so long. Let's go!"[36]

Mel Acheson made a sober and honest assessment of CORE's summer project, which ended on 23 August. CORE had emphasized voter registration as a "safe" project that would provide experience for the youths and enable them to move on to desegregation projects, Acheson explained. But he admitted that the young workers had little interest in voter registration, and only action could break the grip of fear. "The negroes are still very much afraid of the Klan and similar groups, as well as the police," said Acheson. "But the fear is beginning to channel itself into action instead of the paralysis we found when we came to Ferriday . . . the determination of the youth, and their example of overcoming fear, has begun to catch hold of their parents and neighbors."[37]

There was still ample reason for fear, however. The Klan renewed its attacks as soon as CORE left Ferriday. In September 1965 Klansmen from Mississippi attacked twelve blacks who were picketing the Arcadia Theater, and night riders firebombed two more homes. The Ferriday Deacons were not much help. Victor Graham had assumed leadership of the chapter, but it was on shaky ground. Graham was unable to organize regular meetings and had difficulty recruiting a sufficient number of adult men.[38]

In the fall of 1965 Robert "Buck" Lewis became president of the Freedom Ferriday Movement and immediately began to reinvigorate the organization. One of the few adults in the FFM, Lewis was also a student at Grambling University. On 20 November the Klan firebombed his house; when Lewis, with a gun at his side, summoned the police, he was arrested for aggravated assault in a subsequent argument with police. Unfazed by the bombing and arrest, the FFM leader led 150 marchers the following Sunday to protest the black Rufus Baptist Church's refusal to allow the FFM to hold meetings at the church. The march, targeting the black middle class, reflected similar class fissures in Bogalusa, Jonesboro, and other towns that attracted Deacons activity. The unwillingness of the local black clergy to aid the movement was a constant problem for Ferriday activists. "So far the Ministers have been making excuses," David Whatley reported to the CORE regional office, "and in general [are] just plain scare[d]."[39]

The Original Knights of the Ku Klux Klan (OKKKK) responded to the FFM campaign by calling on whites to refuse to bargain with the civil rights protesters. The OKKKK distributed a leaflet that chastised government and business leaders in nearby Natchez for negotiating with blacks. Surprisingly, the Klan broadsheet argued that violence was "not the answer" since it would "only produce more violence" (the Justice Department's successful suit against the Klan in Bogalusa, no doubt, forced the night riders to curtail their public threats of violence). Instead, the OKKKK advocated forming an "economic leadership council" and urged Ferriday businesses that were benefiting from commerce created by the Natchez boycott to fire their black employees. Blacks needed the white man to survive, asserted the OKKKK, but "no longer does the White man in Concordia Parish need the Negro." In the world of mechanization, "our cotton crops, our bean corps [sic] and other stable [sic] production can be produced without the Negro hand once touching it." "The gain you are making today is going to be the hand that makes you slave of the very Negro from which You are gaining," the Klan warned.

"The all powerful civic and business groups can stop this if they wish to. They can begin by starting to eliminate the Negro employees now."[40]

Police joined the assault on the struggling Ferriday campaign. On 30 November Deacons Vernon Smith and Joe Davis were patrolling in their vehicle around 10:00 P.M. when city police stopped and arrested them for carrying a shotgun on the back seat and a pistol in the glove compartment. Artis Ray Dawson, a Deacons leader and former CORE worker, and David Whatley went to the jail to inquire about their colleagues, only to be later arrested themselves.[41]

Three days later, on 2 December, racists fired into three buildings in the black community, including Calhoum's Grocery and Whatley's house. On the evening of 18 December, a gas station owned by Deacon Anthony McRaney mysteriously burned down following an explosion just after McRaney's insurance company canceled his insurance. Similar cancellations had occurred in the case of two black churches that had been active in voter registration in Ferriday.[42]

But the attacks on the Deacons backfired, breathing life into the Ferriday chapter. By December twenty-three members were meeting weekly. They conducted all-night patrols equipped with walkie-talkies, personal weapons, and three semiautomatic carbines. A major responsibility was to guard the young activist David Whatley, as it was rumored that the Klan had offered a $1,000 reward for his assassination. The Klan had made Whatley a special target since the fall of 1965, when he single-handedly integrated the local white high school. Whatley endured intense harassment at the school. Teachers left the classroom when he entered. Students screamed racial epithets at him inside the building, placed snakes in his locker, and stuffed his clothes into the toilet during physical education class. When he played football during physical education, his own teammates would tackle him. Traveling to and from school, Whatley had to walk through a gauntlet of Klansmen who routinely waited outside the building to harass him. In response, the Deacons posted guards at his home, which also doubled as the CORE headquarters. Whatley wrote the New Orleans CORE office that he clung to life "only by the grace of God and the tiresome and lonely Gardshifts [sic] that we are undergoing every night from six o'clock until six thirty A.M."[43]

In the early hours of 29 January 1966, Deacons Joseph Davis and Charley Whatley were standing guard at David Whatley's house in the cold black night. The guard shifts lasted for twelve long hours, and by 3:00 A.M. the Deacons were chilled to the bone and decided to go inside the house to warm themselves. Within a few minutes, two cars quietly pulled in front of

Whatley's home. A white man exited one of the cars, lighted the fuse of a dynamite bomb, and tossed it at the house. Joseph Davis heard the suspicious sounds outside and rushed to the door, catching a glimpse of the fleeing bomber. He fired off a round from a .22 caliber pistol and then grabbed a shotgun and fired a second round at the fleeing cars. Seconds later the dynamite bomb exploded underneath the bedroom window where David Whatley and another CORE worker were sleeping. The two young men miraculously survived the bombing unscathed; the first stick of dynamite had ignited prematurely and had blown the fuse off the second stick, reducing the impact of the explosion.[44]

By February 1966 the Ferriday Deacons' chapter slipped into inactivity. But the Klan was not through. On 16 March it held an open rally, and in May it burned several crosses, including one near Deacon Anthony McRaney's recently fire-damaged gas station and another at the high school that David Whatley had integrated.[45]

With the Deacons in disarray, the FFM desperately needed a new defense group. Among the new group of CORE workers who had arrived in Ferriday in 1966 was an African student, Ahmed Saud Ibriahim Kahafei Abboud Najah—known to local activists simply as Najah. Najah helped organize a paramilitary defense group appropriately called the "Snipers." He selected approximately nine young men and provided them training in martial arts. John Hamilton, one of the CORE staffers assigned to Ferriday, encouraged the Snipers and hoped that they might motivate the older Deacons to reactivate. Although never well organized, the Snipers managed to equip themselves with two-way radios and began to provide security for local activists. Seven of the Snipers guarded David Whatley when he and his date integrated the high school prom. In the event of an emergency, Whatley's date concealed a walkie-talkie in her purse so that she could signal the Snipers who were patrolling outside the high school. The prom proceeded without incident, primarily because of a strong presence of law enforcement officials, but the teenage Snipers were poised to act if called upon.[46]

Young people remained the backbone of the militant movement in Ferriday, and by the spring of 1966, with the Snipers in full bloom, there were additional signs that fear was on the wane. In response to a Klan leaflet, an anonymous black poet penned a poem that was printed and distributed in white neighborhoods:

As I began to read it my anger grew and bigger,
Because the first line read, "Dear Nigger."
They've scared the people and have them upset.

But I'll get one of those peckerwoods yet.
They still think I'm scared of ghosts.
But I'll send them to hell with the DEVIL as their host.
When things are good and going alright
PECKERWOOD stay from around my house at night.
Because after reading the FIERY CROSS.
I'm still the boss.
To find out who's the best you need a good distinguisher,
So I hope you understand—THE FIERY CROSS EXTINGUISHER.[47]

The militant spirit of the poem reflected a general shift toward Black Power politics among young African Americans in the summer of 1966. In August Lincoln Lynch, CORE's leading Black Power militant, toured Louisiana for a series of speaking engagements that culminated in CORE's formation of the "Louisiana Youth for Black Power." The new Black Power group had representatives from fourteen parishes—mostly CORE strongholds—with Ferriday's David Whatley serving as its first president.[48]

As the Jonesboro chapter spearheaded the Deacons' expansion in North Louisiana, the Bogalusa chapter took the lead in organizing the southern part of the state. The Bogalusa Deacons visited several towns where CORE had a presence and developed two chapters and numerous contacts. In Pointe Coupee Parish, where CORE had done some organizing, the Deacons had at least one very interesting member: Abraham Phillips, a leftist and veteran organizer who had once worked as a labor organizer for the Communist-run Share Croppers Union. There was also a scattering of places farther south along the Mississippi River where the Deacons advised and assisted local activists. Among these was Plaquemine, a longtime CORE stronghold, Buras, and Donaldsonville. Although the Deacons did not establish functioning chapters in any of these communities, the visits did provide an opportunity to popularize their philosophy of self-defense.[49]

New Orleans was the site of the first Deacons chapter in South Louisiana. The chapter was founded by Aubrey Wood, a Texan who had served in the army during World War II and settled in San Francisco afterward. Wood became involved in civil rights protests in San Francisco in 1947; by the time he arrived in New Orleans in 1956, he was a seasoned activist. While working as a longshoreman, Wood met the Reverend Avery Alexander, a legendary figure in the local civil rights movement. Working with Alexander, Wood became active in the New Orleans movement and eventually left the docks to establish a small restaurant at Jackson and Dryades, in the heart of the black shopping district. During the Consumer League's boycott of white businesses on Dryades Street, he directed the picket committee; he also advised the NAACP Youth organization when its members began picketing stores on Canal Street, the city's premier shopping district. When CORE descended on New Orleans in 1962, it set up an office in the same building that housed Wood's restaurant. Wood extended his hospitality to the young activists; frequently the only meal they ate was the free repast offered by Wood.[50]

Wood first learned about the Deacons when he traveled to Jonesboro with Oretha Castle, a New Orleans CORE leader, to help install plumbing in the new buildings that replaced two churches destroyed by arson in January 1965. He admired what the Deacons had accomplished: "To be where they were, and have the feeling of courage to do what they did, yeah, they impressed me very much." Wood discussed forming a New Orleans chapter while staying in Jonesboro for several days. "I started talking to the Deacons up there and I got a copy of their charter," he recalled. "Their charter was in line with my thinking, so I became involved with them."[51]

Wood formed the New Orleans Deacons chapter in the spring of 1965 and became its first and only president. But there was little for the chapter to do. The Klan was never strong in the Cradle of Jazz, and mob violence on the picket line had disappeared by 1965. So most of the New Orleans chapter's activities centered on assisting the Bogalusa chapter and transporting visitors between New Orleans and Bogalusa, with Wood traveling to Bogalusa almost every week.[52]

Wood recruited approximately fifteen members for his chapter, many of them longshoremen, personal friends, and drinking buddies who frequented the Dew Drop Inn on LaSalle Street. The executive committee met weekly, general members monthly. Dues were modest, to cover gas and other expenses. Wood remembered his experience with the Deacons with unabashed pride. "When you're a Deacon," he said, "you walk tall."[53]

Law enforcement in New Orleans also took note of the Deacons. After the passage of the Voting Rights Act, Wood would visit the Registrar of Voters' office to help register new voters. These visits often led to confrontations with city officials. On one occasion Wood started "raising hell" and "talking loud," and soon found himself handcuffed and arrested. "When I got back to the first precinct, they was going through my wallet to see if there was any identification," he recalled. "And when they seen that membership card for the Deacons for Defense, they said, 'Oh. This nigger here is the one. He's a Deacon.'"[54]

The New Orleans chapter helped spread the Deacons' creed of self-defense through speaking events and television appearances. Charlie Sims and Wood made a presentation at the International Longshoreman's Association Hall on Claiborne Avenue in 1965. Wood also appeared on a local television show. When the interviewer asked him what he thought of communism, Wood replied tersely, "I don't know nothing about no communism. I don't know nothing about our capitalistic system we have here, because you ain't allowed me to participate."[55]

In February 1966 Joseph P. Henry Jr., executive secretary of the New Orleans chapter, made a strange request of the FBI. Henry contacted the New Orleans FBI office and asked for a representative to participate in a public debate on "law and citizenship," which the Deacons were organizing. The proposed debate was to include the mayor of New Orleans and representatives of several civil rights organizations. The FBI declined the invitation, instead offering to send the Deacons several copies of an official FBI pamphlet entitled, "The FBI, Guardian of Civil Rights." It was an ironic gesture by a law enforcement organization that had worked assiduously to deprive the Deacons of their rights.[56]

The New Orleans chapter experienced some difficulties as a consequence of the July 1965 Alton Crowe shooting. After the incident, Henry Austin, the Deacon assailant, was moved out of Bogalusa for his own protection and assigned to the New Orleans chapter. Wood was not pleased with his new colleague. "They kind of disorganized us here, by him being here," he explained. "When the publicity got out that he was in New Orleans and that he was a Deacon, well that kind of frightened off some of our people." Despite the problems posed by his presence, Austin assisted the New Orleans chapter in several intrepid organizing forays into adjacent Plaquemines Parish, the dominion of legendary racist Judge Leander Perez. The New Orleans Deacons contemplated organizing chapters in Buras and Boothville in Plaquemines Parish, but the level of interest was insufficient. In addition, geography worked against creating any chapters in Plaquemines. The parish is a narrow strip of land that follows the Mississippi River to the Gulf of Mexico. Only one highway runs through the parish; and with the river on one side and an alligator-infested swamp on the other, the highway made a poor escape route. The Deacons had engaged in enough high-speed chases with the Klan to understand the importance of multiple escape routes. Austin thought that it was "suicide" to establish a chapter unless local members would be willing to shoot their way out of the parish, and, in his opinion, they would not.[57]

By the end of 1965, the Deacons had adherents and self-proclaimed members spread across Louisiana. The new organization was both upholding and radically changing a tradition of self-defense in the state. "Black people always did protect their young, but on the q.t. [quiet]," said Virginia Collins, a longtime New Orleans black activist. But the Deacons had transformed this covert tradition into an open, united movement. "It had an impact on all of Louisiana," according to Collins.[58]

Louisiana was only the beginning. The Bayou State shared a long border with Mississippi, and it was not long before the Deacons trained their sights on the Magnolia State. On 29 August 1965 Charlie Sims and a nine-man delegation of Deacons traveled to Jackson to attend a meeting of the Mississippi Freedom Democratic Party (MFDP). The MFDP, an electoral civil rights organization led by Aaron Henry, had attracted national attention at the 1964 Democratic National Convention. The *New York Times* covered the Deacons' appearance at the Jackson meeting, which was organized by Ed King, a white teacher and civil rights activist at Tougaloo College in Jackson. Although the MFDP's invitation to the Deacons reflected the growing disenchantment with nonviolence, the Mississippi group was not ready to fully embrace armed self-defense. When pressed by the media to explain the MFDP's relationship with the Deacons, Ed King said that the MFDP was not endorsing the Deacons but merely providing them a forum. "The Mississippi Negro is very interested in them," King told the press.[59]

More than three hundred people filled the Negro Masonic Hall and exploded in thunderous applause when Sims was introduced. Sweating profusely in his Sunday suit in the sweltering 99-degree heat, Sims entertained the crowd with his trademark gritty bravado. The Deacons leader taunted the White Knights of the Ku Klux Klan and scoffed at threats of violence. "I've been shot five times, and shot at ten times," he boasted. "So I'm not scared to come to Jackson." His message was a clarion call to manhood, bluntly challenging black men to prove their mettle against the Klan. "It is time for you men to wake up and be men," Sims declared. He also spoke of plans to organize a chapter in Jackson and suggested that interested parties confer with him after the meeting. The next day teams of Bogalusa Deacons spread across Mississippi to begin recruitment.[60]

Mississippi was a formidable challenge for the Deacons. Conditions were so desperate that even NAACP leader Medgar Evers seriously considered the idea of guerrilla warfare in the state. Both Medgar and his brother Charles were deeply impressed with Jomo Kenyatta and the Mau Mau uprising in Kenya in 1952. "Talk about nonviolent," Ruby Hurley said of the young Medgar, "he was anything but non-violent: anything but! And he always wanted to go at it in Mau Mau fashion." In her memoir, *For Us, the Living*, Medgar's wife Myrlie recalls that "Medgar himself flirted intellectually with the idea of fighting back in the Mississippi Delta. For a time he envisioned a secret black army of Delta Negroes who fought by night to meet oppression and brutality with violence." Evers went well beyond mere fantasies of a Mississippi Mau Mau; he and his brother Charles actually began to stockpile ammunition for a guerrilla war. Their father eventually discovered their plans and quickly put an end to the nascent rebellion.[61] Now Charlie Sims and the Deacons were preparing to resurrect Medgar's dream of a secret black army in the heart of Klan country.

CHAPTER

Mississippi Chapters

11

ON FRIDAY, 27 August 1965, at 12:30 P.M., George Met-
calfe casually strode to his car in the parking lot of the Armstrong Tire and
Rubber Company in Natchez, Mississippi. Weary, he had just finished an
exhausting twelve-hour shift at the plant where he worked as a shipping
clerk. Outside the factory gates Metcalfe was well known in his role as
president of the Natchez chapter of the NAACP. His visibility had increased
dramatically in the past weeks. He had led a delegation to the city school
board demanding that the schools desegregate in conformance with the
Civil Rights Act. He had also been recently named as a defendant in a suit
filed by the Natchez mayor to prevent the NAACP from picketing his store.
Repression was so severe in Natchez that when George Greene, field secretary of the Student Nonviolent Coordinating Committee (SNCC), arrived in
1963, he had abandoned all hope of organizing and restricted himself to
documenting incidents of racist violence. The city's well-organized Ku Klux
Klan had engaged in systematic guerrilla warfare against Adams County's
black residents since 1964. Robed hooligans bombed churches and flogged
and tortured blacks without fear of consequence. By 1965 the situation had
grown so critical that the U.S. Commission on Civil Rights conducted hearings in Mississippi to investigate the wave of violence and intimidation.
Compounding the danger for Metcalfe was that tensions had increased at
Armstrong Tire and Rubber following the recent desegregation of the company cafeteria.[1]

Metcalfe eased into his car, put the key into the ignition, and turned the
switch. A tremendous explosion rocked the windows of the plant as a bomb
ripped apart the vehicle and mangled Metcalfe's legs and arms. The civil
rights leader clung precariously to life as his blood-soaked body was rushed
to the Jefferson Davis Memorial Hospital. As he lay in critical condition in his

hospital bed, the explosion began to reverberate in the black community. But instead of immobilizing it with fear, the bomb detonated a new combative consciousness among Natchez African Americans. News of the bombing swept through the black community like a firestorm, burning away the bonds of passivity and fear. "I think one of the greatest mistakes [whites] made was when they bombed George Metcalfe's car," recalled James Young, who became a leader in the Natchez Deacons. "Well, that made everybody in this area feel like, 'Whether I'm a part of it, they're just subject to do the same thing to me, so I'm coming out front.'"[2]

If, as Thomas Aquinas once suggested, anger is the precondition of courage, then his maxim was borne out in Natchez the night of 27 August. Rage electrified young blacks throughout the community. Indignation metamorphosed into courage, courage into action. Decades of humiliation, frustration, and resignation gave way to a new militant consciousness. Sober and established black community leaders detected danger in the restive mood and worked frantically to control and redirect the youthful passions. The situation was so grave that NAACP state field secretary Charles Evers rushed to Natchez to assist.

Evers quickly found himself entangled in the awkward role of conciliator and peacemaker. A group of angry young blacks, armed with pistols and rifles, had gathered early Friday night near Metcalfe's home, which also served as the NAACP headquarters. Evers attempted to calm them, empathizing with their vengeful mood. "If they do it anymore, we're going to get those responsible," warned Evers. "We're armed, every last one of us, and we are not going to take it." But Evers tempered his threats with a plea for restraint and order. "We want no violence," he implored the crowd. "We want no violence."[3]

"America thinks the Negroes in Natchez are afraid . . . we're here to let them know we aren't afraid," Evers told reporters who had gathered in the street. One newsman approached a black minister holding a rifle. "What's going to happen here?" he asked. "I'll tell you," the old preacher said grimly, "right now, from the way that practically all the Negroes feel, they feel that the thing that's about to happen is what happened in California," he said, referring to the Watts riot, "a war, or a race riot, or whatever it is, that's about to happen here."[4]

Years later Evers admitted that he had arranged for national television crews to tape the minister bragging about how he was prepared to shoot white men. "This is the sort of thing that frightens white people," said Evers. "They expected me to say it, but a local jackleg [self-taught] preacher would really have some effect on them." Evers said that Natchez's black community was ready for full-scale war. "We had guns and hand grenades, and everything it took to work—and we meant to use them if we had to."[5]

Later that night Evers spoke at a rally at the NAACP headquarters. Behind him stood several men armed with pistols and rifles, most of whom would later become leaders in the Natchez Deacons. "I know all of us are angry and no one's more angry than I am," said Evers in measured tones. "We all are tired of being mistreated and we know who's responsible for this. We know who's responsible for this and we must use the weapon—that we are soon going to have—to get rid of them." The crowd began to shout in exalted response. "Now that weapon," he continued—and as he spoke, a man standing behind Evers thrust his pistol into the air and the crowd erupted in a roar of approval. "The weapon," Evers went on, a little puzzled by the commotion and still unaware of the gun displayed behind him, "the most effective weapon, will be as you know, the vote." The crowd moaned in disappointment. One man shouted, "No! That won't do no good!" Evers had lost his audience.[6]

James Stokes, an NAACP member, had spent the day helping Evers at the NAACP office in the wake of the bombing. Stokes was typical of the working-class men who were the backbone of the Natchez NAACP. He worked at a local paper mill making egg cartons, had leadership experience as a union steward, and was an army veteran.[7] The Metcalfe bombing had sent the NAACP office into a flurry of activity, and Stokes, after putting in a long day at the NAACP office, had retired to his house for a few hours' rest. Late that night he was abruptly aroused from his sleep by a loud pounding. Two friends were at the door. "Come on let's go," they urged, "all hell broke loose downtown."[8]

It was an apt description. The serene jewel on the Mississippi had shattered into violence. As the night wore on, hundreds of enraged black youths filled the black business district. Primed for battle, they had armed themselves with rocks, bottles, pistols, and rifles. James Stokes remembered arriving on the scene and seeing snipers firing from rooftops, "shooting at everything that was moving." Groups of young blacks roamed the streets, shouting threats at white motorists and hurling bricks, bottles, and tomatoes at police cars. Stokes and some NAACP members quickly joined Evers as he attempted to restore order. The improvised security group gave as much attention to protecting whites as it did blacks, preventing the agitated crowd from attacking innocent whites who accidentally drove into the fray. But its principal objective was to deter white police from assaulting young blacks. Stokes and his compatriots were on the streets "to keep our eyes on police officers" and "to make sure if they shoot somebody, we going to shoot them."[9]

Stokes could empathize with the mob's rage toward the police. As a young boy in rural Adams County, he had witnessed police complicity with barbaric racism. "One of my neighbors was running a little social club," he recalled, "and the Klan ran down on this club and took this man out, and cut his penis out and drug him up and down the road." Law enforcement officials participated in the grisly torture. "That night, it was some members of the sheriff's force, police force," said Stokes. "All of them was Klan."[10]

The day after the bombing, Natchez teetered on the edge of open rebellion. In the morning a mass meeting was held to draw up a list of demands. The bombing had galvanized the black community around a militant program for equal opportunity. The demands included hiring at least four additional black policemen to complement the two currently on the force; desegregating public facilities, schools, parks, hospitals, playgrounds, and the city auditorium; naming a black representative to the school board; cooperating in a poverty program with funds divided evenly with whites; and publicly denouncing the White Knights of the Ku Klux Klan and another local white supremacist group, Americans for the Preservation of the White Race.[11]

In an unusual move, the black leadership also demanded that city employees be required to address blacks with "courtesy titles." For decades whites had addressed blacks with condescending and degrading titles, such as "auntie," "missie," "boy," "hoss," and "uncle." The leadership insisted that city employees use the respectful titles of "Mister" and "Missus." Civil equality was insufficient; Natchez blacks wanted dignity and respect as well.[12]

But the black leaders' demands did little to dampen the temper of the young community. As the sun slipped into the Mississippi hills on Saturday, 28 August, the tide of anger rose once again. Young men flocked into the streets to vent their rage. A rock sailed through the air shattering a police car window. Four grim city policemen brandishing shotguns faced off in a tense confrontation with the undaunted crowd. At an open-air rally that night, some participants openly spurned the pleas for nonviolence. As community leaders spoke to the crowd, one group began a chant that grew into a defiant chorus: "We're going to kill for freedom," rose the chant, "We're going to kill for freedom."[13]

Two days of rioting changed the terms of the conflict in Natchez. Prior to 28 August, whites could expect blacks to respond peacefully and lawfully to Klan terror and police brutality. Blacks now had a new bargaining chip.[14]

Set upon a bluff on the winding Mississippi, Natchez stood like a sentinel over the sprawling river bottomlands. In the nineteenth century it had prospered as a key commercial and financial center for Mississippi's slave economy. By 1965 Natchez had survived the demise of King Cotton and transformed itself into a bustling industrial city. Wood products and rubber manufacturing had given rise to a highly unionized and sophisticated black working class, largely independent of the white power structure.[15]

As in the case of Jonesboro and Bogalusa, Natchez's mill-town culture produced strongly independent and courageous black men and women. Their independence derived in part from the protection offered by unions. Trade unions, despite their poor record on racial equality, generally safeguarded the right of black members to participate in the civil rights movement without fear of employer reprisal. Typical of this practice was the United Rubber Workers Union local at the Armstrong Tire and Rubber Company. "There would have been many a one of us that would have been fired from Armstrong," noted James Young, "but the union wasn't going to stand for it. So that's what saved us."[16]

Ironically, the relative freedom from economic coercion may have contributed to Klan violence. In contrast to black sharecroppers, whites could not intimidate unionized black industrial workers by threatening to deprive them of income or shelter. White elites and competing white workers were forced to turn to terrorist violence to discipline the black working class. To a significant degree, the revitalized Klan and the Deacons were both products of the decline of the agricultural oligarchy and its traditional social control mechanisms.

Despite being insulated from some reprisals, voter registration policies prevented blacks from translating economic independence into political power. In 1965 Natchez was a black majority city still dominated by a white minority; 12,300 blacks lived under the rule of 11,500 whites. Attempts to implement the 1964 Civil Rights Act had failed miserably as Natchez whites clung tenaciously to the old traditions.[17]

In the summer of 1965 Natchez became a battleground between the local moderate NAACP chapter and the more militant SNCC-dominated Mississippi Freedom Democratic Party (MFDP). An offshoot of SNCC's Freedom Summer project in 1964, the MFDP was headed by a young black SNCC leader, Lawrence Guyot, who pressed ahead with voter registration work, freedom schools, and development of community leaders, often circumventing the entrenched and cautious local NAACP leadership. Both organizations dug in during the summer of 1965 to win the hearts and minds of Natchez blacks. But the young SNCC pacifists faced a politically savvy foe in the NAACP's Charles Evers. Evers, though always favoring his middle-class minions in the local NAACP chapter, sought to meld a coalition across fissures of class and competing interests in the black community. He had the benefit of political experience and the community's loyalty to the NAACP, which, despite its shortcomings, was an old and familiar institution; as one historian once observed, "People prefer the trouble they have to the trouble they may have." Moreover, Evers had an important tactical advantage over the pacifist SNCC. He had been weaned on Jomo Kenyatta, not Mohandas Gandhi; although Evers preferred nonviolent tactics, when necessary he could accommodate—indeed advocate—the use of force.[18]

In June 1965, two months before the Metcalfe bombing, civil rights activists launched the first coordinated protest in Natchez—a boycott of white businesses, especially stores owned by Natchez mayor John Nosser. The mayor's relatively moderate politics had incurred the wrath of the Klan, but the black community also targeted him for refusing to integrate the clerical staff at his four stores. The boycott failed to generate enthusiasm among blacks and dragged on through the summer, little more than symbolic protest. Women and children walked the picket line as black men kept their distance. James Jackson, another Deacons leader, had difficulty recruiting men to the picket line. "Ever since the two civil rights projects came to Natchez," he noted, "Negroes would sit around and discuss how they want to fight for their freedom and how they were ready to die for it." Yet when Jackson asked them to join the picket line, suddenly they had places to go and funerals to attend. "Nobody never dies until there's going to be a march or a picket," said Jackson laconically. "It started me thinking that the Negro was just fooling himself[,] that he was still ready to do nothing."[19]

The day after the Metcalfe bombing, the Bogalusa Deacons announced in Jackson that they planned to travel to Natchez to develop a Deacons chapter. The presence of Louisiana Deacons in Mississippi posed a dilemma for Charles Evers. Though he would benefit by their protection, to welcome the Deacons into Mississippi could be taken as a sign of weakness on the part of the NAACP and invite organizational competition. Evers was already fending off a serious challenge to his leadership by young militants in SNCC and the MFDP. Another organization on his left flank would only add to his troubles.[20]

Evers had only a short time to weigh his options. The media was pressuring him to comment on the Deacons' planned campaign in Mississippi. Evers finessed the issue by repudiating the Deacons but not armed self-defense. The NAACP leader told the *New York Times* that Mississippi did not need the Deacons because the "state's Negroes are arming and organizing in their own way."[21]

Natchez was a political tightrope for Evers. Even his hesitant endorsement of self-defense appeased militants at the cost of rankling the NAACP national leadership. Roy Wilkins, the NAACP's national director, told the *New York Times* that the national office had not approved Evers's comments on violence. Evers ignored Wilkins and continued to raise the specter of retaliatory violence, a few days later announcing again that Natchez blacks were arming themselves and were prepared to "fight back."[22]

Evers's comments provoked a volley of criticism from NAACP leaders in addition to Wilkins. But his decision to ignore the admonitions was a shrewd maneuver. If Wilkins pressured Evers too strongly, the national office might alienate him and lose control of the Natchez campaign. Competing forces were already descending on Natchez. Within a few days of the bombing, Martin Luther King sent Andrew Young to the troubled city. Young was assessing the possibility of making Natchez the centerpiece of a campaign for federal legislation against killing a person engaged in civil rights activities. If the NAACP national office could accommodate Evers, the Natchez campaign promised to regain prestige lost to younger and more militant groups such as SNCC and CORE.[23]

The factional maneuvering of the national organizations did not divert Natchez's rank-and-file activists from the task at hand. They saw the need for organized self-defense, and the Deacons were the only visible organization prepared to meet the challenge. Stokes, James Young, and the rest of the informal self-defense group that activated following the Metcalfe bombing ignored Evers's rebuke to the Deacons and began to take steps to organize a Natchez chapter.[24]

Earlier that summer, John Fitzgerald, a local black middle-class leader, had organized a meeting to form a Deacons chapter but failed to activate the group and call subsequent meetings. James Jackson, a twenty-five-year-old barber and civil rights militant, suspected that Evers had discouraged Fitzgerald from continuing with the Deacons. Evers could be a ruthless infighter with other civil rights organizations, and he took pains to prevent competitors from invading his turf.[25]

The Metcalfe bombing and the slow pace of the NAACP leadership had pushed James Jackson to the brink. "Man, I done been to 135 meetings, and that's all they ever did was meet," Jackson complained to his friend Otis Firmin. "You know what I'm talking about? And never does nothing. Just planning. Negroes is the planningest people I've ever seen, boy. We plan too damn much, man; and never do nothing."[26]

Jackson contacted a representative of the Bogalusa Deacons and was deeply impressed by what he heard about Charlie Sims. "He got fear into the whole town, man," Jackson told Firmin. Firmin was eager to learn more about Sims's defense group. "They say they got souped-up cars, man?" asked Firmin. "Yeah, fast cars, man, fast cars . . . shit, they got to be fast," replied Jackson. "Say for instance we're guarding this place, someplace, and some guy comes by and shoots. We got to catch him, man, and shoot him to kill him." Jackson paused, then backed off a bit. He remembered that Sims said not to shoot to kill at first. "You can wound him, like in the leg or shoot his tires, stop him, burn him in the leg, take him right on down to the police station, man," said Jackson. The Deacons would not stop whites for simply driving through the community. "This is just for defense. If a car comes into the Negro community just watch him and that's it, man. You know you can't stop people from driving on the streets."[27]

Historians have been blessed with an extraordinary source for what transpired in the first Natchez Deacons meeting held on 10 September 1965, conducted in the back room of James Jackson's barber shop. Filmmaker Ed Pincus, shooting a cinema verité documentary on the Natchez movement, filmed the meeting in its entirety. The transcript provides remarkable insights into the consciousness and organizing methods of ordinary black workers in the Deep South—free of the constraints of middle-class leaders and pacifist doctrine—trying to make sense of the events around them and groping for a purpose and role for the working-class man in the social revolution.

Jackson and Firmin led the meeting. Both men were charismatic and brilliant organizers—trained in the streets rather than movement workshops—adroit at reading the community's fears and aspirations and crafting an appeal that could resonate and inspire confidence.[28]

"I believe just like Martin Luther King and everybody else, I believe in non-violence," Jackson assured the five men assembled. "I really do, man. I think that non-violence is the only way to solve the problem, you know. On the other hand, I believe that our people should stop getting killed." The police had failed to protect the black community, Jackson pointed out, so the responsibility fell to the Deacons.

The Deacons were not motivated by hatred of whites. "I'm not prejudiced, man," Jackson asserted. "I like white people; I like green people; I like any color people. I'm not doing this because I dislike white people. I love white people . . . but when people is killing me off, killing my mother and my sister off . . . the Ku Klux Klan—that's who I'm against completely. . . . It's time for us to do something. If there is anyone in this room that isn't serious, now is the time to say it." A commitment to the group was a commitment for good. "So, you guys, if there is anyone else in here that isn't serious, speak now, cause after you get it going, there ain't no out."

Firmin raised the stakes. "You may have to come into hand-to-hand combat with some of them white cats. You may have to shoot somebody. It's as simple as that, man." The Deacons were up against the Klan. "You know about the klans. No one have to tell you about them. So you got to know the risk that you're taking." Fear was their enemy, the fear of ordinary black men. "They leave Mississippi and they was afraid of the white man. They was afraid to fight the white man. Then they go over there to Vietnam and they fight. Then they come home and they be afraid to stand up for their rights. And I can't see it." So the Deacons were going to fight for their rights. "Right here, now," declared Firmin.

The Deacons membership was to remain a secret, at any cost. In a society that afforded little honor for black men, their word would be their honor. "Your tongue is the worst weapon against you," Firmin warned the group. "And I want to say this, and I mean it from my heart. That I swear before God, may He kill me now if I don't mean it: For something as important as this, I'd burn [kill] my brother. I'd blow his damn brains out." He would expect the Deacons to do the same to him if he betrayed its members. "I'm not directing anything to any one individual, you understand, because I would want everybody in here to feel the same way about me."

The men were to tell no one, not even their families, that they were in the Deacons. The same went for the police. "So if he puts this gun beside my head and say, 'I'm going to blow your damn brains out,' well, shit . . . don't tell him a damn thing," said Jackson. "Just let him blow it out, because you going to get it blowed out one way or the other." Firmin agreed. "Yeah, that goes back to like I said in the beginning. If they don't blow it out—and you get out—one of us will. And I want you to do the same thing to me."

This was the tough talk of street warriors; cool, stoic, and resolute. The testimonials of courage and self-abnegation served to forge bonds between the men and identify membership with the virtues of honor, sacrifice, and love of community. The Deacons were facing a dangerous enemy; secrecy and loyalty offered the security necessary to win recruits.

"This is one thing where we have an advantage on the Klan," pointed out Jackson. "Like, we know all the klans, just about, right? The point is that they don't know who is a Deacon. That's the advantage, man. Like they may know two or three Deacons, but they don't know who else over there is a Deacon. They don't know who we are."

It would be perilous work—but not too perilous. While emphasizing the risks enhanced the Deacons' appeal as a crucible for manhood, Jackson and Firmin did not want to scare the men off. "You got a time set to die," said Jackson, invoking the detached fatalism of the street hustler. "Like Metcalfe.

Metcalfe's car got blowed all to pieces—and he's still alive. It wasn't time for him to die." It was all in the hands of destiny. "So by taking chances—like we fixing to take chances—that don't mean you going to die . . . by taking a risk, that don't mean you going to get hurt."[29]

The Deacons would restore a sense of community and pride. "We're going to respect each other," promised Firmin. "We going to learn to love each other. To live together; to drink together; and above all, fight hard together. Push, man push, you know. All of us, pushing in the same direction."

Talk soon turned to the logistics and duties of the Deacons. "We don't participate in any demonstrations, any marches, anything like that," said Firmin. "We be around, we watch, and we observe, and protect them if they need protecting." They would find security in numbers, and, like Klansmen, they would be part of a regional organization in which local chapters would come to the aid of one another. The chapter would get two-way radios. "Do you reckon we can get permits to tote a weapon?" asked one of the recruits. "I don't think we going to be looking for permits to tote a weapon," replied Firmin wryly. "We just going to tote a weapon."

Though the chapters were ostensibly organized to defend the movement against the Klan, the majority of the meeting was devoted to discussing how the Deacons could discipline their own community, especially the middle-class "Uncle Toms" who were breaking ranks and undermining the boycott. "Are we going get in on this other thing," asked one of the recruits, "like the people that—like downtown there's a boycott now—are we going to take care of the peoples that has been warned three or four times or are we going to let somebody else do that?" The Deacons would handle it, said Jackson. "Like certain people been warned five or six times not to go back into the stores." The Deacons would "put the finger on him and shake him up, to teach him, man, teach him a little lesson." This kind of action would be done as individuals, not formally as the Deacons.

"I am pretty sure that we all physically fit," said Firmin, "and I know that everybody in here is ready to go to war and whup the average frail man that go in any of them stores." Jail was no problem. "Let them put me in jail. I just pay my fine for fighting and disturbing the peace." He would not use a weapon. "Not going to hit him with anything but my fist. Just put a whupping on him. And when I get him on that ground, I'll stomp him. And while he's down there, I'll tell him what it's for."

Jackson knew an army veteran who was a karate expert. He was going to begin to train the men the next week. "This is why this karate and judo is needed . . . we may pick you to just go and fight the man, just walk up to him and beat him," said Jackson. "Flat out beat him with your bare hands. O.K.? It's not but $35 for fighting and disturbing the peace. You give him a good whupping, then we pay the $35."

This talk of violent beatings did not sit well with one recruit. "I don't know if I can whup anybody as bad as you say," he confessed. "Stomping them and all that." No problem, said Firmin, if the recruit would not do it, then Firmin would take on the job personally. "It's not but $35 for disturbing the peace," Jackson pointed out again. Another recruit weighed in. "I'll tell you all what, I have to be honest. I'd have to be in on that [beating] too, because if someone is doing something that shouldn't be done, that is hindering the advancement of colored peoples in Mississippi, I'd have to do it, man. If not, I'd have to give it a good try."

The Deacons would be effective against Uncle Toms "because when this type thing happen, we going to be harder on him than we are on a Klansman if we caught him messing around," warned Firmin. "We'll take a hose pipe and beat his life out." People feared the Klan, but the Deacons would make a boycott breaker "more afraid of us than he is of them." The next time an Uncle Tom contemplated breaking the boycott, "they'll think, 'the white man might come by and he'll shoot into the air; or he might throw a brick and run. But that *nigger* is going to kill me—that *nigger* is going to whip my tail.'"

"Once you find one that's leading the people astray," continued Firmin, "that's keeping the people confused, or that's getting people hurt by going back telling things, and hurting innocent people, then maybe he don't deserve to die. But maybe he don't deserve to see. Or hear. Or even talk any more. I believe in that kind of stuff. I really do."

The focus on how to handle middle-class collaborators was not unique to the Natchez chapter and, in fact, characterized the Deacons wherever they emerged. In Natchez, as elsewhere, the concern with "Toming" reflected a measure of class conflict within the black community. Jackson admitted that there was opposition to the Deacons in the community, primarily among black businessmen, but the Deacons would "give our service to everybody, whether they go along with us or not."

Jackson and Firmin had skillfully orchestrated the meeting, presenting the Deacons as an elite organization reserved for men of honor and courage, and offering the recruits a way of participating in the movement that would allow them to keep their dignity as well as their lives. It all made sense. Rather than one black man against a lynch mob, they would be part of a secret organization that could match the Klan in tactics and breadth. They would end the three-hundred-year white monopoly on fear. "This has just got to happen," Firmin said as the meeting ended. "I swear, this is our chance, when we are older, to be able to say, 'We helped to build Natchez.' Not only Natchez—but Mississippi." One of the recruits concurred. "It has to be a great thing," he said with obvious pride. "Everybody here is serious about the thing. It has to be a great thing."

Following that initial organizing meeting, the Natchez chapter elected officers: James Jackson, the group's founder, became president; Isaac Terrell, a sawmill millwright, was elected vice president; Sandy Nealy became treasurer; and James Stokes, the NAACP militant who had assisted in quelling the riot after the Metcalfe bombing, was appointed spokesman. The secretary was James Young, a coworker of Metcalfe's at Armstrong Tire and Rubber. Young had guarded Metcalfe in the hospital and, like most of the Deacons, was an army veteran, having served as a demolition technician in the South Pacific during World War II.[30]

The rapidly unfolding events provided the Deacons with considerable work. Mayor Nosser had rejected the demands presented by the black leaders during the first week of September. When the leaders threatened a series of marches, Nosser persuaded Governor Paul Johnson to send 650 national guard troops to Natchez. The invading force converged on the city on 3 September and promptly sealed off the black community. A strict 10:00 P.M. to 5:00 A.M. curfew was imposed. Although Prohibition was already in effect in Natchez, city officials banned the previously tolerated bootlegged liquor trade in the black community. They also ordered several black-owned businesses to close on the theory that they threatened civil order by allowing blacks to congregate on their premises.[31]

Given that the riots had subsided before the National Guard arrived, many blacks felt that its presence was intended to discourage legal protest—not violence. On their arrival, the National Guardsmen mounted .50 caliber machine guns in the downtown area. Evers and other black leaders debated whether to defy the guns and march. They were confronted with a grim choice. James Young recalled that a Guard official told them, "If you march, we will open fire." Evers wisely canceled the march and charged that the National Guard was in Natchez with one purpose: to "beat and kill" black citizens if they exercised their right to demonstrate.[32]

The National Guard never had an opportunity to confirm Evers's fears. In response to protests by Aaron Henry, head of the MFDP, Governor Johnson withdrew the troops three days later, on 6 September. The Guard's departure cleared the way for the first of a series of marches in a bitter four-month boycott campaign. Negotiations over black demands soon reached an impasse as city officials remained intransigent. Instead of negotiating in earnest, city fathers grasped for a legal instrument to suppress protest. On 30

September they succeeded temporarily when they secured an injunction from the Chancery Court prohibiting demonstrations.

The injunction set off a wave of mass arrests. During 1–7 October 544 blacks, including Charles Evers, were charged with violating the injunction. The arrests—another shameful chapter in Mississippi history—nonetheless attest to the impressive breadth of the local movement. Prisoners were herded into buses and shipped two hundred miles to the infamous state prison at Parchman, where guards subjected the protesters to unspeakable abuses. The wife and daughter of Deacons leader James Stokes were both arrested and imprisoned. Stokes's wife never recovered from the trauma, and she died shortly afterward.[33]

Evers suspended the demonstrations on 7 October after city officials agreed to consider a revised list of NAACP demands. The boycott of downtown stores continued, however, and by 12 October Mayor Nosser admitted that business was down by as much as 50 percent. Demonstrations resumed briefly in mid-October, when local officials and black leaders failed to reach a settlement. The business community's support for segregation was quickly eroding; by the end of October most of its resistance to black demands was due to Klan threats and intimidation.[34]

The boycott and the marches firmly secured Evers's leadership of the movement. The SNCC activists, working through the MFDP, were marginalized—in good measure because of Evers's ruthless campaign against them—but also because their efforts to impose nonviolence alienated rank-and-file community members. The problem became manifest in a meeting in early September at the Bright Star Baptist Church, when the MFDP activists attempted a final revival of their faltering movement. Approximately one hundred local people attended and listened politely to the speeches. After SNCC activist Bill Ware finished, a black woman rose from the audience and addressed the speakers. "I don't want to march on this accord," she said with great solemnity. "If a man or woman hits me, I'm going to hit back. And so I don't want to get in there since it's non-violent. I don't want to get in there and upset your plans that you have before you . . . I'm not afraid to march, but if he hold my hand, if he stand in front of me, I'll spit on him. I'm not afraid of them."[35]

The response of the SNCC activists was a case study in misguided idealism. First, SNCC leader Lawrence Guyot replied to the woman by castigating her cohorts for "being quiet and doing nothing." As he continued to reproach the audience, a large group rose and began to walk out. Guyot continued, "You're being understood by simply being quiet and sitting back and staying in your places." More people filed out. "The most cowardly thing I have ever heard," Guyot declared, his voice growing tense, "is for someone to say, 'I would go with you all but I ain't non-violent.'"[36] The audience had heard enough. By the end of Guyot's speech, the church was nearly empty.

SNCC never recovered from the church meeting, and Evers now had solid control of the movement. In truth, the people who SNCC had rebuked as cowards ultimately did demonstrate—under Evers's leadership and in numbers and with courage unparalleled in Mississippi organizing. The source of SNCC's difficulties was its emphasis on federal intervention. Although the organization endeavored to develop local leadership and encouraged participatory democracy, it also, like other national civil rights groups, pursued a strategy designed to create confrontations that would force federal intervention. It was a strategy deeply embedded in SNCC's origins. "The youth must take the freedom struggle into every community in the South without exception," Martin Luther King had announced at the group's founding conference in 1961. "Inevitably this broadening of the struggle and the determination which it represents will arouse vocal and vigorous support and place pressures on the federal government that will compel its intervention." When Dorie Ladner, a seasoned SNCC staffer, attempted to get Natchez residents to march to the courthouse in a spontaneous protest, people were reluctant to participate in what they viewed as a small, symbolic protest that would have little effect on city leaders and likely end in arrests and police violence. One local woman told Ladner, "Yeah, I want to march, and when everybody else march, I'm going to march too. But I'll be damned if I'm going down there by myself . . . when it be done, we're going to do it together." Ladner's rejoinder spoke volumes about the federal interventionist approach: "If they start jumping on you," she retorted, "the president of the United States can federalize them like he did in Alabama." But the Natchez community was not going to depend on some fabled avenging angel from the banks of the Potomac. It would rely on its own power to compel concessions from the city. A similar desire to force the federal government to secure rights underpinned the Freedom Summer strategy that flooded Mississippi with young white volunteers. Reflecting back on the movement years later, COFO leader Dave Dennis said the belief was that America would only respond to "the death of a white college student." The Natchez movement had rejected the federal interventionist strategy of appealing to northern conscience through suffering; instead, it emphasized gaining power locally through direct force and coercion—the organizing model developed by the Deacons in Louisiana.[37]

Beginning with the boycott, initiated in September 1965, the Natchez Deacons served as the black community's informal police force (the city police were more accommodating to the dead than the living; funerals were the only occasion when blacks were guaranteed a police escort). The Deacons regularly patrolled the black community by car and on foot to prevent Klan attacks, maintaining contact through a CB radio network. The patrols effectively discouraged Klan harassment without resorting to gunfire, as was necessary in Bogalusa and Jonesboro. They stopped white interlopers and politely yet firmly told them to leave the area. "A guy driving through first, you wouldn't say nothing to him," recalled James Young. "You didn't bother him. But now if he just constantly driving through, back and forth, then you stopped him . . . we'd tell him unless he has some business through that way, don't come through no more." The Deacons also guarded the homes of civil rights activists and provided escorts for visiting activists and supporters.[38]

Most of the Deacons' activity centered on guarding demonstrators during the scores of pickets and marches. The Natchez Deacons were always armed—often openly. James Young walked along the marches sporting a pistol in a side holster. White hecklers lined the streets, but generally the display of resolve and firepower was a sufficient deterrent. "Just the presence of the Deacons kept a lot of things from happening that would have happened," said Young. Occasionally a white antagonist disregarded the danger. In one incident a white man attempted to disrupt a march by steering his car into the line. Within seconds the Deacons converged on the car with weapons drawn, detained the startled driver, and delivered him to the police.[39]

As the boycott proceeded, the organizational life of the Natchez Deacons fell into a regular pattern. Monthly meetings were scheduled, but during the height of the campaign, they met daily if necessary. The chapter operated in a modified democratic style. As a quasi-paramilitary organization, the Deacons found it necessary to delegate authority to a leader for swift command. But they reserved the right to overrule the leader's decisions. As Young described the process, "The leader would make the decision, or he would say that this is the way that he thinks it should be. Well, if we felt like it was meant to be a little different than that or what not, we would discuss it, and whatever we come up with was what we would do."[40]

Approximately fifteen men comprised the core of the chapter, regularly attending meetings and performing duties. Complementing this core was a network of roughly one hundred men who considered themselves members, either formally or informally, and who assisted the chapter when they were needed.[41]

The Natchez Police Department's stance toward the Deacons differed markedly from the belligerent policy of Bogalusa authorities. In general,

Police Chief J. T. Robinson followed a neutral approach, declining to harass the Deacons with arrests or intimidation. Indeed, James Stokes had a surprisingly cordial relationship with Chief Robinson. At one point a Deacon was arrested and assessed a fine following a scuffle with police. Stokes asked Robinson to intervene, and he complied, paying the Deacon's fine and promising to prevent future incidents.[42]

Robinson's policy was not all that mystifying. In truth, the police benefited from having a disciplined defense group in the black community. "Well really, the Chief always looked to us to help him to keep law and order," said Young. The Deacons' purpose was not to provoke confrontations with the Klan, but rather to minimize conflict. "We were out to see that there were law and order carried out." Nevertheless, Chief Robinson was not averse to manipulating the group. On one occasion a black deputy brought Stokes a message offering him a police department job if he would quit the Deacons. Stokes was polite but firm. "I'll tell you like this: I really don't need that job."[43]

From the outset, the Natchez chapter maintained their independence from the Louisiana Deacons, probably to please Charles Evers, who jealously guarded his territory from outsiders, and also because the national Deacons required a $100 chapter membership fee and 10 percent of collected dues to defray national organizing costs. The Natchez chapter's independence was not anomalous; typically, most chapters regarded themselves as an autonomous local organization within a loose federation. This relationship mirrored the independent and democratic nature of most organizations in southern black communities. Baptist ministers served at the pleasure of the church laity, unlike Roman Catholic, Methodist, and other hierarchical denominations. Segregation gave rise to a wide range of locally organized mutual self-help organizations, including benevolent associations and insurance and burial societies. Additionally, the community was honeycombed with self-organized recreational clubs, including social and pleasure clubs and travel clubs. These highly independent, localized organizations provided a model for the relationships between the national Deacons organization and its local chapters. In fact, members of the Natchez and Jonesboro Deacons frequently referred to the organization as a "club."[44]

To ensure that state officials would accept their application for a corporate charter, the Natchez group decided to organize under a name other than the Deacons. It chose the innocently deceptive name "Natchez Sportsmen Club." The name was not without irony, as the Klan frequently named their klaverns "sportsmens" clubs to conceal their identity. In public fund-raising appeals the Natchez chapter acknowledged the subterfuge, explaining that "the name 'sportsmen club' is used in order to obtain a Mississippi state charter."[45]

As in Jonesboro, the Deacons charter in Natchez carried a special significance for the members. They believed that the charter gave them the right to carry firearms and defend their community. "In the charter, we had to protect people's property and churches and so forth," Stokes pointed out, "and therefore couldn't no one take our weapons from us. So we could carry our weapons just like the local law enforcement officers carry theirs." When the police challenged Stokes's right to carry a weapon, the Deacons leader would stand fast, produce the charter like a talisman, and demand that the police honor his rights.[46]

The Natchez Deacons maintained strict membership standards and sought mature recruits, fearless men capable of sound judgment and restraint. The front line against the Klan was no place for hotheads and impulsive youths. The chapter generally attracted men of character and good standing in the community. The mission of the organization appealed to men independent in spirit and mind. "If we thought that they were the type of person who was easily persuaded or swayed, we didn't want that type of person," noted Stokes. Most recruits were stable family men, often in their thirties; nearly all were members of the NAACP. As mill workers, log haulers, barbers, and contractors, most Natchez Deacons enjoyed the security of professions that shielded them from economic retaliation.[47]

A typical member was the chapter's secretary, James Young. Young was forty-one years old when he joined the Deacons in 1965. He had lived his entire life in Adams County. His memories of Mississippi in the 1930s were of an arduous yet peaceful childhood with few incidents of racial harassment. His sharecropper parents lived among poor whites, and the children played together unencumbered by the prejudices of their parents. Young dropped out of high school in the ninth grade to work in the fields; he perhaps would have lived out his life on the farm had not the dogs of war invaded the slumbering world of rural Mississippi.

In September 1943 Young joined the army and soon found himself loading bombs onto warplanes in the South Pacific. The demolition training he received paid few dividends later in life; more profitable were the lessons learned about the power of discipline and collective action. Returning to segregation in Mississippi was a painful and degrading experience for the young soldier. Young sought refuge on his parents' farm to avoid Natchez and the inevitable humiliations attendant to contact with whites. Young described the solace of the farm: "It was kind of hard at first," he said. "The main thing about it is you just have to adjust. . . . I spent most of my time out there. I didn't even come around to town." The military had taught him to accept the bitterness in life. All he could do—all any man could do—was "adjust and fall in line."[48]

After risking life and limb for a nation that denied them full citizenship, black veterans like Young returned with rising expectations for democracy and declining tolerance for Jim Crow. "This is what started changing," explained Stokes. "Men vowed, 'If I go to Korea, or Vietnam, I'm damn sure not going to go back home to nothing like the other soldiers did in World War One and Two.' "[49]

Not all black men were prepared to fight for their freedom. There were Deacons who faltered under the pressure of their duties and quit. "The wives was scared," explained Stokes. "Or the fellows was scared that they were going to get killed or go to jail—when they were the sole provider." Fear was even more pervasive in the small towns dotting the hills and the delta in Mississippi. Accompanying Charles Evers as bodyguards on organizing drives, the Deacons frequently arrived at a courthouse rally to find only one or two people there. These visits to remote communities offered an opportunity for the Deacons to spread the gospel of self-defense and recruit new members, but first they had to overcome the ever-present nemesis of fear. "We had to sort of get the fright out of any county that we went into," admitted Stokes. "We had to get the fright out of those guys."[50]

The gun was the Deacons' principal organizing tool in these isolated communities. Rural blacks could not help being impressed by the Deacons' audacity. "We would go to their town, and they would watch us in action, doing *our* job with *our* guns," explained Stokes. "Police officers didn't bother us. If he did, he was in trouble. So therefore, that made him [the black man] not be afraid." The Natchez Deacons were always armed. "There wasn't no certain time; we were armed day and night," said Young, "and everybody knew that, and I think that's what made it so much the better." The willingness to defend themselves bred confidence. "I didn't want to come to the point to have to pull a gun to use it on nobody," Young remarked, "but knowing that you had the gun was a bit of relief because it was more forceful that way."[51]

To some observers, the Natchez Deacons did more than bear arms; they recklessly flaunted them. Members of the Natchez chapter developed a reputation for brandishing their weapons, a practice that disturbed their counterparts in Bogalusa. Royan Burris was the Bogalusa chapter officer who initially helped organize the Natchez Deacons. On several occasions he returned to Natchez as a liaison to the Mississippi chapters. He was troubled by the brazen display of weaponry. "The Deacons in Natchez really got violent," recalled Burris. "We had to, kind of call their hand because they felt like 'because we had a charter,' they could just walk around with guns . . . guns everywhere they went. Just like it wasn't nothing. And that wasn't our purpose. They said they just needed to do it because that was the only way they could walk the streets at the time." Burris's plea for discretion had little effect. The Natchez chapter, according to Burris, continued to swagger through the streets "with guns hanging outside like cowboys."[52]

Like James Jackson and other Deacons leaders, most of the men recruited by the Natchez chapter regarded nonviolence as a futile strategy. James Stokes equated nonviolence with the passivity exhibited by preceding generations. "They [old people] believed in nonviolence," he pointed out. And the Klan "had gone out and caught old people who believed in nonviolence, killed them, set them afire, cut their penis out and stuffed it in their mouth, drug them up and down the roads, whipped them with barbed wire." History had turned Stokes against nonviolence. "I believe if you shoot at me, I'm going to shoot at you." Nor was Stokes impressed with the partisans of nonviolence. "Those crazy rascals would lay down in the street and so forth," he mused. "The NAACP got rid of CORE and SNCC. After a few people got killed, we just asked them to pack up and leave and let us take care of everything ourselves. Thank you but no thank you." Under Evers's leadership, the NAACP gave the Deacons ample berth. "The NAACP was a fully nonviolent organization," said Young, "and they still stood for that. But they didn't stand in the way of no one else that decided that it took some violence to protect yourself. They didn't stand in the way of this, no way."[53]

Although the Natchez Deacons came to an understanding with the NAACP and Evers, not all segments of the black community accepted them. When they encountered opposition within the black community, fear changed from adversary to ally for the Deacons. As they had planned in their first organizing meeting, the Natchez Deacons frequently used violence to discipline critics and collaborators within their own ranks. It was a pattern of anti–middle-class violence that was a signature of the Deacons throughout the region. Local authorities implicated the Deacons in shootings and assaults against their black detractors in Bogalusa and Port Gibson, but they were never convicted of the crimes.

In Natchez, this internal intimidation was carried out by the Deacons—as they had planned in their first meeting—but also by independent community members under the direction of the Deacons. A vigilante group of women and men frequently attacked blacks who violated the boycott by making purchases at targeted stores. "There was a little group that would go around," said Young, "and if they had violated the boycott, whatever they had, they took it from them and possibly would whup them up." In addition to boycott violators, informants within the black community caused problems by providing whites with critical information about organizational plans and internal conflicts. Because of their regular contact with whites, black domestic workers sometimes came under suspicion. In these cases, the Deacons encouraged women members of the NAACP to take measures against informants. "So we'd have these women, that wasn't members of our organization—they were people in the NAACP—they would go catch them and beat them up," said Stokes. The vigilante groups also attacked black ministers whom they thought had betrayed the community by providing information to the white community. Stokes, who eventually became a minister, charged that some black clergy sold information and campaign endorsements to white politicians. "It almost makes you feel somewhat embarrassed to say you are a minister, because of the things you see ministers do. Every four years they put black people on sale."[54]

While the Natchez Deacons countenanced women enforcing the boycott, they had no place for them within their own ranks. Unlike the prominent formal leadership role played by women in Bogalusa and Jonesboro, the NAACP prevented women from representing the black community in Natchez. Jessie Bernard, a young African American NAACP staffer, crossed swords with Charles Evers and local NAACP members over this policy during one encounter at the NAACP office. Bernard pointed out to Evers that women led the movement on the picket line. "It's these ladies, people like Mrs. Duncan, Mrs. MacNeilly, Mrs. Muzeek, Mrs. Jackson . . . they are the people who are really getting the job done around here," declared Bernard. "Look, I think if you're going to be a man, I think you should be a man all the way." Women were the ones who had endured arrests and "fought off those dogs" on the picket line, yet men had assumed control of negotiations with city officials. "Not one of them walked out there on the picket line," complained Bernard, "and yet when it's time to go around to the City Hall, they can sit down there and make decisions. How can they make decisions when they really don't know what's going on?"[55] As with the NAACP, whenever the Deacons assumed political leadership, their exclusion of women had the effect of limiting women's participation at the leadership level.

The Natchez Deacons had ample funds to carry on their work thanks to Clifford Boxley, a Natchez native who made his home in Redwood, California. Boxley, a postal worker, returned to Natchez for a visit during the height of the boycott and was impressed by the Deacons' work. He arranged for a fund-raising tour in California for James Stokes in November 1965. Stokes was a natural choice as a spokesperson for the Deacons. A well-spoken, articulate man with a flair for the dramatic, he had honed his leadership abilities as a church deacon and choir director and union steward, and he had traveled extensively around the world in the army's entertainment unit from 1953 to 1955.[56]

Born in 1928, Stokes grew up on a dusty sharecropper farm on the Linwood Plantation, a few miles outside of Natchez. For generations, his ancestors had toiled as slaves and sharecroppers on the plantation. All they had to show for their labor was a small family cemetery atop a hill on the plantation. In the 1960s a highway was charted to carve through the cemetery. The Stokes family had long since left the plantation, and despite the desecration, the plantation owners warned Stokes to stay away from the cemetery and keep off the property. One morning Stokes strapped on his gun, drove out to the plantation, and defiantly marched up the hill to the cemetery. He came down the hill with his mother's small tombstone on his shoulder. He took the stone to the cemetery and placed it beside his father's stone, finally laying them to rest together. His defiance toward the white plantation owner was a trait acquired early in life. "My mother used to be afraid for me to leave home, and afraid when I came back," recalled Stokes. "Because, even in my teen-age days, I would say something. I don't know. Maybe I was too crazy to be scared."[57]

Stokes exhibited the same outspokenness as a fund-raiser for the Deacons during his tour of California. On 9 November 1965 Stokes delivered a speech at San Mateo College. A handbill distributed at the event noted that the Deacons' purpose was to "protect the lives and property of negro citizens from hooded night riders." The leaflet requested contributions "to purchase such items as Walkie Talkies, Radio Equipment, Uniform Equipment, and cars that are radio equipped to patrol the negro neighborhood." Though the circular omitted mention of weapons, the FBI reported that in his speech Stokes said that funds would also be used to buy weapons. Years later Stokes confirmed the report and frankly admitted that the objective of the fund-raising tour was to "buy guns."[58]

Stokes traveled throughout California for approximately a week, speaking at several churches in Redwood and appearing at fund-raising events in Los Angeles, Oakland, and San Francisco. He returned to Natchez with contributions totaling $7,000, several guns, and a donated automobile. All of the money went for additional guns and radios.[59]

Stokes's successful fund-raising enabled the Deacons to give their full attention to the boycott, which was entering its third month in November. Since the Metcalfe bombing, militants such as Charles Evers, Rudy Shields, NAACP director Archie Jones, and the Reverend Shead Baldwin had displaced the older moderate leaders, and the aggressive new spirit was undermining unity in the white community. The wintry winds of December finally brought a sober reappraisal of the situation by the white power structure. The boycott had effectively eroded business class solidarity to the extent that twenty-three merchants had already hired blacks as clerks or cashiers. Finally, on 3 December city government and local businessmen formally conceded defeat. The white elite agreed to comprehensive racial reforms, acceding to virtually all of the original NAACP demands. Evers hailed the agreement as the "greatest concession" ever made in the civil rights movement—and he was certainly right as far as Mississippi was concerned. Whereas virtually every other local campaign had ended in failure during the civil rights movement in Mississippi, the Natchez project had mobilized an entire community and exacted sweeping concessions from the white establishment—without benefit of federal intervention. When Evers and Mayor Nosser announced the accord at a joint press conference, Evers took the occasion to dance on the grave of Jim Crow. The black movement had set out to make Natchez a "whipping boy," he bragged, and now the rest of Mississippi needed to "take heed."[60]

The concessions made by city government and business leaders were considerable and went well beyond civil equality reforms. The white establishment agreed to integrate all city-operated facilities, including schools and hospitals; hire more blacks and upgrade current jobs; enforce building codes to eliminate slums; create a biracial committee to advise the City Council; and even implement a beautification program in black neighborhoods. The merchants that the boycott had targeted also agreed to open sales clerk positions to blacks. Although not consenting to mandatory courtesy titles, government and businesses promised to discharge clerks if they addressed blacks with demeaning terms.[61]

The Natchez campaign was the single greatest community victory for the civil rights movement in Mississippi, though historians have never given it the credit it deserves. By any standard of community organizing, the campaign was a sterling success: the organizers united and inspired a community to courageous action (more than five hundred demonstrators were arrested in one week) and secured dramatic legal and economic reforms. In comparison, the projects in McComb, Clarksdale, and Jackson failed to win any significant demands and frequently left the black community demoralized and in disarray (the McComb project, e.g., registered only six voters in six months).[62]

What blinds many observers to the Natchez success is Charles Evers. Competing national civil rights organizations universally reviled Evers, and few of his critics would begrudge him a victory—even decades later. Nonetheless, he deserves credit for his accomplishment. Evers did not pioneer the strategy he used in Natchez: he simply employed the strategic model for community organizing that the Louisiana Deacons had perfected before the Natchez campaign. It was a strategy that eschewed appeals to northern conscience and instead forced local concessions through a combination of legal protest, economic coercion, and, most importantly, militant force—in the form of armed self-defense and community discipline.[63] Moreover, it was a strategy that succeeded where others had failed.

The end of the boycott completed the Deacons' work in Natchez, and the chapter now turned its attention to civil rights campaigns in the surrounding area. On one occasion the chapter provided security for Martin Luther King in Jackson, Mississippi, and later offered to assist him in McComb. Some of the Natchez Deacons were deputized by Charles Evers and provided security for Evers as he organized in Southwest Mississippi, including during trips to McComb, Hazelhurst, and Brookhaven. Although Evers had initially rebuked the Deacons, he quickly integrated the Natchez chapter into every aspect of his organizing. By the spring of 1966 Evers had boycotts planned in the uncharted territories of Fayette and Port Gibson. "Deep down in himself, he knew he needed this protection," said James Stokes. "Because he wasn't going to get it from nowhere else. Nobody else was going to protect him." Evers's assistant, Rudolph "Rudy" Shields, an ex-boxer from Yazoo, Mississippi, served as liaison to the Deacons. Though he was reluctant to discuss his use of force at the time, years later Evers admitted that he relied on armed guards and offensive violence in his Mississippi organizing. "We had our protective squad," Evers wrote in his autobiography, *Evers*. "We had our guns. We didn't go around bragging about it, but we were ready to enforce those boycotts, to die if necessary. And they knew we were ready."[64]

Between 1965 and 1968 Charles Evers's extensive local campaigns provided the main framework for Deacons organizing in Mississippi. The Natchez Deacons went on to organize several Deacons chapters and informal groups in Port Gibson, Fayette (where Evers was eventually elected to office), Vicksburg, Kosciusko, Woodville, Centreville, and St. Francisville, Louisiana. Three of the informal Deacons groups that Natchez organized— in Fayette, Kosciusko, and Vicksburg—had little activity. Fayette, a tiny, predominantly black town a short drive from Natchez, was the site of a NAACP boycott of white stores. Little is known about the Fayette chapter, other than that J. D. Washington headed it. The Vicksburg chapter consisted of only a few members and had little success. The same was true for the Kosciusko chapter. In response to the Klan murder of Vernon Dahmer, a black leader in Hattiesburg, Mississippi, the Bogalusa Deacons organized a chapter known as "the police unit" in Hattiesburg in 1966. Contacts there helped the Bogalusa group to form another chapter in Laurel, Mississippi—one that extended its activities into the labor movement. In addition, the Bogalusa Deacons organized chapters in Tylertown and Columbia—bringing the total number of Mississippi chapters to eight.[65]

Port Gibson became one of the strongest Deacons chapters in Mississippi. In January 1966 the town was still completely segregated, untouched by the Civil Rights Act. When white leaders learned that Charles Evers was planning a campaign there, they quickly sought out a group of compliant black leaders to negotiate a compromise. In response, local activists organized a NAACP chapter to represent the community, but the increasingly militant community considered even the new NAACP chapter, led by a local minister, too accommodating. "He was a minister there, but the black community felt like he could be no spokesman for them," said George Walker, a Port Gibson Deacons leader, "because whatever they [whites] told him, he was going to do that."[66]

In the spring of 1966, activists presented a list of demands to local authorities but failed to receive an acceptable response. On 1 April Evers announced a boycott of all white-owned businesses in Port Gibson, hoping that white merchants would, in turn, pressure municipal and county government officials to accept the demands.[67] To assist with the boycott, Rudy Shields helped form the Port Gibson Deacons chapter in July 1966. Shields became a chapter member and served as the liaison between Evers and the chapter. A retired professional fighter and streetwise operator, Shields was a popular and accomplished grassroots organizer. Like Evers, he had lived in Chicago for several years and returned to his native Mississippi to organize in the movement.[68] Although officially a Deacons chapter, the Port Gibson group quickly acquired the name "Black Hats of Claiborne County," owing to their habit of wearing black hats to identify themselves to police and community members. George Walker, a lifelong resident of the county, became the chapter's first president.[69]

Walker had learned responsibility at a young age on a sharecropper farm. When he was nine, Walker took over farming the cotton crop while his father staved off starvation by doing "public work," that is, logging and other forms of hired labor. "We didn't never do nothing but work," remembered Walker. "Didn't think about nothing else. And just trying to do what we was supposed to do: take care of each other." Walker served three years as an army corpsman in Korea, then returned to a job at the Thompson Funeral Home. He supplemented his income with masonry and electrical work.[70]

In his youth, segregation had seemed natural and immutable to Walker. He never entertained the thought of challenging Jim Crow. "It never dawned on me," said Walker. "I just thought this was a way of life." But in the 1960s, when he saw the movement unfolding around him, his outlook on segregation changed radically. "And then after I got involved with everything else, everything started coming out. Looked like the sun was coming out where I could see. And it come to me—well maybe things not supposed to be like this."[71]

As the head of the Port Gibson Deacons, Walker was preoccupied with ensuring that the black community complied with the boycott. Most blacks did, but a few were intractable. The NAACP resorted to forceful tactics to rein in boycott violators. At the regular Tuesday night NAACP meetings, Evers would read aloud a list of violators and warn them that the "spirit's going to get you." In most cases the "spirit" assumed the form of a brick flying through a window.[72]

Early in the campaign Evers recruited a group of "store watchers" to enforce the boycott, many of whom eventually made up the Port Gibson Deacons chapter. The watchers frequently used strong-arm tactics. They routinely stopped shoppers and intimidated them into not patronizing the store. If the shoppers had already made their purchases, the watchers would seize and destroy the items. Boycott breakers received threatening calls, and on two occasions assailants fired guns into their homes.[73]

The Deacons aided the store watchers in enforcing the boycott, clearly crossing the line between defensive and offensive force. Their actions won them the enmity of many, particularly middle-class blacks and ministers. "The ministers, in general, they were opposed," related Walker. "Some people hated us." Within a few months the Deacons found themselves blamed for any act of intimidation that occurred. Walker maintained that the Deacons "got labeled for harassing people" because of their association with Evers, but he denied that the Deacons were intimidating people. "We were just there to see that the people were protected."[74]

The Claiborne County sheriff's office thought otherwise. It suspected that the Port Gibson Deacons were involved in at least one shooting attack on a black boycott breaker. One night a car cruised by the home of Ed Gilmore and fired several shots into his house. Gilmore, a mechanic, had been one of the high-profile boycott breakers. Within minutes, sheriff's deputies stopped

Elmo Scott as he and two other Deacons were driving on Highway 61 but later released them for lack of evidence.[75]

The Port Gibson chapter held regular meetings at several sites, including the First Baptist Church. Before meeting they would check the church for bombs and then post guards on the roof of an adjacent building. The chapter charged dues to pay for ammunition, and individual members paid for their own weapons and CB radios used to coordinate actions and monitor Klan activities. The chapter conducted both motor and foot patrols and organized regular target practice at a target range south of Port Gibson. "We had our weapons everywhere we went," said Walker. But like the Jonesboro chapter, the Port Gibson Deacons did not publicly display them.[76]

In addition to patrolling, their duties included guarding marchers and keeping a watchful eye on picketers at stores. They occasionally exported their guard services to other towns such as nearby Tillman. By staying in contact by CB radios in their cars and homes, the chapters in Port Gibson, Natchez, and Fayette comprised a regional defense network that could instantly summon assistance and communicate alerts.

The CB transmissions could be a source of fear as well as solace. Walker recalled a white man who spewed an unending torrent of threats on the CB radio. "He stayed on his walkie-talkie and he was always talking about how he was going to 'send them monkeys back to Africa . . . going to send them to the moon before June.' The whole situation was scary for me." The murder of civil rights workers in Neshoba County also haunted Walker and the Deacons. "Didn't nobody really know what was going to happen. The three fellas had just got killed up there. It constantly stayed on all our minds and all our thoughts."[77]

In Port Gibson, the Klan went beyond mere insults and threats. A gang of armed whites assaulted Deacon Alfred Lee Davis while he was picketing the Jones Furniture Store. Davis refused to back down in the face of a gun, and within minutes George Walker and several other Deacons went to his aid. With reinforcements at his side, Davis told one of the white men that he did not have "nerve enough to shoot him." Fortunately, the sheriff intervened and defused the situation.[78]

As in other places, the mere presence of the Deacons transformed the role of the NAACP in Port Gibson. "NAACP officials realized that the presence of the Deacons made the NAACP a more appealing negotiating body and enhanced their effectiveness," observes Emilye Crosby in her study of Port Gibson. With the Deacons fighting back against the Klan, the town negotiated an agreement that the Deacons would disarm if the Klan would, too. The mutual stand-down was a remarkable achievement for the Deacons and testi-fied to the effectiveness of their approach to secure reform on the local level. The boycott became a landmark legal case when white merchants sued the NAACP for conducting an illegal secondary boycott. The merchants claimed that the NAACP had no valid complaint against their establishments, that the civil rights groups had targeted their businesses only to pressure town and county officials to accept their demands. On 9 August 1976, after a pro-longed court battle, Hinds County chancellor George W. Haynes awarded a $1,250,699 settlement to the white merchants and issued a permanent in-junction against several forms of boycotts. The decision was later overturned by the U.S. Supreme Court.[79]

Charles Evers's role in Port Gibson ended ignominiously when he sum-marily called off the boycott, raising suspicions that he had accepted a deal with the white establishment. The black community asked him to leave, and the community, unlike many other civil rights–era projects, survived the loss of outside leadership and sustained a vibrant, effective organization. Ac-cording to Walker, the Deacons chapter finally dissolved in 1968 in response to complaints that it was intimidating blacks in the community. The Port Gibson NAACP had summoned the Deacons to answer a charge that they had thrown a brick at Alexander Collins's barbershop. The Deacons were in-censed at having to defend themselves. "We done put our lives on the line out here. If they think that low of us, then we'll just let what happens happen." The need for self-defense did not end with the demise of the Deacons. Only one year later a shooting incident at a church led to a riot and shoot-out between blacks and the Mississippi State Highway Patrol.[80]

The Deacons also found fertile organizing soil in Wilkinson County in Southwest Mississippi. In 1965 James Stokes from the Natchez chapter formed the Woodville chapter, which eventually recruited approximately forty members from Woodville, Centreville, and rural areas in Wilkinson County. William "Bilbo" Ferguson served as president of the Woodville chap-ter; other officers included Edward Caine, the chapter's spokesperson, and Herman Burkes, vice president. Ferguson was a thirty-two-year-old scrap metal worker who had been reared by his grandparents. Family members es-caped sharecropping by buying their own land in the 1940s. They lived a humble but relatively independent life raising cotton, sweet potatoes, corn, and a few livestock. A Mason and a churchgoer, Ferguson joined the NAACP in 1964.[81]

Ed Caine was a self-employed carpenter. Caine paid a price for his associa-tion with the Deacons: he lost all of his white customers after word circu-lated of his Deacons membership. Other chapter members included Henry

Jones, another carpenter; Benjamin Groom, a logger; Elmo McKenzie, a sawmill worker; William Davis; and Earnest Tollivar. Nearly all of the men were also Masons.[82]

The Woodville Deacons worked closely with the NAACP and conducted monthly meetings at the Negro Masonic Temple. Attendance varied from a dozen to just two or three members. Although organized in 1965, the Woodville Deacons primarily assisted with marches in Natchez for the first two years of its existence. Then in August 1967, blacks became upset when they failed to win any county posts in the Democratic primary. In September the Wilkinson County branch of the NAACP led a series of protests and launched a boycott in Woodville to secure a new election and the appointment of blacks to the Wilkinson County Election Commission. The NAACP was particularly disturbed with a Board of Education election in which a white candidate defeated a popular black leader, Anselm Joseph Finch, in part, because several black teachers had supported the white candidate. The controversy sparked a protest led by James Joliff, president of the Wilkinson County NAACP, a tough uncompromising militant, who called for a boycott of white merchants until a new election could be held.[83]

On 4 September 1967 Joliff led a group of two hundred blacks and a contingent of armed Deacons in a march to the Wilkinson County Training School on the outskirts of Woodville. The NAACP was demanding that school officials fire "Negro teachers there who did not favor Negroes running in the Democratic primaries." "We are going to have to bury those Negroes who have sold themselves out to the white people," Joliff told the marchers at a rally. Forty-five grim members of the State Highway Patrol confronted the marchers on the way to the school. In a subsequent skirmish, patrolmen arrested three Deacons for possession of illegal weapons. Later in the day Joliff and the Deacons traveled the twenty miles to neighboring Centreville and staged a second march of approximately two hundred blacks. This time a white man emerged from a gas station along the march route and menaced the demonstrators with a rifle. In an instant, twenty-five Deacons pulled weapons—carbines, 30-30s, and pistols—and surrounded the bewildered white gunman, who retreated back into the gas station. Ferguson was philosophical about the confrontation. "It would have been my time or theirs."[84]

The Deacons' armed action at the march brought Charles Evers into the controversy. Evers arrived in Woodville the following day and addressed a gathering of one thousand blacks at a Methodist church. In typical high-handed fashion, he ordered an end to the marches and other demonstrations but promised that the boycott would continue. Deacons president Bilbo Ferguson later met with law enforcement officials to discuss the march incident. To mollify the police, the Deacons promised to dismiss members involved in the incident, but Ferguson never followed through with the dismissal. Five Deacons, including Earnest Tollivar, were later arrested on charges arising from the 4 September incident.[85]

Lenox Forman, district attorney for the Southwestern District of Mississippi, who witnessed the 4 September march, was perturbed by the spectacle of the openly armed Deacons walking the streets. Forman authorized the State Highway Patrol to confiscate the Deacons' firearms—a move reminiscent of Louisiana governor John McKeithen's attempt to disarm the Bogalusa Deacons. The NAACP protested the flagrant violation of the Second Amendment, pointing out that the highway patrol was disarming the Deacons but not whites. Confiscating the Deacons' weapons at the 4 September march was not difficult, but Forman had a problem carrying out his policy in the following months. The Woodville Deacons maintained strict secrecy, and law enforcement officials failed to learn the identity of all of the members. As a result, the State Highway Patrol began to indiscriminately confiscate the firearms of any blacks they encountered. Trampling on the Bill of Rights with impunity, Mississippi law enforcement agents arbitrarily stopped blacks in Wilkinson County—sportsmen and Deacons alike—and seized their weapons.[86]

Over the next several months the Deacons guarded NAACP meetings equipped with walkie-talkies and CB radios. "They wouldn't have no meeting without the Deacons," recalled Ferguson. Although the Woodville chapter performed admirably, its record was marred by two shooting incidents. At one Deacons meeting a young member of the chapter argued with Ed Caine, then drew a revolver and shot and wounded Caine. In a second incident Leon Chambers, a Woodville Deacon, was convicted of shooting a black deputy sheriff, Aaron Liberty. Although Gable McDonald, another Wilkinson County man, confessed to the crime, Chambers remained in prison for several years.[87]

In addition to strong chapters in Port Gibson, Natchez, and Woodville, Deacon groups and individual members were spread throughout Mississippi. The Bogalusa and Jonesboro chapters recruited most of these contacts during organizing sorties in Mississippi from 1965 to 1966. Recruiters visited Greenville, Poplarville, Canton, Jackson, Meridian, Tougaloo, Columbia, Hattiesburg, Lexington, Edwards, and Holmes County. Sometimes the Deacons merely advised local groups on how to set up their own security force. On other occasions they actually recruited members and established nominal chapters.[88]

Typical of Bogalusa's organizing efforts were its activities in Columbia,

Mississippi, located in Walthall County. After receiving several requests for assistance from Columbia, Royan Burris and Henry Austin, the Deacon who had shot the white man who attacked the march in Bogalusa, traveled to the Mississippi town—only an hour's drive from Bogalusa. The Columbia civil rights activists told Burris and Austin that the Freedom House had been damaged by arson; that whites drove by and fired shots into the house. "So we asked them, what was they doing, just sitting there letting people shoot at them," recalled Burris. "And they said, 'Well we don't have no other choice. If we shoot, the police arrest us.'" Burris had little patience for this rationale. He told the Columbia men, "If I can walk out there and slap you, and you not going to slap me back, then I'll slap you anytime I get ready. But if I figure I'm going to slap you, and I'm going to be slapped back, I'll be skeptical about it."[89]

Burris and Austin began guarding homes in Columbia and organizing a local chapter. To discourage the drive-by shootings without firing at the Klan, Austin worked with local men to booby-trap the road. They drove nails into wooden planks, attached ropes to the planks, and then placed them in the road. They waited three nights until a carload of Klansmen fell into the trap, which flattened all of their tires. The Klan never returned. The Deacons' guns had a chilling effect on the night riders too, said Burris. The Klan "found out that the same type of guns that they had could kill them—just like they would kill us."[90]

In addition to Mississippi, there were reports that the Bogalusa Deacons were recruiting individuals and forming chapters in Alabama. Clayborne Carson documents a chapter in Lowndes County, Alabama, a SNCC stronghold and the birthplace of the Lowndes County Black Panther Party, which became the namesake of Huey Newton's California-based organization. Charles Sims traveled to Eutaw, Alabama, a small city in Greene County, another SNCC base, and claimed to have established a chapter there. Henry Austin also visited the area. FBI reports give a different version of events, indicating that local blacks had deliberately spread a false rumor that the Deacons had organized a chapter as a form of "psychological retaliation to combat the parading and demonstrating of Klansmen in and around Greene County."[91]

The Deacons also organized in Tuskegee, Alabama, the site of the Tuskegee Institute. A local man sent a letter to Tuskegee residents soliciting membership in the Deacons organization. At least one meeting was held, but the extent of further organizing is unknown. CORE had several projects in the Carolinas, and the connection between CORE and the Deacons soon brought the Deacons to the Southeast. Deacons from Atlanta were sent to provide protection at a voter registration demonstration on 14 August 1965 at Plymouth, North Carolina. The Deacons offered their assistance again in September, but apparently their August visit had achieved the desired results.[92]

A militant movement in St. George, South Carolina, led to questions about the links between the Deacons and another shadowy self-defense group, the Saints of St. George. The FBI suspected that the Saints were "affiliated" with the Deacons but failed to uncover a link. There was also Deacons activity south of St. George in Jacksonboro. The leader of the Jacksonboro Deacons was Bobbie Cox, a longtime civil rights activist and military veteran. It appears that the activists in Walterboro, Jacksonboro, and neighboring towns coordinated defense activities in the region. In April 1966 fourteen black men claiming to be Deacons attacked and beat two Klansmen who were putting up posters for a Klan rally. One of the Klansmen was Kelly Morris, the owner of a local cafe. All of Morris's black employees had quit when Morris advertised that the profits from his cafe would go to the Klan. In addition, blacks and some local whites boycotted the restaurant. Morris's luck got even worse when he and the Klan subsequently parted ways and Morris himself became the target of a Klan cross burning.[93]

There were reports of Deacons' organizing efforts in several other states, including Georgia and Florida. At least one report indicates that there were Deacons in Atlanta, although these may have been members from other chapters visiting the city. The Deacons also claimed to have chapters in North Florida. An FBI investigation revealed that the Deacons had indeed stirred interest in the region. In July 1965 local blacks gave serious thought to forming a chapter in Jefferson and Madison Counties, but there is no evidence that the chapter ever existed.[94]

The Deacons' record in the Deep South was impressive. They developed several effective chapters and recruited hundreds of members. But more important than size was their influence on the grassroots movement. Like a single cottonwood tree whose thousands of seeds are carried aloft to distant lands, the Deacons' message traveled far and wide across the fertile crescent of the Black Belt. In 1965 Earnest Thomas and Charlie Sims seemed to be everywhere. They crisscrossed Louisiana, Mississippi, and Alabama, visiting scores of cities and spreading the gospel of self-defense. CORE organizer Ronnie Moore recalled that the Deacons were widely known in the region—by whites as well as blacks. "I think that the greater white community became afraid," said Moore. "You have to understand that the Klan in the

South had a free hand with no threat of retaliation in any organized fashion until the Deacons were announced. And just the thought that there might be a legitimate, or reactionary response to Klan activities made the white community afraid."[95]

The Deacons had neutralized the Klan in the South. Their next stop was the North.

Heading North

EARNEST THOMAS THOUGHT Elijah Muhammad was rude. In the spring of 1966 Muhammad, leader of the Black Muslim Nation of Islam, invited Thomas to his palatial home for several Sunday dinners. Thomas had become something of a celebrity in nationalist and leftist circles, and the Muslims were determined to recruit the Deacons leader. It was an impressive experience for Thomas: a bountiful meal in a luxurious setting, complete with famous dinner guests like Muhammad Ali. But one of Elijah Muhammad's habits annoyed Thomas. At their first dinner, the Muslim leader was fasting and did not join Thomas in eating. Thomas, the small-town southerner, was offended that Muhammad would not share the meal. When the guests finished their repast, Thomas told Muhammad that it made him "feel bad" to be eating while his host ate nothing. The next time Thomas was invited, Muhammad joined in the meal.[1]

But the food and flattery did little to win Thomas to Islam. When Muhammad finally asked him to join the Nation of Islam, Thomas said that the Muslims would only be gaining a hypocrite, not a convert. "I smoke, I drink, and I don't have any intention of quitting either of them," he told Muhammad. But Thomas had some trepidation about the Muslims, as well. He had heard the dark rumor that Fard Muhammad, Elijah Muhammad's mentor, had mysteriously disappeared and that some suspected foul play. The Deacons leader also objected to the Muslims' separatist political program. Thomas sought justice within America, not without. "I don't want no separate state," he told the Muslims. The Muslims also told Thomas that if he joined them, he would have to learn Arabic so that he could read the Koran. That was too much. "I can hardly speak English," said Thomas years later, "and they wanted me speaking Arabic."[2]

The incident was emblematic of a problem the Deacons would encounter in their forays into the North. They were an indigenous southern organization, steeped in rural southern folkways: pragmatic, independent, and stubborn. By 1966 they were resolute opponents of nonviolence and, compared to the national civil rights organizations, had a radically different approach to winning equality. But they were not ideologues or revolutionaries. They were simple hardworking men—barbers, mill hands, factory workers, church deacons—who wanted nothing more than equality and justice within the framework of the traditional American dream. Their pragmatism would confound their nationalist and leftist suitors, but it also shaped the Deacons' brief but extraordinary sortie into national politics and would take the organization from the mansions of Chicago to the streets of Peking.[3]

The Deacons initially went north for one reason—money. In their early stages, the organization derived most of its financial support from local sources: chapter fees, membership dues, and community contributions. It is impossible to determine the precise amount of the Deacons' income. Few chapters kept financial records, and most of the income was collected and controlled by Earnest Thomas and Charlie Sims, neither of whom kept records. Chapters did not closely monitor the treasury nor did they require receipts for reimbursements. Sims and Thomas casually disbursed cash for travel and other expenses.[4]

By the summer of 1965 both Sims and Thomas had become full-time organizers for the Deacons, and both felt justified in compensating themselves for their work with funds they had raised for the Deacons. Sims normally collected chapter fees himself, so he had wide discretion on how to use the money. Neither Sims nor Thomas grew rich off the Deacons, but their haphazard bookkeeping and indiscriminate spending raised questions about their motives and fueled rumors of self-aggrandizement.[5]

As the Deacons expanded and traveled extensively to assist local projects and recruit members, funding needs soon outstripped local support. National fund-raising not only represented a new source of revenue, but it also presented an important opportunity for the Deacons to publicize their unique approach and win political support. The first major contribution to the Deacons from outside of Louisiana came from a Los Angeles fund-raising effort headed up by black journalist Louis Lomax. Lomax raised $15,000 for the Bogalusa movement after Sims appeared on Lomax's Los Angeles television show in June 1965. Fifteen thousand dollars was a staggering windfall for a small organization like the Bogalusa Civic and Voters League and comparable to nearly two years' income for a mill worker. Although Lomax's contribution went directly to the Voters League, some of the funds underwrote the Deacons' activities as well (Charlie Sims was the league's treasurer).[6]

CORE organized most of the Deacons' fund-raising forays to the West Coast. In July 1965 it was Earnest Thomas's turn to tap California for support. By this time Thomas was billing himself as "Regional Vice-President and Director of Organization" for the Deacons for Defense and Justice, a self-appointed title that gave him autonomy from the Jonesboro chapter. Thomas arrived in San Francisco during the last week of July to raise funds and set up a "Friends of the Deacons" organization that would serve as a permanent fund-raising support group. He spoke at a CORE-sponsored reception in Berkeley on 24 July 1965 and at a rally at the Macedonia Baptist Church in San Francisco the following day. On 5 August he attended a reception at the Sun Reporter Newspaper Building to raise funds for bail for eighteen persons jailed in Jonesboro. The two-week trip also produced a sympathetic article in the *San Francisco Chronicle*: "Rights Army—The Angry 'Deacons.'" While in California, Thomas also met with Bobby Seale, a member of the Revolutionary Action Movement (RAM), who later helped found the Black Panther Party. Seale was impressed with Thomas and the Deacons and raised the possibility of forming a Deacons chapter in Los Angeles. Thomas let the subject drop, judging Seale to be too "radical" for the Deacons.[7]

The Deacons next turned their eyes north to Detroit. The Motor City had long been a center of black nationalist activity, dating back to the Marcus Garvey movement in the 1920s. Malcolm X had spent a great deal of time in Detroit, where his brother directed an important mosque for Elijah Muhammad's Nation of Islam. One of the most prominent black nationalist organizations in Detroit was the Group on Advanced Leadership (GOAL), led by Richard Henry, which had close ties to Malcolm X and other nationalists. Like most black nationalist groups, GOAL admired the Deacons for their willingness to challenge the nonviolent orthodoxy. "Birmingham shows . . . you just can't change the white man by letting him beat you over the head every day," said GOAL leader Reverend Albert B. Cleage in 1963. "I'm sick and tired of singing 'We Shall Overcome.'" Socialist as well as nationalist, GOAL charged that white liberal institutions controlled the mainstream black civil rights movement and were steering it to voter registration and desegregation and away from radical economic and political change.[8]

Like numerous southern communities, Bogalusa had lost many of its black citizens to the industrial behemoth of Detroit. In August 1965 former Bogalusa residents Clement Johnson, Melvina Dexter, and Dexter's wife arranged for GOAL to sponsor a "freedom dinner" in Detroit to honor Bob Hicks and raise funds for the Voters League. The league's attorneys had advised the league to maintain a clear distinction between its organization and the Deacons—although overlapping membership made the distinction a legal fiction. To comply with their attorneys' advice, Hicks attended the Detroit event as a representative of the Voters League and Charlie Sims attended as the Deacons' official spokesperson.

Hicks and Sims may have been regarded as "militants" in Bogalusa, but their self-defense rhetoric paled by comparison to the revolutionary fervor of their hosts in Detroit. GOAL leader Richard Henry, who would later head the separatist Republic of New Africa, told the audience of three hundred that violence was the only way "of 'letting Mr. Charlie' know that the black people were tired of being pushed around." As a sign of the changing attitudes toward nonviolence, Congressmen John Conyers and Charles Diggs both ascended the podium to praise the Deacons and defend the principle of self-defense, with Diggs observing that new situations called for "new techniques."[9]

Hicks and Sims sounded moderate themes of reconciliation and racial harmony. Sims told the audience that the "white man" respects three things: money, the vote, and force. The Deacons were going to fight until they had the "whole hog," since they were "backed up to the river and will drown or fight." The dinner raised $509 for the Voters League.[10]

Sims went on the road again in September 1965, this time with A. Z. Young, to attend a San Bernardino, California, fund-raiser for the Voters League. Their old supporter Louis Lomax had organized a "Freedom Festival" at the Swing Auditorium to benefit the Bogalusa movement and the "victims of Watts rioting." Lomax had recruited an impressive lineup of entertainers for the festival, including actor Dick Van Dyke and comedians Bill Cosby and Godfrey Cambridge.[11]

But plans began to unravel as the event drew near. Some of the festival's sponsors and stars withdrew at the last minute because, according to Lomax, the John Birch Society was applying "incredible pressure." The extremist right wing in San Bernardino was familiar with the Deacons: the city was home to the Reverend Connie Lynch, the racist leader who had spoken in Bogalusa at the height of civil rights activities in July 1965. Lomax and the festival promoters desperately fought to salvage the event in the face of mounting pressure. A. Z. Young appeared on local television and later spoke at a Unitarian church, where he was introduced as a member of the Deacons. Young tried to deflect the criticism that the funds raised by the event would help purchase guns and ammunition. He announced that contributions would go only for children's clothes and fines and bail for protesters. He told his television audience that the Klan was "on the way out" in Bogalusa. "They still ride, but now they are careful when they ride and where they ride." Despite Lomax's countermeasures, the right wing's campaign to discredit the Deacons in San Bernardino had considerable effect. A disappointingly small crowd of six hundred attended the festival, entertained by Dick Gregory, singer Sally Jones, and a handful of local groups.[12]

The Deacons also attracted financial and political support from an assortment of Marxist organizations, including the Communist Party USA, the Socialist Workers Party (SWP), the Workers World Party, and the Sparticist League. The more revolutionary of these groups, such as the Workers World Party and the Sparticists, admired the Deacons' use of armed violence and viewed the defense group as a harbinger of the coming revolution. It was not long before these leftist groups arrived in Bogalusa offering assistance and support.[13]

The Sparticist League, a small and highly disciplined Trotskyite faction, was the most radical of the predominantly white leftist groups courting the Deacons. The New Orleans Sparticist chapter arranged a meeting with Charlie Sims and Henry Austin in 1965. The young Marxists began the meeting by melodramatically pulling their guns from under their shirts and laying them on the table. Austin was not impressed. He thought the Sparticists went overboard with "a lot of flattery and praise that the Deacons were the vanguard of the coming revolution and this general kind of crap." Austin regarded the leftists as irresponsible dilettantes. "Their attitude was, regardless if it was necessary to have a bloodbath in Bogalusa, they wanted to start a revolution right then and there." The Sparticists offered to assist the Deacons with defense duties and provide them guns if necessary. Though Sims politely declined their offer to help with patrols, he was not one to turn down money. The Sparticists publicized the Deacons in their national paper and organized a "buy a bullet for the Deacons" fund-raising campaign that generated some contributions.[14]

The FBI suspected that the Sparticists had found an even more lucrative funding source for the Deacons: Fidel Castro. In the fall of 1965 an unidentified source contacted the FBI and charged that the Sparticists were financing the Deacons and speculated that Robert F. Williams was using the Sparticists to channel funds from the Cuban government to the Deacons. Williams had fled to Cuba following the Monroe, North Carolina, riot, and in 1962 he began to broadcast a radio program in Cuba entitled "Radio Free Dixie." The program was beamed to the United States and could be heard in many areas of the Deep South. Williams took to the airwaves preaching a doctrine of armed revolution to blacks in the South, so it was logical that the FBI suspected a relationship between the Cuban government and the Deacons. Although there was no evidence that the Cubans ever funded the organization, the Deacons' close ties to revolutionary black nationalists and white leftists continued to raise suspicions in the intelligence community.[15]

Another leftist ally and funder of the Deacons was the New York–based Workers World Party. The group viewed the Deacons as the political heirs of Robert F. Williams and the vanguard of a growing self-defense movement. The *Workers World* newspaper opined that the Deacons were a sign that despite "continuous propaganda of 'turn the other cheek' encouraged by the white ruling class, armed defense will be adopted by the black masses all over the U.S." When Henry Austin shot Alton Crowe in July 1965, *Workers World* praised Austin's actions as "commendable." "Henry Austin, his fellow Deacons for Defense and all who take up arms along with them deserve the respect and support of every honest friend of Black Freedom."[16]

The Deacons' connection to the Workers World Party introduced the Bogalusa chapter to the rarified world of left-wing politics in New York. In the fall of 1965 Workers World organized several New York fund-raising tours for the Deacons, featuring Charlie Sims and Bob Hicks. Workers World kicked off the project in September, operating under the auspices of the John Brown Commemoration Committee, with two fund-raising dances.[17]

In the same month the Deacons established a base in New York by creating a support organization, the Friends of the Deacons for Defense and Justice (FDDJ), housed at 271 West 125th Street. The FDDJ chapter was coordinated by Ricque LeSeur, a CORE member who had the title of "Special New York Assistant to Charles Sims." It was during these New York trips that Hicks and Sims made links to many black nationalists in Harlem, including Jesse Gray, Leroi Jones (Amiri Baraka), and Mae Mallory. Mallory, an African American woman, had become a notable on the left after she was arrested in the Monroe, North Carolina, riot that forced Robert F. Williams into exile. In New York, Mallory spoke at several rallies to help raise funds to purchase weapons for the Deacons.[18]

Foremost among the Deacons' new black nationalist suitors was the Revolutionary Action Movement. RAM had its roots in a loose confederation of revolutionary black nationalists that began forming in 1961 during a National Student Association (NSA) conference in Madison, Wisconsin—at the same meeting that gave birth to the premier white antiwar organization, the Students for a Democratic Society (SDS). At the conference, Donald Freeman, an African American student at Case Western Reserve College in Cleveland, met several other black students who shared his emerging militant and nationalist viewpoint, including Max Stanford, a student at Wilberforce College. The fledgling black nationalist network that emerged from the Madison meeting comprised young blacks radicalized by the civil rights movement in the South, as well as former members of the Nation of Islam and African nationalist organizations.[19]

In 1964 Freeman and Stanford joined forces with a Philadelphia black study group led by Stan Daniels and Playthell Benjamin and formed RAM. The secretive cadre posed itself as a radical alternative to the mainstream black civil rights movement. It published two periodicals, *Black America* and *RAM Speaks*, and worked with a wide range of black organizations, including Richard Henry's GOAL in Detroit and the Student Nonviolent Coordinating Committee (SNCC) in the South. Fusing nationalism and socialism, RAM became an openly Maoist communist organization devoted to overthrowing capitalism. The group adopted a twelve-point program, which included a call for rifle clubs and the creation of an underground vanguard.[20]

Robert F. Williams was an icon for the young nationalists, and, accordingly, RAM named him its first international chairman. Don Freeman became the executive chairman and Max Stanford the executive field director. Detroit radicals played a prominent role in the organization, with James Boggs serving as the ideological chairman and his wife, Grace Boggs, as executive secretary. In addition, Detroit GOAL leader Richard Henry, whom the Bogalusa Deacons had worked with, and his brother Milton Henry were both active in RAM.[21]

RAM's birth in 1964 coincided with several other watershed events in the development of the black nationalist movement. In March 1964 Malcolm X left the Nation of Islam and began forming a secular nationalist alternative, which gave impetus to nationalist organizing in general. In the same year Robert F. Williams published an influential article in RAM's *Crusader* entitled "Revolution without Violence." Williams departed from his previous position advocating self-defense and now argued for urban mass rebellions and guerrilla warfare. Among influential black activists and intellectuals, black nationalism had become a significant political challenge to the nonviolent and integrationist orthodoxy by 1964. Indeed, though historians often date the birth of the Black Power slogan as the 1966 Meredith March, in 1965 an umbrella group of militant organizations had already assumed the name "Organization for Black Power" and had convened a major national conference in Detroit.[22]

Black nationalists began a concerted effort to influence students in the civil rights movement as early as 1964. In the spring of 1964 RAM and the Black Liberation Front (BLF) sponsored the Afro-American Student Conference on Black Nationalism at Fisk University, Nashville. At the conference, RAM sharply criticized SNCC, CORE, and other mainstream nonviolent groups. But while the black nationalists were publicly attacking the non-violent movement, RAM was simultaneously infiltrating CORE and SNCC to set up armed self-defense projects and win recruits to the nationalist movement. As a result of their factionalizing inside CORE and SNCC, RAM seriously antagonized black-white relations within the groups.[23]

RAM's attempt to import self-defense groups to the South was not unique. In March 1964 Malcolm X had issued a call for blacks to form "Negro rifle clubs" to resist racist attacks, proclaiming that the black man should "fight back whenever and wherever he is being unjustly and unlawfully attacked." Malcolm's clarion call went unheeded with one notable exception. When a white clergyman was crushed by a bulldozer in a civil rights protest in Cleveland, the tragedy sparked the development of the Medgar Evers Rifle Club in Cleveland, led by a local black housing inspector, Louis Robinson. In July 1964 Malcolm X, growing impatient with the lack of response to his call for rifle clubs, publicly offered to provide defense for Martin Luther King and James Farmer in Mississippi during the Freedom Summer. Following Malcolm X's lead, RAM publicly called for northern blacks to form an army of rifle clubs to defend blacks in the South in the coming "civil war." Richard Henry took to the airwaves in the summer of 1964, calling for the "formation of rifle clubs by Negroes all across the North." The rifle clubs were critical, according to Henry, because blacks in the South "will very shortly begin guerrilla warfare against white terrorists" and "white bigots will react by slaughtering wholesale, helpless Negroes—men, women and children." Ironically, with all their political sophistication and experience, RAM, Robert F. Williams, and Malcolm X all foundered in their efforts to develop a broad self-defense organization in the Deep South, while a handful of working-class black men in Jonesboro found the Holy Grail.[24]

RAM saw great promise in the Deacons. The Marxist organization believed that black rifle clubs would provide the infrastructure for a revolutionary army, and it was determined to recruit the Deacons to its brand of revolutionary nationalism. But the black nationalists would have no more success converting the Deacons than had the New York white leftists. "They were very unpolitical," complained Virginia Collins, a RAM member and a lifelong Garveyite nationalist from New Orleans. Collins, the only female RAM member in the South, met with the Deacons in Jonesboro and Bogalusa but had little luck in moving them toward black nationalism. She found them independent, stubborn, and unwilling to advance beyond their political views. And, according to Collins, the Deacons were beset with the attitude that "women can't tell you nothing." When Collins abandoned her plan to recruit the Deacons, national RAM officials implored her to renew her effort; they were confident that the Deacons could be "politicized" to a revolutionary viewpoint. "If you think so," Collins responded curtly, "then you politicize them." RAM eventually gave up on the Deacons; in truth, they never had a chance of winning the pragmatic group to revolution. "I'm not a left winger," Thomas once said. "I'm just a capitalist that don't have a damn thing."[25]

In addition to fund-raising, Thomas and Sims attempted to build Deacons chapters in the North, working through contacts they had made with revolutionary groups and black nationalists. For the most part, the northern organizing was not coordinated between the Jonesboro and Bogalusa chapters. Thomas organized when and where he pleased, regardless of Sims's wishes, and even independent of the Jonesboro chapter—much to its consternation.

The North proved inhospitable terrain for the Deacons. A short-lived Boston chapter was formed in August 1965, controlled by the Boston Action Group (BAG), a local organization with links to the Maoist-Communist Progressive Labor Party. A chapter was also established in Cleveland, in 1965, with local activist Harlell Jones serving as spokesperson, once again linked to RAM. It appears that RAM attempted to organize a Deacons chapter in Philadelphia in 1966—with Charlie Sims's blessing, but it came to nothing. Similarly, in the spring of 1966 Thomas was also pursuing a chapter in Washington, D.C., this time through local militant activist Julius Hobson.[26]

Chicago became the Deacons' strongest foothold in the North. On 15 October 1965 the *Chicago Daily News* carried a story that gave the first warning that the Deacons were heading north. "Militant Negroes Here Forming Armed Unit to Fight the Klan" announced the headline of a story based on an interview with Earnest Thomas. News reports in preceding days had detailed the resurgence of the Klan in nearby Indiana and Wisconsin, and Thomas was pointing to the renewed Klan activity as justification for the Deacons' expansion northward.[27]

"We believe there are Klansmen active in this city and we're confident they have thousands of sympathizers," Thomas told the *Daily News*. His claim of a mounting Klan resurgence was met with considerable skepticism by blacks and whites alike. Chicago had its share of racists, as the response to Martin Luther King's campaign would soon demonstrate, but the Windy City's most violent racists were more likely to wear a badge than a sheet. Racism in the North manifested itself in police brutality and discrimination, but seldom as vigilante violence. Thomas was still struggling to transform the Deacons from an essentially southern black self-defense organization into a militant nationwide organization. He clearly had no ideological blueprint, but, like scores of other militant leaders following the Watts riot, he knew that he could not successfully organize in the North with a strategy based on non-violence, civil rights, and a legislative coalition with white liberals. Bobby Seale and Huey Newton were moving in the same direction on the West Coast, as were the Henry Brothers in Detroit and the Associated Community Teams (ACT) group, an umbrella organization of militants from around the nation. But the challenge facing the Deacons was substantial: the urban ghettos of the North were a different world from Jonesboro and Bogalusa. "Watts wasn't suffering from segregation, or the lack of official rights," said one participant in the Watts riot. "You didn't have two drinking water fountains." When Lyndon Johnson signed the 1964 Civil Rights Act, the participant added, "nobody even thought about it in Watts. . . . It had nothing to do with us."[28]

In Chicago the Deacons focused on issues of self-defense against police brutality and opposition to political corruption. Thomas told the *Daily News* that the Deacons would also "operate freedom patrols" that would "be alert for police brutality against Negroes"—a tactic that the Black Panthers eventually adopted. In addition, they would "campaign against shady deals that are often pulled off on us Negroes." Thomas emphasized that the Deacons were law-abiding and peaceful. "We don't teach hatred."[29]

Following months of futile attempts by the Deacons to fit their philosophy into the Procrustean bed of nonviolence, Thomas's opening salvo in Chicago marked a turning point in the Deacons' political thinking. Evoking the spirit of Malcolm X, Thomas bluntly criticized Martin Luther King and the nonviolent orthodoxy. "Talk doesn't solve anything," scoffed Thomas. "We Negroes are not going to gain our freedom by talking. We Negroes can't continue to let the Klan and similar hate groups trample on us." He speculated that the difference between him and King was the difference between local and national organizing. "King and I really live in two different worlds," said Thomas.[30]

Chicago's black press had supported the Deacons' actions in the South but now balked at the idea of importing an armed black movement to Chicago. The respected *Chicago Defender* sharply rebuked the Deacons, ridiculing the idea that the Klan posed a threat in the city. "I don't know these fellows or anything about their activities," Timuel Black of the Negro American Labor Council told the *Defender*. "We don't run with this kind of people." The Reverend Lynward Stevenson, militant president of the Woodlawn Organization, dismissed the Deacons as vigilantes who were ignorant about democratic politics. The Deacons only "know how to get rid of the Klan," Stevenson asserted. "They don't know anything about law and order and the ordinary ways of achieving justice."[31]

The hostile reception by the black political establishment did not alter Thomas's plans. During his October visit he appeared on two black radio programs: the Lou House Show and—along with Nahaz Rogers, who eventually became a leader in the Chicago Deacons chapter—the Wesley South Show on WVON radio. On the WVON program, Thomas boasted that he could bring ten thousand Deacons to Chicago to confront the Klan. Listeners were dubious. Some callers challenged his assertion that the Klan was a menace in Chicago; others chided him for professing that he had ten thousand Deacons at his disposal. Grasping for a role in the North, Thomas suggested that the Deacons could protect demonstrators from attacks by police, as the Deacons had done in the South. Chicagoans were not convinced.[32]

Though the radio interview went poorly for Thomas, he did give a coherent explication of the Deacons' critique of nonviolence, which had been evolving over the last year. He told listeners that many civil rights organizations were training blacks into submission. In contrast, the Deacons instilled manhood in black men—a quality missing in most blacks "over the age of twenty-one." Manhood depended on the willingness to protect oneself. For Thomas, the Deacons' philosophy was clear: Freedom for black men depended on manhood, and manhood meant the willingness to use force to defend one's family and community. Black men could not attain manhood through the strategy of nonviolence, since nonviolence prohibited the use of force. And without manhood status, rights were meaningless. For black men to be free, whites had to fear as well as respect them.[33]

On Sunday, 24 October, the Deacons for the first time engaged the partisans of nonviolence in public debate. The West Side Organization (WSO), a Chicago black activist organization, invited Thomas and Nahaz Rogers to participate in a discussion of "Non-violence vs. Self-Defense." Their opponents were two of the ablest representatives of the Southern Christian Leadership Conference (SCLC), the Reverend C. T. Vivian and James Bevel. In many respects, Thomas and Rogers were badly mismatched in the WSO debate. Vivian and Bevel were brilliant, eloquent, and formally educated. Thomas had a sharp mind, but he was hardly a polished orator of Vivian's caliber. Rogers, like Thomas, was intellectually nimble but lacked the erudition of his opponents.[34]

Thomas suspected that the debate was part of an effort by Martin Luther King to discredit the Deacons before they could get a foothold in Chicago. In the fall of 1965 King was taking his first steps toward organizing in Chicago, and Thomas believed that "the man"—the white political establishment— had anointed King leader of the movement in the North. "Well they was trying to ostracize me," charged Thomas years later. "You know, King and them was moving into Chicago. I don't know why he was moving into Chicago, but he was moving in and they had the blessing of the man."[35]

Thomas and Rogers had a sympathetic urban audience at the debate. In the wake of the Watts riot, SCLC would have had a difficult time selling nonviolence to any northern black audience. Thomas thought that he fared well. "They brought their best speaker, and that's Vivian," he recalled. "And this little country boy, they was going to eat me alive. But they made a mistake. The audience was more with me." The Deacons could be reasonably criticized on many issues, but SCLC had challenged them on their strongest point: the right of blacks to defend themselves against violent attacks. "They couldn't shoot a hole in that, because everyone had a right to protect home and family," said Thomas. "They never tried that again."[36]

During his speaking tour of Chicago, Thomas met Edward "Fats" Crawford and Claudell Kirk, two local activists who began assisting Thomas in quietly recruiting members for a Chicago Deacons chapter. Crawford, a seasoned community activist who was heavily involved in Chicago electoral politics, would eventually become the primary driving force for the new chapter. But it was several months before Thomas galvanized the Chicago chapter. In the interim, he continued to publicize the Deacons in the North through speaking events in the Chicago and Detroit areas. In the same way that the Workers World Party had adopted Charlie Sims and the Bogalusa Deacons in New York, white leftists in the Midwest became patrons of Thomas. The Socialist Workers Party, another Trotskyite Marxist organization, assiduously courted Thomas, inviting him to speak at several forums. On 18 February 1966 Thomas was the featured speaker at the "Friday Night Socialist Forum" in Chicago. The Deacons had over five hundred armed members and sixty-two chapters, Thomas told the audience, and the new Chicago chapter would become the regional headquarters of the North. Reflecting his leftward shift, Thomas laced his speech with a class analysis of black problems, arguing that the social welfare legislation of the Great Society was a ploy by the rich to perpetuate their own power. For him, the problem was no longer a few Klansmen, but rather the entire American ruling class.[37]

The nonviolent movement's reliance on direct action was a diversion from effective change, Thomas told his audience. Civil rights demonstrations were a "game" and antipoverty legislation had been enacted to placate black people. The only people benefiting from reform legislation were "fat politicians." "They get the cream while the masses get the non-fat milk."[38]

Thomas ridiculed the idea that education would bring economic equality—another deception of the nonviolent strategy, he charged. Racial discrimination was the culprit, not the lack of skills. But inequality had its price.

Thomas predicted a "black revolution" in Chicago during the coming summer that would make it unsafe for whites to travel in black neighborhoods. He was no longer talking self-defense; at one point in his address Thomas warned that for every Deacon killed, the Deacons would respond by killing three whites. Turning to foreign policy, he criticized the U.S. role in Vietnam, pointing out that a high percentage of soldiers in Vietnam were black and hinting at a genocidal plot. "I guess the power structure feels if they can kill off seven or eight million of us that will solve the problem."[39]

Two months later, as part of his tour to raise funds for a Chicago Deacons chapter, Thomas spoke at another SWP forum in Detroit. Here he laid out plans to make Chicago the training center for a Deacons organization that would have chapters in every major northern city by the summer of 1966. Similar to his performance at the Chicago forum, Thomas departed from the "self-defense" rhetoric and ominously hinted that the Deacons would retaliate against FBI or CIA informants in the organization.[40]

The Detroit speech marked the end of Thomas's short relationship with the SWP. The socialists had asked to see his comments before he spoke in Detroit—a thinly veiled effort to censor his remarks. Thomas balked at the attempt to muzzle him. "I told them my speech is in my head," recalled Thomas. And even if he could produce written remarks, his new socialist friends should not expect him to share their views. He had made his point. "I never had an invitation from them again," said Thomas.[41]

By April 1966 Thomas had yet to establish a Chicago chapter, and he soon found himself competing with the Bogalusa chapter in efforts to organize in Chicago. Thomas had isolated himself from the Louisiana chapters when he severed relations with Jonesboro and anointed himself "Vice-President and Regional Organizer" for the Deacons. The leaders of the Jonesboro Deacons were too conservative for his growing radical tastes, and he wanted the latitude to organize his own chapters in the North without interference from Jonesboro or Bogalusa. But his decision to strike out on his own antagonized relations with both chapters. Soon the Bogalusa Deacons were on their way to Chicago to test the waters themselves. In April 1966 Charlie Sims, Sam Barnes, and A. Z. Young held a press conference at the Chicago home of Lavernon Cornelius, a Bogalusa native. Cornelius announced that the Deacons had been clandestinely recruiting for six months and had established a Chicago chapter at the request of the Olive Branch Masonic Lodge of the Prince Hall Masons (Cornelius served as Grand Master of the branch). Cornelius was joined by Ray McCoy, a wealthy Chicago funeral home owner and also a native of the Bogalusa area. Cornelius said that Chicago needed "a Negro Group that believed in defense and justice at any price." The Deacons were "primed to fight a war to protect Negro rights." He noted that "only last week a cross was burned on a lawn in Waukegan. There's no doubt that we need a chapter here." Cornelius also suggested that the Deacons might provide defense at polling places.[42]

But things began to quickly unravel for the Bogalusa group. Whereas Cornelius clearly stated that the Deacons would conduct armed activities in Chicago, Hicks and Young later characterized the Chicago chapter as merely a support group for the southern movement. On 6 April the *Chicago Daily News* published a second article on the Deacons, bearing the headline, "Not Trying to Start Movement in North" and "Negro Vigilantes Here Will Aid Dixie Fight." Sims reportedly told the *Daily News* that the Deacons were only establishing a branch "to help in the struggle in the South. . . . We're not trying to come up here and start a movement." Young said that they hoped to raise money for the defense of ninety children and six adults arrested the previous fall; he also mentioned that the Bogalusa group was seeking support for a 105-mile march to Baton Rouge. "We're going to clean up the whole state of Louisiana. The whole state is out of line."[43]

The Chicago press conference underscored the growing schism between Thomas and the Bogalusa Deacons. As Thomas inclined to black nationalism, his Bogalusa cohorts remained pragmatists. Whereas Thomas openly vilified Martin Luther King, Young crafted a more moderate image for the Deacons, one in which the defense group complemented the civil rights movement. In Chicago, Young went to great lengths to affirm the Deacons' loyalty to the nonviolent movement and to extend an olive branch to King. His group wanted to confer with the SCLC leader and "ask his support in our struggle in Bogalusa." According to Young, "King has been misled about Deacons and the Voters League in Bogalusa. The Bogalusa Voters League is non-violent, just like Dr. King's organization. And the Deacons are nonviolent—up to a point." Emphasizing the Deacons' peaceful objectives, Charlie Sims suggested that the Chicago chapter might get involved in voter registration and could endorse Dick Gregory, who was planning a run for mayor. "We're a defensive organization, organized to defend people," Sims emphasized. "We have a constitutional right to defend our home, our children's lives. In the South the [white] man is making us pick up arms in order to live. . . . While the Northern Negro can use ballots instead of bullets, there's a need for Deacons anywhere in the country where black men exist."[44]

The Chicago press conference and subsequent rally backfired on the Deacons and created more controversy than benefits. Election officials publicly protested against the Deacons' announcement that they planned to provide armed guards at polling places. Oscar Stanton DePriest, Grand Master of the

Prince Hall Masons, disputed Lavernon Cornelius's claim that the Masons had requested the Deacons to form a Chicago chapter. DePriest ordered a "sweeping investigation" of the Olive Branch Masonic Lodge and ordered Cornelius to "cease and desist" any activity connected with the Deacons. Masonic leaders also canceled a planned financial contribution to the Deacons. The Bogalusa group had failed to form their Chicago chapter. A. Z. Young found the experience discouraging. "I raised more money in San Francisco when I was there by myself than we have been able to scrape up here," he complained afterward.[45]

One month after the Bogalusa chapter's abortive organizing effort, Thomas appeared on the pages of *Newsweek* touting plans for a Chicago chapter. He did not hesitate to berate Martin Luther King's efforts to import his nonviolent strategy to Chicago. "I don't see where in hell nonviolence is going to solve anything," Thomas declared. "When you deal with the beast, you better deal with him appropriately." Thomas punctuated his attack on nonviolence with a call for blacks to arm themselves. "The black man is a fool if he doesn't have a gun or two—and ammunition in abundance." The Watts riot in Los Angeles was an argument for more violence rather than less. "Throwing bricks is going out of style," said Thomas. "Thirty black people and only four whites died in Los Angeles [in the riots]. We've learned from that—it won't happen again."[46]

Newsweek questioned how successful the Deacons' anti-Klan strategy would be in Chicago, given that "racial discrimination there goes in many guises, but bed sheets are not among them." Exhibiting the same ambiguity that undermined the Bogalusa chapter's foray into the North, Thomas insisted that the Chicago chapter would primarily support the movement in the South, through fund-raising and—a new twist—bringing blacks, instead of whites, into the South. He picked Chicago because the Deacons could raise money for southern operations through initiation fees of ten dollars, membership dues of two dollars a month, and selling "Friends of the Deacons" bumper stickers for fifty cents. But he intimated that the Deacons might get involved in armed actions as well. "Chicago is no different from anywhere else," said Thomas. "The Southern red-neck lets you know where he's at. The Northern red-neck is a little smarter; but they are still exploiting my people." Echoing Malcolm X's famous dictum, he added, "I believe in freedom by any means necessary."[47]

The Chicago chapter began to take form, and in May 1966 Thomas officially opened a Deacons for Defense and Justice office at 1230 Pulaski on the West Side. Thomas, who was now living in Chicago, served as president, Fats Crawford as vice president, and Claudell Kirk as secretary. The first public appearance of the Chicago chapter was on 23 May, when Thomas appeared for a second time on Wesley South's radio program. During the interview Thomas made a series of claims that tested the credulity of his black listeners. He claimed that 455 members had already joined the Chicago chapter since he began recruitment in October 1965, and that the Deacons now had sixty-seven chapters nationwide. Thomas also bragged that he was taking 2,000 Deacons to Washington, D.C., for the June demonstration protesting the White House Conference on Civil Rights (in fact, no Deacons attended the demonstration). He followed up with the dubious claim that he was summoning 15,000 Deacons to Chicago in the next three months. The hyperbole only prompted black listeners to call in and openly deride his obvious exaggerations.[48]

During the summer of 1966 the Pulaski Street headquarters began to come to life, taking on the trappings of northern militants such as the emerging Black Panther Party. The storefront window featured a rifle balancing the scales of justice. Some of the Deacons donned berets like the Panthers, and the local chapter offered free training in martial arts. Comprising ten to fifteen active members, the Chicago chapter attempted to establish offices in surrounding communities, including Harvey and Evanston. The FBI kept a close watch on the Chicago chapter, and when a small riot erupted on 4 August in nearby Harvey, the bureau suspected that the Deacons had supplied weapons to youths involved in the shooting, though there was no evidence that they had done so.[49]

The Chicago chapter did not restrict its activities to support of the southern movement, as Thomas had promised, but also got involved in local black issues. In August 1966 a Chicago court issued an injunction preventing Martin Luther King and SCLC from marching through the volatile white neighborhoods of Gage Park and Cicero. In response, the Deacons and several other militant groups threatened to defy the order and march. A planned march on 28 August through Cicero, a racist stronghold, particularly troubled law enforcement officials because of the potential for violent attacks by whites and retaliation by blacks. Rumors spread that young blacks were practicing with weapons in preparation for the protest. But when King acceded to the injunction and pledged a moratorium on the marches, SCLC condemned the militants' plan for the Cicero march. In the end, the protest failed to materialize.[50]

The Chicago chapter's relationship with King was cloaked in mystery. Beginning in July 1966, the Chicago Deacons, led by John Harris and Fats Crawford, provided security for King at speaking events in Chicago and when King traveled in the South. Harris later said that King's lieutenants were divided over the role of the Deacons, with Jesse Jackson adamantly opposed to any contact between King and the Deacons. In the end, King acquiesced on the condition that his new bodyguards would not be publicly identified as Deacons. Fats Crawford and the Deacons, working through intermediaries like activist Bennett Johnson, contrived to provide inconspicuous security for King through 1968.[51]

By the fall of 1966 Thomas had returned to his family in Jonesboro, leaving the Chicago chapter to the leadership of Crawford. The chapter allied itself with a host of emerging Black Power groups that formed the Community Coalition for Black Power (CCBP). The CCBP linked the Deacons with a broad range of groups: radicalized Chicago chapters of CORE and SNCC; Lawrence Landry and Nahaz Rogers of ACT; the W. E. B. Du Bois Club; activists like Monroe Sharp; and members of the two major youth gangs, the Blackstone Rangers and the Vicelords. Through the CCBP, the Deacons became involved in several community protests with mixed success.[52]

The chapter encountered some police harassment. In one incident the Deacons accused the Chicago police of shooting out the front window of their Pulaski Street office. Some of the chapter's activities skirted the boundaries of the law, especially in the area of fund-raising. White businesses on the West Side, desiring good relations with the militants, supplied a significant portion of the Deacons' funds. In the process of soliciting funds from businesses, the Deacons walked a thin line between fund-raising and extortion. At least one local business accused them of extorting money, though no charges were filed. The Deacons became involved in another controversial incident in nearby Gary, Indiana. Richard Hatcher, a black political leader, was running for mayor when another black candidate with the same name placed his name on the ballot. It was an obvious attempt to confuse voters and take votes from Hatcher. The Chicago Deacons were called in to assist. What they did in Gary remains a mystery. All that is certain is that the second candidate withdrew his name from the ballot, complaining that he had been "coerced" by unnamed parties.[53]

The Chicago chapter's dilemma was the same one that vexed all of the Deacons chapters in the North. The Deacons' call for manhood through physical courage in the face of Klan terror had little appeal in the North, where African Americans were relatively free from vigilante violence. Given their origins in the civil rights movement, the Deacons had framed their politics in the language of rights and liberties—not issues that resonated in the North. Moreover, unlike the Black Panthers, the Deacons did not project a revolutionary image that could attract militant young blacks. Even with the adjustments made to adapt to the concerns of northern blacks, the

Deacons' mix of self-defense rhetoric, community organizing, and racial pride could not compete with the Panthers' romantic revolutionary image and distinctive reputation as opponents of police abuse.

The Deacons' venture into the North had failed. They had experimented with a variety of issues—police brutality, economic discrimination, electoral politics, and humanitarian and political aid for southern blacks. But none of the approaches struck a chord with northern blacks. Meanwhile, black militants were flocking to the Black Panthers and other Black Power organizations that projected far more confrontational images.

The Deacons' emphasis on the right of self-defense was both their strength and their weakness. While it provided credibility in the South, where the foe was vigilante violence, it failed in the North, where racial domination and violence were cloaked in the legitimacy of state authority. The Deacons' program rested on a belief in constitutional rights (obedience to federal law and authority) rather than revolutionary rights (the right to disobey law and authority). The latter path, taken by the Panthers, had its own perils.

CHAPTER

13

Black Power—Last Days

BY 1967 THE Bogalusa movement looked nothing like it did in January 1965, when it conducted peaceful and polite desegregation tests. Something had changed. On 24 July 1967 A. Z. Young led a group from Bogalusa to the Washington Parish Courthouse in Franklinton, Louisiana, in a protest against continuing inequality and racism. Instead of the pious and reserved James Farmer, who had led several of the marches in the past, this time CORE was represented by militant Black Power advocate Lincoln Lynch. "There's a new movement afoot," Lynch told the rally audience, "it's not civil rights any longer—it's the movement of revolution. . . . Some call it black power, others may call it the black revolution, but it's all the same. If those rednecks in Bogalusa won't hire you, don't picket at their stores anymore, run them out of your neighborhood. The days of black people clapping their hands and singing are over and many of you are going to be asked to kill for freedom—and you'd better be ready to kill."[1]

Young echoed Lynch's revolutionary theme. Referring to the recent release of two white men who had killed a Bogalusa black man, Young told the rally, "There's a penalty for killing birds out of season, but there is never any penalty for killing a Negro—there has never been a white man convicted for killing a Negro in the history of Washington Parish." Young was going to see Governor John McKeithen about the situation. If he did not get any results, "Get Ready, LBJ, to open those pearly gates. They talk about Watts and the burning—everything will burn in the state of Louisiana," shouted Young to an ecstatic crowd. "Burn, Burn, Burn." It was shocking rhetoric from a man who only a year before had assured the media that the "Bogalusa Voters League is non-violent, just like Dr. King's organization." And it was rhetoric that would permeate the work of the Voters League and the Deacons in their final days. Something had changed, indeed, and that change was the Watts riot.[2]

The Los Angeles Watts riot erupted on 11 August 1965, just days after the Voting Rights Acts went into effect. The rebellion permanently changed racial politics in America—and profoundly impacted the work of the Deacons. Watts transformed black political consciousness unlike any event in modern history. For the first time in the twentieth century, racial politics were explicitly shaped by the threat of black civil violence. More than thirty thousand people participated in the riot. They picked their targets selectively, sparing schools, churches, and public buildings, prompting Bayard Rustin to observe that Watts "marked the first major rebellion of Negroes against their own masochism." Watts would dramatically affect the movement in Bogalusa, as Bogalusa had affected Watts. Journalists reported that as the rioters pelted motorists and firemen with rocks, they were shouting, "This is for Bogalusa!"[3]

Of the Watts residents who did not directly participate in the rebellion, the majority sympathized with the rioters and viewed their actions as a political protest. The plight of the urban working class and poor had finally come to the forefront. "We won because we made the whole world pay attention to us," a rioter jubilantly proclaimed. "We made them come." As one writer observed: "The boost that the events of Watts gave to the sense of community, to black stature in the era of black assertion, to black self-esteem was surely enormous. The world had noticed Watts and, in ghettoes throughout the land, other blacks stood up and demanded to be noticed too." The quest for honor and respect was at the heart of the rebellion. "They couldn't call me boy anymore," said another rioter proudly. "I was respected as a man."[4]

Watts shifted the black freedom movement agenda from a campaign for civil and political equality to a focus on economic parity and community empowerment. By 1965 the civil rights movement's singular obsession with civil equality had become an albatross around the neck of the broader freedom movement. The strategy suggested that civil discrimination was the primary cause for racial economic inequality, an argument that conservatives would later exploit in their battle against affirmative action and other compensatory programs. Nothing in the civil rights strategy explained the legacy of racism, nor did it even hint that enormous educational and economic resources would have to be marshaled to reverse the effects of three centuries of oppression. To many African Americans captivated by the events in Watts, organizations identified with the old civil rights agenda seemed hopelessly outmoded. Martin Luther King encountered a hostile reception when he traveled west to help mediate the crisis. As he drove into Watts, one onlooker jeered King: "I had a dream, I had a dream—hell, we don't need no damn dreams. We want jobs."[5]

With these shortcomings, how then did nonviolence become the official movement doctrine? African Americans in the South had never been disposed to pacifism: even James Lawson, one of the foremost advocates of nonviolence, admitted that there "never was an acceptance of the nonviolent approach" in the South. The answer is that, in good part, northern liberals, pacifists, and leftists managed to impose nonviolence on the movement because they possessed superior organizational and funding resources. Nonviolence was also the natural outcome of an organizing strategy that centered on the rural South, where traditional movement leaders were more economically vulnerable and cautious than their northern counterparts. Until 1955, the black freedom movement had pursued campaigns both rural and urban, North and South. Its greatest organizational accomplishment was A. Phillip Randolph's threatened march on Washington during World War II, which aimed to draw on black organized labor in the North and which produced significant concessions on the part of the federal government. Yet the movement strategy came to focus on the South in the 1950s and 1960s. Its rebirth in Montgomery in 1955, with the city's large college-educated sector—uncharacteristic of the rest of the South—meant that the movement was midwifed by the black middle class, with its genteel aspirations, meritocratic beliefs, and indifference to the political and psychological tasks of transforming black men in the working class and rural agricultural regions.[6]

Some spontaneous organizing in the South was beyond the control of movement organizations and prompted by the exigencies imposed by Jim Crow, as, for example, the Montgomery Bus Boycott and the lunch counter sit-ins. But the key organizing initiatives after 1960—Freedom Rides, desegregation campaigns, and voter registration—were part of a calculated strategy to make the South the battleground of the black freedom movement—and, in the case of the Student Nonviolent Coordinating Committee (SNCC) and CORE, especially the rural South. There was a powerful logic to the choice. Civil inequality was statutory in the South, and the white majority was determined to violently defend its privileged position. What better way to move public opinion and Congress than to confront racism in its most naked form?

But there were substantial obstacles to building a black freedom movement. Rural African Americans lacked the education and economic independence of their northern counterparts. Indeed, no successful reform movement in the United States began by organizing its most impoverished, economically dependent, and educationally deprived constituency. The 1930s organized labor movement—the other great social movement of the twentieth century—established its beachhead where its constituency was strongest. The militant Congress of Industrial Organizations (CIO) chose Flint and Detroit, Michigan, to stage their successful sit-down strikes.

Although the South presented formidable obstacles to creating self-sustaining movement, it did offer something that movement strategists came to value: a stage where protest would provoke the latent violence that propped up the caste system. This racist violence, in the age of television, had the potential to embarrass the United States in the Cold War, win sympathy from northern liberals, and eventually galvanize a national legislative coalition that could secure federal intervention or legislation on behalf of black equality.

For these media images of violence to be effective, it was critical that the black victims remain passive and not exhibit behaviors that would evoke white stereotypes of black impulsiveness and violence—or cause observers to confuse perpetrators for victims. Michael Clurman, a veteran of three summer projects—in both SNCC and CORE—described the strategy succinctly: Nonviolence was ideal for the civil rights movement because, more than any other struggle for freedom, the movement depended "a great deal on the action of the federal government, which in turn depends on white northern public opinion," Clurman told an interviewer in 1965. And northern opinion "has to be won by showing that in every instance not only that the Negroes are right, but that they're absolutely right, and that all the right-doers are on one side and all the wrong-doers are on another side."[7]

This kind of political theater could not have succeeded in the urban North, where African Americans were economically independent and had a stronger tradition of self-defense and combativeness. The agrarian South was more hospitable terrain, with its small, isolated black populations and a host of police and vigilantes who historically acted with impunity. And so the stage was set. The drama went as planned, and the guilt and pity followed as predicted, but not without detrimental consequences. However necessary it may have been to shape the national legislative agenda, the political theater of nonviolence did not bring about the profound changes in psychology and political consciousness that were the precondition of meaningful black freedom: changes in identity and perceptions for both blacks and whites.

Moreover, nonviolence's singular focus on Jim Crow in the South deflected national attention from economic and social forces that reproduced inequality and racism—for example, discrimination in employment, housing, and education—as well as less visible but more insidious forms of institutional and cultural racism. Nonviolence equated racism with civil and political discrimination, the two more obvious forms of racism in the South. For the southern black middle class, lifting these civil and political barriers did, in fact, remove most of their obstacles to equality. Even Martin Luther King recognized the class bias of his own strategy. Evaluating the successes in public accommodations and the vote, King later lamented that "we must face the fact that progress has been limited mainly to the Negro middle class." Blacks had "gotten great new job opportunities in this country" but "they have applied mainly to the Negro middle class." What is more, King added, "the great problem we face today is that the economic plight of the Negro poor is worse today than before." For poor and working-class blacks, the legacy of slavery would require solutions far more substantial than a stool at the lunch counter.[8]

The Watts riot had been a black working-class referendum on nonviolence and the civil rights strategy—and King had lost decisively. Hundreds of thousands of African American men and women who had refused to participate in the nonviolent movement finally found a strategy that they believed could compel reforms. The Watts rebellion infused a new militancy in young African Americans, and that militancy soon found its way to Bogalusa.

The Deacons' vigorous organizing and fund-raising efforts across the nation had paid dividends for the group, but the movements in Bogalusa and Jonesboro were still their paramount concern. The Bogalusa campaign in the summer of 1965 had been a key test of the federal government's commitment to free speech, equal treatment, and an end to vigilante racist terror on a mass scale in the South. The Deacons could say, with deserving pride, that they had played a key role in compelling Washington to restore the Constitution in the Deep South. But by the fall of 1965 the Deacons were becoming victims of their own success in Bogalusa. They had popularized attitudes that gave birth to a new assertive and uncompromising black identity—one that elicited both fear and grudging respect from whites. As community people internalized the Deacons' values of courage, pride, and self-reliance, the community became more willing to defend itself—and the Deacons became less necessary.

In the fall of 1965 young blacks began to assert their authority over the movement in Bogalusa, impatient to "take it to the streets" and do battle directly with town officials. In October several hundred students boycotted classes and marched to the annual Washington Parish Fair. The students were protesting a school policy that released white students from classes for three days to attend the fair, while black students were given only one day. The students marched through the fair grounds, drawing little more than a few critical stares from the hundreds of whites in attendance. The protest also targeted black teachers who had crossed the picket line at the fair to work on an exhibit. It was the second time students had singled out middle-class leaders; earlier in the year Bogalusa students had marched in protest against black ministers who refused to participate in the movement or honor the downtown boycott.[9]

One week later the Deacons became embroiled in a controversial school boycott. School integration had never been a paramount issue for the Bogalusa movement; instead, the October school boycott focused on demands for equal distribution of resources. The Voters League's Youth Organization demanded improved facilities, equal expenditures, new books (rather than castoff books from white schools), and foreign language course offerings. The youth group also called for more and better teachers and disciplinary action against teachers who were perceived as hostile toward the movement. In addition, the students demanded an end to the degrading practice of forcing black students to cut the lawn at the school superintendent's home. Leading the student boycott was Don Expose, son of Voters League officer Gayle Jenkins. After the school board rejected the demands, students boycotted classes, picketed the school gates, and staged militant marches to the school board offices.[10]

The school board countered with a new tactic. With the Ku Klux Klan in retreat, local courts and police now became the principal instruments of repression. At the request of the school board, on 19 October District Judge Jim Warren Richardson signed an injunction prohibiting the Voters League from encouraging or assisting school children to absent themselves from school. Simultaneously, Washington Parish district attorney W. W. Erwin filed a criminal bill of information against leaders of the Voters League charging them with contributing to the delinquency of school children.[11]

Undeterred by the legal actions, the next day Voters League and Deacons leaders joined a group of more than two hundred for a protest march to the school board building. A few minutes before the march was to begin, city police swooped down on the site and arrested virtually all of the leaders. Among those jailed were nearly all the Deacons' elected officers: Charlie Sims, Royan Burris, and Sam Barnes. Police also arrested Voters League leaders Robert Hicks and Gayle Jenkins. A. Z. Young, who was hospitalized at the time, was the only leader to escape arrest. All were charged with contributing to the delinquency of a minor.[12]

If the city fathers had hoped to thwart the movement by beheading its adult leadership, they had seriously underestimated the determination and organization of the youth. When informed that they could not march, two hundred students began shouting, "Let's go to jail." They forged ahead with the demonstration, forcing police to arrest forty-six students, including march leader Don Expose. A second march staged later that day led to another twenty-one arrests.[13]

By nightfall all of the adult leaders, with the exception of Sims, remained in jail. The arrests sent tempers flaring in the black community. At 10:00 P.M. an angry crowd of approximately 250 blacks gathered at the Negro Union Hall and began a spontaneous march to protest arrests earlier that day. Charlie Sims was the lone remaining adult leader on the scene; he was joined by Henry Austin, who had heard of the arrests and had traveled from New Orleans to lend a hand. When the police learned that the marchers were moving toward the downtown area, they quickly sent all available units to the scene. There the police were confronted by a mob that was a far cry from the polite, nonviolent marchers that had walked the picket line the summer before. "You could have heard them for three or four blocks, whooping and hollering, calling us cowards," bristled Chief Claxton Knight. The crowd began chanting "Freedom, Freedom, Freedom" and then more ominously "War, War, War."[14]

Police claimed that the demonstrators tossed beer bottles at them. Whatever the provocation, there is little doubt that law enforcement grossly overreacted. Instead of asking the marchers to disperse, Chief Knight sent the police into the crowd to scatter it. The result was nothing short of a police riot. Police officers stormed through the black community, arresting anyone in their way: innocent bystanders, people returning from work, people eating in restaurants, even business owners in their own establishments. When police found Henry Austin in the Bamboo Club, they dragged him out and brutally beat him with clubs. "You niggers aren't going to rule this town," one policeman screamed at Austin. Police indiscriminately clubbed and manhandled children and pulled hapless passersby from their cars and beat them. After going to the police station to bail out his son-in-law, the Reverend Nathan Lewis was stopped, roughed up, and arrested for possession of a pocketknife. One policeman told the minister that he might be found with "a weight around your head in the Pearl River."[15]

"Bloody Wednesday," as the police riot came to be known, posed a challenge for the federal government. Using the injunction that it had won in federal court, *Hicks v. Knight*, the Justice Department filed charges against several officers, including Vertrees Adams, Sidney J. Lyons, and John Hill. At the hearing, Judge Herbert W. Christenberry aptly described the events of the night as "more like East Germany than the United States"; he lectured police officials for engaging in a "deliberate scheme to harass these people and throw them in jail." Although *Hicks v. Knight* was primarily intended to compel local officials to protect civil rights activists from vigilante attacks, it had now become an effective tool against police violence. Bloody Wednesday was the first and last police assault on the black community in Bogalusa.[16]

Bloody Wednesday left the Voters League and the Deacons in bad shape. Bail for the arrested marchers drained the league's resources. The boycott had little success, and students soon returned to school. By the end of the year the Voters League shifted its focus from school issues back to equal employment. In November the league launched a new boycott of twenty-four stores that had still not hired blacks. The picketing was effective, and by December Bogalusa shop owners admitted that business was down—although they accused the league of frightening away blacks through threats and intimidation. There was some merit to their claim. For most black Bogalusans, the civil rights movement had ended in the summer of 1965. It is difficult to sustain interest and support for any social movement for long periods, especially when the movement's goals appear to be accomplished. The Christmas holidays were approaching, and, for some, the temptation to slip downtown for a little holiday shopping was irresistible. It became difficult for the league to recruit pickets, and the group increasingly used threats to enforce the boycott.[17]

One leaflet distributed by the league read: "Warning, Warning, Warning. Any persons found shopping at any of these stores will have to pay *the penalty*. Cooperate and together we shall overcome. Don't cooperate and we shall overcome *you* along with the *white man*." During a rally in January 1966, A. Z. Young berated the black community for lack of participation in the movement. "I am not getting the cooperation you promised me," he said. "You promised 24-hour-a-day cooperation. I have been embarrassed at marches and rallies by your not turning out." Young accused the Voters League Youth Organization of "dragging its feet," and he laid the blame on parents who prevented their children from participating. "You had better join me," Young warned his audience. "If you don't join me, we are out to get you, baby."[18]

Occasionally the Deacons made Young's threats a reality. On 16 April 1966 unknown assailants fired several shots at the home of the Reverend Herrod Morris, a longtime black critic of the Voters League, and black resident Raleigh Lucas. Several weeks later Sam Barnes, the Deacons' vice president, and George Skiffer were arrested and charged with attempted murder for the shooting incident at the Morris home. Although there was enough evidence to indict them, the case never went to trial. Barnes, the fifty-five-year-old Deacons officer, died of a heart attack a few weeks after his arrest.[19]

In the fall of 1965 the Klan was also having trouble sustaining interest, having lost the ability to organize mass marches and counterprotests. The night riders were reduced to an occasional skirmish with local blacks. In September, only a few days before the federal hearing of the Original Knights of the Ku Klux Klan (OKKKK) was scheduled to open, police arrested Klansman Saxon Farmer for brandishing a .38 caliber pistol during a brawl between blacks and whites at the Bogalusa Dairy Queen.[20]

In September federal court proceedings commenced against the Klan in New Orleans. Faced with defiant Klan leaders Saxon Farmer and Charles Christmas who refused to reveal the names of Klan members, the special three-judge panel composed of Christenberry, Robert A. Ainsworth Jr., and John Minor Wisdom gave the Grand Dragon and his Grand Titan a choice: names or jail. Farmer and Christmas quickly caved in and delivered a list of 87 names, later supplemented by the Justice Department with a second list of 151 names—including the name of Bogalusa city attorney Robert Rester. But the full extent of the Klan's terror campaign in Bogalusa never came to light at the hearing. To spare themselves the embarrassment of a public airing of their crimes, Farmer and Christmas admitted to most of the counts against the OKKKK, including the numerous assaults and intimidations against civil rights workers, business people, judges, congressmen, and even Governor McKeithen. The evidence that did emerge indicated that the Klan had been behind most of the seemingly spontaneous violence in Bogalusa. FBI special agent Frank Sass, whose memory had failed him in previous hearings, now recalled that he had seen Klansman Adrian Goings Jr. dispense baseball bats and two-by-four clubs to a group of young white teenagers in a parking lot near a civil rights protest. Armed with the bats and clubs, the teenagers were then apparently deployed for attacks by Randle C. Pounds, the Klansman who had assaulted James Farmer.[21]

The hearings did not go well for the Klan, and on 22 December the three-judge panel issued a permanent injunction against the OKKKK. Naming a total of 234 OKKKK members in Washington Parish, the injunction prohibited Klansmen from harassing and intimidating blacks who were exercising their civil rights or voting rights, or pursuing equal employment. Klansmen would face fines or jail if they threatened or intimidated blacks, business owners, or city officials and employees. The court also ordered Farmer and Christmas to maintain a record of members of the OKKKK and post copies of the injunction in a conspicuous place where they met. Federal marshals fanned out around Washington Parish in the following weeks and served the injunction papers on all 234 Klan members. Saxon Farmer remained defiant in the face of defeat. "So what?" Farmer said of the injunction, "I think the decision was actually rendered before we entered into the hearing."[22]

Deprived of their secrecy, the OKKKK withered away within days. That it took so little to destroy the Klan in Louisiana begs the question, why didn't the Justice Department take decisive measures against racist terrorist organizations earlier? The statutes and constitutional provisions used to destroy the Klan in Bogalusa had been available to the department from the beginning of the civil rights movement. The truth was that the Kennedy administration failed to vigorously prosecute the Klan for a simple reason: the president feared that aggressive federal intervention would alienate southern voters and lose him the White House in 1964. Moreover, Kennedy needed the cooperation of the South's powerful congressional delegation in order to pass his legislative initiatives. His assassination led to a national mandate for civil rights legislation, but Lyndon Johnson, despite his leadership on civil rights, also fell short of using his power to ensure the safety of people seeking to enjoy these rights. Civil rights leaders implored Johnson to enact special federal legislation to protect rights workers in the South, but their entreaties went unheeded. In the wake of Viola Liuzzo's murder in the Selma protests, President Johnson had publicly declared "war" on the Klan, but he took his time making his way to the battlefield. Even after the Neshoba County murders, the Justice Department limited its anti-Klan campaign to identifying Klan members and their activities and placing informants in several Klan groups. The Civil Rights Division assigned nine lawyers to investigate the Klan terror campaign in southwestern Mississippi; it failed to produce a single criminal or civil case. The FBI carried out a secret Counter Intelligence Program (COINTELPRO–WHITE HATE) to disrupt the Klan groups but did not aggressively build cases against the vigilantes. These low-profile, unobtrusive actions were simply a continuation of the Justice Department's policy of remaining invisible in the South. As might be expected, the strategy proved to be totally ineffective: the Klan continued to spread like wildfire throughout 1964–65.[23]

In announcing his "war" on the Klan, Johnson called for a thorough investigation of the organization. He quickly disappointed civil rights activists when he inexplicably handed over the investigation to the House Un-American Activities Committee (HUAC)—a body dominated by unreconstructed segregationists (the hearings took more than a year to get off the ground). Johnson continued to ignore the Klan problem until the Deacons left him no options in Bogalusa.[24]

The successful Bogalusa injunction against the Louisiana Klan deprived the night riders of their secrecy and their ability to mobilize large-scale demonstrations and public violence with impunity. The remaining Klan loyalists retreated into a world of fragmented, clandestine cells that carried on intermittent acts of terror. But the most immediate and telling development was the way that the Deacons had turned the tables on the Klan and inspired a paranoid panic among hooded vigilantes in the Deep South.[25]

In November 1965 J. H. Wood, a member of the United Klans of America (UKA), contacted Washington County deputy sheriff Earl Fisher of Greenville, Mississippi, to relate a bizarre tale of a black conspiracy and an imminent race war. Wood told Deputy Fisher that he and his associates had discovered that the Deacons and the Black Muslims were smuggling guns, automatic weapons, and thousands of rounds of ammunition into Mississippi through the Gulf of Mexico. The Klan was convinced that the Deacons and the Muslims had joined forces to foment a violent revolt against whites in the South. Though dubious, Fisher began investigating the allegations and talked to other UKA members who had staked out the Delta Memorial Gardens Cemetery outside the city limits of Greenville. The Klansmen claimed that they had observed several suspicious black burials in recent months. One burial was mysteriously attended by only one person; in the case of another burial, there allegedly was no record of a recent death. The Klansmen were convinced that the Deacons were concealing weapons and ammunition in empty graves. The Alcohol, Tobacco, and Firearms Department also became interested in the allegations and interviewed Earnest Thomas about them.[26]

The Klansmen made Fisher an offer. They would lead him to the graves where the weapons were hidden if the Klan would receive a portion of the guns and ammunition to protect whites against the planned uprising. They also insisted that if weapons were found, the State Highway Patrol should post guards at every black cemetery in the state. The Klan was in a panic over the prospects of a race war and even offered to help the highway patrol contain the Deacon-Muslim conspiracy. "One of our members is in tears out there thinking about those guns," said UKA Kleagle Ernest Gilbert.[27]

Deputy Fisher grew concerned that the rumor of a black revolt might spread in the white community. His fears were well founded. Paranoid fantasies of bloody and vengeful black revolts were deeply embedded in the southern white psyche, dating back to the time of slavery when revolt was a real threat. The Deacons had jogged the phantom memory to the surface. Compounding the problem was the Klansmen's insistence on massive publicity to unmask the black insurrection. "They wanted ABC, NBC, CBS, and the Jackson newspapers on hand when the graves were opened," said Fisher. Fearing a riot if the rumors reached the white community, the anxious deputy contacted the state attorney general, who authorized the investigation to continue. Fisher then secured permission to exhume the grave of an elderly black man where the Klan believed that weapons were hidden. To minimize publicity, the police dug up the grave at night under armed guard. At last they reached the coffin and anxiously pried off the lid. Inside they found the remains of James Turner, a sixty-four-year-old black man who had been buried on 4 November. There were no guns. The next day Fisher invited the local media to examine the ridiculous scene. "This was done to disprove once and for all that Negroes are not stashing guns," Fisher solemnly announced. "The Black Muslims and the Deacons for Defense and Justice are not in here creating an uprising." The photograph accompanying the news story showed three slightly befuddled deputy sheriffs peering into a gaping and harmless grave. To add insult to injury, Fisher stated that his office was now opening an investigation of the Klan.[28]

Amusing as the Mississippi Klan panic was, it demonstrated the power of the "New Negro" image that the Deacons had helped create. Moreover, it testified to the effectiveness of this image in discouraging open Klan violence.

By the end of 1965 the Klan in Louisiana was virtually dead. That year its campaign of terror had included hundreds of cross burnings and assaults, twenty-two shootings, twenty-eight bombings, and arson. The Klan's last attack in Bogalusa occurred on 27 January 1966, when James Farmer returned to the city for the first large march in several months. In response, the Klan held a rally and—under cover of darkness—lit four small crosses in a circle around Ebenezer Baptist Church. Initially, the Voters League decided to retaliate by donning Klan robes and parading through Bogalusa to ridicule the night riders as cowards. The shocking idea electrified the black community as much as it terrified whites. It also attested to the sweeping psychological transformation that the Deacons had produced in ten short months. The provocative plan was dropped, but a rally on 29 January provided a forum for the league to issue a stern threat to the Klan. "Thursday there were four crosses burned in the Negro section of town," A. Z. Young told the rally audience. "They don't scare us," he continued. "But if any more are burned, we'll strike a match on you baby." The crowd roared its approval. Charlie Sims warned local authorities that if the city attempted a repeat of "Bloody Wednesday," the Deacons would "come off of defense and go on offense." As the rally ended, Fletcher Anderson joined Sims on the stage and donned a wrinkled sheet with a pointed Klan hood painted with the letters "KKK." Anderson pronounced the Klan officially dead and pranced around the stage in his costume—to gales of laughter from the audience.[29]

On 5 June 1966 James Meredith began a quiet 220-mile protest pilgrimage from Memphis, Tennessee, to Jackson, Mississippi. Now a Columbia University Law School student, Meredith had first attracted international attention during his efforts to integrate the University of Mississippi in 1962. The iconoclastic and inveterate loner set off on his pilgrimage joined by only a few supporters. Meredith's goal was to encourage black voter registration and increase national awareness of "the all-pervasive and overriding fear that dominates the day-to-day life" of blacks in the South. On the second day of his journey, a white man emerged from the brush along the highway near Hernando, Mississippi, and fired three shotgun blasts at the civil rights leader. Meredith miraculously survived the attack with only superficial wounds. But the shooting triggered a major reaction by national civil rights organizations, who were determined to use the incident to call for additional voting rights and poverty legislation and to highlight the failure of state and local governments to provide the promised rights. On 7 June Martin Luther King, representing the Southern Christian Leadership Conference (SCLC), Floyd McKissick, the new national director of CORE, and Stokely Carmichael, chairman of SNCC, announced that the three organizations would continue Meredith's march to Jackson. The subsequent "Meredith March against Fear" was the last great march of the modern civil rights movement, stretching out for nearly three weeks and covering 260 miles.

Deacons from both South and North became immediately involved in the march. When the news of the Meredith shooting reached Chicago, Earnest Thomas departed the city with a contingent of Deacons bound for Memphis. They planned to join forces with Deacons from Mississippi and Louisiana. Thomas pulled his van into the Lorraine Motel and quickly caught the attention of Memphis police as the Deacons piled out with M-1 rifles and bandoliers. A police superintendent questioned the Deacons and ran arrest warrant checks. The group checked out clean, but the superintendent was still wary of the surly looking armed gang. He asked Thomas why they were so heavily armed. "That's the only way I'm going to Mississippi, sir," replied Thomas coolly.[30]

That night Thomas talked briefly with Martin Luther King. Although the two had crossed swords in the media in the past, Mississippi had a way of making friends of old enemies. They appeared to put aside their differences, and King even took to calling Thomas "Deac." Tuesday night Dick Gregory told Thomas that there was a meeting in King's room at the Lorraine. As soon as they crossed the threshold, Hosea Williams, an SCLC aide, protested Thomas's presence. "Well I'm going to tell you right now, there ain't going to be no Deacons on the march," Williams announced. Tempers flared for a moment as King calmly sat on the edge of his bed quietly eating a steak. Stokely Carmichael and Floyd McKissick, who supported the Deacons, were also there, along with Roy Wilkins of the NAACP and Whitney Young of the

National Urban League. The NAACP and the Urban League were appalled at the idea of armed guards in the march and adamantly opposed the Deacons. Thomas fumed at Williams and warned him that SCLC risked losing the support of rank-and-file blacks, "because you getting people hurt, and you get back on them god-damn planes and you fly off and forget about them." The Deacons were not going to allow that to happen again. This was going to be a "different march," promised Thomas. King looked surprised and stopped carving his steak for a moment. "Deac, you mean you're going to march?" asked King. "I don't have no intention of marching one block in Mississippi," Thomas told King. "But we're going to be up and down the highways and the byways. And if somebody gets shot again, they going to have somebody to give account to for that."[31]

The Mississippi Delta was SNCC country, and King could ill-afford to alienate the young radicals. He would need their support and organizational network in the region if the march were to succeed. To many who listened to the debate at the Lorraine that night, King's silence appeared to be tacit support for SNCC and the militants. SNCC not only demanded that the Deacons be invited to guard the march, but also argued that the focus of the demonstration should be "an indictment of President Johnson over the fact that existing laws were not being enforced." Reflecting the growing Black Power politics in SNCC, Carmichael demanded that whites be excluded from the march. Wilkins and Young opposed SNCC's strategy as divisive—and they wanted nothing to do with the gun-toting Deacons. The two moderates left the meeting, and the remaining organizers drafted a march "manifesto" that contained much of SNCC's militant rhetoric. By the end of the night King reluctantly agreed that the Deacons could remain in the march.[32]

Why King consented to having the Deacons on the march remains a mystery. He may have assumed that they would not become a media issue, given Thomas's assurances that the Deacons would not carry weapons. Still, it was a risky concession for King. The media was alert to symbols of a growing political schism in the movement over nonviolence. NAACP leader Charles Evers received deafening applause when he told a Mississippi rally that he and his followers were going to Meredith's aid like the popular matinee gunslingers Buck Jones and Tim McCoy. Meredith himself bluntly repudiated nonviolence while recuperating from his wounds. He told reporters that before the march he had debated whether to bring a gun or a Bible. To his regret, he chose the Bible. "I was embarrassed because I could have knocked the intended killer off with one shot if I had been prepared," said Meredith. "I will return to the march . . . and I will be armed unless I have assurances I will not need arms. I believe in law and order, but if the whites continue to kill the Negro in the South, I will have no choice but to urge them [Negroes] to go out and defend themselves." Meredith had little to say about the Deacons other than he did not "favor" the Deacons—or any group for that matter. The Deacons would be there to protect Meredith just the same. "If a white man starts shooting again," Thomas told reporters, "you'll know where to find him."[33]

As the march continued, the Deacons positioned themselves in cars in front of and behind the marchers. Some Deacons walked in the march guarding King, but without weapons. They scouted the march route, guarded campsites, and escorted travelers to the Memphis airport at night. Charlie Sims brought a contingent of Deacons from Louisiana, and the New Orleans and Jonesboro chapters also sent members. "I was carryin' two snub-nosed .38s and two boxes of shells," recalled Sims, "and had three men ridin' down the highway with semi-automatic carbines with thirty rounds apiece. . . . See, I didn't believe in that naked shit, no way." Although there were rumors that 350 Deacons were at the march, the figure was probably closer to 30. As promised, the Deacons kept a low profile.[34]

Despite their efforts to remain out of the public eye, the Deacons' role in the march soon surfaced in the media. On 13 June Thomas got involved in a heated debate with a white pastor who had objected to the Deacons carrying weapons at the march campsite. Thomas told the pastor that he was wrong to tell blacks not to fight back when their lives were at stake. The argument spread among marchers throughout the camp until CORE field secretary Bruce Baines admonished the group not to air their dispute in front of the press. It was too late. The *New York Times* carried a story on the argument and quoted Thomas as saying that the Deacons were guarding the campsite at night "with pistols, rifles and shotguns" and providing armed escorts of marchers who traveled at night to the Memphis airport. "But we don't take guns with us when the people are marching," said Thomas. "The march is nonviolent." Floyd McKissick attempted damage control by telling the *Times* that he had no knowledge of weapons around the campsite and that he had talked "way into the night" telling the Deacons and the marchers that the march "must remain nonviolent."[35]

Tension began to grow between SCLC and the Deacons. On 21 June King asked Thomas if the Deacons could set up a series of radio base stations along the march route. King said that he feared that there were "dark days ahead" for the march, and the communication system would aid security (pay phone lines were frequently cut along the route). Thomas agreed and left for Jonesboro to retrieve the radios. In his absence, King left the Meredith March and took approximately twenty persons to Philadelphia, Mississippi, to attend a memorial service for the three civil rights workers slain there two years before. In Philadelphia, King led an impromptu march that was quickly surrounded by a mob of several hundred armed whites. A group of twenty-five whites broke away from the mob and viciously assaulted the marchers. Half a dozen black marchers vainly fought back as police and FBI agents looked on for several minutes. Later that night marauding whites made four gunfire attacks on the black community, including an attack on the headquarters of the Mississippi Freedom Democratic Party. Blacks at the headquarters returned fire during two of the attacks and wounded one of the white assailants.[36]

Thomas was furious with King when he learned of the detour to Philadelphia and the subsequent debacle. Right or not, Thomas suspected that the radio errand was a ruse to prevent him from accompanying King to Philadelphia. "This is the end of this," Thomas told King's aides in disgust. Relations between King and the Deacons were clearly strained by the incident. The same day as the Philadelphia attack, the Meredith March arrived in Indianola, where SNCC field secretary Charles McLaurin led marchers in a chant for "black power"—a chant that Carmichael had first introduced in the march at Greenwood. King flew from Philadelphia to Indianola, where he addressed a rally that night. He took the opportunity to bitterly condemn the Deacons and the Black Power advocates. "Some people are telling us to be like our oppressor, who has a history of using Molotov cocktails, who has a history of dropping the atom bomb, who has a history of lynching Negroes," said King. "Now people are telling me to stoop down to that level. I'm sick and tired of violence."[37]

King repeated his attack on self-defense throughout 1966, arguing in the pages of *Ebony* that "it is extremely dangerous to organize a movement around self-defense" because the "line between defensive violence and aggressive retaliatory violence is a fine line indeed. When violence is tolerated even as a means of self-defense there is a grave danger that in the fervor of emotion the main fight will be lost over the question of self-defense." King emphasized that the movement should not rely on self-defense in marches, but rather suffer bloodshed for the greater good. Ultimately, "violence, even in self-defense, creates more problems than it solves."[38]

The Meredith March ended without incident, though it lay bare for the public the divisions between the old civil rights leaders and the new Black Power militants. The march had involved scores of Deacons from several chapters and served to strengthen ties between the defense group and leaders of the emerging Black Power movement. The influence of nationalists was evident in the new rhetoric and tactics of the Deacons in Bogalusa. Black

Power as a political movement has often been dismissed as a doctrine of hatred and racial separatism. "It was born from the womb of despair and disappointment," said Martin Luther King. "Black Power is a cry of pain. It is in fact a reaction to the failure of White Power to deliver the promises and to do it in a hurry." Its advocates engaged in "disruption for disruption's sake," argued King, and failed to offer a program for change because they believed "that evil has so engrossed itself in the society that there is no answer within the society."[39]

Black Power was admittedly an ambiguous term, but it was much more than a cry of pain. Most Black Power activists advanced a program of community control of police and economic resources and a strategy of force and coercion rather than moral appeals to secure these reforms. They believed that blacks had to control their own organizations of liberation, in contrast to interracial groups like CORE, or organizations financially dependent on white liberals and trade unions, such as the NAACP and SCLC. But racial separatism was a means, not an end. "The concept of Black Power rests on a fundamental premise," said Stokely Carmichael in 1967: "*Before a group can enter an open society, it must first close ranks.*" Regardless of the intended meaning of the term, historical hindsight makes clear its political impact. Black Power conveyed to white people that African Americans were no longer willing to behave politically in ways prescribed by white liberals. In contrast to the popular nonviolent image of peaceful and polite supplicants, swaying to song and prayer, Black Power presented a gritty coercive image of black men and women, defiant, proud, exalting in their blackness, and impervious to white expectations and entreaties. Black Power leaders like Stokely Carmichael viewed nonviolence as a form of cultural imperialism in which white people had imposed their own culturally preferred method of social change. "For black people to adopt *their* methods of relieving *our* oppression is ludicrous," said Carmichael. Black Power was fundamentally a movement for self-definition. "We blacks must respond in our own way, on our own terms, in a manner which fits our temperaments. The definitions of ourselves, the roles we pursue, the goals we seek are *our* responsibility." Far from a puerile tantrum or nihilistic hate, Black Power was a lucid alternative to nonviolence that had a calculated effect on white and black consciousness and an implicit message about how change occurs in America.[40]

The Deacons who participated in the Meredith March were profoundly influenced by Black Power, and when they returned home they soon began to employ the militant rhetoric of confrontation. During an interview on WDSU television in New Orleans on 16 September, Bob Hicks bemoaned the slow pace of change and intimated that violence was necessary. "The federal government won't do anything, the state government won't do anything, so somebody has to die," said Hicks. "It won't do any good for a Negro to die, so somebody else has got to die." A. Z. Young took the same tack at a subsequent rally. "If you own a gun buy plenty of ammunition for it and get ready to use it," Young said, "because we might have to burn this baby down." These threats provoked a near-hysterical response by Bogalusa whites. Gayle Jenkins did her best to defuse the situation. "You know A. Z. as well as I do," Jenkins told reporters. "He makes all those kinds of statements."[41]

But Robert Rester, Bogalusa city attorney and Klan member, was unwilling to forgive Young's statements. Rester announced that he would ask the Twenty-second District Court to convene a Washington Parish Grand Jury to investigate the Deacons and "inflammatory" statements by the Voters League. The investigation would determine if the league "advocates violence" and if the Deacons "have violated state statutes on purchase, sale, or possession of firearms." Rester's threats never bore fruit, but they represented the white political establishment's new strategy of using the courts to neutralize the Voters League and the Deacons. In the fall of 1966 city officials sued several league and Deacon members.[42]

The last armed confrontation between the Deacons and the Klan occurred on 12 September 1966, the same day as Hicks's television appearance. A rumor had spread that James Meredith had been invited to speak at the newly integrated Bogalusa Junior High. Black and white students had been involved in a series of fights in recent days, adding to the tension. Fifty white men and twelve women, many of them Klan members, assembled outside the school a few hours before classes began. They were led by Paul Farmer, leader of the Citizens Council and brother of Klan leader Saxon Farmer. Hicks, Young, and about twenty members of the Voters League and the Deacons arrived at the school. Guns were drawn, but police eventually persuaded the two groups to leave. It was the last time that the Klan attempted to use force to intimidate the black community in Bogalusa.[43]

Voters League protests revived briefly in August 1967 with a dramatic 105-mile march from Bogalusa to Baton Rouge—through the heart of Klan country—led by A. Z. Young. It was a surreal scene: a handful of marchers, stoked by fiery Black Power rhetoric, walking in a slow, deliberate gait into the lion's den. Though it attracted hardly any followers, the march became the focus of enormous media coverage and sparked fears of black rioting. On 10 August Young commenced the march from Bogalusa, with plans to end with a rally at the state capitol featuring Black Power advocates H. Rap Brown and Lincoln Lynch. The protest began with a meager forty-four participants and a handful of Deacons.[44]

The last leg of the march tested the mettle of even the bravest demonstrators. Livingston Parish stood between the marchers and Baton Rouge, with only a small contingent of state troopers standing guard. A Klan stronghold with virtually no black population, Livingston Parish had a deserved reputation as dangerous to blacks. The militant tone of the march had attracted statewide attention, and Governor McKeithen blustered with threats to arrest anyone at the Baton Rouge rally who made "inflammatory statements." In the small town of Satsuma a group of whites broke through state troopers and attacked the marchers. The next day McKeithen dispatched 150 state police to guard the march, which had dwindled to only six participants.[45]

After more attacks occurred, McKeithen was forced to call out the National Guard and order in state troopers to ensure the marchers' safety. By the time the marchers reached the outskirts of Baton Rouge, they were accompanied by a formidable army of nearly 1,000 troops: 825 Louisiana National Guardsmen and 170 state police. National guard helicopters roared overhead as a magnetic sweeper cleared the highway of roofing nails scattered by the Klan. Wilting in the 97-degree August heat, Guardsmen lined the highway with rifles with fixed bayonets. State police stood by nervously fingering submachine guns with live ammunition. Law enforcement officials discovered sections of wire under the twin spans crossing the Amite River on Highway 190, apparently intended to blow up marchers. "If they hadn't had the Louisiana National Guard, it would have been a slaughter camp," Young said later.[46]

With black nationalist H. Rap Brown as the major speaker for the rally ending the march, Louisiana's white power structure feared a major rebellion in Baton Rouge's simmering slums. To cool passions Governor McKeithen took to the airwaves with a statewide address. When the marchers arrived in Baton Rouge on Saturday, they were greeted by fifteen hundred National Guardsmen standing by for the rally with express orders from the governor to "shoot-to-kill" if a riot erupted. McKeithen told state police officials that if any speaker made "treasonous or seditious statements" they were to "arrest them on the spot."[47]

Ignoring McKeithen's threats, several hundred blacks attended the rally, which turned out to be law-abiding and peaceful (Rap Brown had been arrested on a firearms charge and could not attend). At one point about 150 blacks splintered off from the main rally and threatened to conduct a sit-in on the state capitol steps. In a strange role reversal, it was Charlie

Sims, now billing himself as national chairman of the Deacons, who intervened and persuaded them to abandon their plan and rejoin the rally. Later that night spontaneous violence did break out in the city's black neighborhoods, as gangs of youths roamed the streets breaking windows and hurling firebombs.[48]

The march to Baton Rouge ushered in the twilight of the Deacons organization. As the march had demonstrated, local law enforcement agencies were living up to their obligation to protect activists. The Klan had been defanged, and black communities now turned to the task of working within the political system to acquire resources and power. The Voting Rights Act offered new opportunities to influence local government, and many Deacons made bids for elective office. In Jonesboro, Earnest Thomas ran for sheriff; in Bogalusa, several former Deacons launched campaigns for school board and municipal offices in the late 1960s and early 1970s. None were successful; warriors seldom make good statesmen.

Of all the Deacons, only A. Z. Young remained in the public eye. The Baton Rouge march had made Young a legend across the state, and in 1972 he campaigned vigorously for Edwin Edwards in the gubernatorial race. When Edwards won with a unique coalition of blacks and blue-collar whites, he awarded Young a plumb appointment in his administration. Young remained in state government for the rest of his life; he was serving as assistant to the commissioner of elections at his untimely death in 1993. The Louisiana Department of Social Services' building in Baton Rouge now bears his name and, in a final twist, a "no guns allowed" sign is prominently affixed to the front door.[49]

Bob Hicks stayed active in local politics and made history by becoming the first black supervisor at the Crown-Zellerbach plant. As a commentary on the limits of the civil rights laws, when Hicks retired he was, because of workforce reductions, still the only black supervisor at the plant. Charles Sims, the old lion, retired to a quiet life of odd jobs and bartending. He grew bitter with the years, disappointed that young people had failed the struggle—that they had "let it fall back in the same shape." He was also convinced that unscrupulous journalists had exploited his story without financially compensating him. Plagued by health problems in his final years, Sims died quietly in Bogalusa in 1989.[50]

Henry Austin, the young Deacon who shot Alton Crowe in the Bogalusa march, left Bogalusa in exchange for Washington Parish officials dropping charges against him. Austin continued his efforts to organize Deacons chapters in the North and briefly attended college, but his subsequent life became a struggle against his own demons.

Frederick Douglas Kirkpatrick, one of the original founders of the Jonesboro Deacons, went on to a life with several fascinating turns. He left his position at Grambling to become a coordinator for SNCC in Houston while attending Texas Southern University. Kirkpatrick founded a Deacons chapter and was involved in efforts to stop a riot at the school in 1967. He later worked with King's SCLC. During the antiwar movement he became a well-known folk singer and later started the "Hey Brother Coffee House" at Hunter College in New York—a place to combine politics and friendship. He remained active in various social justice movements as a singer and "cultural worker" until his premature death in 1987. There was one sweet irony in Kirkpatrick's later life. In the 1970s he made several singing appearances on PBS's *Sesame Street* as "Brother Kirk" and later released an album of music from the program. Little did the millions of children viewing the show suspect that the gentle and warm folk singer was also the founder of a militant black armed organization that once fought pitched battles with the Ku Klux Klan in the dusty hot streets of little towns in the Deep South.[51]

Earnest "Chilly Willy" Thomas also had a remarkable life. In 1966 he traveled to Cuba to visit exiled black nationalist leader Robert F. Williams. On arriving in Havana, Thomas learned that Williams had left the previous day for the People's Republic of China by way of North Vietnam. Williams had become deeply disillusioned with Castro's Cuba and was looking for a more hospitable home for exile.[52]

Cuban officials assigned an interpreter to Thomas and arranged a series of tours, including of the Cuban countryside. He soon tired of the official tours and political propagandizing and spent much of his time walking the streets of Havana, chatting with ordinary people. He met bricklayers (his old trade) and learned that they earned a paltry eighty-five cents an hour—yet were forced to pay twenty-four dollars for a fifth of rum—a profound injustice to a drinking man like Thomas.[53]

The Cuban government treated Thomas considerably better than they treated their bricklayers, providing him with a free hotel, sumptuous meals, and all the perks of a visiting dignitary. He met with military officials, including a Cuban general, "Commandant Bayou," who had received training in New Orleans. The general, who had been treated as a white during his stay in segregated New Orleans, recounted how his American superiors had once reprimanded him for politely stepping off the sidewalk to allow a black couple to pass. Later Thomas attended the annual ceremony commemorating the 26 July Revolution and was assigned a prestigious seat only a few rows from Fidel Castro. The barroom hustler from Jonesboro was coming up in the world.[54]

But Thomas never received an introduction to Castro, and after a few days in Cuba he began to run afoul of the government. Part of his difficulties arose from his characteristic frankness. Thomas had noticed early on that a distinct color line divided blacks and whites in Cuba. When Cuban officials inquired about his impression of Cuba compared to the United States, Thomas replied indelicately: "I see the same thing. I see a lot of black people working on the farm and I see all the white folks got the best jobs. I don't see no difference." His criticisms did not endear him to his hosts.[55]

Thomas asked Cuban officials to allow him to travel to China to meet with Williams, but the government dragged its feet in providing an exit visa, no doubt a consequence of increasing tensions between the Chinese and Soviet blocs. Growing impatient with the bureaucratic delays, Thomas attempted to secure an exit through several of the embassies in Havana. He had little luck with the African embassies, but the North Vietnamese offered to help on the condition that he would urge black u.s. troops to refuse to fight in Vietnam. "I said shit with that. I can't do that," recalled Thomas. Finally he went to the Chinese embassy, which, after contacting Williams in China, arranged to expedite his departure. After four weeks in Cuba, Thomas left for China by way of Europe.[56]

Thomas rendezvoused with Williams in China and began another long tour of official sites: military bases, war museums—or, in Thomas's words, "nothing of interest." He admired the Chinese for not attempting to proselytize him as the Cubans had. After two weeks in China, Thomas departed for the United States. Originally he planned to arrive through New Orleans, but the Chinese government warned that he might encounter difficulties with u.s. officials, so he returned through Canada and drove across the border.[57]

The news that Thomas had traveled to Cuba and China sent the FBI into a paroxysm of frantic memos and international cables. The bureau knew that the Deacons had close contact with revolutionary nationalists and suspected that they had purchased hundreds of automatic weapons. After Thomas returned to the United States via Canada, the FBI received information that he had served as a courier for Chinese funds for the Revolutionary Action Movement (RAM) and other radical groups. FBI headquarters sent their forces scurrying from London to Hong Kong to determine where Thomas had been and whether he had been a conduit for Chinese money to RAM or other u.s. revolutionaries. J. Edgar Hoover ordered the New Orleans field office to look into the rumors. The New York field office was instructed to see if Thomas had had contact with RAM since his return, and Hong Kong was queried about Thomas, RAM, and connections to China. Thomas denied that he served as a courier, and Williams declined to comment on the matter.[58]

As it turned out, the FBI was right. Three years after Thomas's China trip, Williams returned to the United States to face charges arising from the Monroe riot. The charges were soon dropped, and Williams withdrew from the movement and moved to rural Michigan. He spent time briefing the U.S. State Department on China, and in the fall of 1970 he was called before the House Un-American Activities Committee to give testimony on his activities in China. Though Williams initially balked at the subpoena, he eventually turned over personal financial records and testified before the committee. He was a reluctant witness and did his best not to provide HUAC with names of other U.S. citizens residing in China. But the CIA and other government investigators had amassed detailed evidence that Williams was funneling money from China into the United States for revolutionary groups. Among Williams's records was a $1,200 payment to Earnest Thomas intended for RAM.[59]

The Cuba-China trip had been an amazing adventure for Chilly Willy—hailed as a revolutionary leader and immersed in cloak-and-dagger operations in the Far East. Rubbing shoulders with Third World revolutionaries had some effect on Thomas, but it had not changed his political views. He did not return home a Marxist-Leninist; he was too firm in his convictions to succumb to revolutionary politics. He would have been a prize catch for any of the leftist groups, but they all found his political stubbornness impenetrable. "Everyone was trying to get a hold of him," remembered RAM leader Virginia Collins, but "Chilly Willy just couldn't catch on."[60]

In 1967 Thomas cut back his organizing activities for the Deacons and began traveling and speaking with Stokely Carmichael, as well as serving as Carmichael's bodyguard. In May 1967 Thomas returned to Louisiana, guarding Carmichael during a speaking engagement at Southern University in Baton Rouge. In an incident outside the university, police arrested him on a concealed weapons charge. When Thomas failed to appear for a 14 June hearing, he was found in contempt of court and received a sentence of fifteen days in jail and a $500 fine.[61]

By 1968 Thomas had left the Deacons for a new career. On his way back from China, he had met football and movie star Jim Brown at the London airport. The two developed an instant rapport, and Brown soon asked Thomas to be his bodyguard. Thomas jumped at the opportunity and shortly left for California, leaving the Deacons and the civil rights movement in his past. He later started a successful trucking company in Los Angeles and retired to a comfortable life of playing the money markets.[62]

Many of the Bogalusa Deacons insist that the organization never disbanded. It is still alive, they assert, only awaiting the call to arms. The sentiment is more metaphor than fact, but a metaphor rich in meaning. The Deacons understood—better than any civil rights organization of their time—that rights are no more secure than our willingness to defend them. Charlie Sims was once asked how long the Deacons would be needed in the civil rights movement. "In 1965 there will be a great change made," Sims said, alluding to the Voting Rights Act. "But after this change is made, the biggest fight is to keep it," he continued. "My son, his son might have to fight this fight and that's one reason why we won't disband the Deacons for a long time. How long, Heaven only knows. But it will be a long time."[63]

The Myth of Nonviolence

SEVERAL YEARS AGO I was discussing the history of the civil rights movement with Dr. J. L. Garret, a respected African American leader in Hammond, Louisiana. Garret is a middle-class professional who takes great pride in how he ushered in change in the 1960s through patient and quiet negotiations with the town's leading white citizens. He is, by no stretch of the imagination, a militant or a nationalist. As we talked, I asked if he had heard of the Deacons. His eyes lit up and a smile spread across his face. "Do you know who H. Rap Brown was?" he asked. Yes, I replied, he was the Black Power firebrand whom the Deacons and the Bogalusa Voters League had invited to speak at a night rally in Baton Rouge in 1967. At the time, Brown struck terror in the hearts of white people and his threatened appearance panicked the Louisiana political powers and prompted paranoid fears of riots and mayhem. Brown had a way of making nettlesome activists like Garret look appealingly conservative to the white establishment. Garret took a sip of his coffee and looked at me across the table. "Rap Brown did a great favor for black people in Louisiana," he said with deliberation. "You understand what I am saying?" "Yes," I said; I thought I understood his point. "The Good Book says that sometimes the Devil can do God's work," he added with a wink. "That's who Rap Brown was. He was God's Devil."[1]

According to conventional wisdom, nonviolence provided the impetus for change during the civil rights movement. In some quarters it has become heresy to suggest otherwise. Historians, for the most part, continue to labor under this truism. But the experience of the Deacons—and the other "God's Devils" of the period—stubbornly contradict the myth of nonviolence.

Nonviolence as the motive force for change became a reassuring myth of American moral redemption—a myth that assuaged white guilt by suggesting that racism was not intractable and deeply embedded in American life, that racial segregation and discrimination were handily overcome by orderly, polite protest and a generous American conscience, and that the pluralistic system for resolving conflicts between competing interests had prevailed. The system had worked and the nation was redeemed.

It was a comforting but vacant fiction. In the end, segregation yielded to force as much as it did to moral suasion. Violence in the form of street riots and armed self-defense played a fundamental role in uprooting segregation and economic and political discrimination from 1963 to 1965. Only after the threat of black violence emerged did civil rights legislation move to the forefront of the national agenda. Only after the Deacons appeared were the civil rights laws effectively enforced and the obstructions of terrorists and complicit local law enforcement agencies neutralized.[2]

Nonviolence did have its day. Nonviolence unquestionably defined the black freedom movement from 1954 to 1963—through the Montgomery Bus Boycott, the lunch counter sit-ins, and the Freedom Rides. But by the end of 1962 Martin Luther King and the more militant nonviolent organizations had fallen victim to state repression and terrorism. The Student Nonviolent Coordinating Committee (SNCC), CORE, and Southern Christian Leadership Conference (SCLC) had all failed to secure local reform, voting rights, or protective federal legislation. Appeals to the conscience of whites had foundered in the South and were having limited success in the North. By the beginning of 1963 the Kennedy administration was backtracking on promised civil rights legislation. Terrorism and legal repression so demoralized the movement that activists concluded that federal intervention was their only salvation. Activists were learning that the myth of nonviolence rested on a perilous underestimation of racism and a misplaced confidence in the American conscience and democratic institutions.

Then came the Birmingham campaign in 1963 and, more important, the Birmingham riots. The first riot occurred on 3 May after police opened up with water cannons on protesters. Young black men, nonpacifists who had previously lingered on the sidelines, now retaliated with bricks and bottles. On 4 May three thousand blacks, most of whom were uninvolved in nonviolent marches, assembled in downtown Birmingham and clashed with police again.[3] Three days later a peaceful protest sparked more displays of force by nonmovement blacks, including several hundred who encircled two police officers.[4] Finally, in the early hours of 12 May a massive riot broke out in response to two Ku Klux Klan bombings the night before. For the first time in the history of the civil rights movement, working-class blacks took to the streets in a violent protest against police brutality and Klan terror. The young blacks who defied King's strictures irreversibly altered the strategy of the civil rights movement, raising the specter of massive black civil violence and ultimately forcing the first real concession in the form of the Civil Rights Act. From Birmingham forward, every peaceful nonviolent protest carried the threat of black violence. The Birmingham riots marked the end of nonviolence and the advent of a movement characterized by both lawful mass protest and defensive violence.[5]

The May riots were followed by another riot in Birmingham on 15 September 1963 in response to the bombing of the 16th Street Baptist Church. All of these riots were essentially acts of *defensive violence*, that is to say, collective acts intended to protect the black community from police or white terrorist violence. In this sense, these forcible collective protests were part of the same countermovement against nonviolence represented by the Deacons and their armed self-defense philosophy. The tactic of collective force spread rapidly after the May riots in Birmingham. In the summer of 1963—in the middle of what is traditionally viewed as the nonviolent phase of the movement—black civil violence against police and white vigilantes exploded in Lexington, North Carolina; Savannah, Georgia; Charleston, South Carolina; and Cambridge, Maryland. During 1964–65 more black riots erupted in southern cities, including a second uprising in Cambridge and disorders in St. Augustine, Florida; Natchez, McComb, and Jackson, Mississippi; Jacksonville, Florida; Henderson, North Carolina; Princess Anne, Maryland; and Bogalusa, Louisiana. Numerous "near-riots" occurred in Nashville, Atlanta, and other cities.[6]

Urban rebellions in the South placed enormous pressure on national policymakers, but they also dramatically affected local power relations. Significantly, the southern riots contributed to civil rights victories in many cities—in some cases, months before the Civil Rights Act went into effect. Desegregation settlements were quickly negotiated in Charleston, Savannah, Cambridge, Lexington, and St. Augustine. McComb, Mississippi, lived under a siege by white terrorists from 1962 to 1964, despite two separate SNCC campaigns. After a series of bombings in September 1964, McComb blacks abandoned nonviolence and staged a riot. Within days, President Johnson brought pressure to bear on state officials, and the Klan was soon out of business. "Whatever the speculation," writes John Dittmer, "the fact remains that until the end of September the Klan had its way in McComb, and the bombers were arrested only after blacks engaged in retaliatory violence and after both the president and the governor had threatened to send troops to occupy McComb."[7]

The phenomenon of the defensive street riot also casts light on the role of black men in the freedom movement. Throughout the South, most black men boycotted the civil rights movement; the campaigns in Birmingham, New Orleans, Bogalusa, and Jonesboro became movements of women and children.[8] Many civil rights leaders explained the absence of men as some character failing—apathy, alienation, or fear.[9] Yet black men did participate in the black freedom movement in the Deep South—but not under the discipline of nonviolent organizations.

The numerous instances of black violence in response to police brutality and Klan terror constituted a form of collective political behavior—one that attracted thousands of black men. These collective acts of force were, in every sense, an integral part of the African American freedom movement. But for many leaders of the national civil rights organizations, the nonviolent movement was the *only* movement. When SCLC's James Bevel tried to disperse rioters who were taunting Bull Connor's troops in downtown Birmingham, Bevel shouted, "If you are not going to respect the policemen, you're not going to be in the movement." Contrary to Bevel, the crowd was very much a part of the movement—but a movement beyond the control of the pacifists.[10]

This conflation of nonviolence with "the movement" blinded many to a new social movement unfolding before their eyes. "No longer can white liberals merely be proud of those well-dressed students, who are specialists in non-violent direct action," wrote Bayard Rustin in the days after Birmingham. "Now they are confronted with a Negro working class that is demanding equal opportunity and full employment."[11]

Even the role of black students in the movement was changing. During the 1964 Freedom Summer, SNCC lamented the lack of participation by southern black men and college students. But earlier that year, nearly one thousand black Mississippi students—men and women—risked life and limb in a militant demonstration and riot against police at Jackson State College. Although police wounded three protesters, the students were determined to march the following day and confront the police again; they were deterred only when Charles Evers and James Meredith intervened.[12] The hundreds of young people who participated in these protests were no less courageous or motivated than the passive resisters and no less part of a movement. But their actions made it clear that they believed that repression would only yield to force. One study concluded that black working-class parents of CORE volunteers were less concerned with the possibility that their children would end up in jail and more concerned with the perils of pacifism. "Most of the working parents—like with the CORE members—just object to the nonviolence," said one CORE leader. "That's what they disapproved of most. They wished we were taking guns."[13] It was the genius of the Deacons that they recognized this sentiment and offered black men a way to participate in the movement while maintaining their concept of male honor and dignity.

"The lesson of Birmingham," Malcolm X once observed, "is the Negroes have lost their fear of the white man's reprisals and will react with violence, if provoked."[14] One of the great ironies of the civil rights movement was that black collective force did not simply *enhance* the bargaining power of moderates; it was the very *source* of their power. This was evident even at the March on Washington, long heralded as the apogee of the nonviolent movement. Although the day at the reflecting pool was tranquil, the weeks preceding the march provoked considerable anxiety over fears of violence. The city banned liquor sales, President Kennedy mobilized 4,000 troops and placed another 15,000 paratroopers on alert in North Carolina. Authorities in Washington, according to one King biographer, feared that "Negroes might sack the Capitol like Moors and Visigoths reincarnate."[15]

Later in the day of the march, King met with Kennedy, accompanied by several other civil rights leaders and labor leader Walter Reuther. Reuther's remarks to the president offer a glimpse at how the fear of violence was shaping white opinion. Reuther took it upon himself to advise Kennedy on how to get the business community to support the pending civil rights legislation. In Detroit, Reuther said, he had pigeonholed automobile executives and told them bluntly, "Look, you can't escape the problem. And there are two ways of resolving it; either by reason or riots." As King looked on, Reuther pushed home his point. "Now the civil war that this is gonna trigger is not gonna be fought at Gettysburg," Reuther warned. "It's gonna be fought in your backyard, in your plant, where your kids are growing up."[16]

Black violence, in the form of riots and militant armed self-defense, fundamentally changed the meaning of nonviolence and the role of King and moderate leaders; it provided moderates with a negotiating power that they had never enjoyed before.[17] It was the threat of black violence, not redemptive suffering and moral suasion, that was now making the political establishment take notice of nonviolent protest. King understood the changing dynamics and readily deployed apocalyptic images of black violence in his speeches and writings. In his famous "Letter from Birmingham City Jail" written in April 1963, King posed nonviolence as the only alternative to an impending violent revolt that was being fomented by the forces of "bitterness and hatred" in the black movement. If nonviolence "had not emerged I am convinced that by now the streets of the South would be flowing with floods of blood," wrote King. "And I am further convinced that if our white brothers dismiss as 'rabble rousers' and 'outside agitators'—those of us working through the channels of nonviolent direct action . . . millions of Negroes, out of frustration and despair, will seek solace and security in black ideologies, a development that will lead inevitably to a frightening racial nightmare."[18]

King added that the black man had "many pent-up resentments and latent frustrations" that needed to be released through nonviolent marches, sit-ins, and Freedom Rides. "If his repressed emotions do not come out in these nonviolent ways," he warned, "they will come out in ominous expressions of violence. This is not a threat; it is a fact of history."[19]

Following the March on Washington, King returned to his Birmingham theme. "Unless some immediate steps are taken by the u.s. government, to restore a sense of confidence and the protection of life, limb, and property," he told an audience, "my pleas [for nonviolence] will fall on deaf ears and we shall see in Birmingham and Alabama the worst racial holocaust the nation has ever seen." At times, King's message was multilayered and seemingly contradictory, conveying different meanings to different audiences. His preachments against violence were intended for blacks, while his allusions to retributive violence were intended for whites.[20]

King's words were not wasted on the nation's leaders. What the Kennedy administration feared was not peaceful protest, but the black violence that might accompany it.[21] After the Birmingham riots, Attorney General Robert Kennedy expressed concern that police violence "could trigger off a good deal of violence around the country, with Negroes saying that they've been abused for all these years and they are gonna have to start following the ideas of the Black Muslims and not go along with the white people." President Kennedy, in his famous 11 June 1963 speech calling for civil rights legislation, spoke of "a rising tide of discontent that threatens the public safety." Social chaos would be the price of complacency. "The fires of frustration and discord are burning in every city, North and South, where legal remedies are not at hand," Kennedy warned. "Redress is sought in the streets, in demonstrations, parades, and protests which create tensions and threaten violence and threaten lives." Unless Congress acted, the only remedy blacks had was "in the street." In his message to Congress one week later the president revisited his apocalyptic images, speaking of the "fires of frustration and discord" now burning "hotter than ever" and conjuring up images of a nation wracked by "rancor, violence, disunity, and national shame." Kennedy's argument was explicit: nonviolent protest had become violent, and civil rights legislation was the only way to end the protests and avert black violence.[22]

Force and coercion also contributed to the 1965 Voting Rights Act. Although African Americans protested peacefully in Selma, Alabama, by 1965 most whites believed that the nonviolent civil rights movement had disappeared. The summer before, riots had erupted in Harlem; Rochester, New York; Jersey City, Paterson, and Elizabeth, New Jersey; Chicago; and Philadelphia—in which 2,483 rioters were arrested and more than 1,000 stores destroyed. By the time of the Selma march, many white Americans feared that behind every gospel-singing nonviolent protester stood a menacing street thug ready to hurl a firebomb.[23]

The experience of the Deacons lays bare the myth of nonviolence, testifying to the crucial role of defensive violence in securing enforcement of the law of the land. The Deacons' greatest accomplishment was in Bogalusa, where their willingness to retaliate against Klan violence ultimately forced the federal government to enforce the Civil Rights Act and the Bill of Rights, assert federal supremacy, and destroy two major pillars of white supremacy—local police repression and Klan terror. Since the beginning of the movement in 1960, rights activists had pleaded with the federal government for protection, to no avail. Not even the assassination of black deputy O'Neal Moore in June 1965 aroused the government to action. But when Deacon Henry Austin shot Alton Crowe in defense of a lawful civil rights march, the White House finally decided that violence had become a problem in the South. After years of appeasing white supremacists—a policy that led to a decade of unmitigated terrorism, marked by a score of assassinations and thousands of vicious beatings and imprisonments—it finally took the blood of one white man to change the course of history.

The Deacons' tactical flexibility gave them an immense advantage over doctrinaire nonviolent organizations. The national civil rights organizations like SCLC, SNCC, and CORE succeeded in drawing national attention to the plight of black southerners, exposing the latent violence concealed within segregation and winning federal civil rights legislation. They were courageous and visionary, and their members served as exemplary models of moral commitment. But the hard truth is that these organizations produced few victories in their local projects in the Deep South—if success is measured by the ability to force changes in local government policy and create self-governing and sustainable local organizations that could survive when the national organizations departed. Indeed, time and again SNCC's local voter registration projects ended in demoralization and defeat. The celebrated McComb voter registration campaign of 1962, which established the template for future SNCC organizing in Mississippi, resulted in registering only six new voters in six months.[24]

In contrast, the Deacons' campaigns frequently resulted in substantial and unprecedented victories at the local level, producing real power and self-sustaining organizations. Their willingness to use force, unlike the national civil rights organizations, was a vital part of their strategy. In Jonesboro, the Deacons made history when they compelled Louisiana governor John McKeithen to intervene in the city's civil rights crisis and require a compromise with city leaders—the first capitulation to the civil rights movement by a Deep South governor. In Bogalusa, the Deacons scored a dramatic victory in May 1965 when they forced city officials and business leaders to agree to abolish all segregation laws, provide equal protection under the law for protesters, integrate city government and police, and carry out physical improvements in the black neighborhoods. When the Klan blocked the agreement, the Deacons were, again, the first organization to successfully compel the federal government to intervene against the Klan and official intransigence. Across the state line, the Natchez campaign, employing the Deacons' organizing model, was undoubtedly the greatest success of the civil rights movement in Mississippi: its mobilization of the entire black community led to massive marches, hundreds of arrests, and a devastating boycott that brought the city fathers to their knees. Similarly, the Port Gibson Deacons ensured the success of the boycott of town businesses and helped build local organizing capacity to the point that when local activists decided to part ways with Charles Evers, the community emerged from the crisis even stronger than before. No other civil rights–era organization could claim these kinds of achievements. Force made the difference between success and failure.

In addition to appreciating the role of force, the Deacons understood the importance of respect and honor in the social revolution in the South. For black men to become equal in the eyes of whites, they had to acquire the respect that comes with fear. The Deacons believed that by encouraging armed self-defense, they were not only unshackling black men from the chains of fear and passivity, they were also vanquishing a submissive stereotype that fostered white supremacist attitudes and violence.[25] Implicit in their actions was a belief that black self-respect and dignity depended on the ability to defend themselves against white violence.[26] Self-defense became the sine qua non of black dignity. Nonviolence was the path to self-respect and personal dignity for many African American men—but not all. Segregation and the caste system in the South rested on violence—state and vigilante violence. White violence could not be overcome through an increased sense of worth; self-respect never stopped a lynch mob. To overcome white terror, blacks had to gain respect through fear. The black image in the white mind had to change. "You have to put some injury on your enemy to get respect," said CORE leader Dave Dennis in the wake of the murder of three civil rights workers in Philadelphia, Mississippi.[27]

Moreover, for many black men, especially the nonpacifist working-class men who found the Deacons appealing, nonviolence posed a serious dilemma. Profound psychological changes were required for black men to transform their social identity and emancipate themselves—including overcoming passive and submissive stereotypes. In the minds of southern whites, the ritual of nonviolent protest, centering on the interplay of domination and submission, only reinforced the stereotype of black men as passive, timorous, and childlike. Robert F. Williams, the president of the militant Monroe, North Carolina, NAACP, who once castigated nonviolence as "ritual sado-masochism," summarized the misgivings that many black men had about nonviolence. "There are many liberals and many organizations in the North that are dumping hundreds of thousands of dollars into our struggle in the South," said Williams:

> This money is sent into the South to convert us to nonviolence, to make us pacifists. But you see, the thing is that we've always been submissive. We've served in slavery; we were submissive then. We've gone through a period of lynching, of all types of brutal exploitation. And our children have been denied the right to grow up, to develop as total human beings. Our women have been raped and our men deprived of the right to stand up as men. . . . Nobody spends money to go into the South and ask the racists to be martyrs or pacifists. But they always come to the downtrodden Negro who is already oppressed, who's already too submissive, and then ask him not to fight back.[28]

If black men wanted to effectively counter vigilante violence, they had to maintain a "credible threat of violence" in the eyes of whites. According to the southern white code of honor, passivity was cowardice and cowards were inherently inferior. Honor required a man to defend his family and home—something that nonviolence prohibited. Southern whites could not respect, let alone fear, a man without honor. Without fear of reprisals, white terror and the caste system would continue, and southern whites would never regard blacks as their equals. The experience of black abolitionist and former slave Frederick Douglass illustrates how both slaves and slave masters linked self-defense to self-respect. One day as a young man Douglass refused to be beaten by his overseer, Edward Covey the "Negro Breaker." "It was a glorious resurrection, from the tomb of slavery to the heaven of freedom," wrote Douglass in a memoir. "My long-crushed spirit rose, cowardice departed, bold defiance took its place; and I now resolved that, however long I might remain a slave in form, the day had passed forever when I would be a slave in fact. I did not hesitate to let it be known of me, that the white man who expected to succeed in whipping me, must also succeed in killing me." Douglass believed that he had restored his manhood; as one historian observed, when Covey walked away from Douglass, "he had implicitly accepted Douglass's assertion of his liberty and equality." The same could be said for what happened when the Klan walked away from the Deacons.[29]

Northern whites had stereotypes about southern blacks as well, though they were anchored in the hoary images of noble suffering savages or docile helpless children. Nonviolence was never intended to help African Americans counter passive or impulsive stereotypes, nor overcome the psychological barriers that prevented an effective assault on economic and social inequality. It was a strategy devoid of racial pride, masculine honor, and self-reliance—all crucial qualities for the birth of the New Negro in the South. From the outset, nonviolence implicitly conceded the white stereotype of African Americans as violent, impulsive, and lacking self-restraint: they were either beast or child (one could argue that the popular myth that the black freedom movement lunged blindly from peaceful protest to violent riots was the political representation of this dualistic cultural stereotype). Many northern whites were convinced that blacks were fundamentally different: that they lacked the internal psychological restraints and self-discipline that were the hallmarks of civilization; that blacks had failed Cicero's dictum, "let the passions be amenable to reason." They believed that blacks, unlike themselves, could not move between conflicting emotional states and behaviors: hate and forgiveness, violence and peace.

Martin Luther King had hoped that nonviolence would allay white liberal fears of black vengeance and retaliation in the aftermath of freedom by demonstrating that blacks were unwilling to respond with force to the gravest assaults and provocations. But the failure to challenge and eradicate this stereotype continues to haunt American race relations in two important ways. First, by winning sympathy through conformance with white expectations of passive behavior, passive behavior became the condition for continuing support—which helps explain why white liberal support evaporated so rapidly during the Black Power period. Second, since the 1960s opponents of the black policy agenda have adroitly mobilized support by deploying images of blacks as an intemperate people lacking the virtues of self-denial: sobriety, thrift, and delayed gratification. These "intemperate" stereotypes have found their way into virtually every social policy debate on the causes and remedies for poverty, crime, drugs, education, and employment. Black pacifism may have pricked the conscience of northerners and assuaged their fears of black violence, but it did little to subvert the negative images that hobbled black social and economic progress. White guilt came at the expense of black dignity.[30]

The Deacons' strength was that they were the *only* southernwide organization created and controlled by the black working class during the civil rights movement. It is no coincidence that it was crystallized around a challenge to the doctrine of nonviolence, which, as a matter of principle, deprived African Americans of an indispensable means of countering white terror. The Deacons reflected the reality that there were competing forces in the black movement based on class and geography, with conflicting views of how black liberation should be achieved. The Deacons' strategy gave the movement a new ability to determine the terms of the conflict in the South. Previously, the nonviolent organizations had conceded to the federal government the exclusive right to use force and, by doing so, surrendered strategic control of the black movement to the government. The federal government alone—not the movement—had the right to decide when to use force against racist terror. The Deacons ended this practice by using the threat of force to appropriate the right to choose their own battles. This gave the black movement the flexibility and power to redefine its strategy toward the Klan, manifest in Bogalusa where the Deacons' decision to confront Klansmen compelled the federal government to intervene—according to the Deacons' terms and timing.

The Deacons did not see their self-defense activities as mutually exclusive of nonviolent tactics and voter registration. Viewing themselves as part of the broader civil rights movement, they did not oppose nonviolent direct action—indeed, they supported it, employed it as a tactic, and expended most of their energy defending its practitioners. What the Deacons opposed was the dogmatic idea that nonviolent direct action precluded self-defense. The Deacons evolved a more flexible strategy—similar to the 1930s labor movement—that employed tactics of nonviolence, direct action, symbolic protest, and the judicious use of defensive force. The choice confronting the black movement was not, as Martin Luther King and his disciples maintained, strictly a choice between nonviolence and violence. By cloaking their pragmatic legislative strategy in religious pacifist trappings, the partisans of nonviolence could take the high moral ground and dismiss their critics as being pro-violence. It was a clever use of language. But the Deacons never advocated violence. It was quite possible to follow a peaceful path, while rejecting nonviolence's inflexible passive strictures and legislative reform strategies. What pacifists disparaged as *violence* was in fact *force*—the willingness to coerce change rather than win consent from one's enemies.

That many of the national civil rights organizations rejected the Deacons is not surprising. The national organizations had a narrow conception of what comprised "the movement," so confining that it excluded hundreds of thousands of African Americans who were also fighting racism. The civil rights movement was only part of a much broader black freedom movement that contained a variety of strategies that were simultaneously competing for the loyalty of African Americans. This parallel movement was comprised of public figures like Malcolm X and organizations like the black nationalists and the Deacons. It also encompassed what Malcolm called "the brothers in the streets," those thousands of southern working-class blacks who had taken to the streets for defensive violence in cities like Birmingham, Mc-Comb, and Natchez; and they were the hundreds of students who had rebuked the nonviolent movement and fought back against police violence at Jackson State University in Mississippi. These defensive street rebellions from Birmingham forward, though not plotted out in seminaries and foundation offices, were conscious strategies, as well, with clear ideas about how to counter police and vigilante terror and how to force the white majority to correct injustices. There was a common thread that united the armed self-defense movement, the Black Power movement, and the thousands of working-class blacks who shunned nonviolence and participated in collective civil violence. All these disparate groupings shared what might be called a "black autonomist" strategy. Black autonomists were defined by their refusal to allow their political behavior to be dependent on maintaining a coalition with white liberals or the federal government. Largely anchored in the black working class, the black autonomists acted without concern for alienating white liberals or accommodating white fears of black violence.[31] This stance was reflected in the Deacons who, like Malcolm X, used rhetoric and exemplary courage to counter fear and resignation. For the Deacons, the imperative was psychological liberation, even if it jeopardized the black-liberal coalition.

The autonomist movement had its own problems. Riots and street rebellions lacked leadership and discipline and were prone to reckless violence, needlessly endangering lives and property. Ironically, because of its inflexibility, nonviolence ultimately delivered young people into the hands of street violence, since there was no organized alternative to the middle-class dominated civil rights organizations until 1965. The Deacons were the first indigenous southern organization to offer a middle path, *tertium quid*, that attracted people who doubted the effectiveness of nonviolence but had no taste for riotous behavior (on more than one occasion the Deacons played a role in quelling riots).

In the end, Martin Luther King crafted a successful strategy for winning legislative civil reforms, but it came at the expense of challenging economic inequality and changing the attitudes, practices, customs, and institutional systems that also sustained inequality. Nothing in the rhetoric of nonviolence helped white Americans understand the social and economic legacy of three centuries of racism—and the government resources and compensatory policies that would be necessary to reverse its effects. The limitations of nonviolence rhetoric came back to haunt the black movement in the decades following the Civil Rights Act. By equating rights with freedom, opponents of the black agenda could claim that racism had been vanquished since the civil barriers to progress had been lifted; the playing field had been leveled and merit alone determined success or failure. Any remaining economic inequality was the result of defects in blacks' values and character—the lack of industry, thrift, and self-discipline (here again, the stubborn stereotypes that nonviolence left unchallenged).

In a final twist of irony, King's "content of our character" phrase became a rallying cry against any race-conscious policy intended to remedy inequality. The single-minded focus of nonviolence on legislative coalition building to win civil reforms came at a high price. Nonviolence ultimately subsumed economic equality under a civil reform agenda that served the interests of white liberals and middle-class blacks. For the next three decades the nation would pay the price in the form of persistent urban poverty, profound inequalities in education, and a host of social and economic equity issues. Remarkably, even the lion of the nonviolent movement displayed an uncanny appreciation for the shortcomings of the strategy he had pioneered for ten years. In November 1966 King told an SCLC staff retreat that the civil rights movement "did not defeat the monster of racism." Blacks needed "to see that racism is still alive in our country" and that "the roots of racism are very deep in America." Legislative and judicial victories against the caste system "did very little to improve the lot of millions of Negroes in the teeming ghettos of the North." The civil rights victories—integration of public accommodations and enforcement of equal voting rights—"were at best surface change, they were not really substantive changes." Voting rights and desegregation had primarily benefited the black middle class by opening new job opportunities, but the millions of poor blacks in the nation's ghettos had seen their condition actually worsen. "Now what I want to say is that we are now making demands that will cost the nation something," King continued. In effect, King was admitting that the legislative reform strategy had erred in equating civil inequality with racism.[32]

There is one final contribution that the Deacons made to the black freedom movement, and that is in the realm of black consciousness. Only when blacks felt entitled to their rights would their rights be secure. These changes in consciousness were far more significant than laws and judicial decisions, for without these changes, whites and blacks would have inevitably slipped back into the old roles, habits, and customs. Blacks had to construct a new political personality. It is in this realm of consciousness changing that Malcolm X and Black Power groups excelled over nonviolent organizations. In the final analysis, the most important elements of contemporary black political identity and consciousness—group identity, racial pride, militance without regard for white approbation, and the will to defend rights at all costs— owe more to Malcolm X than to Martin Luther King.[33]

No small measure of the Deacons' success came from their emphasis on changing consciousness over changing laws, and in this regard they shared much in common with black nationalism. Changing black consciousness was a paramount concern for Malcolm X and the nationalist current of the freedom movement that predated the rise of Black Power. Nationalists were defined by a core of shared and interrelated beliefs: the power of group identity; the notion that rights are natural and inalienable rather than a reward conditioned on good behavior; a willingness to use coercion and force to secure these rights with little concern for winning sympathy or approval from the ethnic majority; the conviction that these rights can only be won and secured by transforming the consciousness of the oppressed— engendering self-respect, courage, confidence, and a sense of entitlement— rather than depending on the goodwill of the oppressor; a belief that power for the dispossessed depends more on fear than guilt; and the idea that real freedom is found in the struggle for freedom—that psychological liberation is the precondition of political freedom. For nationalists, the fundamental choice confronting the black movement was between guilt or coercion.[34]

Nationalists rebelled against whites dictating the terms of the movement and defining the emerging black political identity. Violence and separatist rhetoric served to drive whites out of the movement, providing blacks with the organizational independence necessary to change black consciousness. As a consequence, the source of power for blacks in America today is not only civil rights laws, but also a new black political identity derived from Black Power consciousness that emphasized racial pride, self-respect, militancy, coercion, and a resolute belief in rights entitlement. These changes in consciousness among ordinary blacks were critical to making economic advances and protecting rights following the civil rights movement. The Deacons served as a unique bridge between the civil rights movement and the burgeoning nationalist groups. While continuing to identify with the older goals of the civil rights agenda, the Deacons saw their principal project as creating new black men and women who confronted whites on their own terms. "When you're dealing with the wolf," said Deacons militant Henry Austin, "you have to speak the language of the wolf."[35]

The Deacons—and the Black Power movement that followed them—represented a decisive shift from the politics of the past. The new militants swept away old ideologies, deposed old leaders, and forged a new black identity. They operated on the premise that to bring about real social and economic equality, the social costs of disruption had to exceed the social costs of inequality.[36] The significance of the Deacons' strategy is even more evident when contrasted with the accommodationist politics that preceded them. Fear and resignation posed real obstacles to the movement. It is noteworthy that even the most militant campaigns in Louisiana—Jonesboro and Bogalusa—occurred in communities that, prior to the Civil Rights Act and the arrival of CORE, never engaged in a single organized public protest against segregation laws. To ignore this reality is to miss how radically the Deacons departed from the politics of the past, and to diminish the magnitude of their contribution to the African American freedom movement.

Somewhere along the way the Deacons were forgotten—and for a reason. They simply did not fit into the myth of nonviolence. They stood as an embarrassing testimonial to the level of force that was necessary to bring African Americans into full citizenship.

Violence is a controversial and emotional subject. Americans would like to believe that change has always been peaceful and orderly. We like to believe that each generation learns from the past, and we fear that young people will learn the wrong lessons from history; that in an age of numbing violence, a story about people who took the law into their own hands is a misguided fable.

But the story of the Deacons is at heart a cautionary tale and a compass for finding more peaceful ways to remedy injustice in the future. Moral appeals to the conscience of America were indispensable to the success of the movement. They won millions to the cause of racial justice, and, for those who were not so moved, moral arguments gave an enduring ethical legitimacy to the new laws and their underlying principles. But moral suasion reached its limits as the movement began to demand change that undermined white privilege. When change came, it was because some Americans hoped to buy salvation, while others only hoped to buy social insurance against disorder. In the end, both love and fear animated the social revolution of the 1960s.

In an ideal world, rational argument and moral suasion should settle all conflicts. But that was not the history of the civil rights movement. We can predict with the precision of science that problems of inequality and ethnic competition for power and resources will persist well into the future. What the Deacons tell us is that when appeals to reason and morality fail, oppressed people will turn to coercive methods of disruption, force, and violence. We delude ourselves as a nation if we think we can remain indifferent to these inequities and injustices without paying a price. We have the historical hindsight and the means to stop this cycle of violence.

Finally, there is something inspiring in a story of people who stood up to injustice when everyone around them was afraid. That is a fable that will always serve us well.

Notes

Abbreviations

airtel	air telegram
ARC	Amistad Research Center, Tulane University, New Orleans
BDN	*Bogalusa Daily News*
CORE	Congress of Racial Equality
CORE (FFM)	Ferriday Freedom Movement Files, CORE Papers, SHSW
CORE (Jackson Parish)	Jackson Parish Files, CORE Papers, SHSW
CORE (Microfilm)	CORE Papers, Microfilm, ARC
CORE (SHSW)	CORE Papers, SHSW
CORE (SRO)	Southern Regional Office, CORE Papers, SHSW
GMHP	Gwendolyn Midlo Hall Papers, ARC
LHM	Letterhead Memorandum
LW	*Louisiana Weekly*
MFP	Miriam Feingold Papers, SHSW
MHS	Minnesota Historical Society, St. Paul
MLK	Martin Luther King Jr.
NOT-P	*New Orleans Times-Picayune*
NYT	*New York Times*
PSCSUA	Project South Collection, Stanford University Archives, Stanford, Calif. (Glen Rock, N.J.: Microfilming Corp. of America, 1975)
SAC	Special Agent in Command
SHSW	State Historical Society of Wisconsin, Madison
SNCCP	Student Nonviolent Coordinating Committee Papers, MLK Center for Nonviolent Social Change, Atlanta
TDC	Tom Dent Collection, ARC
WFO	Washington Field Office, FBI

Introduction

1. Burris interview by author (quotations); *LW*, 24 September 1966; *NOT-P*, 14 September 1966. Tension was exacerbated at the school by a rumor that civil rights activist James Meredith had been invited to speak there. See Sobel, *Civil Rights*, 407.

2. Burris interview by author.

3. Ibid.

4. There are abundant cases of individual African Americans defending themselves and communities against racist attacks before and during the civil rights movement. Some scholars offer these incidents as evidence of political resistance to oppression, a break from subjugation, or a conscious effort to subvert white supremacy. But individual acts of self-defense did not in themselves constitute a sign of militancy or a leap of consciousness. Physically defending oneself can be motivated by nothing more than common sense and the instinct to survive. Armed self-defense had no political significance until it became collective and public and openly challenged authority and white terror. Unlike individualized resistance, collective and public self-defense was an assertion of group rights and equality, and, as we shall see with the Deacons, had the potential to effectively counter police violence and white terrorism. The Jim Crow system frequently tolerated individual acts of self-defense against random white invasions of homes. But *collective* armed defense was the kiss of death for African Americans in the South, because it implicitly claimed social and civil equality. The real sea change in consciousness occurred when African Americans transformed this isolated, covert practice into a well-organized public movement— and asserted the same right to collective armed defense that whites possessed. The proscriptions against black collective armed self-defense date back to Reconstruction. Kantrowitz ("One Man's Mob," 67) concludes that in South Carolina "black men's right to vote and bear arms in collective struggle represented a revolutionary challenge to white patriarchal authority."

Because I draw an important distinction between the Deacons and the covert, pragmatic self-defense groups that preceded them, I do not devote space to documenting the history of these earlier self-defense activities. But the accounts of these incidents of armed self-defense are substantial. An overview of informal armed self-defense groups can be found in Tyson, *Radio Free Dixie*. See also Tyson, "Robert F. Williams," 543 (n. 4). There was nothing clandestine about Tyson's subject: a militant North Carolina activist, Williams was the first figure in the modern civil rights movement to publicly practice and endorse what he called "armed self-reliance." The definitive account of Mississippi self-defense activities is contained in Umoja, "Eye for an Eye." Umoja uncovers a large number of clandestine and informal self-defense groups throughout Mississippi, operating in virtually every community where the Student Nonviolent Coordinating Committee (SNCC) was active. Accounts can also be found in Dittmer, *Local*

People; Payne, *Light of Freedom*; and Youth of the Rural Organizing and Cultural Center, *Mind Stayed on Freedom*. Dent's interviews in the TDC contain a wealth of references to armed self-defense in Mississippi; see esp. interviews with Charlie Cobb, Jerome Smith (on Choctaw Indians in Lee County, Miss., aiding the black community), June Johnson, and Mary Hightower. In Meridian, Miss., in 1964, Rev. R. S. Porter organized a self-defense organization that included one white member, Bill Ready; see Nelson, *Terror in the Night*, 108–9. A study of the remarkable Columbia riot of 1946, in which African Americans engaged in extensive self-defense, is found in O'Brien, *Color of Law*. Accounts of self-defense groups in Louisiana can also be found in Meier and Rudwick, *CORE*, 263–64. At their national meeting in June 1964, SNCC staffers reported widespread armed self-defense activities in Mississippi. See Staff Meeting Minutes, 10 June 1964, box 7, folder 8, SNCCP. On armed guards in King's house, see Fairclough, *To Redeem the Soul*, 24–25 (Glenn Smiley said that the "whole movement is armed in a sense, and this is what I must convince him [King] to see as the greatest evil" [25]), and Belfrage, *Freedom Summer*, xvii.

5. To this day, the Deacons remain an important part of African American lore in the Deep South. Akinyele Umoja credits the Deacons with pioneering the organized self-defense movement in the region. In his study of armed self-defense in Mississippi, Umoja ("Eye for an Eye," 186, 194) concludes that the "Deacons of Defense and Justice provided the paradigm for protection of the Movement and the Black community in general" and "served as a model for Blacks interested in armed self-defense in Mississippi and throughout the South." Also according to Umoja ("Repression Breeds Resistance," 5), the Deacons were "considered by many to be the armed wing of the civil rights movement from 1965 through 1969." Among the definitive works on the mainstream nonviolence groups are Garrow, *Bearing the Cross*; Fairclough, *To Redeem the Soul*; Branch, *Parting the Waters* and *Pillar of Fire*; Meier and Rudwick, *CORE*; Carson, *In Struggle*; and Kluger, *Simple Justice*. See also Tushnet, *The NAACP's Legal Strategy against Segregated Education*. Fairclough's book on Louisiana, *Race and Democracy*, touches briefly on the Deacons in Bogalusa.

6. Brink and Harris, *Negro Revolution*, 72–74, 206–7. Lerone Bennett Jr. addresses the additional dynamic of emotional repression and self-hatred. "But the harsh fact is that the choice for most Negroes is not between hating or loving, but between hating and hating," wrote the black intellectual in 1964, "between hating themselves or hating their oppressors. You cannot deny people the basic emotions of rage, resentment and, yes, hate. Only slaves or saints or masochists love their oppressors. If you humiliate a man, if you degrade him, if you do this over and over for hundreds of years, he will either hate you or hate himself." Bennett, *Negro Mood*, 146.

7. Scholarly interest in the role of local organizing began with community studies like Garrow, *Protest at Selma*; Thornton, "Challenge and Response"; Norrell, *Reaping the Whirlwind*; Chafe, *Civilities and Civil Rights*; and Colburn, *Racial*

Change. Early community studies of the civil rights movement revealed the distinctions between local and national movements; see Eagles, *Civil Rights Movement,* esp. Carson's essay, 19–32. Regional studies have expanded significantly in recent years with works like Dittmer's *Local People* and Payne's *Light of Freedom.*

8. Tyson, *Radio Free Dixie.* NAACP leaders spared no efforts in ostracizing Williams, including bribing Little Rock activist Daisy Bates to condemn Williams—despite her own use of armed guards. See ibid., 159. On Williams's view of the 27 August 1961 Monroe riot, see his *Negroes with Guns.* An illuminating first-person account of the riot can be found in Mayfield, "The Monroe Kidnapping." Williams did not attempt to build separate self-defense organizations outside of Monroe, though he did much to publicize his criticism of nonviolence in his publication *Crusader* and his book *Negroes with Guns.* He later broadcast his philosophy across the South on his Cuban radio program, "Radio Free Dixie." None of the Deacons interviewed recalled hearing of Williams before they joined the organization, but Williams was widely known among CORE and SNCC activists. When Sam Block, Willie Peacock, and other SNCC workers were arrested in June 1964, authorities found a large number of copies of the *Crusader*; see Tyson, *Radio Free Dixie,* 290.

9. McMillen, *Citizens' Council.*

10. On the distinction between the Council and the Klan, see ibid., 359–63.

11. I define the region of the Klan Nation as encompassing the Third Congressional District in southwestern Mississippi and the adjoining Sixth Congressional District in southeastern Louisiana—sometimes referred to as the "Florida parishes." Normally the historiography of the civil rights movement makes African Americans the subject of history, as, indeed, they were. There is some benefit, though, to viewing the period as a defense of caste privilege, rather than simply motivated by "hatred" as most paradigms suggest. Viewing poor whites in this sense underscores how important white terrorism was in support of the caste system and how any efforts to dismantle that system without neutralizing white terrorism—the Kennedy-Johnson strategy—were doomed to fail. On the Klan's meteoric growth during 1964–65, see U.S. House, *Present-Day Ku Klux Klan* and *Activities of Ku Klux Klan.*

12. On Jim Crow remaining the "rule rather than the exception" after the Civil Rights Act, see Dittmer, *Local People,* 390.

13. Cashmore's *Dictionary of Race and Ethnic Relations,* 63–64, offers a typical example of the nonviolence myth in publications for the general public. The Civil Rights Act was due "in large part to the sustained, nonviolent campaigns of the civil rights movement and the ability of King to negotiate at the highest political levels" reads the entry on the civil rights movement. "Whereas King and his movement brought, through peaceful means, tangible gains and a heightening of self-respect for blacks, the new movement [Black Power] was based on the view that no significant long-term improvements could be produced through working peacefully with the political system—as King had done."

14. The portrayal of King as naive idealist–turned-pragmatist—or a shrewd pragmatist all along—underpins most of the recent works on King and the movement; see Garrow, *Protest at Selma*, esp. the chapter, "The Strategy of Protest and the SCLC at Selma," 212–36. Garrow characterizes King as moving from a "moral commitment to nonviolence" to a more pragmatic strategy designed to win the broader populace. He takes the "idealist to pragmatist" a step further, suggesting that King deliberately sought to provoke white violent reactions to protest in order to garner sympathy in the North. The failed Albany campaign convinced him that nonviolence was "unrealistic and ineffective" and moved him toward a strategy of "coercive nonviolence" as opposed to "persuasive nonviolence." The new coercive strategy was intended to win "external allies" and force through federal legislation—and the path to federal legislation lay in national news media (pp. 221–22, 224–25). Fairclough (*To Redeem the Soul*, 52–53) argues that King was never an idealist; that he "never made an unqualified assertion that nonviolent protest succeeded through moral suasion," and that the notion of redemptive suffering was "marginal" to his strategy.

What King believed and what he said may have been two different things; but in social movements, one's public expressions are all that matters; it is what defines the movement's image, message, and appeal. King's constant public exhortations to nonviolence leave little question about his public image. On his first and most definitive publication on nonviolence, see MLK, *Stride toward Freedom*.

15. Clayborne Carson offers that local organizations "were more concerned with local issues, including employment opportunities and political power, than with achieving national legislation"; they were not "designed to persuade and coerce the federal government to act on behalf of black civil rights." Carson, "Civil Rights Reform," 24, 27.

16. The idea that whites could be won by moral argument by exploiting the tension between American principles and practice is expressed in Myrdal, *American Dilemma*.

17. MLK, *Stride toward Freedom*, 215–17.

18. Garrow, *Protest at Selma*, 224–25 (King); *LW*, 17 July 1965. King never wavered in his public preachments for pacifism as a response to white violence. In the aftermath of the worst police violence in the Birmingham campaign, he took the pulpit at New Pilgrim Baptist Church to sermonize that the guiding ideal of the movement should be based on the Greek notion of *agape*—"an overflowing, redemptive love toward all men." Quoted in Fairclough, *To Redeem the Soul*, 138–39.

19. Fredrickson, *Black Liberation*, 232. There is clearly a need for a full study of the pragmatic reformist roots of nonviolence in the civil rights movement. King himself knew full well the pitfalls of Christian pacifism and was profoundly affected by his reading of Nietzsche's *Genealogy of Morals*, which criticized Christian otherworldliness and the precepts of suffering, piety, and humility. See McCartney, *Black Power Ideologies*.

20. Bennett, *Negro Mood*, 30–31.

21. Lynch quoted in *NYT*, 22 June 1966.

22. Popularized historical treatments of Martin Luther King's theological and political education—based largely on his autobiographical work—have perpetuated this identification of nonviolence with philosophy and religion. It is noteworthy that some scholars have concluded that King's core beliefs on social change and the role of the church—the "social gospel" doctrine—originated not from white theologians and philosophers, but rather from the pragmatic "African-American folk religion" that King learned from his father's sermons and activities at Ebenezer Baptist Church. King's later study of the works of Niebuhr, Rauschenbusch, Fosdick, and Gandhi clarified and gave intellectual force to his ideas, but they were not the original inspiration for his political strategy. His first principles were rooted in folk religion, black middle-class reformism, and pragmatism. On the influence of black folk religion on King, see Baldwin, *Balm in Gilead* and Keith D. Miller, *Voice of Deliverance*, 58–66, 88. Branch (*Parting the Waters*, 138–40) suggests that King initially seized upon the theme of nonviolence in the Montgomery Bus Boycott primarily to distinguish the black boycott from the coercive and violent white Citizens Council boycotts. The criticism that nonviolence was a conciliatory political strategy masquerading as religion dates back to the anticolonial movement in India. Gandhi's Muslim adversaries often dismissed nonviolence as Hindu accommodation to British imperialism.

23. Nonviolence is a difficult term to define in part because there is no scholarly consensus on the meaning of its antithesis—violence. Gandhi himself argued that nonviolence meant the primacy of means over ends; that nonviolence was not a means to a goal, but the goal itself; that success should not be measured by the achievement of political reforms, but by a permanent change in the human spirit. For Gandhi, nonviolence was the path of purification—means and ends were identical. "Take an instance of untruth or violence," he wrote, "and it will be found that at its back is the desire to attain the cherished end." This otherworldly "primacy of means" concept would later pose problems for civil rights activists who attempted to employ nonviolence as a pragmatic political reform strategy. See Bell, *CORE*, 117; Hanigan, *King . . . and the Foundations of Nonviolence*; and Bondurant, *Conquest of Violence* (Gandhi). Bondurant discusses Gandhi's ends-means concept on pp. 229–32. In his seminal *Reflections on Violence*, Georges Sorel argued that the distinction between legitimate state authority and violence was artificial; that ruling elites used violence cloaked in the authority of the state. For ruling elites, force equals authority and violence equals revolt. By naming his strategy as "nonviolence," Gandhi was conceding the ruling elite's notion that any force on behalf of the oppressed was illegitimate "violence." The distinctions between coercion, force, and violence are subtle yet critical to understanding the role of nonviolence in the civil rights movement. See Ronald B. Miller, "Violence, Force, and Coercion," 9–44. Anthony Oberschall (*Social Conflict*, 332–33) argues that violence is "but one of several means of

conducting conflict" and that conflict can be pursued through a mixture of collective (civil) violence, nonviolence, coercive and noncoercive means. He defines violence as "the use of force with the intent of inflicting damage or injury upon one's opponent in order to coerce him against his will."

Chapter One

1. Thomas interview by author.

2. Shugg, *Origins of Class Struggle*. The impact of automation in discussed in Zieger, *Rebuilding the Pulp . . . Union*. On the role of blacks in the paper industry, see Northrup, *The Negro in the Paper Industry*.

3. Daniel Mitchell to Ronnie M. Moore, "Jackson Parish and Jonesboro, Louisiana: A White Paper," [September 1964], Jonesboro, Monroe Project Files, CORE (SHSW) (hereafter cited as Daniel Mitchell, "White Paper").

4. Census data cited in ibid.

5. Ibid.

6. Ibid.

7. For a summary of the literature on black fraternal orders, see Fahey, *Black Lodge*, 5–12.

8. Daniel Mitchell, "White Paper."

9. Ibid.; Kirkpatrick interview by Hall.

10. Daniel Mitchell, "White Paper." On the campaign to destroy the NAACP in Louisiana in the 1950s, see Fairclough, *Race and Democracy*, which also contains a comprehensive history of the Louisiana NAACP. Local NAACP chapters often enjoyed a great deal of independence from the national NAACP, and Voters Leagues also served to keep the national organization at a distance. Similar state studies of the movements in Mississippi and Georgia draw the same conclusion on the local NAACP chapters. On Mississippi, see Payne, *Light of Freedom*, and Dittmer, *Local People*; on Georgia, see Tuck, *Beyond Atlanta*. Louisiana had a significantly higher percentage of black voters who were registered in comparison to surrounding states. Black voter registration in 1960 was 30 percent for Louisiana, 14 percent for Alabama, and only 6 percent for Mississippi. Twenty-seven counties with substantial black populations had no registered voters, including four in Louisiana. See Doar and Landsberg, "Performance of the FBI," 6:955.

11. Kirkpatrick interview by Hall; Daniel Mitchell, "White Paper." The clientelist relationship between black political machines and the white power structure was noted early on by Myrdal, *American Dilemma*, 498–99.

12. "Weekly Report—August 1–August 4," [August 1964], Clinton, La., box 4, folder 13, CORE (SRO). The role of the black middle class in local movements in the South was a complex one that changed throughout the 1950s and 1960s. Part of the difficulty in assessing its contributions and failings is that the category of middle class cannot be easily assigned by income or profession. While indepen-

dent black business people had the same or better incomes than teachers, they were not as vulnerable to economic retaliation by the white establishment. Gail Williams O'Brien (*Color of Law*, 246–47) found particular militance among black proprietors who played a role in the 1946 Columbia, Tenn., riot. Educational and professional training also shaped the attitudes of middle-class blacks toward the movement, as did community size and proximity to larger urban areas and black institutions of higher education. Different sectors of the middle class had strengths and weaknesses depending on the task at hand: negotiating with the white power structure, winning incremental changes, confrontational politics. The leadership in the local movement included a panoply of social categories with subtle but important differences in political disposition: ministers, church deacons, women church leaders, fraternal order leaders, proprietors, etc. A concise, perceptive description of the diversity of the black middle class by a movement veteran is found in Carmichael and Hamilton, *Black Power*, 101.

13. On mass meetings as a method of leadership control, see the account of Bogalusa mass meetings in Chapters 5–9 of this book, where the old leadership was displaced, and even the new militant leadership was occasionally reigned in; see also Morris, *Origin of the Civil Rights Movement*, 23, 166. In Montgomery, according to Jo Ann Gibson Robinson (*Montgomery Bus Boycott*, 56), the initial mass meetings were used to control community protest.

14. Dittmer, *Local People*, 76 (Evers); Eskew, *But for Birmingham*, 229 (King). John Dittmer (*Local People*, 75–76) notes that in Mississippi "the institutional church did not stand in the forefront of civil rights activity, and black ministers were conspicuously absent from the front ranks of movement leadership."

15. Nixon quoted in Branch, *Parting the Waters*, 136.

16. On black fraternal orders in the South, see the introduction in Fahey, *Black Lodge*.

17. An overall history is covered in Meier and Rudwick, *CORE*. Regrettably, there are still no state studies of the organization, particularly in Louisiana. In contrast, several state studies of NAACP local chapters and state organizations in Louisiana, Mississippi, and Georgia are contained in Fairclough, *Race and Democracy*; Dittmer, *Local People*; Payne, *Light of Freedom*; and Tuck, *Beyond Atlanta*. For a comprehensive history of the SCLC, see Fairclough, *To Redeem the Soul*; Garrow, *Bearing the Cross*; and Branch, *Parting the Waters* and *Pillar of Fire*. SNCC studies include Carson, *In Struggle*, and the state studies of Dittmer and Payne cited above.

18. Meier and Rudwick, *CORE*. CORE's roots in the World War II pacifist movement gave it a much stronger commitment to nonviolence than SNCC, even as the strategy began to falter in the South. As early as 1961, some SNCC activists began to privately question Gandhian principles; see Carson, *In Struggle*, 54, 62, 82, 95.

19. Meier and Rudwick, *CORE*.

20. Laue, *Direct Action*, 85–86 (King), 87 (Lawson).

21. "An Interview with John Lewis: The Chairman of SNCC Discusses the Negro Revolt, Its Problems and Prospects," *Dialogue Magazine* 4, no. 2 (Spring 1964): 7–9, reprinted in Meier, Rudwick, and Broderick, *Black Protest Thought*, 355–56. Bob Moses discussed his opposition to armed defense in Greenwood and Amite County in an interview with Akinyele K. Umoja; see Umoja, "Eye for an Eye," 124 (n. 22). References to SNCC activists carrying weapons are found in Umoja, 169, and throughout the Dent interviews.

22. Quotations from the Atlanta debate on armed self-defense are found in Staff Meeting Minutes, 10 June 1964, box 7, folder 7, 12–15, SNCCP. For RAM's self-defense project in Greenwood, see Ahmad, *History of RAM*, 15, 20, 28, and Forman, *Making of Black Revolutionaries*, 374–75. The Freedom Summer volunteer orientation sessions, conducted during 12–27 June 1964, were organized by the National Council of Churches (NCC), Commission on Religion and Race, with the stated purpose of teaching "the art of nonviolence and interpersonal relations." (Unbeknownst to the participants, Edwin Espy, general secretary of the NCC, secretly turned over a list of all orientation participants to the FBI, including field workers and grassroots attendees.) By midsummer, Mississippi was flooded with nonviolent partisans; in addition to the 800–1,000 Freedom Summer volunteers, the NCC sent 275 of its own volunteer ministers to Mississippi to serve as "counselors." Findlay, *Church People in the Struggle*, 85–87, 89. Clayborne Carson locates the shift away from Gandhism and appeals to liberal conscience among SNCC staff beginning as early as the fall of 1961; he argues that by 1963 most SNCC staff had soured on nonviolence. Dave Dennis, a leader of the Congress of Federated Organizations (COFO) in Mississippi, and other movement leaders set the date of the disillusionment much later—the fall of 1964 following the disappointing Democratic National Convention; Carson, *In Struggle*, 55, 62, 82, 95, and Dennis interview by Dent. David Garrow (*Bearing the Cross*, 171) maintains that King also realized that nonviolence "could not be simply a tool of persuasion for convincing southern whites of the evils of segregation."

23. Dennis interview by Dent; Muse, *American Negro Revolution*, 160 (CORE oath); Moore interview by author; James "Mice" Williams interview by anonymous (Tallulah volunteer). The microfilm edition does not carry names of interviewees; these can be gleaned from the collection container list for the Project South Collection available from http://www.oac.cdlib.org/dvnaweb/ead/stanford/uarc/sco066/@Generic; Internet; accessed 11 November 2002. On armed self-defense in West Feliciana Parish, see Meier and Rudwick, *CORE*, 263–64. Garrow (*Protest at Selma*, 215–18, 220–21) discusses Seifert's and Lipsky's theories on the impact of nonviolence on reform protest. According to Seifert, violence on the part of protesters delegitimates their claims, whereas unprovoked violence inflicted on undeserving victims wins sympathy. Garrow believes that King reached the same conclusion and shrewdly applied these insights to the movement. The counterpoint to this "undeserving victim" theory of reform are those social science theories that argue that radical movements employing coer-

cion can also win reforms by enhancing the appeal of moderates. Two of the greatest victories for the black freedom movement, the Fair Housing Act and President Richard Nixon's affirmative action policy, came on the heels of the massive riots in 1968 at the height of the Black Power movement—which had thoroughly alienated the white majority. This "radical flank" theory is cogently argued in Haines, *Black Radicals*.

24. Moore interview by author; Umoja, "Eye for an Eye," 92–93 (Flug).

25. Mike Lesser, "Report on Jonesboro-Bogalusa Project," March 1965, box 5, folder 5, CORE (SRO); Meier and Rudwick, *CORE*, 266–67.

26. Lesser, "Report."

27. Catherine Patterson Mitchell interview by author.

28. Ibid.

29. Anonymous CORE volunteer interview by anonymous; Daniel Mitchell, "White Paper." The conditions in Louisiana constantly tested the convictions of many CORE volunteers. "I came down here thinking, as I still do, that nonviolence is the way for all men and is the only way that any peace will be achieved," said CORE volunteer Lorraine Roy in 1965. But she was having her doubts. "And until nonviolence as a tactic . . . begins to prick the conscience of the [southern] white, if that doesn't happen soon, people are going to chuck it completely, because it's not defending their families and it's not securing justice. It hasn't been working. It's all been pricking the Northern white conscience, but we're all coming down here." Roy, anonymous interviewer.

30. In a remarkably insightful study of nonviolence and the attitudes of activists, Inge Powell Bell (*CORE*, 43–44) makes a persuasive argument that nonviolence was adopted to legitimize black protest in the eyes of whites and was a concession to whites' unwillingness to accept blacks as fully equal and deserving of the right to use coercive measures to gain their rights. For a comparative study of nonviolence in the United States and South Africa, see Fredrickson, *Black Liberation*, esp. 225–76.

31. Daniel Mitchell, "White Paper."

32. Catherine Paterson Mitchell interview by author.

33. Thomas and Annie Purnell Johnson interviews by author. Any history of a semiclandestine organization like the Deacons must rely heavily on oral interviews. With the exception of a few reprinted news interviews, there are few accounts of the Deacons in published memoirs. First-person accounts of the movement are a growing part of the literature, including CORE and SNCC leaders' contributions such as Farmer, *Lay Bare the Heart*, and Forman, *Making of Black Revolutionaries*. See also Lyon, *Memories of the Southern Civil Rights Movement*; Sutherland, *Letters from Mississippi*; Moody, *Coming of Age in Mississippi*; Reavis, *If White Kids Die*; and various activists' recollections in Cheryl Lynn Greenberg, *Circle of Trust*. The interviews with CORE staff and volunteers found in the Project South Collection at the Stanford University Archives are some of

the most illuminating. Almost all of the interviews touch on the Deacons and nonviolence. There is a marked difference between the Stanford interviews, which were conducted contemporaneously with the movement, and interviews like those in the Tom Dent Collection, which were conducted many years later. The contemporaneous interviews give more emphasis to problems of fear, passivity, and apathy in the rural African American community. See esp. Fred Lacey and James Bell interviews by anonymous. In his interview Bell, a young black community recruit, talks about the "mental block" of deferential attitudes in older African Americans and credits CORE with being a catalyst for change: "The organizations such as CORE have come in, and I think this has changed it . . . has removed the mental block." See also Annie Purnell Johnson interview by author.

34. Sutherland, *Letters from Mississippi*, 44–45.

35. CORE's organizers in Jonesboro were true believers in nonviolence, but the debate in CORE over how to use nonviolence—as mere tactic or overarching strategy—had been going on privately for several years. CORE staffers' doubts about nonviolence were frequently prompted by the militance they encountered among young local black activists whom they had recruited. "Most everyone, especially the kids who have been the most active, are disillusioned with nonviolence, and see the situation very much running toward violence," wrote CORE staffer Miriam Feingold in 1963. "They think that we must do as the masses feel— and if that means violence, then that's what we do." Feingold hastened to add, "But never fear—we've decided that non-violence is still the most viable tactic at the moment." Feingold to Parents, 17 July 1963, Plaquemine, La., MFP. See also armed self-defense groups and the debate on nonviolence in West Feliciana Parish in Rudwick and Meier, *CORE*, 263–64.

36. Lawson interview in 1969 quoted in Estes, "'I AM A MAN!,'" 164 (n. 42).

37. Catherine Patterson Mitchell interview by author.

38. Moore interview by author.

39. Catherine Patterson Mitchell and Thomas interviews by author. The role of masculine honor and violence has primarily been the purview of anthropologists and ethnographers. Here the literature is vast, though generally focused on Europe and the Mediterranean. See, e.g., Péristiany, *Honour and Shame*. Historians have suggested that African American honor and manhood values most likely derived from both African social traditions and the influence of the honor-bound white society in the South. Bertram Wyatt-Brown's study of honor in the Old South, *Southern Honor*, leaves little doubt of the centrality of the code of honor for the white patrician classes. In his most recent work (*Shaping of Southern Culture*), Wyatt-Brown argues that honor played an important role among slaves as well, especially in the chapter, "Dignity, Deception, and Identity in the Male Slave Experience." Honor and violence are inextricably linked in the southern experience; writers and scholars have long speculated on the causes

of excessive violence in the region. See Cash, *Mind of the South*; McWhiney, *Cracker Culture*; Moore, *Frontier Mind*; and Ayers, *Vengeance and Justice*. See also Fischer, *Albion's Seed*, on Celtic culture in the South.

For many African American men, the Civil War became the first opportunity to test their manhood using the same martial values of courage and valor that informed white masculine identity. Violence and militarism have been at the heart of honor studies of the Old South, beginning first with works such as Franklin, *Militant South*; McWhiney and Jamieson, *Attack and Die*; and Bruce, *Violence and Culture*. On honor and southern politics, see Kenneth S. Greenberg, *Masters and Statesmen*. Whereas Wyatt-Brown's early works on honor centered on the southern upper classes, other scholars have posited the idea that honor also animated plebian violence. See Ayers, *Vengeance and Justice*, 21; Ownby, *Subduing Satan*; Gorn, "'Gouge and Bite'"; and McWhiney, *Cracker Culture*, esp. the chapter, "Violence," 146–70. A broader cultural study is made in Kenneth S. Greenberg, *Honor and Slavery*. For an opposing view that attributes southern violence to politics more than honor, see Vandal, *Rethinking Southern Violence*. A series of essays that address the intersection of honor and masculine values in early African American life can be found in Hine and Jenkins, *A Question of Manhood*. The literature on honor and the twentieth-century African American freedom movement is virtually nonexistent. See the discussion of honor and masculine values in Tyson, *Radio Free Dixie*, 140–43.

40. Defending one's family was a requisite of white masculine honor in the South. A traditional southern saying was, "Every man should be sheriff on his own hearth." Nisbett and Cohen, *Culture of Honor*, 5. Nonviolence also posed recruitment problems for SNCC in its earliest project in Mississippi. Attacks on SNCC in Greenwood "brought no significant outcry" from blacks, according to Akinyele Umoja. As in Jonesboro, those participating in marches "had to commit themselves to nonviolence and not to be armed on the march"; this inevitably excluded some local residents. SNCC activist Hollis Watkins recalled that "some of the local brothers and sisters said 'I can't give up my stuff so I wont be on the march, I'll be on the side.'" Umoja, "Eye for an Eye," 107–9.

41. Ed Pincus, "Black Natchez," film transcript, Pincus Collection, ARC. On local women exhorting black men to protect the community, see also Tyson, *Radio Free Dixie*, 148–49.

42. Ibid. The relationship between black masculine values and patriarchy has recently attracted some scholarly attention, drawing heavily on gender studies of white male identity in the nineteenth century, especially Gail Bederman's *Manliness and Civilization*. Bederman combines race and gender to draw a link between male dominance and white supremacy. The obsession with a new "primal" manliness in the late nineteenth century—in contrast to earlier notions of manhood that were anchored in Victorian restraint—was intimately connected to the idea that white males deserved to rule the world (a notion that she believes African Americans resisted). But imposing Bederman's paradigm onto twentieth-

century black masculinity has its own perils. Bederman herself cautions against viewing manhood as a fixed set of traits and attitudes; she posits that manhood is a dynamic "historical, ideological process" in which "concrete individuals are constituted as members of a preexisting social category—as men" (p. 7). See esp. chap. 1, "Remaking Manhood through Race and 'Civilization,'" 1–44. See also Rotundo, *American Manhood*, and Kimmel, *Manhood in America*. A related work on manhood ideals and patriarchy is Hoganson, *Fighting for American Manhood*. See anthropologist David Gilmore (*Manhood in the Making*) on how courage and loyalty in the role of protector are linked to honor. See also Carnes's *Secret Ritual*, which looks at the fraternal lodge movement in the same late-nineteenth-century period and concludes that the lodges were a response to the growing influence of women in the domestic sphere and religion. Jacquelyn Dowd Hall (*Revolt against Chivalry*) offers insights on the chivalric tradition and racism and patriarchy in the early twentieth century. Given this connection between manhood and patriarchy in white middle-class society, a key challenge for students of the modern civil rights era is to determine how the black masculine ideal differed from the white ideal. For perspectives on this question for nineteenth-century African Americans, see Hine and Jenkins, *A Question of Manhood*, which contains a variety of viewpoints on how black men constructed manhood and expressed masculinity while resisting the dominance of white middle-class male identity. I will return to this question in later chapters.

43. Catherine Patterson Mitchell interview by author.

44. For the Voter Education Project, voter registration, and direct action, see Chapter 2.

Chapter Two

1. This account is drawn from Thomas, White, and Mitchell interviews by author and Kirkpatrick interview by Hall.

2. Kirkpatrick interview by Hall.

3. Ibid.

4. White and Thomas interviews by author.

5. Thomas interview by author.

6. Danny Mitchell, "VEP Field Report," 24 June 1964, 124–770, CORE (Microfilm); Hunter interview by anonymous.

7. On SNCC and community demands for desegregation, see Belfrage, *Freedom Summer*, 179–241.

8. Danny Mitchell, "A Special Report on Jonesboro, Louisiana," July 1964, box 1, folder 10, CORE (Jackson Parish).

9. Ibid.

10. Ibid.

11. This account is drawn from ibid. and Moore interview by author.

12. Moore interview by author.

13. "Chronology on Jonesboro, July 1964–January 1965," reel 20, CORE (Microfilm); Daniel Mitchell to Ronnie M. Moore, "Jackson Parish and Jonesboro, Louisiana: A White Paper," [September 1964], Jonesboro, Monroe Project Files, CORE (SHSW) (hereafter cited as Daniel Mitchell, "White Paper").

14. "Chronology on Jonesboro"; *NYT*, 21 February 1965.

15. Daniel Mitchell, "White Paper."

16. Ibid.

17. Ibid.; Annie Purnell Johnson interview by author.

18. "The M and D Restaurant and Cafeteria, July 29, 1964," GMHP; Kirkpatrick interview by Hall.

19. "The M and D Restaurant and Cafeteria, July 29, 1964," GMHP.

20. Daniel Mitchell, "White Paper"; Ed Hollander, "Jonesboro Swimming Pool Arrests," 29 July 1964, Jonesboro, GMHP; Willie Swafford Jr., "A Statement by Willie Swafford, Jr. of Jonesboro, July 1964, Jonesboro, Louisiana," GMHP; *LW*, 31 July 1964.

21. Thomas and White interviews by author; Kirkpatrick interview by Hall.

22. The jail incident account draws on Rudwick and Meier, *CORE*, 267–68, and *LW*, 8 August 1964.

23. Thomas, White, and Harvey Johnson interviews by author; Kirkpatrick interview by Hall. The precise date of this first meeting is unclear, though it probably was 31 July 1964.

24. Annie Purnell Johnson interview by author.

25. Several published sources mistakenly cite this initial meeting as the official beginning of the Deacons for Defense and Justice. The meeting was certainly the impetus for the Deacons, but the organization did not develop a name, an organizational identity, and a formal structure until November 1964. Throughout its life, it interchangeably used the name Deacons *of* Defense and Justice and Deacons *for* Defense and Justice. In this book I use the latter.

26. Will Palmer Jr., "A Statement by Will Palmer Jr. of Jonesboro," 3 August 1964, GMHP.

27. Rev. Y. D. Jackson, "Statement by Y. D. Jackson," 4 August 1964, GMHP.

28. Catherine Patterson Mitchell interview by author.

29. Danny Mitchell, "VEP Field Report."

30. Daniel Mitchell, "White Paper."

31. The shift from direct action protest, such as the lunch counter sit-ins and Freedom Rides, began in 1961 through the VEP, a program funded by several liberal foundations. The Kennedy administration engineered the strategic maneuver, hoping to steer CORE and SNCC away from the highly public and disruptive direct action confrontations that were pressuring the White House to intervene in the South. The shift nearly split SNCC, where a significant number of staffers viewed voter registration as a retreat from the kind of militant direct action of the lunch counter sit-ins and Freedom Rides that had inspired a generation of new activists. Scholars differ over the importance of this programmatic

shift; most recent histories of SNCC and CORE treat the move to voter registration as insignificant, and some, like Adam Fairclough, view voter registration— and even litigation—as simply another form of direct action. Fairclough writes that "white authorities drew no distinction between direct action and 'conventional' activities like litigation and voter registration. They treated both equally harshly. Voter registration *was* direct action in that it directly challenged white supremacy and evoked severe repression. So was litigation, as many a black plaintiff found out to his or her cost." Fairclough, "Civil Rights Movement in Louisiana," 15–28 (quotation, p. 25). For Fairclough, virtually any political activity passes for meaningful and subversive resistance to oppression. In his effort to exonerate the black community of criticism of accommodation, Fairclough blurs the very real distinctions between militant and direct confrontation with authority—which was the motive force of the movement—and far less inspiring and transformative activities like voter registration and litigation. In Louisiana, the shift to voter registration was a strategic sea change and did indeed reduce disruptive protests as the Kennedys had hoped for. It also placed CORE at odds with local militants eager to directly challenge segregation, as the Jonesboro and Bogalusa cases bear out. In both communities, white authorities and racist vigilantes responded much more violently to desegregation. Ronnie Moore opted for voter registration precisely because he understood that desegregation protests provoked a more violent response from local whites. In Plaquemine, La., Moore said that "I thought voter registration was dangerous enough down here, that's all I wanted to do." But when voter registration failed to capture the enthusiasm of local people, he altered his course. "Since voter registration was such a frustrating thing," Moore explained, "we weren't getting anybody to register anyway, no matter how many people we took down, we decided to get involved in other things [direct action protests]"; Moore interview by author.

Dittmer's and Payne's studies of Mississippi both assign less importance to the move away from direct action. On the Kennedy administration and the VEP, see Dittmer, *Local People*, 119–20. For a Kennedy administration insider's view, see Wofford, *Of Kennedys and Kings*, 159–60. Payne (*Light of Freedom*, 108–11) also argues that voter registration was "at least as problematic" as direct action protest for the Kennedys in Mississippi. James Laue (*Direct Action*, 114–17) gives a very different account of the VEP controversy and SNCC's strategic move, one in which SNCC leader Tim Jenkins, assisted by SNCC chairman Charles McDew and field secretary Charles Jones, carefully engineered a "takeover" of SNCC to move it away from direct action protest. Jenkins was convinced that the success of the black movement hinged on suffrage and that SNCC need to ally with the Justice Department to destroy the southern white electoral bloc. During the summer of 1961 Jenkins arranged for a series of special meetings between SNCC Executive Committee members and the Justice Department; he capped off his campaign with a month-long training seminar attended by most of SNCC's staff in Nashville, 30 July–26 August. Far from "grassroots training," the "Special

Southern Student Leadership Seminar" was led by a team of academics and was designed to give SNCC "a solid academic approach to understanding the movement." According to Jenkins, the seminar served as a catalyst for the SNCC takeover; following the seminar, SNCC placed voter registration on an equal footing with direct action. Laue, *Direct Action*, 114–17.

32. For a characteristic African American perspective on the civil rights movement in the fall of 1964, see "Worst of Racial Strife over in South, Some Say," *Jet*, 15 October 1964, 4.

33. Kirkpatrick interview by Hall.

34. LHM, 25 March 1965, Deacons file 157-2466-13, FBI Files.

35. Fenton interview by author; Donovan Bess, "Torture in a Louisiana Jail," *Louisiana–Summer 1964*, n.p., Moore Collection, ARC. Fenton was not a religious person and found his inspiration in more secular sources. Nonviolence has its roots in Christianity and Hindu-derived Gandhism, but also in the nineteenth-century philosophy of Leo Tolstoy and Henry David Thoreau: see *Tolstoy's Writings on Civil Disobedience* and Gandhi, *Non-Violent Resistance*. On Gandhian nonviolence, see Sharp, *Gandhi as a Political Strategist*. See also Kapur, *Raising Up a Prophet*. On the influence of Gandhi, Walter Rauschenbusch, and Reinhold Niebuhr on Martin Luther King, see Ansbro, *Martin Luther King Jr.*

36. Fenton interview by author.

37. Ibid.

38. Ibid.

39. Ibid.

40. Ibid.

41. Ibid.

42. Ibid.

43. There are no studies of the role of women in the self-defense movement, though it would be a fascinating and useful subject.

44. Annie Purnell Johnson interview by author. Jackie Hicks in Bogalusa was said to have organized target practice for a women's group.

45. Fred Brooks to Ronnie Moore, "Field Report 11-1-64 to 11-15-64, Jonesboro, Louisiana," box 5, folder 4, CORE (SRO); Charles Fenton and Willie Green, "Field Report of Jackson Parish," November 1965, Jonesboro, La., box 1, folder 7, CORE (Jackson Parish).

46. Kirkpatrick, *Black Music*.

47. Kirkpatrick, Harvey Johnson, and Catherine Patterson Mitchell interviews by author. The first recorded use of the Deacons' name was in a 6 January 1965 FBI memorandum based on an interview with Percy Lee Bradford. See SAC New Orleans to Director, 6 January 1965, Deacons file 157-2466-1, FBI Files. Kirkpatrick's tendency to revise the history of the Deacons deserves some explanation. He, along with other Deacons, failed to mention in interviews that the Deacons evolved, in part, from a volunteer police squad. In the late 1960s anti-

police sentiment was at a fever pitch in the movement, especially among the Black Power and antiwar groups that Kirkpatrick associated with. Kirkpatrick was understandably reluctant to admit his service as a policeman. Moreover, it would have been difficult to elevate the Deacons to icon status if it were known that they had originated, in part, as a police squad.

48. Fred Brooks to Oretha Castle, Monroe, La., n.d., box 3, folder 2, CORE (SRO); Brooks to Moore, "Field Report."

49. Fenton and Green, "Field Report."

50. Belfrage, *Freedom Summer*, 170, 175. Many CORE workers interviewed for Project South in 1965 strongly complained that Freedom Summer had reproduced the condescending dynamic of white people telling poor African Americans what was best for them, especially by emphasizing registration in the Mississippi Freedom Democratic Party (MFDP). Ickes, interview by anonymous. Ickes believed that the MFDP project had diverted attention away from the felt needs of local people. See also Lacey, interview by anonymous; but the criticism runs throughout the interviews.

51. The community organizing model became official CORE policy by January 1965. One document widely circulated in CORE clearly delineated this line of debate: Jimmy Garrett, "Who Decides," *The Movement*, April 1965, reprint in box 1, file 9, CORE, "Bogalusa, Louisiana, Records, 1965–1966," CORE (SHSW). See also Ronnie Moore, "Discussion Draft on Louisiana Project," January 1965, box 4, folder 2, CORE (SRO). Moore argues, "Rather than institutors of pre-selected programs, the staff should present the full array of alternatives and allow the community to shape its individual project." Indeed, by 1965 several former SNCC volunteers had joined CORE in Louisiana because of its focus on local control and leadership. Harold Ickes, who ended up in CORE in 1965, had worked with SNCC the previous summer; he felt that "when you start comparing actual method of operation to the line that's preached, I think there's a wide division." Ickes, interview by anonymous. Payne gives a comprehensive account of SNCC's community organizing model in *Light of Freedom*.

52. Dennis, interview by anonymous; Lesser, interview by anonymous.

53. Belfrage, *Freedom Summer*, 174–75, 178.

54. Oretha Castle, "Field Report, December 6, 1964 to December 12, 1964," Monroe, La., box 4, folder 2, CORE (SRO); *Wall Street Journal*, 21 February 1965.

55. Investigative report, 17 August 1965, Deacons file 157-2466-41, FBI Files.

56. White interview by author. The fear and reluctance to act that Charles Fenton witnessed was not unique to Jonesboro. Whereas most recent studies of African American life in the twentieth century emphasize cultural resistance and downplay the role of fear, resignation, and fatalism, scholars studying poor whites in the South offer illuminating analyses of these attitudes and behaviors in the white community, viewing them as "functionally positive" adjustments to poverty. "Such folk did not expect much from life," writes I. A. Newby, "at least in

a material sense, because experience discouraged expectation, and they wanted to avoid the disappointment of unrealized hope." Their numerous encounters with "prejudice and discrimination necessitated behavioral strategies to avoid humiliation and a consequent sense of inadequacy." These survival behaviors took the form of noncompetitiveness, low aspirations, and attraction to paternalism. By limiting their sense of pride, they limited their definition of success and protected themselves from feelings of inferiority. The failing of this adaptive behavior, though, was that "in keeping their hopes low and expectations realistic, plain folk helped perpetuate the system that exploited them." Plain folk were ultimately concerned with their self-image, and although they were not "debased" or "demoralized," there was widespread guilt and shame because they could not live up to the values they shared with other southerners: "They were supposed to be . . . independent, unrestrained, and beholden to no one." Newby, *Plain Folk in the New South*, 456–57, 454–55, 458–60.

57. Ibid.

Chapter Three

1. *LW*, 2 January 1965.

2. "Chronology on Jonesboro," [1965], box 5, folder 4, CORE (SRO); *LW*, 9 January 1965.

3. SAC New Orleans to Director, 6 January 1965, Deacons file 157-2466-1, FBI Files; LHM, "Deacons for Defense and Justice, Jonesboro, Louisiana, Percy Lee Bradford, President," 6 January 1964, Deacons file 157-2466-2, FBI Files.

4. LHM, "Deacons for Defense and Justice."

5. This broader, more fluid notion of "membership" is addressed by Deacons leader Henry Austin (interview by author).

6. A similar phenomenon occurred with the Black Panther Party. By 1970 there were thousands of self-proclaimed Black Panthers scattered around the nation, most of whom had never formally joined the party or, for that matter, even met a party member.

7. White, Thomas, and Burris interviews by author. The autonomous Deacons chapter that spontaneously formed in Port Gibson is representative of this latter trend. For membership estimates, see Thomas and White interviews by author. In some reports the FBI estimated total membership at 15,000—an obviously inflated number.

8. SAC New Orleans to Director, 6 January 1965, Deacons file 157-2466-1, FBI Files.

9. "Chronology on Jonesboro"; Annie Purnell Johnson, Jacobs, and Lewis interviews by Feingold; *LW*, 4 December 1965.

10. LHM, "Deacons for Defense and Justice, Inc., Jonesboro, Louisiana, March 26, 1965," Deacons file 157-2466-13, FBI Files.

11. Annie Purnell Johnson interview by author.

12. Ibid.; Kirkpatrick interview by Hall.

13. *NYT*, 21 February 1965.

14. Ibid.

15. Ibid.

16. Ibid.

17. Moore interview by author.

18. On informal, clandestine self-defense groups, see Introduction (n. 4), above.

19. On SNCC's McComb campaign, see Dittmer, *Local People*, 102–14 (voter registration total, p. 114). The theme that civil rights workers were not building organizations that could be sustained by local members runs throughout the Stanford University's Project South Oral History interviews with CORE workers in Louisiana. See esp. Miriam Feingold transcript, Clinton, La., 5 July 1965, reel 0124–0125, PSCSUA. One CORE volunteer commented on how activists frequently reinforced old patterns of racial deference. There were "many projects that were sort of messed up by well-intentioned but nevertheless white people who set up organizations . . . and then left, and left a community that was maybe a little bit worse off than before, for having yes-ma'amed and no-ma'amed another summer." Roy, interview by anonymous.

20. Viewing violence as primarily an ethical question obscures its political function. Georges Sorel argued that violence guaranteed the political independence of the working class by driving away middle-class leaders who favored orderly and lawful reform. Though the Deacons were far from a revolutionary vanguard, their advocacy of violence accomplished the same end—it kept white liberals and middle-class blacks at a distance. See Sorel, *Reflections on Violence*, 99, 105, 132.

21. Thomas's activities in New York are drawn from Thomas interview by author. Special thanks to Virginia Collins (Dara Abubakari), Lawrence Landry, and Gwendolyn Midlo Hall for their insights on New York's black political groups. See also Landry interview by author.

22. On Thomas's contact with RAM, see Thomas interview by author. On Thomas, the Deacons, and RAM, see FBI Files: SAC Detroit to Director, 10 June 1965, airtel, Deacons file 157-2466-LHM; Enclosure, "Revolutionary Action Movement[,] June 10-1965," app. "Revolutionary Action Movement [RAM])"; SAC WFO to Director, 9 September 1965, airtel, Deacons file (unnumbered), and enclosure, LHM, "Organization for Black Power (OBP)," Washington, D.C., 9 September 1965, Deacons file 157-3022-156; Director to SAC New Orleans, 12 October 1966, Deacons file (unnumbered); John Edgar Hoover, Director of FBI, to Director of CIA, 13 October 1966, originally serialized as Deacons file 157-3022-156; Cleveland SAC to Director, 28 February 1967, airtel, Deacons file 157-2466-200; and Mr. W. C. Sullivan to R. W. Smith, memorandum, 29 September 1967, Deacons file 157-2466-243. Sullivan recommends "that monographs be prepared on several black extremist organizations, including the Deacons, that would be

circulated to law enforcement agencies." He describes RAM as a "fanatical all-Negro hate group that follows the Red Chinese Marxist-Leninist line."

23. The Articles of Incorporation are contained in SAC New Orleans to Director, 26 March 1965, Deacons file 157-2466-13, FBI Files.

24. Ibid.

25. The charter listed Bradford as president, Thomas as vice president, Charlie White as secretary, Cossetta Jackson as treasurer, and Elmo Jacobs as a member of the Board of Directors. Thomas's listing as vice president introduced the first public note of discord in the organization. Henry Amos had served as vice president since the group's formation in November 1964, but Thomas managed to substitute his name for the position in the incorporation papers—a maneuver that angered Bradford and other officers and led to a permanent rift between Thomas and the rest of the Jonesboro chapter. Thereafter, Thomas identified himself as the Deacons' *national* vice president. See Harvey Johnson interview by author.

26. Quotation from Anonymous CORE members and Deacons interview by anonymous. Teachers in Homer, La., who wanted to join the Deacons also labored under this misapprehension. See ibid.; Cottrol and Diamond, "Second Amendment," 336–37, 355; and Stokes interview by author.

27. Harvey Johnson interview by author.

Chapter Four

1. King quoted in Weisbrot, *Freedom Bound*, 132.

2. The accommodationism of teachers and ministers is a recurring theme in interviews with the Deacons. See Harvey Johnson and Whatley interviews by author and Kirkpatrick interview by Hall. See also Owen Brooks, June Johnson, and Hightower interviews by Tom Dent. On the conservative role of black educators in Mississippi, see Dittmer, *Local People*, 37, 44, 110, and Payne, *Light of Freedom*, 129, 138, 177. Principals of black schools provoked student protests in other Deacon strongholds such as Bogalusa and Woodville (see later chapters).

3. This elitism and complacency were evident in small and medium communities in the Deep South but seemed to be mitigated in larger urban areas, as evidenced by the leading role of black women educators in the Montgomery Bus Boycott. See Robinson, *Montgomery Bus Boycott*. In her interview with Tom Dent, Mary Hightower, a grassroots activist from Lexington, Miss., confirmed the meritocratic ideas of middle-class blacks. Hightower said that middle-class blacks felt that they were "above" the movement because protesters were demanding what the middle class had already achieved through education and being a "good citizen."

4. Whatley interview by author.

5. Annie Purnell Johnson interview by author.

6. Ibid.; Oretha Castle, "Activities in Jonesboro, Louisiana," n.d., box 5, folder 4, CORE (SRO).

7. Alvin Adams, "3-Week School Boycott Gets Results in Jonesboro, La.," *Jet*, 15 April 1965, 46–48.

8. Ibid.

9. Ibid.

10. Castle, "Activities in Jonesboro"; Mike Lesser, "Report on Jonesboro-Bogalusa Project," March 1965, box 5, folder 5, CORE (SRO).

11. On this incident, see Lesser, "Report on Jonesboro"; Thomas interview by author; "Statement by Ernest [*sic*] Thomas regarding Events of March 11, 1965," box 5, folder 4, CORE (SRO); and *Jet*, 15 April 1965, 46–48.

12. "Statement by Ernest [*sic*] Thomas regarding Events of March 11, 1965."

13. Ibid.

14. Ibid.

15. Thomas interview by author.

16. This account is drawn from Frederick Brooks and Annie Purnell Johnson interviews by author.

17. Ibid.

18. *NOT-P*, 15 March 1965.

19. "Statement by Cossetta Jackson on Arrest of March 15, 1965," box 5, folder 4, CORE (SRO); Castle, "Activities in Jonesboro."

20. Gale to Belmont, 15 March 1965, memorandum, Deacons file 157-2466-10, and Director to SAC New Orleans, 19 March 1965, Deacons file (unnumbered), FBI Files. I am indebted to David Garrow and retired FBI agent Clifford Anderson for their assistance in interpreting the Deacons' FBI Files.

21. Harvey Johnson interview by author.

22. Thomas, Bradford, and White had all been paper mill workers. A similar change in leadership occurred in the Bogalusa movement.

23. Castle, "Activities in Jonesboro"; SAC New Orleans to Director, 26 March 1965, Deacons file 157-2466-13, FBI Files.

24. *BDN*, 23, 25 March 1965.

25. This account is drawn from SAC New Orleans to Director, 26 March 1965; Castle, "Activities in Jonesboro"; and Thomas interview by author.

26. SAC New Orleans to Director, 26 March 1965; Castle, "Activities in Jonesboro"; Thomas interview by author.

27. Sobel, *Civil Rights*, 304.

28. *NOT-P*, 27 March 1965. On the FBI, COINTELPRO, and black activists, see O'Reilly and Gallen, *Black Americans*, 48–52. The FBI documents on COINTELPRO operations against the Klan are in Counterintelligence Program, Internal Security, Disruption of Hate Groups, 157-9-33, FBI Files.

29. Daniel Mitchell, "A Special Report on Jonesboro, Louisiana," July 1964, box 1, folder 10, CORE (Jackson Parish).

30. Castle, "Activities in Jonesboro."

31. *NOT-P*, 28 March 1965.

32. *BDN*, 29 March 1965; *NYT*, 26 April 1965.

33. SAC New Orleans to Director, 3 March 1965, Deacons file 157-2466-9, FBI Files.

34. Ibid.

35. *Jet*, 15 April 1965; *BDN*, 29, 30 March 1965; Castle, "Activities in Jonesboro."

36. Castle, "Activities in Jonesboro."

37. Catherine Patterson Mitchell interview by author.

38. Simpson, *Simpson's Contemporary Quotations*, 195.

39. Moore interview by author. Scholarship on southern values among the nineteenth-century upper class defines honor as a set of values and attitudes including honesty, courage, trustworthiness, and moral probity. Anthropologists define plebian honor differently, linking it directly to the readiness to fight: the ability to protect one's family and property in one's absence—a trait found in societies marked by stiff competition, scarce resources, and limited government. This was particularly true for the Scotch-Irish herdsmen who peopled the Celtic South. Unable to constantly monitor their widespread herds, the Celts relied on maintaining a credible threat of violence that guaranteed that any theft would be mercilessly avenged. This was also "true wherever gaining resources, or keeping them, depends on the community's believing that the individual is capable of defending himself against predation," according to Richard Nisbett and Dov Cohen. Potential predators will avoid the risk of someone "who knows how to defend himself and his possessions and who appears not to be afraid to die." Honor served the same purpose in the black community, where the absence of legal protection made masculine honor an important deterrent to vigilante violence. On honor and Celtic culture, see Nisbett and Cohen, *Culture of Honor*, xv; on Celtic culture, see McWhiney, *Cracker Culture*; on fighting and the South, see Gorn, " 'Gouge and Bite.' " Ultimately, a person's honor depended on what other people thought of him or her. As Edward Ayers (*Vengeance and Justice*, 13) has written, honor is "a system of values within which you have exactly as much merit as others confer upon you."

40. Castle, "Activities in Jonesboro."

41. This account is drawn from ibid. and Jacobs interview by Feingold.

42. Jacobs interview by Feingold.

Chapter Five

1. Quick, "History of Bogalusa." On the Balltown Riot, see Bond and Bond, *Star Creek Papers*, 10, 141 (n. 5). An excellent overview of the early history of Bogalusa and its labor relations can be found in Norwood, "Bogalusa Burning," which also contains an account of the IWW's 1919 campaign. Norwood concludes that the campaign "marked the only time during the first half of the twentieth century when white workers picked up guns to protect black rights" (p. 627).

2. Quick, "History of Bogalusa."

3. John Fahey, "Will Bogalusa Survive?," *NOT-P*, 28 August 1977.

4. "The Bogalusa Negro Community," 16 May 1965, box 7, folder 6, CORE (SRO).

5. The unionization of the Bogalusa mill was not unusual for two reasons. First, papermaking was a continuous process and mill owners wanted a minimum of labor stoppages. Second, the mills were capital-intensive operations and had a low ratio of mill worker costs to total costs. This capital-intensive nature of paper production exacerbated racial tension in the 1950s, when black employment declined as a result of automation. The recessions of 1958 and 1961 compounded labor cutbacks and caused whites to "harden the opposition" to black job opportunities. Northrup, *The Negro in the Paper Industry*, 14, 48, 54; on the Bogalusa mill, see 95–104.

6. Fahey, "Will Bogalusa Survive?"

7. Rony, "Bogalusa."

8. Ibid., 235–36.

9. Paul Good, "Klantown, USA," *Nation*, 1 February 1965, 110–13.

10. Bond and Bond, *Star Creek Papers*, 11, 5, 12.

11. Lori Davis, Mimi Feingold, and Howard R. Messing, "Summer Parish Scouting Report, Washington Parish," [Summer 1964], box 7, folder 6, CORE (SRO). Much of the scholarly literature on the civil rights movement has been dominated by the "resource mobilization" theory, which stresses the movement's reliance on local traditions and resources and continuity between the old and new organizations. The experience of the Deacons, with their dramatic break from old organizations and established ideologies, clearly argues against this continuity thesis; see McAdam, *Political Process*, and Morris, *Origin of the Civil Rights Movement*. Adam Fairclough's study of Louisiana emphasizes the continuity theme, arguing that in Louisiana "the NAACP provided the backbone of the civil rights struggle." Fairclough, *Race and Democracy*, xiv–xv. On the role of the black church, see Morris, *Origin*, xiii, 77. For an alternative perspective on the spontaneity of the social movements, see Piven and Cloward, *Poor People's Movements*.

12. Hicks interview by Feingold.

13. On the May CORE announcement, see Hill, "Character of Black Politics," 65.

14. Davis, Feingold, and Messing, "Scouting Report."

15. Hill, "Character of Black Politics," 65.

16. Moore to Cutrer, 18 July 1965, box 7, folder 5, CORE (SRO).

17. Davis, Feingold, and Messing, "Scouting Report."

18. Ibid.

19. Good, "Klantown," 110–13. The May rally is referred to in U.S. House, *Activities of Ku Klux Klan*, 3:2413. The social composition and political appeal of the Klan has been the subject of recent debate. Most scholarly works on the Klan

in the twentieth century have focused on the "second klan" of the 1910s and 1920s. Early influential writers like John Moffat Mecklin (*Ku Klux Klan*) characterized the Klan as an organization of antimodern misfits: violent, white supremacist, and rural. Richard Hofstadter and other scholars in the 1950s continued to employ the Mecklin thesis, but beginning in the 1960s, authors such as David Chalmers (*Hooded Americanism*) and Kenneth T. Jackson (*Ku Klux Klan in the City*) challenged the paradigm. In recent years a populist-civic school argued that the "second klan" was not a group of aberrant, low-status reactionaries, but rather ordinary people who saw themselves as upholders of the moral order. Their nativist and racist attitudes were typical of the times; they were not particularly violent, nor were they driven by white supremacist ideas. See Lay, *War, Revolution* and *Invisible Empire*; Jenkins, *Steel Valley Klan*; Gerlach, *Blazing Crosses in Zion*; and Lutholtz, *Grand Dragon*. See also MacLean, *Behind the Mask*. A scholarly study of the 1960s Klan ideology is found in Rich, "Klan Ideology." One of the few studies of the "third klan" of the 1960s is Newton, *Invisible Empire*, though Newton fails to use oral history interviews with Klan members that would have produced a useful social history. The proceedings of the 1965 HUAC hearings on the Klan remain a rich source of material on the 1960s Klan; see U.S. House, *Present-Day Ku Klux Klan* and *Activities of Ku Klux Klan*. The OKKKK in Bogalusa was quite unlike the "second klan" described by the populist-civic school. It was overtly white supremacist, unrelentingly violent, and largely working class—though the leadership was comprised of small business proprietors.

20. Rony, "Bogalusa," 238.

21. *NOT-P*, 6 January 1965; *BDN*, 6 January 1965.

22. "Fact Sheet on Bogalusa, Louisiana," 17 February 1965, reel 25, CORE (Microfilm); Good, "Klantown," 110–11. For earlier Klan leaflets attacking Talley and Lou Major, see "Published by the Original Ku Klux Klan of Louisiana," [September 1964], box 7, folder 6, CORE (SRO), and Klan leaflet text in U.S. House, *Activities of Ku Klux Klan*, 3:2421–22.

23. Good, "Klantown." On the OKKKK name change, see *NOT-P*, 7 September 1965.

24. Linder, *Bending toward Justice*, 7.

25. U.S. House, *Present-Day Ku Klux Klan*, 106–7, and *Activities of Ku Klux Klan*, 3:2525–29; *BDN*, 17 June 1965; *LW*, 31 July 1965. Lee was found guilty by a federal court in New Orleans and sentenced to three years in prison in June 1965.

26. Good, "Klantown," 111–12.

27. U.S. House, *Activities of Ku Klux Klan*, 3:2487–88 (18 December meeting); Good, "Klantown," 111 (doggerel). A copy of a Klan leaflet, dated 27 December 1964, can be found in U.S. House, *Activities of Ku Klux Klan*, 3:2454; several other Bogalusa Klan leaflets appear on pp. 2454–58; on the Klan in the Bogalusa auxiliary police, see p. 2549.

28. Good, "Klantown," 111.

29. Ibid.

30. Leroy Collins to Hubert Humphrey, 13 August 1965, 150-E-7-10-F, Humphrey Papers, MHS; "Field Report, Tangipahoa Parish, Hammond, Spring 1964," ca. 1964, Hammond, La., box 7, folder 2, CORE (SRO).

31. Badger, "Fatalism, Not Gradualism," 87–88.

32. Heilbron interview by author.

33. *BDN*, 5 January 1965.

34. *BDN*, 3 January 1965; Good, "Klantown," 110–11.

35. *BDN*, 6 January 1965.

36. *BDN*, 8 January 1965.

37. *NOT-P*, 12 January 1965.

38. Crown-Zellerbach's role in staging the tests is documented in "Crown-Zellerbach in Bogalusa," 16 May 1965, box 7, folder 6, CORE (SRO), and Rony, "Bogalusa," 238. See also "Field Report, January–June 1965," GMHP.

39. Good, "Klantown," 112; "Fact Sheet on Bogalusa, Louisiana"; *BDN*, 29 January 1965.

40. Hill, "Character of Black Politics," 67–70; "Summary of Incidents: Bogalusa, Louisiana, January 28–July 1, 1965," box 7, folder 6, CORE (SRO).

41. *BDN*, 29 January 1965; *NOT-P*, 29 January 1965; "Summary of Incidents: Bogalusa, Louisiana, January 28–July 1, 1965."

42. Miller interview by author.

43. *BDN*, 29 January 1965.

44. Hill, "Character of Black Politics," 67–70; Miller and Hicks interviews by author.

45. The account of the events at the Hicks's home is drawn from Hicks and Miller interviews by author and "Fact Sheet on Bogalusa, Louisiana."

46. Hicks interview by author.

47. Ibid.

48. Ibid.

49. Ibid.; "Fact Sheet on Bogalusa, Louisiana."

50. The Klan's pressure on Mayor Cutrer is documented in "Federal Complaint," *United States of America, . . . v. Original Knights*, and Miller interview by author.

51. Hicks interview by author. The new militancy evident in Jonesboro and Bogalusa can be attributed to the failure of old strategies and to many structural developments following World War II, including mechanization of agriculture that led to northern and urban migration, increased unionization, the abolition of the white primary, de-legitimization of racist theories, the Cold War, rising expectations of veterans, and military discipline. Morris, *Origin of the Civil Rights Movement*, 73–77, 79–81; Payne, *Light of Freedom*, 431. On the impact of the 1940s and the Cold War on the black movement, see Korstad and Lichtenstein, "Opportunities Found and Lost."

52. Hill, "Character of Black Politics," 70.

Chapter Six

1. *BDN*, 3 February 1965.

2. This account is drawn from Miller and Hicks interviews by author and "Federal Complaint," *United States of America, . . . v. Original Knights.*

3. Miller interview by author.

4. Ibid.

5. Ibid. Miller's sudden disillusionment with nonviolence is representative of the popular narrative of the civil rights movement as a journey from nonviolent idealism to disillusioned Black Power. It is a quintessentially middle-class narrative of the period: whereas middle-class activists were indeed disabused of their faith in moral suasion, the black working class did not labor under this illusion.

6. Ibid.

7. Ibid.

8. Ibid.

9. Ibid.

10. Ibid.

11. *BDN*, 5 February 1965; *NOT-P*, 5 February 1965.

12. Hill, "Character of Black Politics," 67–68.

13. Program for "A. Z. Young Civil Rights March 25th Anniversary Commemoration," 12 November 1992, Louisiana Legislative Black Caucus, in author's possession. Military service deeply affected a generation of African American men, raising their expectations for full citizenship and teaching them the power of collective and disciplined action. See MacGregor, *Integration of the Armed Forces*; Wynn, *The Afro-American and the Second World War*; Donaldson, *History of African-Americans in the Military*; and McGuire, *Taps for a Jim Crow Army.*

14. On the nonviolent mandates of the national organizations, see Carson, *In Struggle*; Meier and Rudwick, *CORE*; Fairclough, *To Redeem the Soul*; Garrow, *Bearing the Cross*; and Branch, *Parting the Waters* and *Pillar of Fire.*

15. On Klan strategy and wrecking crews, see *NOT-P*, 8 September 1965, and "Federal Complaint."

16. *NOT-P*, 8 September 1965; "Federal Complaint"; "Summary of Incidents: Bogalusa, Louisiana, January 28–July 1, 1965," box 7, folder 6, CORE (SRO). Charles Ray Williams was the only assailant who was not a Klan member.

17. "Summary of Incidents: Bogalusa"; "Federal Complaint."

18. "Summary of Incidents: Bogalusa." Ovied Dunaway, a supervisor at the telephone company in Bogalusa, was the exalted Cyclops of the Bogalusa klavern of the OKKKK. Dunaway spoke at a United Klans of America rally near Poplarville, Miss., on 17 July 1965; U.S. House, *Activities of Ku Klux Klan*, 3:2463.

19. "Bogalusa, Louisiana, Incident Summary: January 25–February 25," [February 1965], box 7, folder 5, CORE (SRO); "Summary of Incidents: Bogalusa"; "Federal Complaint."

20. On the Blumberg incident, see "One Man's Stand," *ADL Bulletin*, May 1965,

1; *NOT-P*, 20, 23 March 1965; "WBOX and the KKK," *Newsweek*, 16 August 1965, 75; and Blumberg's testimony in U.S. House, *Activities of Ku Klux Klan*, 3:2415–38.

21. "One Man's Stand."

22. *NOT-P*, 20, 23 March 1965; *BDN*, 23 March 1965.

23. "WBOX and the KKK," *Newsweek*, 75.

24. *BDN*, 16, 21, 17 February 1965.

25. The account of the first visit to Bogalusa by the Jonesboro Deacons is drawn from Miller, Thomas, and Taylor interviews by author; Kirkpatrick interview by Hall; SAC New Orleans to Director, 23 February 1965 (Deacons file 157-2466-3), 24 February 1965 (Deacons file 157-2466-4), and 26 February 1965 (Deacons file 157-2466-6), FBI Files; and "The Deacons," *Newsweek*, 2 August 1965, 28–29.

26. Miller interview by author.

27. Fenton interview by author.

28. Ibid.

29. "The Deacons," *Newsweek*, 28.

30. Ibid.

31. Ibid.

32. Ibid. Thomas's reference to machine guns later provided the FBI a pretext to launch an investigation of the Deacons and illegal firearms. There were also rumors that the Deacons had imported 420 Czech machine guns to Baton Rouge in July 1965. In both cases, the FBI never uncovered any evidence of illegal firearms. See SAC Los Angeles to Director, 25 April 1966, Deacons file 157-2466-129, FBI Files.

33. SAC New Orleans to Director, "Deacons for Defense and Justice," 24 February 1965, Deacons file 157-2466-4, FBI Files.

34. The FBI later seized on these remarks to argue that the Deacons went beyond defensive force and encouraged attacks on police. See ibid. and SAC New Orleans to Director, "Deacons for Defense and Justice," and March 1965, Deacons file 157-2466-8, FBI Files.

35. Fenton interview by author.

36. Ibid.

37. Ibid.

38. Ibid.; Kirkpatrick interview by Hall.

39. Hicks interview by author.

Chapter Seven

1. SAC New Orleans to Director, "Deacons for Defense and Justice," 23 February 1965 (Deacons file teletype 157-2466-3), and 24 February 1965 (Deacons file 157-2466-4), FBI Files; *Los Angeles Times*, 2 August 1965.

2. LHM, "Deacons for Defense and Justice, Jonesboro, Louisiana Percy Lee Bradford," 4 March 1965, Deacons file 157-2466-8, FBI Files.

3. Hicks interview by author. In August 1965 Sims identified Hicks as a "public relations man for the Deacons." Sims interview by Price.

4. *BDN*, 12 July 1965; Louie Robinson and Charles Brown, "The Negro Feared Most by Whites in Louisiana," *Jet*, 15 July 1965, 14–17; Sims interview by Price (quotation).

5. "Deacons Chief Defends Aims on Visit to L.A.," *Los Angeles Times*, 14 June 1965; Robinson and Brown, "Negro Most Feared by Whites" (quotation).

6. "Deacons Chief Defends Aims on Visit to L.A."

7. Ibid.

8. Ibid.; Hicks interview by author.

9. Deacon Henry Austin once described Sims as a consummate "bullshit artist." Though the term is normally pejorative, in this instance it had a positive implication. The black man most capable of defying whites in the era of Jim Crow had to be skilled at confrontation, bluff, and trickery. Sims the street hustler was a master of that style. Austin interview by author.

10. Hicks interview by author.

11. Thomas interview by author.

12. SAC New Orleans to Director, "Deacons for Defense and Justice," 3 March 1965, Deacons file 157-2466-8, FBI Files.

13. Ibid.

14. SAC New Orleans to Director, 3 March 1965, Deacons file 157-2466-9, FBI Files.

15. A. H. Belmont to J. H. Gale, 15 March 1965, Deacons file 157-2466-9, FBI Files.

16. Director to SAC New Orleans, "Deacons for Defense and Justice," 26 February 1965, Deacons file 157-2466-6, FBI Files.

17. A March memo indicated that the New Orleans Office had been instructed to conduct these interviews "for deterrent value such interviews have." See Baumgardener to Sullivan, memorandum, 20 March 1965, Deacons file 157-2466-12, FBI Files; "Additions to Bogalusa Intimidation List," [March 1965], box 7, folder 5, CORE (SRO).

18. Burris interview by author; "Summary of Incidents: Bogalusa, Louisiana, January 28–July 1, 1965," box 7, folder 6, CORE (SRO); "Statement by Mr. Royan Burris," n.d., box 7, folder 5, CORE (SRO); *BDN*, 25 February 1965; "Additions to Bogalusa Intimidation List."

19. "Summary of Incidents: Bogalusa"; "Additions to Bogalusa Intimidation List."

20. Hamilton Bims, "Deacons for Defense," *Ebony*, September 1965, 25–30; *NOT-P*, 20 July 1965; "Statement by Mr. Royan Burris"; Burris interview by author.

21. *NOT-P*, 15 March 1965; *BDN*, 15 March 1965.

22. *BDN*, 15 March 1965.

23. *BDN*, 26 March 1965.

24. "Additions to Intimidation List"; "Summary of Incidents: Bogalusa."

25. *NOT-P*, 27 March 1965; *BDN*, 28, 29 March 1965.

26. *BDN*, 26, 28, March 1965; "Caught in the Civil Rights Crossfire," *Business Week*, 7 August 1965, 102–6.

27. Robinson and Brown, "Negro Most Feared by Whites.

28. Ibid.

29. Hicks interview by author.

30. Ibid.

31. Ibid.

32. *BDN*, 7, 8 April 1965, 4 April 1965.

33. The account in this and the next two paragraphs is drawn from "Summary of Incidents: Bogalusa"; *New York Post*, 8 April 1965; "Bogalusa Riflemen Fight Off KKK Attack," *Jet*, 22 April 1965, 5; Austin interview by Hall; Austin interview by author; *BDN*, 8 April 1965; *NOT-P*, 9 April 1965; and *New York Post*, 8 April 1965.

34. *BDN*, 8 April 1965; *NOT-P*, 9 April 1965.

35. *New York Post*, 8 April 1965.

36. *BDN*, 8 April 1965.

37. *NOT-P*, 9 April 1965; *BDN*, 9 April 1965; "Letter to Police Jury et al.," reel 20–43, CORE (Microfilm).

38. *NOT-P*, 9 April 1965; *BDN*, 9 April 1965.

39. *NOT-P*, 9 April 1965.

40. "Summary of Incidents: Bogalusa."

41. *NOT-P*, 9 April 1965.

42. Accounts of the attack are in *BDN*, 9, 13 April 1965, and *NOT-P*, 10 April 1965. Police made no arrests at the time, but four days later Klansman Randle C. Pounds was arrested for attempted assault on Farmer. Charles McClendon, Latimore McNeese, and Klansman Bill Alford Jr. were arrested on charges of disturbing the peace for their involvement in the incidents. See *BDN*, 14 April 1965, and "Federal Complaint," *United States of America, . . . v. Original Knights*.

43. *NOT-P*, 10 April 1965.

44. *NOT-P*, 10, 11 April 1965; *BDN*, 9, 11 April 1965.

45. Heilbron interview by author.

46. *BDN*, 14 April 1965.

47. *NOT-P*, 14 April 1965; "Summary of Incidents: Bogalusa."

48. *NOT-P*, 29 June 1965; *BDN*, 29 June 1965; Will Ussery to Ed Hollander, 16 April 1965, box 7, file 6, CORE (SRO).

49. *NOT-P*, 16 April 1965.

50. *BDN*, 16 April 1965; *NOT-P*, 17 April 1965.

51. *LW*, 1 May 1965.

52. Accounts of the rally can be found in *NOT-P*, 23 April 1965, and *BDN*, 23 April 1965. See also *NOT-P*, 17 April 1965.

53. *BDN*, 2, 3 May 1965; *NOT-P*, 4 May 1965; *LW*, 15 May 1965.

54. *NOT-P*, 2 April 1965.

55. *NOT-P*, 23 April 1965; *BDN*, 23, 25 April 1965.

56. *NOT-P*, 21 April 1965.

57. *NOT-P*, 23 April 1965; *NYT*, 26 April 1965.

58. *NOT-P*, 25, 24, 28 April 1965; *BDN*, 28, 30 April 1965.

59. *NOT-P*, 6, 7 May 1965.

60. *BDN*, 9 May 1965.

61. *NOT-P*, 17 May 1965; *BDN*, 17 May 1965.

62. This account of the Cassidy Park assault is drawn from Hicks interview by author; *BDN*, 20 May 1965; *NYT*, 20 May 1965; *NOT-P*, 20 May 1965; and "Federal Complaint." Klan leader Virgil Corkern and his two teenaged sons were part of the white mob. See "Federal Complaint."

63. Hicks interview with author.

64. *NOT-P*, 21 May 1965.

65. *NOT-P*, 24 May 1965.

66. *LW*, 30 May 1965; *BDN*, 24 May 1965.

67. "Telephone Report from Mike Jones, May 24, 1965," box 7, folder 6, CORE (SRO).

Chapter Eight

1. On the Wilson lynching, see Bond and Bond, *Star Creek Papers*, 123–29.

2. *BDN*, 24, 25 May 1965; *NOT-P*, 25 May 1965.

3. *BDN*, 27 May 1965; Mike Jones to Ed Hollander, 26 May 1965, box 7, file 6, CORE (SRO); *States-Item*, 1 July 1965.

4. *BDN*, 30 May 1965.

5. *NOT-P*, 31, 30 May 1965; *LW*, 5 June 1965.

6. John Stewart to Hubert Humphrey, 15 June 1965, Humphrey Papers, MHS; "Summary of Incidents: Bogalusa, Louisiana, January 28–July 1, 1965"; *NOT-P*, 1 June 1965; *BDN*, 1, 4 June 1965. McKeithen's secret meeting with the Klan is documented in J. Edgar Hoover to David B. Filvaroff, 2 June 1965, attached memorandum, "Racial Situation: Bogalusa, Louisiana," Humphrey Papers, MHS.

7. *NOT-P*, 8, 10, 6 June 1965.

8. *Newsweek*, 14 June 1965, 38; *NOT-P*, 4, 7, 29 June, 4 July 1965.

9. *NYT*, 6 June 1965.

10. Ibid.

11. Ibid.

12. Ibid.

13. "Guns, Pickets Down: Talks Begin in Bogalusa Racial Crisis," *Jet*, 24 June 1965, 8–11.

14. *NYT*, 6 June 1965.

15. Ibid.

16. Ibid.

17. Joyce, "The 'Double V' Was for Victory," 107.

18. *Los Angeles Times*, 13 June 1965.

19. Two representative FBI reports on this meeting are SAC New Orleans to Director, 23 February 1965 (Deacons file 157-2466-3) and 24 February 1965 (Deacons file 157-2466-4), FBI Files.

20. *Los Angeles Times*, 13 June 1965.

21. Ibid.

22. Ibid.

23. Ibid.

24. Ibid.

25. Ibid.

26. *Los Angeles Times*, 14 June 1965.

27. SAC Los Angeles to Director, 15 June 1965, and LHM, "Deacon for Defense and Justice," 15 June 1965, Deacons file 157-2466-16, FBI Files.

28. Shana Alexander, "Visit Bogalusa, and You Will Look for Me," *Life*, 2 July 1965, 28.

29. Ibid.

30. Ibid.

31. Ibid.

32. Ibid. Many CORE volunteers had the same ambivalence about the Deacons. Joan Grieco was hoping not to be assigned to Bogalusa, but "when I heard about the Deacons, I heaved a huge sigh of relief, and I thought, gee. I'm going to have some protection. And it relieved me so that's why I'm kind of mixed up on my theories on non-violence now." Grieco interview by anonymous.

33. "Guns, Pickets Down."

34. *NOT-P*, 26 June 1965; *BDN*, 27 June 1965; *Hicks et al. v. Cutrer et al.*

35. *NOT-P*, 2, 3 July 1965; *BDN*, 2 July 1965.

36. "WATS Report," 6–28 to 7–65, box 4, folder 2, CORE (SRO); "Summary of Incidents: Bogalusa, Louisiana, January 28–July 1, 1965"; *BDN*, 1 July 1965; *NOT-P*, 30 June 1965; "WATS Line Report," [July 1964], box 7, folder 6, CORE (SRO); *States-Item*, 1 July 1965.

37. On the planned marches, see Hill, "Character of Black Politics," 83, and *BDN*, 30 June 1965. The CORE convention and Thomas's comments are reported in "Core Shifts to Politics: Tackles Needy Money Problem," *Jet*, 22 July 1965, 8–9. Many CORE members disagreed with the new policy that allowed the pacifists to accept armed protection: "I can't see letting someone else do it for you," said one CORE volunteer working in Louisiana. "If you're going to be non-violent, you have to refuse their protection it seems to me." Peters interview by anonymous.

38. *NOT-P*, 10 July 1965.

39. On the Sims arrest, see "WATS Line Report, July 5, 1965," box 7, folder 6, CORE (SRO); *BDN*, 8 July 1965; *NYT*, 8 July 1965; and *NOT-P*, 7 July 1965. The 7 July meeting is found in "CORE and Bogalusa Civic and Voters League Meeting," 7 July 1965, reel 0104, Bogalusa, La., transcript, PSCSUA. At the meeting A. Z.

Young expressed surprise that members of Bogalusa's Italian community had joined in on the attacks and reminded the audience that the Sicilians had been on the same side of the color line with blacks: until recently, Italians were buried in the "colored cemetery."

40. Austin and Hicks interviews by author; Austin interview by anonymous. Austin joined the Deacons before July 1965 but publicly denied membership on occasion.

41. Austin interview by author.

42. The account of this incident is drawn from Austin interview by Hall; Austin interview by author; *NOT-P*, 9 July 1965; *BDN*, 9 July 1965; and *Newsweek*, 19 July 1965, 25–26.

43. Austin interview by author.

44. Ibid.

45. Ibid.

46. Ibid.

47. Ibid.; *NYT*, 15 August 1965. Austin admitted to police that he was a Deacon. See *Newsweek*, 19 July 1965. Accounts of the CORE/League meetings are also drawn from "CORE and Bogalusa Civic and Voters League Meeting," Bogalusa, La., transcript, PSCSUA, reel 0104, 8 July 1965 (Sims), reel 0108, 9 July 1965, and reel 0047, 10 July 1965.

48. *BDN*, 9 July 1965; *NOT-P*, 10 July 1965.

49. *NOT-P*, 25 January 1966.

50. Fred Zimmerman, "Race and Violence: More Dixie Negroes Buy Arms to Retaliate against White Attacks: Non-Violence Coming to End?," *Wall Street Journal*, 12 July 1965.

51. *BDN*, 19 July 1965.

52. Hamilton Bims, "Deacons for Defense," *Ebony*, September 1965, 25–30; *NYT*, 11 July 1965.

53. *NYT*, 11 July 1965.

54. *LW*, 17 July 1965. King made allowances for armed self-defense in a 1959 article published in *Liberation*. In a response to Robert F. Williams, King said, "The principle of self-defense, even involving weapons and bloodshed, has never been condemned, even by Gandhi, who sanctioned it for those unable to master pure nonviolence." MLK, "The Social Organization of Non-Violence," *Liberation*, October 1959; reprinted in Robert F. Williams, *Negroes with Guns*, 11–15. But in the same year King joined the campaign to expel Williams from the NAACP for his support of armed self-defense, saying that armed action "would be the greatest tragedy that could befall us" because it would give "our oppressors . . . an opportunity to wipe out many innocent Negroes." Tyson, *Radio Free Dixie*, 163. By 1965, when the Deacons posed a real threat to the alliance with liberals, King held firm to his position against armed self-defense. Bayard Rustin, a key figure in King's leadership circle, echoed the theme of the liberal alliance in his analysis of the March on Washington. The march "took place because the Negro needs

allies," wrote Rustin in October 1963. Until "the successful completion of the March, the method was on trial," but now the march had succeeded and reassured "our white allies." Rustin, "The Meaning of the March on Washington," reprinted in Meier, Rudwick, and Broderick, *Black Protest Thought*, 1965 ed., 381, 383.

55. *LW*, 17 July 1965; *NOT-P*, 13 July 1965.

56. Richard Haley, "Memorandum: CORE, Deacon, Relationship," [1965], reel no. 19, Southern Civil Rights Litigation Records, Yale University, New Haven.

57. Ibid.

58. *NOT-P*, 11, 12 July 1965. News reports identified the four young black men as Deacons, though Sims appeared to deny that they were. The four were Joe Gatlin, Gerald Simmons, Harrison Andrews, and Lucious Manning. *BDN*, 19 July 1965; *NOT-P*, 19 July 1965; *NYT*, 11 July 1965.

59. *BDN*, 20 July 1965.

60. Zimmerman, "Race and Violence."

61. Ibid.

62. Ibid.

63. Ibid.

64. "The Deacons," *Newsweek*, 2 August 1965, 28–29.

65. *Jet* served as a barometer of concerns and hopes of the black working class during the civil rights period—reflecting its changing identity, ideas, and political debates on movement strategy. That the publication is virtually invisible in most early works on civil rights is an indication of the tendency to view the movement through the perspective of middle-class leaders. Most coverage of the Deacons in the black media was positive. See *LW*, 13 March 1965, 8 May, 19, 26 June, and 17 July 1965. The coverage in *Jet* was extensive; a sampling of articles include "Bogalusa Riflemen Fight Off OKKKK Attack," 22 April 1965, 5; "Guns, Pickets Down: Talks Begin in Bogalusa Racial Crisis," 24 June 1965, 8; Louie Robinson and Charles Brown, "Negro Most Feared by Whites," *Jet*, 15 July 1965, 14–17; "CORE Shifts to Politics: Tackles Needy Money Problem," 22 July 1965, 8–9; and "Deny Deacons Shot Bogalusa White Youth," 22 July 1965, 5.

66. Robinson and Brown, "Negro Most Feared by Whites."

67. Ibid.

68. Ibid.

69. Ibid.

70. Ibid.

71. "Guns, Pickets Down."

72. Ibid.

Chapter Nine

1. *BDN*, 3, 11 July 1965; *NOT-P*, 13, 11 July 1965; *Hicks et al. v. Cutrer et al.*

2. *NOT-P*, 12 July 1965; *BDN*, 12, 15 July 1965.

3. *NOT-P*, 13 July 1965.

4. *NOT-P*, 14 July 1965; *BDN*, 15 July 1965. Lomax had raised at least $5,641 for the league by 9 July 1965. See "Ledger: Bogalusa Voters League," 9 July 1965, Jenkins Papers, CORE (SHSW).

5. *NOT-P*, 13, 15 July 1965; *BDN*, 15 July 1965.

6. *NOT-P*, 14 July 1965.

7. Ibid. Another account of the airport meeting is given in *Time*, 23 July 1965, 19–20.

8. *NOT-P*, 14 July 1965 (McKeithen); *Los Angeles Times*, 14 June 1965 (Sims). McKeithen's attempt to disarm the Deacons was consistent with the tradition of whites controlling black access to weapons. See Cottrol and Diamond, "Second Amendment."

9. *BDN*, 15 July 1965.

10. Ibid.; *NOT-P*, 15 July 1965.

11. *NOT-P*, 15 July 1965; *LW*, 28 August 1965.

12. *Commonwealth*, 29 July 1965, 517; *NOT-P*, 16 July 1965.

13. Doar and Landsberg, "Performance of the FBI," 6:912–21; *United States v. U.S. Klans*. In 1962 the Justice Department had asked Federal Judge Frank Johnson Jr. in Montgomery for injunctions to prevent the Klan from violence against the Freedom Riders and requiring Alabama police to protect the protesters. Johnson issued the injunction but negated its impact by also enjoining CORE and Martin Luther King from conducting Freedom Rides. Unlike the Bogalusa case where the Justice Department used the restraining order to destroy the Klan and compel local police to consistently protect the constitutional rights of activists, the department never sought to enforce the Montgomery injunction. Bass, *Taming the Storm*, 179–82. By 1962 most movement activists believed that there would be no progress in the South unless the federal government protected activists against racist terrorism. John Kennedy had campaigned on the promise that he would enact "effective anti-bombing and anti-lynching legislation" but failed to deliver on his pledge. Protective legislation did not pass until 1968. Mann, *Walls of Jericho*, 300.

14. Scholars differ on how credible the "federalism" defense was. Some believe that the Kennedys genuinely respected the doctrine. Others think that they invoked federalism only to avoid a confrontation with southern segregationists—a confrontation that was both a constitutional and a moral imperative. Taylor Branch (*Parting the Waters*, 721–25) writes that the Kennedys backed out of the Greenwood suit because they feared that southern officials would balk at enforcement, provoking a showdown with Washington across the South. On the Greenwood suit, see Dittmer, *Local People*, 153–55.

15. Quoted in Dittmer, *Local People*, 468 (n. 62).

16. The federal government prosecuted five Klansmen in 1964 for a Florida bombing but failed to obtain a guilty verdict. Newton, *Invisible Empire*, 173–74.

17. "A Report to Governor McKeithen: Louisiana at the Crossroads," 20 July 1965, Community Relations Service, Humphrey Papers, MHS.

18. *BDN*, 18 July 1965.

19. *NOT-P*, 17 July 1965.

20. *BDN*, 19 July 1965; *NOT-P*, 19 July 1965.

21. *BDN*, 19 July 1965; *NOT-P*, 20 July 1965. Klansmen named in the suit were Dewey Smith, Virgil Corkern, Albert Applewhite, Arthur Ray Applewhite, Louis Applewhite, E. J. Dixon, O'Neal Austin Jones, Delos Williams, James M. Ellis, Hardie Adrian Goings Jr., Esley Freeman, James A. Hollingsworth Jr., Randle C. Pounds, Sidney August Warner, Billy Alford, and Rawlin Williams. The Justice Department had filed a similar suit against the Klan in Montgomery in 1962 but never enforced the order. See n. 13, above.

22. *BDN*, 18, 20, 29, 22 July 1965; *NOT-P*, 22 July 1965.

23. *BDN*, 21, 30 July, 6 August 1965; *NOT-P*, 21, 25, 30 July 1965.

24. *NYT*, 19 August 1965; *BDN*, 20 July 1965. On Rester's Klan membership, see *NOT-P*, 12 September 1965.

25. *NOT-P*, 29, 30 July 1965.

26. Forman, *Making of Black Revolutionaries*, 381.

27. *NOT-P*, 28, 29 July 1965.

28. *BDN*, 3 August 1965; *NOT-P*, 8 August 1965.

29. *BDN*, 13 August 1965.

30. *States-Item*, 9 August 1965.

31. Ibid.

32. Roy Reed, "The Deacons, Too, Ride by Night," *New York Times Magazine*, 15 August 1965, 10–24.

33. Ibid.

34. Ibid. The ways in which masculine rhetoric shaped gender roles in the modern civil rights movement have received little scholarly attention. Tim Tyson (*Radio Free Dixie*, 140–43) offers a perspective on masculine rhetoric and patriarchy. "For black men as well as white men," writes Tyson, "the rhetoric of protecting women was an integral part of the politics of controlling women." He cautions that black patriarchy must be placed in "social context" (p. 141). Steve Estes has undertaken the most ambitious effort to apply gender theory to the modern civil rights movement in "Race, Masculinity, and the 1968 Memphis Sanitation Strike" and "'I AM A MAN!,'" Drawing on the work of Gail Bederman and Jacquelyn Dowd Hall, Estes maintains that the masculine rhetoric of the movement was a response to the verbal and physical emasculation of black men. Although appeals to manhood were a powerful mobilizing tool, the concept of manhood also carried with it the idea of female subordination—that "black and white masculinity rested on definitions of womanhood as well as race, age, and class." Estes quotes Martin Luther King telling the Memphis sanitation workers, "We are tired of our men being emasculated so that our wives and daughters

have to go out and work in the white lady's kitchen, leaving us unable to be with our children and give them the time and attention that they need." From this statement Estes concludes that King was relegating women to the mother role and accepting the "patriarchal ordering of the black family." "Race, Masculinity," 154 (King quoted on pp. 160–61). Estes posits that "masculinist liberation strategies" exploited "male insecurities," and though this strategy yielded political victories, it also "circumscribed the roles women could play in the struggle and accepted many of the patriarchal and heterosexist assumptions that underlie American society. " 'I AM A MAN!,' " iii.

Gender role analysis of black manhood ideals deserves more attention, but there are important considerations. First, care should be taken in assuming that the act of protecting women necessarily subordinates them. This may be true in honor and shame societies in the Mediterranean, where the defense of women is inextricably linked to a strict set of prescribed behaviors and punishments imposed on women clearly intended to degrade and control them—that is, where protection is explicitly linked to dominance. But there is no compelling evidence that a comparable social code existed in the African American community. The Deacons were a male-exclusive organization, but they did not, for the most part, attempt to relegate their wives to the domestic sphere. Indeed, many Deacons' wives and children were politically active, and there were women auxiliaries for the Deacons in both Jonesboro and Bogalusa, though their role is unclear. Jackie Hicks, wife of Deacons leader Bob Hicks, had armed confrontations with racist vigilantes on more than one occasion and organized target practice for the Bogalusa Deaconesses. See Hicks interview by author and "The Deacons," *Newsweek*, 2 August 1965, 28–29. Moreover, for African American men, slavery imparted a meaning to manhood that was quite different from the white male ideal. Slavery systematically denied African American men the right to protect their loved ones from violence and sexual assault. The frustration, anger, and shame that accompanied this dehumanizing treatment led the freedmen to defend their families to prove their humanity and equality. That the struggle for human dignity was expressed in masculine symbols does not mean that the black masculine ideal possessed the same patriarchal meaning as that found in white society. The freedmen were using the only vernacular at hand to express their hopes and aspirations for dignity. For black men, the desire to protect their families owed more to a sense of filial and community responsibility than to a desire to exert power over others and construct black patriarchy. This is not to say that there were not patriarchal meanings to the newly found manhood, but rather that—in historical perspective—becoming a man had much more to do with fulfilling obligations to family and community than with subordinating women. Ultimately, "manhood" meant a set of virtues and duties that had very real meaning for African American men in the South: it determined how they measured their success or failure as humans and created the basis for self-esteem. For male self-abnegation, honor, and the ideology of masculinity, see Gilmore, *Manhood* in the Making, esp. 121, 229–30. On male honor, violence, and patriarchy in the slave quarters, see Wyatt-Brown, *Shaping of Southern Culture*, and Wilma King, *Stolen Childhood*.

35. Reed, "Deacons, Too, Ride by Night."

36. Ibid.

37. *NOT-P*, 12 April 1965; *BDN*, 31 May 1965; "Caught in the Civil Rights Crossfire," *Business Week*, 7 August 1965, 102–6.

38. *Ebony*, September 1965, 25–30.

39. Ibid.

40. Malcolm X quote in "James Farmer and Malcolm X: A Debate at Cornell University, March 7, 1963"; Burris quote from Reed, "Deacons, Too, Ride by Night."

41. *Ebony*, September 1965, 25–30.

Chapter Ten

1. The quotations in this and the next paragraph are from Hunter interview by anonymous; Clurman interview by anonymous; Acheson interview by anonymous; Peters interview by anonymous; "Louisiana CORE Newsletter," [ca. Summer 1965], MFP; and Meldon Acheson to Mr. and Mrs. Robert Acheson, 22 July 1965, reprinted in "Richland Boy Beaten in Louisiana CORE Mission—Letter to Parents Outlines," a leaflet distributed by the Richland and Ollie Methodist Churches, Richland, Iowa, n.d., Acheson Papers, CORE (SHSW). On the shooting incident at the end of the next paragraph, see "Report 7-21-65 by Jim Peters on Ferriday," 22 July 1965, box 4, folder 7, CORE (SRO). Contrary to scholarship that argues that resistance and armed self-defense were unceasing traditions in the African American community, the Ferriday episode demonstrates the very real problems of fear and passivity that created the need for organizations like the Deacons that could spawn a new consciousness. Similarly, witness the absence of local protest in response to the lynching of Mack Parker in 1959 in Poplarville, Miss.

2. Roy Reed, "The Deacons, Too, Ride by Night," *New York Times Magazine*, 15 August 1965, 10–24. The pattern of development for expansionist organizations emerging from social movement tends to follow three parallel and interrelated courses of action: (1) uniting atomized and episodic protests into a cohesive organization, (2) crystallizing a strategy and philosophy (intellectual labor—which organization frees up people to do), and (3) competing for political legitimacy, followers, and resources.

3. Otis Firmin, quoted in Natchez Deacons Meeting, 10 September 1965, audio tape reels 178, 179, Pincus Collection, ARC.

4. Several factors make it difficult to accurately assess the Deacons' size, the most significant being that the national leadership did not keep records. In addition, while the Deacons leadership was public, most of the membership was

secret and some entire chapters were clandestine. Even the FBI, with its extensive network of informants, frequently failed to uncover chapters until they had been operating for some time.

5. The FBI Deacons files alone indicate suspected organizing activity in fifty-one cities and counties. Affiliated Deacons members who worked alone were more likely to escape FBI attention and be omitted from oral histories with Deacons leaders. For example, although there was no FBI record of Deacons activity in the River Parishes of Louisiana, in a 1999 interview Black Panther leader Geronimo ji Jaja Pratt said that his uncle, Percy Pratt, of Morgan City, La., was a Deacon. Pratt interview by author. The FBI found no evidence of a Deacons chapter in Houston, although an active chapter in the city, operated by Frederick Kirkpatrick, was well known to local police. See Investigative Report, Deacons for Defense and Justice, New Orleans, 27 November 1967, Deacons file 157-2466-250, and SAC Houston to Director, memorandum 157-2466-2455, FBI Files. On Kirkpatrick in Houston, see Justice, *Violence in the City*, 24, 35–37, 119, 128–29.

6. Investigative Report, Deacons for Defense and Justice, New Orleans, 22 November 1966, Deacons file 157-2466-176, FBI Files; *Jet*, 19 May 1966, 7.

7. Fairclough, *Race and Democracy*, 113–19.

8. "WATS Line Report," 30 June 1965, box 7, folder 7, CORE (SRO); Harper interview by author; Meier and Rudwick, *CORE*, 352.

9. "WATS Line Report," 30 June 1965; Meier and Rudwick, *CORE*, 352.

10. Harper interview by author.

11. Ibid.

12. Ibid.

13. Investigative Report, Deacons for Defense and Justice, New Orleans, 28 March 1966, Deacons file 157-2466-120, FBI Files; Harper interview by author.

14. Harper interview by author.

15. Ibid.

16. Ibid.

17. Ibid.

18. Background on the Homer Deacons is drawn from Anonymous Core Members and Deacons interview by anonymous.

19. Lewis interview by Feingold. Background information on the Homer chapter is drawn from Malray and Dodd interviews by author.

20. Pam Smith and Dan Paik, "Follow-up Scouting Report, May 25, 1965," box 4, folder 12, CORE (SRO); "Field Report, April 25 to April 30, 1965," box 4, folder 6, CORE (SRO).

21. SAC New Orleans to Director, 24 June 1965, Deacons file 157-2466-18, and Investigative Report, Deacons for Defense and Justice, New Orleans, 17 August 1965, Deacons file 157-2466-41, FBI Files. Other Homer officers included Otis Chatman, Joe Lester Green, and George Lewis, Fred Lewis's brother.

22. Pam Smith, "Claiborne Parish (Homer), July 12, 1965," and "Homer Report," 15 July 1965, box 4, folder 6, CORE (SRO); Lewis interview by Feingold.

23. "Statement of Harvey Malray," n.d., box 4, folder 6, CORE (SRO); Malray interview by author.

24. "WATS Line Report, June 29, 1965," box 1, folder 9, Monroe Project Files, CORE (SHSW); Malray interview by author.

25. Anonymous CORE members and Deacons interview by anonymous.

26. Lewis interview by Feingold.

27. Harper interview by author.

28. Oretha Castle and Gary Craven to unidentified correspondent, 26 May 1965, box 5, folder 6, CORE (SRO); John L. Gee to David Dennis, [ca. December 1965], Ferriday, La., box 1, folder 1, CORE (FFM). FBI sources confirmed that a chapter had been formed in Tallulah. See Investigative Report, Deacons for Defense and Justice, New Orleans, 28 March 1966, Deacons file 157-2466-120, FBI Files. On the first unsuccessful attempt to establish a Deacons chapter, see Dawson interview by anonymous.

29. Whatley interview by author.

30. *LW*, 2 January 1965; Meldon Acheson to unidentified correspondent, 10 August 1965, Ferriday, La., Acheson Papers, CORE (SHSW); "Chronology of Events in Concordia Parish," 30 January 1966, box 4, folder 7, CORE (SRO).

31. Meldon Acheson to Gary Greenberg, 17 July 1965, Acheson Papers, CORE (SHSW); Whatley interview by author.

32. "WATS line report," 3 July 1965, box 1, folder 3, CORE (SRO).

33. Acheson to Greenberg, Ferriday, La., 27 July, 17 August 1965, Acheson Papers, CORE (SHSW). The youthful FFM found itself competing with an older moderate organization: the Civic League, headed up by Father August Thompson, a black priest, which was attempting to organize biracial talks. See Fairclough, *Race and Democracy*, 401, and Pat Scharber, "Negro Pastor Says People Have Love, but Frustrated," *[St. Paul, Minnesota] Catholic Bulletin*, September 1965, found in box 1, folder 6, CORE (FFM).

34. Archie Hunter, "Report," 24 July 1965, Ferriday, La., box 4, folder 7, CORE (SRO); Whatley interview by author.

35. Acheson to unidentified correspondent, Ferriday, La., 30 July 1965, Acheson Papers, CORE (SHSW).

36. Acheson to Greenberg, Ferriday, La., 17 August 1965, Acheson Papers, CORE (SHSW).

37. Ibid.

38. *LW*, 13 November 1965; "Chronology of Events in Concordia Parish," 30 January 1966. The first efforts to organize a chapter in Ferriday are noted in "Non-Prosecutive Summary Report," New Orleans, 14 October 1965, Deacons file 157-2466-73, FBI Files.

39. "Freedom Ferriday Movement Release," 23 November 1965, GMHP; *LW*,

4 December 1965; Whatley to Rev. Willie Johnson, 29 December 1965, Ferriday, La., box 1, folder 1, CORE (FFM).

40. OKKKK, Realm of Louisiana, Concordia Parish, "The Fiery Cross," November 1965, box 1, folder 15, CORE (FFM).

41. "Statement by Vernon Smith," box 1, folder 14, 30 November 1965, CORE (FFM).

42. "Statement by David Whatley," 3 December 1965, GMHP; *LW*, 4, 25 December 1965; "Negro Gas Station Burned after Insurance Canceled: Violence Continues in Ferriday, LA.," News Release, Ferriday, 19 December 1965, CORE (FFM).

43. Investigative Report, Deacons for Defense and Justice, New Orleans, 30 December 1965, Deacons file 157-2466-102, FBI Files; Whatley interview by author; Whatley, "Autobiography of David Lee Whatley," n.d., n.p., in author's possession, and "Field Report of Concordia Parish, La.," Ferriday, La., 29 January 1966, GMHP. A "guard shift" book is one of the few remaining written records of the self-defense group in Ferriday. See "Guard Note Booklet," ca. December 1965, Ferriday, La., box 1, folder 16, CORE (FFM).

44. Whatley, "Autobiography" and "Field Report of Concordia Parish, La."

45. Investigative Report, Deacons for Defense and Justice, New Orleans, 28 March 1966, Deacons file 157-2466-120, FBI Files.

46. Little is know about Najah or his place of origin. There is a small collection of his papers donated by Miriam Feingold at the State Historical Society of Wisconsin. See Najah Papers, SHSW. On the Snipers, see John Hamilton to Richard Haily [*sic*], 22 March 1966; Hamilton to Mr. Haley, May 1966; Unidentified correspondent to Haily [*sic*], ca. April 1966; Hamilton to Haily [*sic*], 16 April and ca. May 1966—all Ferriday, La., box 1, folder 5, CORE (FFM).

47. "The Fiery Cross Extinguisher," Ferriday, La., Spring 1966, Acheson Papers, CORE (SHSW).

48. *LW*, 27 August 1966. Other officers included Steven Ward (Bogalusa), vice president; Lillie Mae Thompson (Bogalusa), assistant secretary; and Willie Jackson (Lake Providence), treasurer.

49. Kelley, *Hammer and Hoe*, 169 (thanks to Arthur Carpenter for this citation); Burris and Austin interviews by author. Bill Yates reported that in May 1965 Charlie Sims traveled to Donaldsonville on several occasions and met with CORE staff and local blacks. See Yates, "Memo," 6 May 1965, box 4, folder 3, CORE (SRO).

50. Wood interview by author.

51. Ibid.

52. On the New Orleans chapter, see Investigative Reports, Deacons for Defense and Justice, New Orleans, 10 January 1966, Deacons file 157-2466-104; 21 July 1966, Deacons file 157-2466-152; and 27 November 1967, Deacons file 157-2466-250—all in FBI Files.

53. Wood interview by author.

54. Ibid.

55. "Deacons for Defense and Justice Rally," October 1965, broadsheet, Political Ephemera Collection, Special Collections, Tulane University Library, New Orleans; Wood interview by author.

56. New Orleans SAC to Director, 8 February 1966, Deacons file 157-2466-111, FBI Files.

57. Wood interview by author; Investigative Report, Deacons for Defense and Justice, New Orleans, 28 March 1966, Deacons file 157-2466-120, FBI Files; Austin interview by author.

58. Collins [Dara Abubakari] interview by author. The Deacons also formed a chapter in St. Francisville, north of Baton Rouge, which was primarily active in a 1967 boycott protest. On the St. Francisville chapter, see Noflin interview by author, and SAC New Orleans to Director, 27 February 1968, Deacons file 157-2466-264, FBI Files.

59. *NYT*, 30 August 1965; *LW*, 11 September 1965. The FBI's account of the Jackson meeting is contained in SAC Jackson to Director, 3 September 1965, Deacons file 157-2466-59, and 25 October 1965, Deacons file 157-2466-78, FBI Files.

60. *NYT*, 30 August 1965. Recruiters departed for Natchez, Columbia, and Greenville.

61. Dittmer, *Local People* (Hurley), 49–50; Mrs. Medgar Evers and Peters, *For Us, the Living*, 82–84; Charles Evers, *Evers*, 74–75.

Chapter Eleven

1. U.S. Commission on Civil Rights, *Justice in Jackson*; *NYT*, 28 August 1965. On SNCC in Natchez in 1964, see Robert Coles, "Natchez, Lovely Natchez," *New Republic*, 18 February 1967, 31–34. Accounts of the bombing and community response are drawn from *NYT*, 28 August 1965; *NOT-P*, 28 August 1965; *LW*, 4 September 1965; and Young interview by author.

2. Young interview by author.

3. *NYT*, 29, 28 August 1965.

4. "Black Natchez," transcript.

5. Charles Evers, *Evers*, 132.

6. "Black Natchez," transcript.

7. Stokes interview by author.

8. Ibid.

9. *NYT*, 29, 30 August 1965; Stokes interview by author. The Natchez riot was not the first incident of black civil violence in the Mississippi movement. One of the rare integration efforts during the lunch counter sit-in period was on Sunday, 24 April 1960, when blacks tried to integrate the Gulf Coast beach in Biloxi. When a white mob attacked protesters during the day, the black community quickly abandoned the nonviolence that protest organizers prescribed and

launched its own form of collective protest. Before sundown, 200–300 blacks roamed the streets of Biloxi, throwing bottles and bricks at passing cars. After midnight, shooting broke out between blacks and whites, wounding 2 whites and 8 blacks. Police arrested several whites and blacks for fighting. Police Chief Herbert McDonnell closed all white and black bars (though liquor was illegal anyway). The incident portended the coming conflict between nonviolence and the political instincts of the Mississippi black working class. Johnston, *Mississippi's Defiant Years*, 105–11.

10. Stokes interview by author.

11. *NYT*, 29 August 1965.

12. Ibid.

13. Ibid.

14. The Metcalfe bombing was not an isolated event. A wave of racist violence and intimidation swept across the Deep South beginning on 20 August, when Thomas L. Coleman, a member of a prominent Lowndes County family, blasted his shotgun at two civil rights workers in Hayneville, Ala., killing Jonathan Daniels, a 26-year-old white seminarian. Two days later, three white men wounded a Unitarian minister in a similar shotgun attack as he stood outside his apartment house in Jackson, Miss. The bloody assaults were accompanied by a wildfire of cross burnings, including three crosses torched in Philadelphia, Miss.— apparently in protest of plans to desegregate city schools. Klan passions had been inflamed the previous week when officials desegregated Neshoba Central School just outside Philadelphia. Sobel, *Civil Rights*, 360–61; *NYT*, 30 August 1965.

15. Economic, social, and political facts on Natchez are drawn from SNCC Research, "Adams County, Mississippi," 25 October 1965, Atlanta, Ga., Pincus Collection, ARC.

16. Young interview by author.

17. SNCC Research, "Adams County."

18. Untitled report on Natchez Political Groups, ca. 1965, Pincus Collection, ARC. Many young blacks in Natchez were predisposed to Evers's tactical use of force. The Klan threatened filmmakers Ed Pincus and David Neuman when they first arrived in July 1965. Without hesitation, four young black boys appointed themselves guardians, and unbeknownst to the filmmakers, perched on their roof all night with rifles and Molotov cocktails. The boys were unsure how to ignite the fuses on their coke bottle bombs and ended up littering the yard with unsuccessful experiments. When the filmmakers awoke the next morning, they were shocked to find a yard full of Molotov cocktails. They thanked the boys for their concern but convinced them to station their guard farther down the street. Percy Shain, "Story of Change in 'Black Natchez,'" *Boston Globe*, 21 March 1976.

19. "Black Natchez," transcript.

20. *NYT*, 4 September 1965.

21. Ibid.

22. *NYT*, 4, 9 September 1965.

23. *NYT*, 4, 9 September 1965.

24. Stokes interview by author.

25. "Natchez Deacons Meeting," ca. July 1965, audiotape reels 43–44, Pincus Collection, ARC; "Black Natchez," transcript.

26. "Black Natchez," transcript.

27. Ibid.

28. The following quotations from the meeting are from "Natchez Deacons Meeting," 10 September 1965, audiotape reels 178–79, Pincus Collection, ARC, and "Black Natchez," transcript.

29. There are obvious similarities between African American and white beliefs about masculine honor. By linking death with honor and freedom, Jackson was propounding a notion of masculine honor identical to that held a century before by slave masters. According to Kenneth S. Greenberg (*Honor and Slavery*), the willingness to risk death for freedom was central to the code of masculine honor for slave owners. Slave owners believed that slaves could never be men because they were unwilling to risk their lives for freedom. The idea of "slavery as an alternative to death reached deeply into the abstract thought of men of honor," and one of "the distinguishing features of slaves was their inability to confront death without fear or submission. Men of honor believed that every slave had chosen a life of humiliation over an honorable death" (pp. 100, 107, 98).

30. Young interview by author.

31. "Natchez Hurries Bi-Racial Talks as Fear Grips City," *Jet*, 16 September 1965, 14–15; *LW*, 11 September 1965; *NYT*, 4 September 1965.

32. *NYT*, 3, 4 September 1965; Young interview by author.

33. *NYT*, 8 October 1965; Stokes interview by author.

34. *NYT*, 13, 14 October 1965; "Natchez Crisis Eases a Bit; City Fathers Still Evasive," *Jet*, 28 October 1965, 6–7; Francis Ward, "Economic Squeeze Highlights," *Jet*, 4 November 1965, 16–20.

35. "Black Natchez," transcript.

36. Ibid.

37. Ibid.; Laue, *Direct Action and Desegregation*, 85–86 (King); "Black Natchez," transcript (local woman, Ladner); Dittmer, *Local People*, 210 (Dennis). SNCC consistently employed the federal interventionist strategy throughout the civil rights movement. According to Clayborne Carson (*In Struggle*, 37, 128), its reliance on the liberal–federal government coalition did not change until after the 1964 Democratic convention. As the Ladner and Guyot exchanges demonstrate, in some communities SNCC activists continued to adhere to the interventionist strategy well into 1965. In 1965 SNCC joined the Selma campaign, whose explicit purpose was to achieve federal legislation. In Selma, King exhorted his followers to, as Robert Weisbrot (*Freedom Bound*, 132) writes, "fill the jails and 'arouse the federal government' to assure the ballot." On the interventionist strategy in the Greenwood campaign, see Umoja, "Eye for an Eye," 107. John

Dittmer (*Local People*, 199, 209) writes that by 1963 COFO activists had decided that the movement could not make substantive gains as long as "white hoodlums and police could attack black organizers with impunity" and that this could be accomplished only by federal intervention. Opposition to Bob Moses' Freedom Summer proposal came primarily from those activists who favored local organizing and community empowerment over the interventionist strategy. On opposition to Freedom Summer, see Cobb and Peacock interviews by Dent. Cobb, a SNCC leader, feared that the white volunteers would "take over" by virtue of their skills and contacts, and the movement would come to be defined as "white people doing good works." Peacock also saw the Freedom Summer strategy as primarily an attempt to secure federal intervention and viewed the project as a major turning point for SNCC—a move away from "mass education" for economic power. Voting rights were illusory: "After you got the vote, you didn't have nothing . . . you had to have some economic power."

38. "Natchez Crisis Eases a Bit; City Fathers Still Evasive," *Jet*, 28 October 1965; Young interview by author; *NYT*, 31 October 1966.

39. Young interview by author.

40. Ibid.

41. Group size is drawn from Young and Stokes interviews by author.

42. Ibid. Early FBI intelligence on the Deacons substantially underestimated the organization's reach—e.g., the FBI knew virtually nothing about the Natchez Deacons until 1966. See SAC Jackson to Director, 25 October 1965, Deacons file 157-2466-78, and Director to SAC Jackson, 11 January 1966, Deacons file 157-2466-105, FBI Files.

43. Young and Stokes interviews by author.

44. On fees and dues, see Investigative Report, Deacons for Defense and Justice, 17 August 1965, New Orleans, Deacons file 157-2466-41, FBI Files.

45. Director to SAC Jackson, 11 January 1966, Deacons file 157-2466-105, FBI Files.

46. Stokes interview by author.

47. Ibid.

48. Young interview by author.

49. Stokes interview by author.

50. Ibid. The relationship of violence and self-respect—and the emphasis on psychological transformation in social revolution—was first explored by Fanon in *Wretched of the Earth* (see esp. the chapter, "Concerning Violence"). Fanon's argument, often criticized as nihilistic and reckless, goes well beyond self-defense to include therapeutic revolutionary violence. But his central idea of the need for social movements to extirpate internal psychological demons—to liberate consciousness as a precondition of political liberation—is useful in analyzing the civil rights movement. The Deacons employed militant rhetoric and exemplary courage to overcome fear and resignation. This psychological liberation was imperative, even if it had to be done at the expense of destroying alli-

ances with liberals and the government. The teachings of Black Muslim leader Elijah Muhammad framed this theory of social death and rebirth in the biblical imagery of Lazarus. According to Muhammad, slavery and segregation had killed the black man "mentally, culturally, spiritually, economically, politically, and morally—transforming him into a 'Negro.'" The "Negro" remained in the graveyard "of segregation and second-class citizenship" until Elijah Muhammad was summoned to lift Lazarus from the grave. On "social death," see Patterson, *Slavery and Social Death*; on Black Muslim teachings and social death, see Cleaver, *Soul on Ice*, 91–94.

51. Stokes and Young interviews by author.

52. Burris interview by author.

53. Stokes and Young interviews by author.

54. Ibid. That Stokes, Kirkpatrick, and many Deacons were religious men raises the question about the conflict between black Christian pacifism and black masculine honor. The black church played a progressive role in sustaining black resistance and culture, but it also taught the Christian doctrine of "turn the other cheek," an idea clearly at odds with the Deacons' belief in self-defense. In contrast, the fraternal orders that the Deacons belonged to did not promote Christian pacifism and were, in some respects, a retreat from the asceticism, humility, and self-restraint associated with the black church. Masculine honor and Christianity also clashed in the white southern experience. Ted Ownby (*Subduing Satan*, 12) writes that Christian evangelicalism in the nineteenth century "demanded self-control, humility in manner, and harmony in personal relations" whereas southern "honor demanded self-assertiveness, aggressiveness, and competitiveness," all of which violated the norms of evangelical morality. There would be some value in a study of how working-class African American men reconciled their own notions of honor with the teachings of the black church.

55. "Black Natchez," transcript.

56. Stokes interview by author.

57. Ibid.

58. Director to SAC Jackson, 11 January 1966, Deacons file 157-2466-105, FBI Files; Stokes interview by author.

59. Director to SAC Jackson, 11 January 1966, Deacons file 157-2466-105, FBI Files; Stokes interview by author.

60. Ward, "Economic Squeeze Highlights"; *NYT*, 4 December 1965; *LW*, 11 December 1965.

61. Ward, "Economic Squeeze Highlights"; *NYT*, 4 December 1965; *LW*, 11 December 1965.

62. On the ill-fated Jackson protest campaign in the wake of the Medgar Evers shooting, see Dittmer, *Local People*, 166–68; on the Clarksdale defeat, see p. 177; and on the McComb campaign, see p. 114.

63. Evers's reputation took a serious blow with the release of the Sovereignty Commission Papers, which revealed his extensive cooperation with the commis-

sion. Dittmer (pp. 360–61) casts the Natchez campaign in a less positive light, arguing that it secured reforms that were "of little direct benefit" to the black community. He also concludes that "the emergence of Charles Evers was a setback for the Mississippi movement" (p. 178). The 3 December agreement did not end the movement in Natchez. Picketing at stores continued, and on 22 December a fight between a black picketer and a white man resulted in charges of police brutality. The following day Evers announced that the boycott was in effect again. It formally ended on 3 March 1966, when the city agreed to fire two policemen and reinstate several black store employees who had been dismissed in retaliation for the renewed boycott. The Natchez Deacons continued to meet and maintain activities through 1968. The chapter survives at the time of this writing as the "Natchez Sportsmen Club," having made a peaceful transition to a hunting club.

64. On Port Gibson, see Investigative Report, Deacons for Defense and Justice, New Orleans, 27 November 1967, Deacons file 157-2466-250, FBI Files; Stokes interview by author; and Charles Evers, *Evers*, 134.

65. Stokes and Young interviews by author. The Hattiesburg and Laurel chapters are documented in Umoja, "Eye for an Eye," 221–22.

66. Walker interview by author.

67. George Haynes, "Opinion of the Court," "Final Decree," *Claiborne Hardware v. NAACP* (hereafter cited as *Claiborne Hardware v. NAACP*); Walker interview by author. A thorough study of the Port Gibson campaign can be found in Crosby, "Common Courtesy."

68. Crosby, "Common Courtesy," 230.

69. Walker interview by author. Walker was joined by Calvin Williams and Julius Warner, who was later elected chapter president.

70. Ibid.

71. Ibid.

72. *Claiborne Hardware v. NAACP*; Walker interview by author (Evers quotation).

73. *Claiborne Hardware v. NAACP*.

74. Walker interview by author. The Deacons also encouraged rumors about their boycott enforcement actions to bolster their reputation. See Crosby, "Common Courtesy," 234.

75. *Claiborne Hardware v. NAACP*. On the arrests, see Crosby, "Common Courtesy," 319. Although the sheriff's office could never prove that the three Deacons were involved in the shooting, they did make a major find in Scott's car that night. Scott was carrying minutes of chapter meetings and a complete membership list of forty-two Deacons. The incident was a convincing argument for the secrecy practiced by most other Deacons chapters. By keeping written records, the Port Gibson chapter had exposed itself to potential retaliation by police and racist forces. Indeed, the Citizens Councils of America subsequently published the names of all of the Deacons. See *Claiborne Hardware v. NAACP*, and "Blacks

Terrorized into Boycotting White Stores," *Citizen*, November 1976, 4–14. The FBI reported that "members of the DDJ [Deacons for Defense and Justice] organization are again active in Port Gibson, Mississippi" and that "Negroes wearing black hats were on the streets on 14 January 1967, harassing other Negroes." Investigative Report, Deacons for Defense and Justice, New Orleans, 27 November 1967, Deacons file 157-2466-250, FBI Files.

76. Walker interview by author.

77. Ibid.

78. Ibid.

79. Crosby, "Common Courtesy," 232, 250; *NAACP v. Claiborne Hardware Co.*, *United States Reports* 458 (October 1981): 886–940.

80. For many years Evers was dogged with accusations that he had cooperated with Mississippi authorities. The release of the state's files on the Sovereignty Commission—Mississippi's segregation spy agency—confirmed that Evers had cooperated with the agency, though he defended his actions as an effort to protect the movement. On Evers's interactions with the Sovereignty Commission, see Crosby, "Common Courtesy," 316–44; on the 1969 shoot-out, see Crosby, 400–413.

81. SAC Jackson to Director, 29 June 1967, Deacons file 157-2466-234, FBI Files; Ferguson interview by author. For a personal autobiographical viewpoint on Wilkinson County's black community, see Moody, *Coming of Age in Mississippi*.

82. Ferguson and Burkes interviews by author; SAC Jackson to Director, 29 June 1967, Deacons file 157-2466-234, FBI Files.

83. SAC Jackson to Director, 29 June 1967, FBI, Deacons file 157-2466-234, and 6 September 1967, Deacons file (unnumbered), FBI Files; Ferguson interview by author; Investigative Report, Deacons for Defense and Justice, New Orleans, 27 November 1967, Deacons file 157-2466-250, FBI Files.

84. *NYT*, 5 September 1967; Ferguson interview by author.

85. Investigative Report, Deacons for Defense and Justice, New Orleans, 27 November 1967, Deacons file 157-2466-250, FBI Files.

86. SAC Jackson to Director, 6 September 1967, Deacons file (unnumbered), FBI Files; *NYT*, 5 September 1967.

87. Stokes interview by author; *NYT*, 25 February 1973.

88. Recruiting forays are referred to in Thomas, Burris, and Austin interviews by author.

89. Burris and Austin interviews by author.

90. Investigative Report, Deacons for Defense and Justice, New Orleans, 10 January 1966, Deacons file 157-2466-104, FBI Files; Austin and Burris interviews by author; Austin interview by Hall.

91. Carson, *In Struggle*, 164; Burris and Austin interviews by author; Investigative Report, Deacons for Defense and Justice, New Orleans, 28 March 1966, Deacons file 157-2466-120; SAC Birmingham to Director, 2 September 1965, Deacons file 157-2466-56, and 3 September 1965, file 157-2466-576—all in FBI Files.

92. On Tuskegee, see SAC Mobile to Director, 13 September 1965, Deacons file (unnumbered), FBI Files. On North Carolina, see SAC Charlotte to Director, 1 October 1965, Deacons file 157-2466-68, FBI Files.

93. On South Carolina, see SAC Savannah to Director, 25 September 1965, Deacons file (unnumbered), 26 November 1965, Deacons file 157-246-93, and 22 September 1965, Deacons file 157-731, FBI Files. The Klan incident is cited in SAC Columbia to Director, [13 April 1966], Deacons file (unnumbered), and Frazier and Riley interviews by author. Blacks in the lowlands of South Carolina engaged extensively in armed self-defense in Reidsville and Dorchester, according to Victoria Delee (interview by author), a black veteran of the civil rights movement.

94. SAC Mobile to Director, 13 September 1965, Deacons file (unnumbered); SAC Savannah to Director, 15 September 1965, Deacons file 157-2466-58, and 22 September 1965, file 157-2466-65—all in FBI Files.

95. Moore interview by author.

Chapter Twelve

1. Thomas interview by author. It was not Thomas's and the Deacons' first contact with the Muslims. The Muslims had a strong presence in Monroe, La., and frequently traveled to Jonesboro to sell *Muhammad Speaks*. When the Nation of Islam group was harassed by police in Monroe, Thomas led a delegation of Jonesboro Deacons to confront the mayor and police chief. The Muslims were also actively recruiting in Bogalusa as early as 1965.

2. Thomas interview by author.

3. Ibid.

4. Austin interview by author.

5. Ibid.

6. The Lomax windfall gave rise to internal bickering and recriminations about how the funds were used. See Austin interview by author.

7. SAC San Francisco to Director, 21 September 1965, Deacons file 157-2466-67 (article), FBI Files; Thomas interview by author.

8. Larry Still, "Talk Is of a Revolution—Complete with Mixed Blood," *Jet*, 28 November 1963, 14–19.

9. SAC Detroit to Director, 12 August 1965, Detroit "Appearance of Robert Hicks," Deacons file 157-2466-40, FBI Files.

10. Ibid.

11. SAC Los Angeles to Director, 29 September 1965, Deacons file 157-2466-69, FBI Files.

12. Ibid.

13. One of the leftist support groups was the Committee to Aid the Deacons; see SAC San Antonio to Director, 9 August 1965, Deacons file 157-2466-35, and 10 August 1965, file 157-2466-42, FBI Files.

14. Austin interview by author.

15. On the Deacons' Castro money connection, see Director to SAC New Orleans, 14 March 1966, Deacons file 157-2466-115, and SAC New Orleans to Director, 23 March 1966, file 157-2466-117, FBI Files.

16. Phyllis Fishberg, "Klan Stopped Cold When Masses Fight Back," *Workers World*, 29 April 1965; "Black Armed Groups Spread across South," *Workers World*, 10 June 1965.

17. SAC New York to Director, 28 October 1965, Deacons file 157-2466-80, FBI Files; *Workers World*, 14, 28 October 1965.

18. On LeSeur, see SAC New York to Director, 30 June 1966, Deacons file 157-2466-140, FBI Files. The Labadie Collection at the University of Michigan has one item of correspondence from LeSeur written on stationary from the "Deacons for Defense and Justice—New York Chapter." See LeSeur to unidentified correspondent, 7 January 1966, Staten Island, New York, Labadie Collection, University of Michigan Library, Ann Arbor. Thanks to Caroline Melish for this document. On New York fund-raising, see SAC New York to Director, 26 October 1965, Deacons file 157-2466-81, and 24 November 1965, file 157-2466-90; Investigative Report, Deacons for Defense and Justice, New Orleans, 28 March 1966, Deacons file 157-2466-120—all in FBI Files; and *Workers World*, 28 October, 11 November 1965.

19. Ahmad, *History of RAM*, 6–8.

20. Ibid., 10–11, 14–15, 20–21.

21. Ibid., 20.

22. Ahmad, *History of RAM*, 18 (*Crusader* article); Airtel to Director from SAC WFO, 9 September 1965, Deacons file and enclosure LHM, "Organization for Black Power (OBP)" Washington, D.C., 9 September 1965, FBI, Deacons file originally numbered 157-3022-156, FBI Files.

23. Ahmad, *History of RAM*, 15, 20, 28; Forman, *Making of Black Revolutionaries*, 374–75.

24. *NYT*, 13 March 1964; Sobel, *Civil Rights*, 283–84; "North's First Rights Martyr Made in Bloody Cleveland," *Jet*, 23 April 1964, 16–20; Ahmad, *History of RAM*, 28; "Form Rifle Clubs, Militant Detroiter Urges," *Jet*, 16 July 1964, 7.

25. Collins and Thomas interviews by author.

26. On Boston, see SAC Boston to Director, 6 October 1965, Deacons file 157-2466-70, and 3 November 1965, file 157-2466-85; Investigative Report, Deacons for Defense and Justice, New Orleans, 22 November 1966, Deacons file 157-2466-176, and 27 November 1967, file 157-2466-250—all in FBI Files. On Cleveland, see Investigative Report, Deacons for Defense and Justice, New Orleans, 28 March 1966, Deacons file 157-2466-120, and 10 January 1966, file 157-2466-104, FBI Files. The Cleveland chapter became a target for the only COINTELPRO action against the Deacons. See SAC Cleveland to Director, 21 April 1966, Deacons file unnumbered, and Investigative Report, New Orleans, 21 July 1966, Deacons file 157-2466-152, FBI Files. On Philadelphia, see Director

to SACs Newark, New Orleans, Philadelphia, and WFO, 20 April 1966, Deacons file (unnumbered); SAC Philadelphia to Director, 17 April 1966, Deacons file 157-2466-127; SAC WFO to Director, 29 April 1966, Deacons file 157-2466-134; Director to SACs, Chicago, New Orleans, and Philadelphia, 14 September 1967, Deacons file 157-2466-241—all in FBI Files; and *Philadelphia Enquirer*, 17 April 1965. On Washington, D.C., see *Jet*, 21 April 1966, 5; SAC WFO to Director, 31 March 1966, LHM, Deacons file 157-2466-121; and Investigative Report, Deacons for Defense and Justice, New Orleans, 28 March 1966, Deacons file 157-2466-120, and 21 July 1966, file 157-2466-152—all in FBI Files.

Hobson never formed a chapter and only spread the rumor to gain political leverage. A Deacons chapter was successfully organized in Newark—apparently without the knowledge of the national Deacons. See SAC Philadelphia to Director, 18 April 1966, Deacons file 157-2466-128, and SAC Newark to Director, 25 May 1966, Deacons file 157-2466-136, FBI Files.

27. *Chicago Daily News*, 15 October 1965.

28. Viorst, *Fire in the Streets*, 321.

29. "Militant Negroes Here Forming Armed Unit to Fight the Klan," *Chicago Daily News*, 15 October 1965.

30. Ibid.

31. "Rights Leaders Reject Plan to Start Deacons," *Chicago Defender*, 18 October 1965.

32. SAC Chicago to Director, 2 November 1965, Deacons file 157-2466-84, FBI Files. This document contains a complete transcript of the WVON program.

33. Ibid.

34. Rogers interview by author.

35. Thomas interview by author.

36. Thomas and Rogers interviews by author.

37. LHM, 28 February 1966, Deacons file no. 157-2466-113, FBI Files. Thomas (interview by author) confirmed these and the following statements taken from the FBI.

38. Ibid.

39. Ibid.

40. Investigative Report, Deacons for Defense and Justice, New Orleans, 21 July 1966, Deacons file 157-2466-152, FBI Files.

41. Ibid.; Thomas interview by author.

42. Slightly different versions of the news stories of 5 and 6 April were published in different editions of the *Chicago Daily News*: Quoted material here is gleaned from 6 April 1966 and articles quoted in SAC Chicago to Director, 5 April 1966, Deacons file 157-2466-123, and 13 April 1966, file 157-2466-125, FBI Files.

43. *Chicago Daily News*, 6 April 1966.

44. Ibid.

45. *Chicago Daily News*, 8 April 1966; Hicks interview by author; "Deacons Come to Chicago for Money and Muscle," *Jet*, 21 April 1966, 5–6.

46. "The Deacons Go North," *Newsweek*, 2 May 1966, 20–21.

47. Ibid. On the Deacons' Chicago tour, see "Deacons Come to Chicago for Money and Muscle," 5.

48. SAC Chicago to Director, 8 June 1966, Deacons file 157-2466-137; Investigative Report, Deacons for Defense and Justice, New Orleans, 21 July 1966, Deacons file 157-2466-152—all in FBI Files.

49. On the Deacons and the Harvey incident, see SAC Chicago to Director, 10 August 1966, Deacons file 157-2466-158, FBI Files.

50. SAC Chicago to Director, 22, 29 August 1966, Deacon files (unnumbered), FBI Files.

51. Fred Kirkpatrick, one of the Deacons' founders from Jonesboro, worked closely with King beginning in 1966 and eventually worked for SCLC while he was still active in the Chicago Deacons; see Kirkpatrick interview by Hall. The FBI reported that approximately forty Deacons guarded King during a speech in Chicago on 29 July 1966. See Investigative Report, Deacons for Defense and Justice, 22 November 1966, Deacons file 157-2466-176, FBI Files. On Deacons secretly guarding King, see interview with John Harris, a Chicago chapter member, by author. Harris's account is confirmed by Bennett Johnson, a major figure in Chicago black politics, in Bennett Johnson interview by author.

52. SAC Chicago to Director, 7 November 1966, Deacons file (unnumbered), FBI Files.

53. Investigative Report, Deacons for Defense and Justice, New Orleans, 27 November 1967, Deacons file 157-2466-250, FBI Files; Thomas interview by author.

Chapter Thirteen

1. *NOT-P*, 25 July 1967.

2. Ibid.; *Chicago Daily News*, 6 April 1966 (Young).

3. Viorst, *Fire in the Streets*, 334 (Rustin). On the Watts riot and Bogalusa, see Oberschall, *Social Conflict*, 332.

4. Viorst, *Fire in the Streets* (first rioter, writer, 341; second rioter, 338). A study of opinions of Watts residents in the riot curfew area is found in Tomlinson, "Riot Ideology." The study indicated that 15 percent of the community participated in the riot, 50 percent "express[ed] a sympathetic understanding of the views of the supporters," 62 percent viewed the riot as a "protest," 56 percent thought that it had purpose, and 58 percent expected it to have "favorable effects" (p. 418).

5. Lentz, *Symbols*, 17, 186.

6. Lawson quoted in Estes, "'I AM A MAN!,'" Ella Baker leaves little doubt that nonviolence was imported by northern pacifists and leftists. In 1955 Baker, Bayard Rustin, Stanley Levison, and others formed "In Friendship," a liberal–labor coalition to aid school integration in the South. In Friendship became the principal organization fostering nonviolence as the strategy for the modern civil rights movement in the South. Baker said that discussions between members of the

Fellowship for Reconciliation and Martin Luther King "strengthened whatever germ of an idea about a nonviolent movement Martin had." Rustin's "influence became paramount" in what Baker said was the "articulation of the nonviolent concept coming out of Montgomery." The outcome of a series of meetings in Levison's kitchen with Baker and Rustin was the "creation of the Southern Christian Leadership Conference, SCLC." When asked if the "genesis of the idea for SCLC" came out of the North, Baker said, "That's correct." Grant, *Ella Baker*, 102–3. Levison, who eventually became Martin Luther King's closest adviser, was a major figure in the Communist Party in the early 1950s. On Levison, see Barron, *Operation SOLO*, 263–66, and Garrow, "The FBI and Martin Luther King," *Atlantic Monthly*, 80–86, 88. On the Montgomery Bus Boycott's middle-class origins, see Robinson, *Montgomery Bus Boycott*, esp. 7–8. The boycott was initiated and controlled by the black middle class, but the rank and file was the working class. There had been incidents of defiance on Montgomery buses before Rosa Parks, but E. D. Nixon and the Women's Political Committee selected Parks as the test case because her genteel demeanor and respectable profession made her acceptable to the black middle class.

7. Clurman interview by anonymous. Clurman's support for nonviolence was strictly tactical: "I think when homes get shot into, and people go around telling them they should be nonviolent—I think they should shoot back."

8. MLK, Speech at Frogmore, 11 November 1966, box 11966, MLK Papers, MLK Center for Nonviolent Social Change, Atlanta (hereafter cited as "Frogmore speech").

9. *BDN*, 12, 16 October 1965.

10. *BDN*, 18 October 1965; Hill, "Character of Black Politics," 86.

11. *NOT-P*, 20 October 1965.

12. *LW*, 6 November 1965; *NOT-P*, 21 October 1965.

13. *LW*, 6 November 1965; *NOT-P*, 21 October 1965.

14. *NOT-P*, 7, 30 December 1965.

15. *NOT-P*, 7, 30 December 1965; *BDN*, 2 November 1965; Austin interview by author; *NOT-P*, 29 December 1965.

16. *NOT-P*, 28, 29, 30 December 1965.

17. *NOT-P*, 21 November, 8 December 1965; *BDN*, 5 December 1965.

18. "Bogalusa Voters League Boycott List," n.d., box 1, folder 6, CORE, "Bogalusa, Louisiana, Records, 1965–1966," CORE (SHSW); *BDN*, 5 December, 30 January 1966; *LW*, 6 February 1966.

19. *BDN*, 7 June 1966.

20. *BDN*, 3 September 1965.

21. *NOT-P*, 8, 9, 10, 12, 13 September, 4 December 1965. Christmas admitted that the OKKKK had maintained a "bureau of investigations" and a secret "wrecking crew"—which he characterized as peacekeepers. "I guess you might call it the police force." *NOT-P*, 8 September 1965.

22. *NOT-P*, 4 (Farmer), 23 December 1965; *BDN*, 2 February 1966.

23. John Doar's report (Doar and Landsberg, "Performance of the FBI"), though an apologia for the FBI and the Justice Department, gives a good overview of the department's dismal record. In response to the reign of Klan terror in southwestern Mississippi, Doar assigned nine lawyers to investigate the beatings and bombings; they failed to bring a single legal action. As early as 17 July 1964, J. Edgar Hoover had sent the attorney general a list of Klan members in Mississippi and a list of law enforcement officials who were known or suspected Klan members; the Justice Department failed to follow up with any criminal or civil actions. On the Klan's explosive growth in 1964–65, see Doar and Landsberg, "Performance of the FBI," 929–31; Dittmer, *Local People*, 215–17, 305–6; Newton, *Invisible Empire*, 159, 177; and U.S. House, *Present-Day Ku Klux Klan*.

24. *NOT-P*, 25 January 1965. The HUAC hearing resulted in three volumes of testimony and reports, contained in U.S. House, *Activities of Ku Klux Klan* and *Present-Day Ku Klux Klan*.

25. The Mississippi panic finds its echoes in the slave revolt panics that periodically swept across the South in the nineteenth century. In Mississippi the paranoia was heightened by emancipation, as in the case of the 1865 insurrection panic. See Wharton, *The Negro in Mississippi*, 218. In the 1940s similar rumors of murderous black conspiracies were rampant, including the Eleanor Clubs panic. See Odum, *Race and Rumors of Race*.

26. "Miss. KKK Scared Stiff: Say Black Muslims Hide Guns in Graves, Coffins," *Jet*, 2 December 1965, 6–8; Thomas interview by author.

27. "Miss. KKK Scared Stiff."

28. Ibid.

29. *LW*, 29 January, 6 February 1966; *BDN*, 28, 30 (Young) January 1966; *NOT-P*, 29 January 1966 (Sims). The Klan did launch a rash of cross burnings in January 1966 in response to the HUAC hearings.

30. Thomas interview by author.

31. There are several differing accounts of this meeting. I have combined Thomas's recollections with Garrow, *Bearing the Cross*, 477; Oates, *Let the Trumpet Sound*, 397–98; and Sellers, *River of No Return*, 162.

32. Dittmer, *Local People*, 393.

33. "Meredith Threat 'To Arm' Not the Answer, Says Dr. King," *Jet*, 23 June 1966, 16–19.

34. Interview in Raines, *My Soul Is Rested*, 416–23 (Sims, 422); Thomas interview by author.

35. *NYT*, 14 June 1966.

36. Thomas interview by author; *NYT*, 22 June 1966.

37. Thomas interview by author; "Dr. King Scores Deacons," *NYT*, 22 June 1966; *LW*, 17 July 1965 (King).

38. MLK, "Nonviolence: The Only Road To Freedom," *Ebony*, October 1966,

27–30. King also had harsh words for Charles Evers's support of self-defense on the Meredith March. See MLK, Frogmore speech.

39. MLK, Frogmore speech.

40. Carmichael and Hamilton, *Black Power*, ix, 44.

41. *BDN*, 16 September 1966; *NOT-P*, 16 September 1966.

42. *BDN*, 16 September 1966. In July 1967 City Attorney Rester and nine other men were charged with littering for throwing Klan leaflets on lawns. See *BDN*, 28 July 1967, and *NOT-P*, 22 December 1966.

43. Burris interview by author; *BDN*, 16 September 1966; *NOT-P*, 21 September 1966; Sobel, *Civil Rights*, 407.

44. *NOT-P*, 11, 15 August 1967.

45. *NOT-P*, 16, 17 August 1967.

46. *NOT-P*, 18, 19 August 1967.

47. *NOT-P*, 21 August 1967.

48. Ibid.

49. "A. Z. Young: A Leader's Legacy," *NOT-P*, 7 December 1993.

50. Lisa Frazier, "Thank you, Mr. Young," *NOT-P*, 6 December 1993.

51. On Kirkpatrick in Houston, see Justice, *Violence in the City*, 24, 35–37, 119, 128–29. Thanks to Annie Pearl Kirkpatrick and Charlie Fenton for background on Kirkpatrick's life after the movement.

52. Thomas interview by author; Tyson, *Radio Free Dixie*, 292–94.

53. Thomas interview by author.

54. Ibid.

55. Ibid.

56. Ibid.

57. Ibid.

58. SAC Chicago to Director, 19 July 1966, Deacons file 157-2466-153; Director to SAC New Orleans, 12 October 1966, unrecorded; SAC Hong Kong to Director, 20, 28 July 1967, Deacons file (unnumbered)—all in FBI Files; Robert F. Williams and Thomas interviews by author.

59. Williams's financial records and testimony are found in U.S. Senate, *Hearings before the Subcommittee to Investigate the Administration of the Internal Security Act*; payments to Thomas for RAM are documented in pt. 3, 247, 252.

60. Collins interview by author.

61. Investigative Report, Deacons for Defense and Justice, New Orleans, 27 November 1967, FBI, Deacons file 157-2466-250; Thomas interview by author.

62. Thomas's chance meeting with Jim Brown placed the celebrity under added FBI scrutiny. A memorandum from the Cleveland SAC detailed Brown's current movie production and included a transcript of a speech Brown gave in January during a "Jim Brown Farewell Night" at the Cleveland Arena. See SAC Cleveland to Director, 28 February 1967, Deacons file 157-2466-200, FBI Files.

63. Sims interview by Price.

Conclusion

1. Dr. J. L. Garret, conversation with the author.

2. Sidney Hook maintained that nonviolence is never effective by itself: that the threat of violence is what influences those in power, and reform is futile without violence. The popular myth that Gandhi led a nonviolent anticolonial revolution in India is belied by the violence that surrounded his movement. Gandhi constantly launched campaigns he could not control. For example, during the boycott of the visit of the prince of Wales in 1921, Gandhi's followers rioted in Bombay while chanting their leader's name. In 1922 Gandhi called off a noncooperation campaign when volunteers attacked a police station and killed twenty-one police and Chaukidars. Hook cited in Aiyar, "Anatomy of Mass Violence in India," 28. See also Phadke, "Historical Background of Mass Violence in India," 50–51.

3. Eskew, *But for Birmingham*, 268, 270–71.

4. Ibid., 278 (riot of 7 May); Sobel, *Civil Rights*, 181.

5. Eric Arnesen's book on black dockworkers, *Waterfront Workers of New Orleans*, is a case study on how the judicious use of force helped secure black working-class economic gains. In the last decade there has been more interest in the role of organized labor in the civil rights movement. See Honey, *Southern Labor and Black Civil Rights*.

6. For the Lexington, N.C., riot of 5 June 1963, see Sorensen, *Kennedy*, 493, and Sobel, *Civil Rights*, 204; for the Cambridge, Md., riot of 11 June 1963, see Sobel, *Civil Rights*, 196–97; for the Jackson State College, Jackson, Miss., riot of 4 February 1964, see *NYT*, 4, 5 February 1964, and Dittmer, *Local People*, 238; for the Jacksonville, Fla., riot of 23–24 March 1964, see "Shocking Police Action Spurs Negro Students to Strike Back," *Jet*, 9 April 1964, 14–19, Newton, *Invisible Empire*, 173, and Sobel, *Civil Rights*, 252–53; for the Henderson, N.C., riot of 12 July 1964, see Sobel, *Civil Rights*, 253, and Parker, *Violence in the U.S.*, 75; for the Princess Anne, Md., riot of 26 February 1964, see Sobel, *Civil Rights*, 253; for the 1964 McComb, Miss., riot, see Dittmer, *Local People*, 305–10. Violence erupted in the wake of NAACP leader Medgar Evers's assassination in Jackson on 12 June 1963 as a crowd of rock-throwing blacks, chanting "We want the murderer," marched on the downtown business district, resulting in twenty-seven arrests. See Sobel, *Civil Rights*, 191; Linder, *Bending toward Justice*, 2–3. Jackson State erupted a second time on 10 May 1967, when more than one thousand students engaged in a pitched battle against police and the National Guard. See Dittmer, *Local People*, 413. The Cambridge riots began on 11 June 1963, and the National Guard was not withdrawn until 1964. Cleveland Sellers (*River of No Return*, 68, 74) reported that blacks were extensively armed in the spring of 1964 in Cambridge, Md., and that during the April riot a group of armed black men held off advancing National Guard troops with gunfire. For the St. Augustine, Fla., riot, see Newton, *Invisible Empire*, 173.

7. Dittmer, *Local People*, 310.

8. On the dearth of adult African American men in the movement, see Belfrage, *Freedom Summer*, 76. In the Mississippi Delta, SNCC's constituency was primarily the very young and the very old. See Dittmer, *Local People*, 125. As early as the Nashville sit-ins in 1961, young black men were fighting back, says SNCC leader James Forman. There was regrettably "limited participation of young blacks in the student movement precisely because of its nonviolent character." Forman, *Making of Black Revolutionaries*, 376, 95.

9. One researcher found that black CORE activists, frustrated by their organizing failures, often blamed working-class blacks, whom they thought were "too cowardly to stand firm, too brainwashed by the white culture, and too apathetic to support the militant movement." Bell, *CORE*, 99–100.

10. Eskew, *But for Birmingham*, 271.

11. Viorst, *Fire in the Streets*, 222.

12. On the lack of involvement by black students, see Dittmer, *Local People*, 245, and *NYT*, 4, 5 February 1964.

13. Bell, *CORE*, 99. Bell concluded that there was an inverse relationship between socioeconomic status and participation in the movement by black students. Black middle-class students were less likely to participate in protests, often succumbing to pressure from status-conscious parents who regarded jail as a "badge of disgrace." CORE tended to attract more children of the working class, whose parents were less concerned with the stigma of jail.

14. "Freedom Now," *Time*, 17 May 1963, 23–25.

15. Branch, *Parting the Waters*, 872.

16. Ibid., 885.

17. Herbert Haines (*Black Radicals*) makes a strong argument for the "radical flank effect" on mainstream movements, though I would argue that the radical flank effect theory misreads the role of radicals in the black freedom movement. William Van Deburg (*New Day in Babylon*) offers an excellent analysis of the positive impact of Black Power consciousness; he also argues, like Haines, that Black Power rhetoric enhanced the bargaining position of moderates (p. 306). I am arguing that black civil violence did not merely *enhance* the power of moderates: it was the primary source of their negotiating power. The events of the movement demonstrated time and again that the white power structure was unwilling to make any meaningful concessions unless there was a threat of black civil violence. The threat of violence transformed the very role of moderates; they ceased to be moderates when they began to benefit from white fears of black violence. After Birmingham, it was impossible to employ nonviolence in the moral and noncoercive way that Gandhi intended; the threat of violence was ever-present in the minds of whites. The fear of black civil violence was the driving force for the passage of the Civil Rights Act of 1964 and the Voting Rights Act of 1965. Moreover, nonviolent reformers who derived their bargaining power

from the threat of violence were not, in the strict sense, practicing the teachings of Gandhi.

18. MLK, "Letter from Birmingham City Jail," 48–49.

19. Ibid., 49.

20. Loevy, *To End All Segregation*, 63–64. A few weeks later King told a gathering at Howard University, "If the civil rights legislation does not pass, I say to you that this ugly sore on the body politic of segregation suddenly will become malignant, and this nation may live in a long night of darkness and violence." "Dr. King, Others Forecast Violence in Rights Struggle," *Jet*, 21 November 1963, 5.

21. Malcolm X saw a direct link between the Birmingham riots and Kennedy's new civil rights initiative. Malcolm argued that King had met failure in the Albany desegregation campaign in 1962 and was failing again in Birmingham until "Negroes took to the streets"—forcing Kennedy to expedite the Civil Rights Act. Malcolm X, "Message to the Grass Roots," 10 November 1963, in *Malcolm X Speaks*, 13–14.

22. *Public Papers . . .: John F. Kennedy*, 397–98, 483–94. "Everybody looks back on it and thinks that everybody was around this [civil rights] for the last three years," Robert Kennedy once said, "but what aroused people generally in the country and aroused the press was the Birmingham riots in May of 1963." Quoted in Haines, *Black Radicals*, 159, and Eskew, *But for Birmingham*, 392 (n. 24). The 12 May riot is detailed in Eskew, 300–303, and Sobel, *Civil Rights*, 184. President Kennedy's national television address on the heels of the Birmingham riots said nothing about rights or racial justice but instead sounded a "pox on both houses" theme. "The Federal Government will not permit it to be sabotaged by a few extremists on either side who think they can defy both the law and the wishes of responsible citizens by inciting or inviting violence," said Kennedy, equating Klan and police terror with the black response in Birmingham. "I call upon the citizens of Birmingham, both Negro and white, to live up to the standards their responsible leaders set last week in reaching the agreement, to realize that violence only breeds more violence. . . . There must be no repetition of last night's incidents by any group." John F. Kennedy, "Radio and Television Remarks Following Renewal of Racial Strife in Birmingham," 12 May 1964, 9:00 P.M., *Public Papers*, 397–98 (quotation, p. 397). One month later Kennedy appeared before the U.S. Conference of Mayors and once again invoked the threat of black civil violence. He reminded the mayors that during the summer "large numbers of Negroes will be out of work" and the "events in Birmingham have stepped up the tempo of the nationwide drive for full equality—and rising summer temperatures are often accompanied by rising human emotions." If the nation did nothing it would be "inviting pressure and increasing tension, and inviting possible violence." Kennedy, "Address in Honolulu before the United States Conference of Mayors," 6 June 1963, *Public Papers*, 454–59. In his 19 June message to Congress introducing the civil rights bill, Kennedy made eight sepa-

rate references to the threat of violence, six that specifically appealed to white fears of black civil violence. He ended his address by warning blacks that "violence is never justified; and, while peaceful communication, deliberation and petition of protest continue, I want to caution against demonstrations which can lead to violence." Kennedy, "Special Message to the Congress on Civil Rights and Job Opportunities," 19 June 1963, *Public Papers*, 483–94 (quotation, p. 493).

23. *Violence in the City: An End or a Beginning.* White fears of black violence were pervasive by 1964. In the *New York Times Magazine* in November 1964, philosopher and author Eric Hoffer opined: "The Negro seems to say: 'Lift up my arms. I am an abandoned and abused child. Adopt me as your favorite son. Feed me, clothe me, educate me, love me and baby me. You must do this right away or I shall set your house on fire, or rot at your doorstep and poison the air you breathe.'" Conservative cartoonist Al Capp responded to Hoffer's article, saying, "It says aloud what most of America is saying through clenched teeth." Hoffer and Capp quoted in Muse, *American Negro Revolution*, 107.

24. On the McComb campaign, see Dittmer, *Local People*, 114. On SNCC's shift from redemptive suffering to mobilizing the poor, see Carson, *In Struggle*, 62, 82, 155. Voter registration during Freedom Summer is found in Carson's chapter, "Mississippi Challenge."

25. Bell (*CORE*, 111–12, 115) found that even loyal CORE members were ambivalent toward nonviolence, precisely because they feared that it would perpetuate negative passive stereotypes.

26. Nietzsche stated this viewpoint in the extreme when he said, "Self respect depends on being able to make reprisals." Quoted in Mencken, *Nietzsche*, 238. Sorel (*Reflections*) makes a similar argument on the relationship of self-defense and self-respect.

27. Dennis interview by Dent. Richard King (*Civil Rights*, 175) says that the central question for the civil rights movement was, "How are the possibilities of self-respect and dignity created?" See esp. King's chapters, "Self-Interest and Self-Respect" and "Violence and Self-Respect: Fanon and Black Radicalism," and his discussion of the Hegelian master/slave dynamic (pp. 78–81).

28. Schultz, "Interview with Robert F. Williams," 54–55. Thanks to Annie Chamberlain for this citation.

29. Kenneth S. Greenberg, *Honor and Slavery*, 36–37.

30. White conceptions of African American character historically alternated between two contradictory images: on the one hand, the romantic racialist stereotype of blacks as submissive and grateful children; on the other hand, the paranoid image of blacks as violent and treacherous savages. The two stereotypes found expression in the nineteenth century in the popular and conflicting images of "Sambo" and Nat Turner. See Fredrickson, *Black Image*. In the aftermath of the Watts riot, CORE leaders like Dave Dennis recognized what the quid pro quo for liberal support had been. Future violence was "going to do more to antagonize the white liberals than it is to appease them." Liberals looked at

Watts and only saw "ungrateful people." Liberals did not "realize that none of the [civil rights] bills have really spoken to the problems of those people." Dennis interview by anonymous.

31. Rethinking the definition and periodization of the black freedom movement opens up new directions in scholarship. Of the many published interviews reviewed in preparing this book, not one has been with a participant of the Birmingham riots—despite the pivotal role of the event. In the past scholars have attempted to classify the movement using categories of integrationists, assimilationists, gradualists, separatists, nationalists, etc., or by using concepts such as transformative politics and consciousness-changing. My concept of "black autonomism" is not intended to reduce the movement to simple categories, but to link together many currents within the movement that had different goals but a common strategy with respect to coercion and force. Charles Silberman saw coercion at the center of change during the movement: "The tragedy of race relations is that there is no American Dilemma. White Americans are not torn and tortured by the conflict between their devotion to the American creed and their actual behavior. They are upset by the state of race relations, to be sure. But what troubles them is not that justice is being denied but that their peace is being shattered and their business interrupted." Quoted in Carmichael and Hamilton, *Black Power*, 5. Carmichael and Hamilton argue that the coalition with white liberals was at the heart of the difference between Black Power and the national civil rights organizations (pp. 54–84). The notion of a black autonomist movement is reflected in Julius Lester's *Look Out, Whitey!* "Nonetheless, they have been in 'the movement,' often silent and unseen, but affecting the course of events," according to Lester. "In Birmingham in 1963, they were the ones who burned the cars and buildings after the frustration of watching mass arrest of nonviolent demonstrators. In Selma in 1965 they were the ones who lined the curbs, armed, saying 'Go ahead and march. If Jim Clark tries anything this time, we'll take care of him" (p. 25).

32. MLK, Frogmore speech.

33. Historians have never held Black Power in high regard; the movement is usually dismissed as politically divisive and counterproductive; it is even held responsible for the Republican Party's ascendancy beginning with Richard Nixon's election in 1968. See Carson, "Rethinking African-American Political Thought," 122. Carson says that Black Power militancy "survives not as insurgencies but as unthreatening expression of Afrocentrism" and contributed to "a decline in the ability of African-Americans to affect the course of American politics."

34. Here an echo of Fanon's notion that freedom bequeathed without revolt is no freedom at all; that the oppressed must transform themselves in the process of liberation to ensure that they can be self-governing.

35. Austin interview by Hall.

36. Within this trend in history are writings that employ a "culture of resistance" framework. This framework argues that there was a continuous tradi-

tion of cultural resistance to oppression in the African American community, from slavery to the modern civil rights movement. But oppression not only bred cultural resistance; it also bred passivity, fatalism, and internalization of oppressor values. Martin Luther King described this phenomenon as the "force of complacency made up of Negroes who, as a result of long years of oppression, have been so completely drained of self-respect and a sense of 'somebodiness' that they have adjusted to segregation." MLK, "Letter from Birmingham City Jail," 48. That resistance was relegated to symbolic expressions in religion, music, and other cultural forms is evidence of political defeat, not victory. By giving too much weight to symbolic cultural resistance, we lose sight of the only form of resistance capable of liberating people from systems of domination—direct and open confrontation with authority through *political* resistance. Emphasis on cultural resistance and continuity inevitably diminishes the crucial importance of radical leadership and political ideas and expressly political movements that seek to redefine power relationships—e.g., armed self-defense, Black Power, and black nationalism. The overemphasis on culture can lead us to impart politically subversive meaning to quietism, fatalism, apathy, and individualistic self-preservation. (For a representative work arguing the culture of resistance, see Kelley, *Hammer and Hoe*.) Similarly, most recent scholarship minimizes the political differences between nonviolence and Black Power, positing that these movements shared core values, organizational resources, or consciousness-transforming goals. Studies that emphasize the commonalities of black nationalists and the nonviolent movement include Tyson, *Radio Free Dixie*; Richard H. King, *Civil Rights*; and Cone, *Martin and Malcolm*. This search for continuity in militancy and political resistance arises, in part, from a well-intentioned desire to correct the passive images of African Americans portrayed in scholarly literature and popular fiction. Among historians, most "culture of resistance" writers are responding to Stanley Elkins's *Slavery*, published in 1959. For decades historians have been endeavoring to prove Elkins wrong, especially his notion that the "infantalized" slave experience crushed the slave's personality. By framing the debate in an "either-or" dichotomy, scholars have overlooked the way in which passive and rebellious attitudes coexist and compete within the human personality. See Elkins, *Slavery*.

Bibliography

Archival Collections

Ann Arbor, Mich.
    University of Michigan Library
        Labadie Collection
Atlanta, Ga.
    Martin Luther King Jr. Center for Nonviolent Social Change
        Martin Luther King Papers
        Student Nonviolent Coordinating Committee Papers
Madison, Wis.
    State Historical Society of Wisconsin
        Congress of Racial Equality Papers
            Meldon Acheson Papers
            Bogalusa Voters League Files
            CORE, "Bogalusa, Louisiana, Records, 1965–1966"
            Ferriday Freedom Movement Files
            Homer Files
            Jackson Parish Files
            Gayle Jenkins Papers
            Monroe Project Files
            Southern Regional Office Files
        Miriam Feingold Papers
        El Ahmed Saud Ibriahim Kahafei Abboud Najah Papers
New Orleans, La.
    Amistad Research Center, Tulane University
        Congress of Racial Equality Papers, microfilm
        Gwendolyn Midlo Hall Papers
        Lawyers Constitutional Defense Committee Files, Southern Civil Rights
            Litigation Records (SCRLR), microfilm. Published by Wesleyan
            University, Middletown, Conn. 1980.
        Ronnie Moore Collection
        National Association for the Advancement of Colored People Field Director
            for Louisiana Papers

Ed Pincus Collection
Kim Lacy Rogers–Glenda Stephens Oral History Collection
Tulane University Library, Special Collections
Political Ephemera Collection
St. Paul, Minn.
Minnesota Historical Society, Manuscript Collections
Hubert H. Humphrey Papers, Vice Presidential Files, 1965–68, Civil and
Human Rights, Correspondence
Stanford, Calif.
Stanford University Archives
Project South Collection (Glen Rock, N.J.: Microfilming Corp. of America,
1975)

Government and Judicial Documents

Doar, John, and Dorothy Landsberg. "The Performance of the FBI in
Investigating Violations of Federal Laws Protecting the Right to Vote, 1960–
1967." In U.S. Senate, *Hearings before the Select Committee to Study
Governmental Operations with Respect to Intelligence Activities*, 94th Cong., 1st
sess., vol. 6. Washington, D.C.: Government Printing Office, 1976.

George Haynes, "Opinion of the Court," "Final Decree," *Claiborne Hardware v.
NAACP*, 9 August 1976, Case no. 78353, Hinds County Chancery Court,
Mississippi.

*National Association for the Advancement of Colored People et al. v. Claiborne
Hardware Co. et al.*, 10 December 1980, Case no. 51,488, Supreme Court of
Mississippi.

*National Association for the Advancement of Colored People et al. v. Claiborne
Hardware Co. et al.*, 2 July 1982, 458 U.S. 886–940.

Public Papers of the President of the United States: John F. Kennedy, 1963.
Washington, D.C.: Government Printing Office, 1964.

Robert Hicks et al. v. Jesse H. Cutrer et al., Case no. 66-225, Civil Case Files,
U.S. District Court for the Eastern District of Louisiana, New Orleans
Division.

*United States of America, by Nicholas deB. Katzenbach, Attorney General of the
United States, v. Original Knights of the Ku Klux Klan, an Incorporated
Association et al.*, 1965. U.S. District Court, Eastern District of Louisiana. Civil
Action 15793, Case Records, Federal Records Center, Fort Worth, Texas.

United States v. U.S. Klans, Knights of Ku Klux Klan, Inc., 194 F. Supp. 897 (M.D.
Ala. 1961).

U.S. House of Representatives. *Activities of Ku Klux Klan Organizations in the
United States: Hearing before the Committee on Un-American Activities.* 3 vols.
90th Cong., 1st sess., 19–22, 25 October 1965. Washington, D.C.: Government
Printing Office, 1966.

——. *The Present-Day Ku Klux Klan Movement: Report by the Committee on Un-American Activities*. 90th Cong., 1st sess., 11 December 1967. Washington, D.C.: Government Printing Office, 1967.

U.S. Senate. *Hearings before the Subcommittee to Investigate the Administration of the Internal Security Act and Other Internal Security Laws of the Committee on the Judiciary, Testimony of Robert F. Williams*. 91st Cong., 2d sess., pt. 1, 16 February 1970; pt. 2, 24 March 1970; pt. 3, 25 March 1970. Washington, D.C.: Government Printing Office, 1970.

Violence in the City: An End or a Beginning: A Report by the Governor's Commission on the Los Angeles Riots, http://www.usc.edu/isd/archives/cityinstress/mccone/part3.html, (2 December 1965).

Federal Bureau of Investigation Files

Bogalusa Civic and Voters League Files
   17-117
   166-32
   44-0-5411
Congress of Racial Equality Files
   100-225-892
Counterintelligence Program, Internal Security, Disruption of Hate Groups Files
   157-9-33
Deacons for Defense and Justice Files
   157-2466
Revolutionary Action Movement Files
   100-442684

Interviews

Acheson, Meldon. Interview by anonymous, Ferriday, La., ca. July 1965, reel 0290. Project South Collection, Stanford University Archives, Stanford, Calif. Glen Rock, N.J.: Microfilming Corp. of America. Transcript.

Anonymous CORE members and Deacons. Interview by anonymous, Homer, La., ca. August 1965, reel 0207. Project South Collection, Stanford University Archives, Stanford, Calif. Glen Rock, N.J.: Microfilming Corp. of America. Transcript.

Anonymous CORE volunteer (white male). Interview by anonymous, Bogalusa, La., ca. July 1965, reel 0044-1. Project South Collection, Stanford University Archives, Stanford, Calif. Glen Rock, N.J.: Microfilming Corp. of America. Transcript.

Austin, Henry. Interview by anonymous, n.p., ca. July 1965, reel 0333. Project South Collection, Stanford University Archives, Stanford, Calif. Glen Rock, N.J.: Microfilming Corp. of America. Transcript.

——. Interview by Gwendolyn Midlo Hall, tape recording, New Orleans,

8 October 1978. Gwendolyn Midlo Hall Papers, Amistad Research Center, Tulane University, New Orleans.

——. Interview by author, tape recording, New Orleans, 26 September 1994.

Bell, James. Interview by anonymous, Clinton, La., ca. July 1965, reel 0121. Project South Collection, Stanford University Archives, Stanford, Calif. Glen Rock, N.J.: Microfilming Corp. of America. Transcript.

Bradford, Johnnie (Mrs. Percy Lee Bradford). Interview by author, by telephone, 30 August 1994.

Brooks, Frederick. Interview by author, by telephone, 10 August 1993.

Brooks, Owen. Interview by Tom Dent, tape recording, 18 August 1978. Tom Dent Collection, Amistad Research Center, Tulane University, New Orleans.

Bryant, Patrick. Interview by author, New Orleans, 30 June 1993.

Burkes, Herman. Interview by author, by telephone, tape recording, 11 September 1994.

Burris, Royan. Interview by author, tape recording, Bogalusa, La., 7 March 1989.

Clurman, Michael. Interview by anonymous, Ferriday, La., ca. July 1965, reel 0287. Project South Collection, Stanford University Archives, Stanford, Calif. Glen Rock, N.J.: Microfilming Corp. of America. Transcript.

Cobb, Charlie. Interview by Tom Dent, tape recording, 11 February 1983. Tom Dent Collection, Amistad Research Center, Tulane University, New Orleans.

Collins, Virginia [Dara Abubakari]. Interview by author, New Orleans, 15 March 1993.

Cox, Louisa. Interview by author, by telephone, 6 August 1994.

Dawson, Artis Ray. Interview by anonymous, Tallulah, La., ca. August 1965, reel 0335. Project South Collection, Stanford University Archives, Stanford, Calif. Glen Rock, N.J.: Microfilming Corp. of America. Transcript.

Delee, Victoria. Interview by author, by telephone, 6 August 1994.

Dennis, Dave. Interview by anonymous, New Orleans, ca. August 1965, reels 0442-1 and 0443. Project South Collection, Stanford University Archives, Stanford, Calif. Glen Rock, N.J.: Microfilming Corp. of America. Transcript.

——. Interview by Tom Dent, tape recording, 8 October 1983. Tom Dent Collection, Amistad Research Center, Tulane University, New Orleans.

Dodd, George. Interview by author, tape recording, Homer, La., 14 November 1993.

Feingold, Miriam. Interview by anonymous, Clinton, La., 5 July 1965, reels 0124-0125. Project South Collection, Stanford University Archives, Stanford, Calif. Glen Rock, N.J.: Microfilming Corp. of America. Transcript.

Fenton, Charles. Interview by author, by telephone, tape recording, 19 February 1993.

Ferguson, William. Interview by author, tape recording, Percy Creek Community, Miss., 12 November 1993.

Frazier, Lee. Interview by author, Jacksonboro, S.C., 5 August 1994.

Grieco, Joan. Interview by anonymous, Bogalusa, La., ca. July 1965, reel 0045-1. Project South Collection, Stanford University Archives, Stanford, Calif. Glen Rock, N.J.: Microfilming Corp. of America. Transcript.

Harper, James. Interview by author, tape recording, Minden, La., 11 November 1993.

Harris, John. Interview by author, by telephone, tape recording, 23 January 1994.

Heilbron, Jerry. Interview by author, by telephone, tape recording, 12 September 1993.

Hicks, Robert. Interview by Miriam Feingold, tape recording, Bogalusa, La., ca. July 1966. Miriam Feingold Papers, State Historical Society of Wisconsin, Madison.

———. Interview by author, tape recording, Bogalusa, La., 25 February 1989.

Hightower, Mary. Interview by Tom Dent, tape recording, 20 August 1978. Tom Dent Collection, Amistad Research Center, Tulane University, New Orleans.

Hunter, Archie Hunter. Interview by anonymous, Ferriday, La., ca. July 1965, reel 0286. Project South Collection, Stanford University Archives, Stanford, Calif. Glen Rock, N.J.: Microfilming Corp. of America. Transcript.

Ickes, Harold. Interview by anonymous, Tallulah, La., ca. August 1965, reel 0353. Project South Collection, Stanford University Archives, Stanford, Calif. Glen Rock, N.J.: Microfilming Corp. of America. Transcript.

Jacobs, Elmo. Interview by Miriam Feingold, tape recording, Jonesboro, La., ca. July 1966. Miriam Feingold Papers, State Historical Society of Wisconsin, Madison.

Johnson, Annie Purnell. Interview by Miriam Feingold, tape recording, Jonesboro, La., ca. July 1966. Miriam Feingold Papers, State Historical Society of Wisconsin, Madison.

———. Interview by author, tape recording, Jonesboro, La., 15 November 1993.

Johnson, Bennett. Interview by author, by telephone, tape recording, 11 May 2002.

Johnson, Harvey. Interview by author, tape recording, Jonesboro, La., 14 November 1993.

Johnson, June. Interview by Tom Dent, tape recording, 22 July 1979. Tom Dent Collection, Amistad Research Center, Tulane University, New Orleans.

Kirkpatrick, Frederick Douglas. Interview by Gwendolyn Midlo Hall, New York City, notes, 31 October 1977. Gwendolyn Midlo Hall Papers, Amistad Research Center, Tulane University, New Orleans.

Lacey, Fred. Interview by anonymous, Greensburg, La., ca. July 1965, reel 0126. Project South Collection, Stanford University Archives, Stanford, Calif. Glen Rock, N.J.: Microfilming Corp. of America. Transcript.

Landry, Lawrence. Interview by author, Washington, D.C., by telephone, notes, 14 June 1993.

Lesser, Michael. Interview by anonymous, Baton Rouge, La., ca. July 1965, reel

0284. Project South Collection, Stanford University Archives, Stanford, Calif. Glen Rock, N.J.: Microfilming Corp. of America. Transcript.

Lewis, Frederick Douglas. Interview by Miriam Feingold, tape recording, Homer, La., ca. July 1966. Miriam Feingold Papers, State Historical Society of Wisconsin, Madison.

Malray, Harvey. Interview by author, tape recording, Homer, La., 14 November 1993.

Miller, Steven. Interview by author, by telephone, tape recording, 28 August 1994.

Mitchell, Catherine Patterson. Interview by author, by telephone, tape recording, 6 June 1993.

Montgomery, Lucille. Interview by author, by telephone, tape recording, 29 May 1993.

Moore, Ronnie M. Interview by author, tape recording, New Orleans, 26 February 1993.

Noflin, Reverend George. Interview by author, by telephone, 4 September 1993.

Peacock, Willie. Interview by Tom Dent, tape recording, 20 July 1979. Tom Dent Collection, Amistad Research Center, Tulane University, New Orleans.

Peters, James. Interview by anonymous, Baton Rouge, La., ca. August 1965, reel 0210. Project South Collection, Stanford University Archives, Stanford, Calif. Glen Rock, N.J.: Microfilming Corp. of America. Transcript.

Pittman, William J. Interview by author, by telephone, 15 September 1993.

Riley, Reverend James D. Interview by author, by telephone, 5 August 1994.

Rogers, Nahaz. Interview by author, by telephone, tape recording, 13 June 1993.

Roy, Lorraine. Interview by anonymous, Baton Rouge, La., ca. July 1965, reel 0211-1. Project South Collection, Stanford University Archives, Stanford, Calif. Glen Rock, N.J.: Microfilming Corp. of America. Transcript.

Sims, Charles R. Interview by William A. Price, Bogalusa, La., 20 August 1965. Transcript in author's possession.

Smith, Jerome. Interview by Tom Dent, tape recording, 23 September 1983. Tom Dent Collection, Amistad Research Center, Tulane University, New Orleans.

Stokes, James. Interview by author, tape recording, Natchez, Miss., 12 November 1993.

Taylor, Alcie. Interview by author, tape recording, Bogalusa, La., 8 March 1989.

Thomas, Earnest. Interview by author, San Mateo, Calif., by telephone, tape recording and notes, 6, 20 February 1993.

Walker, George. Interview by author, tape recording, Warren County, Miss., 19 April 1994.

Whatley, David Lee. Interview by author, tape recording, Baton Rouge, La., 5 May 1993.

White, Charles. Interview by author, tape recording, Jonesboro, La., 11 November 1993.

Williams, James "Mice." Interview by anonymous, Tallulah, La., ca. August 1965, reel 0313. Project South Collection, Stanford University Archives, Stanford, Calif. Glen Rock, N.J.: Microfilming Corp. of America. Transcript.

Williams, Robert F. Interview by author, by telephone, tape recording, 11 November 1995.

Wood, Aubry. Interview by author, tape recording, New Orleans, 21 February 1989.

Woods, Moses, Sr. Interview by author, Natchez, Miss., 8 June 1992.

Young, James. Interview by author, tape recording, Natchez, Miss., 19 April 1994.

Books and Chapters in Books

Ahmad, Akbar Muhammad. *History of RAM—Revolutionary Action Movement*. N.p., n.d. In author's possession.

Aiyar, S. P. "The Anatomy of Mass Violence in India." In *The Politics of Mass Violence in India*, edited by S. P. Aiyar, 21–33. Bombay: P. C. Manaktalas and Sons, 1967.

Ansbro, John J. *Martin Luther King, Jr.: The Making of a Mind*. Maryknoll, N.Y.: Orbis Books, 1982.

Arnesen, Eric. *Waterfront Workers of New Orleans: Race, Class, and Politics, 1863–1923*. New York: Oxford University Press, 1991.

Ayers, Edward L. *Vengeance and Justice: Crime and Punishment in the Nineteenth-Century American South*. New York: Oxford University Press, 1984.

Badger, Tony. "Fatalism, Not Gradualism: Race and the Crisis of Southern Liberalism, 1944–1965." In *The Making of Martin Luther King and the Civil Rights Movement*, edited by Tony Badger and Brian Ward, 67–95. New York: New York University Press, 1996.

Baldwin, Lewis V. *There Is a Balm in Gilead: The Cultural Roots of Martin Luther King, Jr.* Minneapolis: Augsburg Fortress Press, 1991.

Barron, John. *Operation SOLO: The FBI's Man in the Kremlin*. Washington, D.C.: Regnery Publishing, Inc., 1996.

Bass, Jack, *Taming the Storm: The Life and Times of Judge Frank M. Johnson, Jr., and the South's Fight over Civil Rights*. New York: Doubleday, 1993.

Bederman, Gail. *Manliness and Civilization: A Cultural History of Gender and Race in the United States, 1880–1917*. Chicago: University of Chicago Press, 1995.

Belfrage, Sally. *Freedom Summer*. 1965. Charlottesville: University Press of Virginia, 1990.

Belknap, Michal. *Federal Law and Southern Order: Racial Violence and*

Constitutional Conflict in the Post-Brown South. Athens: University of Georgia Press, 1987.

Bell, Inge Powell. *CORE and the Strategy of Nonviolence*. New York: Random House, 1968.

Bennett, Lerone, Jr. *The Negro Mood and Other Essays*. New York: Ballantine Books, 1964.

Bond, Horace Mann, and Julia W. Bond. *The Star Creek Papers*. Edited by Adam Fairclough. Athens: University of Georgia Press, 1997.

Bondurant, Joan V. *Conquest of Violence: The Gandhian Philosophy of Conflict*. Princeton, N.J.: Princeton University Press, 1958.

Branch, Taylor. *Parting the Waters: America in the King Years, 1954–1963*. New York: Simon and Schuster, 1989.

———. *Pillar of Fire: America in the King Years, 1963–1965*. New York: Simon and Schuster, 1998.

Brink, William, and Louis Harris. *The Negro Revolution in America: What Negroes Want, Why and How They Are Fighting, Whom They Support, What Whites Think of Them and Their Demands*. New York: Simon and Schuster, 1964.

Brown, Cynthia, ed., *Ready from Within: Septima Clark and the Civil Rights Movement*. Navarro, Calif.: Wild Trees Press, 1986.

Bruce, Dickson D., Jr. *Violence and Culture in the Antebellum South*. Austin: University of Texas Press, 1979.

Carmichael, Stokely, and Charles V. Hamilton. *Black Power: The Politics of Liberation in America*. New York: Vintage Books, 1967.

Carnes, Mark C. *Secret Ritual and Manhood in Victorian America*. New Haven: Yale University Press, 1991.

Carson, Clayborne. *In Struggle: SNCC and the Black Awakening of the 1960s*. Cambridge: Harvard University Press, 1981.

———. "Civil Rights Reform and the Black Freedom Struggle." In *The Civil Rights Movement in America: Essays by David Levering Lewis, Clayborne Carson, Nancy Weiss, John Dittmer, Charles V. Hamilton, William Chafe*, edited by Charles W. Eagles and David L. Lewis, 19–32. Jackson: University Press of Mississippi, 1986.

———. "Rethinking African-American Political Thought in the Post-Revolutionary Era." In *The Making of Martin Luther King and the Civil Rights Movement*, edited by Brian Ward and Tony Badger. New York: New York University Press, 1996.

Cash, W. J. *Mind of the South*. New York: Vintage Books, 1941.

Cashmore, Ellis. *Dictionary of Race and Ethnic Relations*, 3d ed. London: Routledge, 1994.

Chafe, William. *Civilities and Civil Rights: Greensboro, North Carolina, and the Black Struggle for Freedom*. New York: Oxford University Press, 1980.

Chalmers, David Mark. *Hooded Americanism: The First Century of the Ku Klux Klan, 1865–1965*. Garden City: Doubleday, 1965.

Cleaver, Eldridge. *Soul on Ice*. 1967. Reprint, New York: Dell Publishing, 1992.

Colburn, David, *Racial Change and Community Crisis*. New York: Columbia University Press, 1985.

Crawford, Vicki, Jacqueline Rose, and Barbara Woods. *Black Women in the Civil Rights Movement: Trailblazers and Torchbearers*. Brooklyn, N.Y.: Carlson Publishing, 1990.

Dittmer, John. *Local People: The Struggle of Civil Rights in Mississippi*. Urbana: University of Illinois Press, 1994.

Donaldson, Gary Donaldson. *The History of African-Americans in the Military: Double V*. Malabar, Fla.: Krieger Publishing Co., 1991.

Eagles, Charles W., and David L. Lewis, eds. *The Civil Rights Movement in America: Essays by David Levering Lewis, Clayborne Carson, Nancy Weiss, John Dittmer, Charles V. Hamilton, and William Chafe*. Jackson: University Press of Mississippi, 1986.

Elkins, Stanley M. *Slavery: A Problem in American Institutional and Intellectual Life*. Chicago: University of Chicago Press, 1959.

Eskew, Glen T. *But for Birmingham: The Local and National Movements in the Civil Rights Struggle*. Chapel Hill: University of North Carolina Press, 1997.

Evans, Sara. *Personal Politics: The Roots of Women's Liberation in the Civil Rights Movement and the New Left*. New York: Random House, 1979.

Evers, Charles. *Evers*. New York: World Publishing Co., 1971.

Evers, Mrs. Medgar, and William Peters. *For Us, the Living*. New York: Ace Books, 1970.

Fahey, David M. *The Black Lodge in White America: "True Reformer" Browne and His Economic Strategy*. Dayton, Ohio: Wright State University Press, 1994.

Fairclough, Adam. *To Redeem the Soul of America: The Southern Christian Leadership Conference and Martin Luther King, Jr.* Athens: University of Georgia Press, 1987.

——. *Race and Democracy: The Civil Rights Struggle in Louisiana, 1915–1972*. Athens: University of Georgia Press, 1995.

——. "The Civil Rights Movement in Louisiana, 1939–54," in *The Making of Martin Luther King and the Civil Rights Movement*, eds. Tony Badger and Brian Ward. New York: New York University Press, 1996.

Fanon, Frantz. *The Wretched of the Earth*. Translated by Constance Farrington. New York: Grove Press, 1968 (originally published by François Maspero, ed., *Les Damne's del la Terre*, Paris, 1961).

Farmer, James. *Lay Bare the Heart: An Autobiography of the Civil Rights Movement*. New York: Arbor House, 1985.

Findlay, James F., Jr. *Church People in the Struggle: The National Council of*

Churches and the Black Freedom Movement, 1950–1970. New York: Oxford University Press, 1993.

Fischer, David Hackett. *Albion's Seed: Four British Folkways in America*. New York: Oxford University Press, 1989.

Fleming, Cynthia Griggs. *Soon We Will Not Cry: The Liberation of Ruby Doris Robinson*. Lanham, Md.: Rowman and Littlefield, 1998.

Forman, James. *The Making of Black Revolutionaries*. Washington, D.C.: Open Hand Publishing, Inc., 1985.

Franklin, John Hope. *The Militant South, 1800–1861*. Cambridge, Mass.: Belknap Press, 1956.

Fredrickson, George M. *The Black Image in the White Mind: The Debate on Afro-American Character and Destiny, 1817–1914*. New York: Harper and Row, 1971.

———. *Black Liberation: A Comparative History of Black Ideologies in the United States and South Africa*. New York: Oxford University Press, 1995.

Gandhi, Mohandas. *Non-Violent Resistance (Satyagraha)*. New York: Schocken Books, 1951.

Garrow, David J. *Protest at Selma: Martin Luther King, Jr. and the Voting Rights Act of 1965*. New Haven: Yale University Press, 1978.

———. *Bearing the Cross: Martin Luther King, Jr. and the Southern Christian Leadership Conference*. New York: William Morrow and Co., 1986.

Gerlach, Larry R. *Blazing Crosses in Zion: The Ku Klux Klan in Utah*. Logan: Utah State University Press, 1982.

Gilmore, David D. *Manhood in the Making: Cultural Concepts of Masculinity*. New Haven: Yale University Press, 1990.

Grant, Joanne. *Ella Baker: Freedom Bound*. New York: John Wiley and Sons, 1998.

Greenberg, Cheryl Lynn. *A Circle of Trust: Remembering SNCC*. New Brunswick, N.J.: Rutgers University Press, 1998.

Greenberg, Kenneth S. *Masters and Statesmen: The Political Culture of American Slavery*. Baltimore: Johns Hopkins University Press, 1985.

———. *Honor and Slavery: Lies, Duels, Noses, Masks, Dressing as a Woman, Gifts, Strangers, Humanitarianism, Death, Slave Rebellions, the Proslavery Argument, Baseball, Hunting, and Gambling in the Old South*. Princeton, N.J.: Princeton University Press, 1996.

Haines, Herbert H. *Black Radicals and the Civil Rights Mainstream, 1954–1970*. Austin: University of Texas, 1988.

Hall, Jacquelyn Dowd. *Revolt against Chivalry: Jesse Daniel Ames and the Women's Campaign against Lynching*. New York: Columbia University Press, 1979.

Hanigan, James P. *Martin Luther King, Jr. and the Foundations of Nonviolence*. Lanham, Md.: University Press of America, 1984.

Hine, Darlene Clark, and Earnestine Jenkins, eds. *A Question of Manhood: A Reader in U.S. Black Men's History and Masculinity*. Vol. 1, "Manhood Rights":

The Construction of Black Male History and Manhood, 1750–1870.
Bloomington: Indiana University Press, 1999.

Hoganson, Kristin L. *Fighting for American Manhood: How Gender Politics Provoked the Spanish-American and Philippine-American Wars*. New Haven: Yale University Press, 1998.

Honey, Michael K. *Southern Labor and Black Civil Rights: Organizing Memphis Workers*. Urbana: University of Illinois Press, 1993.

Jackson, Kenneth T. *The Ku Klux Klan in the City, 1915–1930*. New York: Oxford University Press, 1967.

"James Farmer and Malcolm X: A Debate at Cornell University, March 7, 1963." In *The Rhetoric of the Civil-Rights Movement*, edited by Haig A. Bosmajian and Hamida Bosmajian, 59–87. New York: Random House, 1969.

Jenkins, William D. *Steel Valley Klan: The Ku Klux Klan in Ohio's Mahoning Valley*. Kent, Ohio: Kent State University Press, 1990.

Johnston, Erle. *Mississippi's Defiant Years, 1953–1973*. Forest, Miss.: Lake Harbor Publishers, 1990.

Justice, Blair. *Violence in the City*. Texas Christian University Press, 1969.

Kantrowitz, Stephen. "One Man's Mob Is Another Man's Militia: Violence, Manhood, and Authority in Reconstruction South Carolina." In *Jumpin' Jim Crow: Southern Politics from Civil War to Civil Rights*, edited by Jane Dailey, Glenda Elizabeth Gilmore, and Bryant Simon, 67–87. Princeton, N.J.: Princeton University Press, 2000.

Kapur, Sudarshan. *Raising Up a Prophet: The African American Encounter with Gandhi*. Boston: Beacon Press, 1992.

Kelly, Robin G. *Hammer and Hoe: Alabama Communists during the Great Depression*. Chapel Hill: University of North Carolina Press, 1990.

Kimmel, Michael S. *Manhood in America: A Cultural History*. New York: Free Press, 1996.

King, Martin Luther, Jr. *Stride toward Freedom: The Montgomery Story*. New York: Harper and Brothers, 1958.

———. "Letter from Birmingham City Jail, April 16, 1963," in *The Rhetoric of the Civil-Rights Movement*, edited by Haig A. Bosmajian and Hamida Bosmajian, 37–57. New York: Random House, 1969.

King, Richard H. *Civil Rights and the Idea of Freedom*. New York: Oxford University Press, 1992.

King, Wilma. *Stolen Childhood: Slave Youth in Nineteenth-Century America*. Bloomington: Indiana University Press, 1995.

Kirkpatrick, Frederick Douglas. *Black Music*. N.p., 1980. In author's possession.

Kluger, Richard. *Simple Justice: The History of Brown v. Board of Education and Black America's Struggle for Equality*. New York: Vintage, 1977.

Laue, James H. *Direct Action and Desegregation, 1960–1962: Toward a Theory of the Rationalization of Protest*. Brooklyn, N.Y.: Carlson Publishing, Inc., 1989.

Lay, Shawn. *War, Revolution, and the Ku Klux Klan: A Study in Intolerance in a Border City*. El Paso: Texas Western Press, 1985.

——, ed. *The Invisible Empire in the West: Toward a New Historical Appraisal of the Ku Klux Klan of the 1920s*. Urbana: University of Illinois Press, 1992.

Lentz, Richard. *Symbols, the News Magazines, and Martin Luther King*. Baton Rouge: Louisiana State University Press, 1990.

Lester, Julius. *Look Out, Whitey! Black Power's Gon' Get Your Mama*. New York: Grove Press, 1968.

Linder, Douglas O. *Bending toward Justice: Heroes in Great Trials Involving the Rights of Black Americans*, http://www.law.umkc.edu/faculty/projects/ftrials/trialheroes/doaressay.html, 2001.

Loevy, Robert D. *To End All Segregation: The Politics of the Passage of the Civil Rights Act of 1964*. Lanham, Md.: University Press of America, 1990.

Lutholtz, William M. *Grand Dragon: D. C. Stephenson and the Ku Klux Klan in Indiana*. West Lafayette, Ind.: Purdue University Press, 1991.

Lyon, Danny. *Memories of the Southern Civil Rights Movement*. Chapel Hill: University of North Carolina Press, 1992.

MacGregor, Morris J., Jr. *The Integration of the Armed Forces, 1940–1965*. Washington, D.C.: Center for Military History, 1989.

MacLean, Nancy. *Behind the Mask of Chivalry: The Making of the Second Ku Klux Klan*. New York: Oxford University Press, 1994.

Malcolm X. *Malcolm X Speaks*. New York: Grove Press, n.d.

Mann, Robert. *The Walls of Jericho: Lyndon Johnson, Hubert Humphrey, Richard Russell, and the Struggle for Civil Rights*. New York: Harcourt and Brace, 1996.

May, Henry Farnham. *Protestant Churches and Industrial America*. New York: Harper and Brothers, 1949.

McAdam, Doug. *Political Process and the Development of Black Insurgency, 1930–1970*. Chicago: University of Chicago Press, 1982.

McCartney, John T. *Black Power Ideologies: An Essay in African-American Political Thought*. Philadelphia: Temple University Press, 1992.

McGuire, Phillip, ed. *Taps for a Jim Crow Army: Letters from Black Soldiers in World War II*. Santa Barbara, Calif.: ABC-Clio, 1983.

McMillen, Neil R. *The Citizens' Council: Organized Resistance to the Second Reconstruction, 1954–1964*. Urbana: University of Illinois Press, 1971.

McWhiney, Grady. *Cracker Culture: Celtic Ways in the Old South*. Tuscaloosa: University of Alabama Press, 1988.

McWhiney, Grady, and Perry D. Jamieson. *Attack and Die: Civil War Military Tactics and the Southern Heritage*. University: University of Alabama Press, 1982.

Mecklin, John Moffatt. *The Ku Klux Klan: A Study of the American Mind*. 1924. Reprint, New York: Russell and Russell, 1963.

Meier, August, and Elliott Rudwick. *CORE: A Study in the Civil Rights Movement, 1942–1968*. New York: Oxford University Press, 1973.

Meier, August, Elliott Rudwick, and Francis L. Broderick, eds. *Black Protest Thought in the Twentieth Century*. 1965. Reprint, Indianapolis: Bobbs-Merrill, 1971.

Mencken, H. L. *The Philosophy of Friedrich Nietzsche*. Boston: Luce, 1913.

Miller, Keith D. *Voice of Deliverance: The Language of Martin Luther King, Jr. and Its Sources*. New York: Free Press, 1992.

Miller, Ronald B. "Violence, Force, and Coercion." In *Violence*, edited by Jerome A. Shaffer, 9–44. New York: Daniel McKay Co., 1971.

Mills, Kay. *This Little Light of Mine: The Life of Fannie Lou Hamer*. New York: Dutton, 1993.

Moody, Anne. *Coming of Age in Mississippi*. New York: Dell, 1971.

Moore, Arthur K. *The Frontier Mind: A Cultural Analysis of the Kentucky Frontiersman*. Lexington: University Press of Kentucky, 1957.

Morris, Aldon D. *The Origins of the Civil Rights Movement: Black Communities Organizing for Change*. New York: Free Press, 1984.

Muse, Benjamin. *The American Negro Revolution: From Nonviolence to Black Power, 1963–1967*. Bloomington: Indiana University Press, 1968.

Myrdal, Gunnar. *An American Dilemma: The Negro Problem and Modern Democracy*. New York: Harper and Brothers, 1944.

Nelson, Jack. *Terror in the Night: The Klan's Campaign against the Jews*. New York: Simon and Schuster, 1993.

Newby, I. A. *Plain Folk in the New South: Social Change and Cultural Persistence, 1880–1915*. Baton Rouge: Louisiana State University Press, 1989.

Newton, Michael. *The Invisible Empire: The Ku Klux Klan in Florida*. Gainesville: University of Florida Press, 2001.

Nisbett, Richard E., and Dov Cohen. *Culture of Honor: The Psychology of Violence in the South*. Boulder, Colo.: Westview Press, 1996.

Norrell, Robert J. *Reaping the Whirlwind: The Civil Rights Movement in Tuskegee*. New York: Alfred A. Knopf, 1985.

Northrup, Herbert R. *The Negro in the Paper Industry: The Racial Politics of American Industry*. Report no. 8, Industrial Research Unit, Department of Industry, Wharton School of Finance and Commerce, University of Pennsylvania. Philadelphia: University of Pennsylvania Press, 1969.

Oates, Stephen. *Let the Trumpet Sound: The Life of Martin Luther King, Jr.* New York: Harper and Row, 1982.

Oberschall, Anthony. *Social Conflict and Social Movements*. Englewood Cliffs, N.J.: Prentice-Hall, 1973.

O'Brien, Gail Williams. *The Color of Law: Race, Violence, and Justice in the Post–World War II South*. Chapel Hill: University of North Carolina Press, 1999.

Odum, Howard W. *Race and Rumors of Race: Challenge to American Crisis*. Chapel Hill: University of North Carolina Press, 1943.

O'Reilly, Kenneth, and David Gallen, eds. *Black Americans: The FBI Files*. New York: Carroll and Graf Publishers, Inc., 1994.

Ownby, Ted. *Subduing Satan: Religion, Recreation, and Manhood in the Rural South, 1865–1920*. Chapel Hill: University of North Carolina Press, 1990.

Parker, Thomas F., ed. *Violence in the U.S.* Vol. 1, *1956–1967*. New York: Facts on File, 1974.

Patterson, Orlando. *Slavery and Social Death: A Comparative Study*. Cambridge: Harvard University Press, 1982.

Payne, Charles M. *I've Got the Light of Freedom: The Organizing Tradition and the Mississippi Freedom Struggle*. Berkeley: University of California Press, 1995.

Pearson, Hugh. *The Shadow of the Panther: Huey Newton and the Price of Black Power in America*. Reading, Mass.: Addison-Wesley Publishing Co., 1994.

Péristiany, Jean Georges, ed. *Honour and Shame: The Values of Mediterranean Society*. Chicago: University of Chicago Press, 1966.

Phadke, Y. D. "The Historical Background of Mass Violence in India." In *The Politics of Mass Violence in India*, edited by S. P. Aiyar, 44–52. Bombay: P. C. Manaktalas and Sons, 1967.

Piven, Frances Fox, and Richard Cloward. *Poor People's Movements*. New York: Vintage Books, 1979.

Raines, Howell. *My Soul Is Rested: Movement Days in the Deep South Remembered*. New York: G. P. Putnam's Sons, 1977.

Reavis, Dick J. *If White Kids Die: Memories of a Civil Rights Movement Volunteer*. Denton: University of North Texas Press, 2001.

Robinson, Jo Ann Gibson. *The Montgomery Bus Boycott and the Women Who Started It: The Memoir of Jo Ann Robinson Gibson*. Edited by David J. Garrow. Knoxville: University of Tennessee Press, 1987.

Rothschild, Mary A. *A Case of Black and White: The Northern Volunteers and the Southern Freedom Summers, 1964–1965*. Westport, Conn.: Greenwood Press, 1982.

Rotundo, E. Anthony. *American Manhood: Transformations in Masculinity from the Revolution to the Modern Era*. New York: Basic Books, 1993.

Rustin, Bayard. "The Meaning of the March on Washington," in *Black Protest Thought in the Twentieth Century*, edited by August Meier, Elliott Rudwick, and Francis L. Broderick. 1965. Reprint, Indianapolis: Bobbs-Merrill, 1971.

Sellers, Cleveland, with Robert Terrell. *The River of No Return: The Autobiography of a Black Militant and the Life and Death of SNCC*. New York: William Morrow and Co., 1973.

Sharp, Gene. *Gandhi as a Political Strategist*. Boston: Porter Sargent, 1979.

——. "The Lesson of Eichmann: A Review-Essay on Hannah Arendt's Eichmann in Jerusalem." *Social Power and Political Freedom*. Boston: Porter Sargent Publishers, 1980.

Shugg, Roger W. *Origins of Class Struggle in Louisiana: A Social History of White Farmers and Laborers during Slavery and After, 1840–1875*. Baton Rouge: Louisiana State University Press, 1939.

Simpson, James B., comp. *Simpson's Contemporary Quotations*. Boston: Houghton Mifflin, 1988.

Sobel, Lester, ed. *Civil Rights, 1960–1966*. New York: Facts on File, 1967.

Sorel, Georges. *Reflections on Violence*. Translated by T. E. Hulme and Jay Roth, with an introduction by Edward A. Shils. Glencoe, Ill.: Free Press, 1950.

Sorensen, Theodore C. *Kennedy*. New York: Harper and Row, 1965.

Sutherland, Elizabeth. *Letters from Mississippi*. New York: McGraw-Hill, 1965.

Tolstoy, Leo. *Tolstoy's Writings on Civil Disobedience and Nonviolence*. New York: Bergman, 1967.

Tomlinson, T. M. "Riot Ideology among Urban Negroes." In *Riots and Rebellion: Civil Violence in the Urban Community*, edited by Louis H. Masotti and Don R. Bowen, 417–28. Beverly Hills: Sage Publications, 1968.

Tuck, Stephen G. N. *Beyond Atlanta: The Struggle for Racial Equality in Georgia, 1940–1980*. Athens: University of Georgia Press, 2000.

Tushnet, Mark V. *The NAACP's Legal Strategy against Segregated Education, 1925–1950*. Chapel Hill: University of North Carolina Press, 1987.

Tyson, Timothy B. *Radio Free Dixie: Robert F. Williams and the Roots of Black Power*. Chapel Hill: University of North Carolina Press, 1999.

Umoja, Akinyele Omowale, "Repression Breeds Resistance: The Black Liberation Army and the Radical Legacy of the Black Panther Party." In *Liberation, Imagination, and the Black Panther Party: A New Look at the Panthers and Their Legacy*, edited by Kathleen Cleaver and George Katsiaficas. New York: Routledge, 2001.

U.S. Commission on Civil Rights. *Justice in Jackson, Mississippi: Hearing Held in Jackson, Miss., February 16–20, 1965*. Vols. 1 and 2. New York: Arno Press and the New York Times, 1971.

Vandal, Gilles. *Rethinking Southern Violence: Homicides in Post–Civil War Louisiana, 1866–1884*. Columbus: Ohio State University Press, 2000.

Van Deburg, William L. *New Day in Babylon: The Black Power Movement and American Culture, 1965–1975*. Chicago: University of Chicago Press, 1992.

Viorst, Milton. *Fire in the Streets: America in the 1960s*. New York: Simon and Schuster, 1979.

Weisbrot, Robert. *Freedom Bound: A History of America's Civil Rights Movement*. New York: Norton, 1990.

Wharton, Vernon Lane. *The Negro in Mississippi, 1865–1890*. James Sprunt Studies in History and Political Science, vol. 28. Chapel Hill: University of North Carolina Press, 1947.

Williams, Robert F. *Negroes with Guns*. Edited by Marc Schleifer. New York: Marzani and Munsell, Inc., 1962.

Wofford, Harris. *Of Kennedys and Kings: Making Sense of the Sixties*. New York: Farrar, Straus and Giroux, 1980.

Wyatt-Brown, Bertram. *Southern Honor: Ethics and Behavior in the Old South*. New York: Oxford University Press, 1982.

———. *The Shaping of Southern Culture, 1765–1865: Honor, Grace, and War, 1760s–1890s*. Chapel Hill: University of North Carolina Press, 2001.

Wynn, Neil A. *The Afro-American and the Second World War*. New York: Holmes and Meier Publishers, 1976.

Youth of the Rural Organizing and Cultural Center. *Mind Stayed on Freedom: The Civil Rights Struggle in the Rural South, an Oral History*. Boulder, Colo.: Westview Press, 1991.

Zieger, Robert H. *Rebuilding the Pulp and Paper Makers Union, 1933–1941*. Knoxville: University of Tennessee Press, 1984.

Articles

Cottrol, Robert J., and Raymond T. Diamond. "The Second Amendment: Toward an Afro-Americanist Reconsideration." *Georgetown Law Journal*, no. 80 (1991): 309–61.

Estes, Steve. "Race, Masculinity, and the 1968 Memphis Sanitation Strike." *Labor History* 41, no. 2 (May 2000): 153–70.

Garrow, David J. "The FBI and Martin Luther King." *Atlantic Monthly*, July–August 2002, 80–88.

Gorn, Elliott. " 'Gouge and Bite, Pull Hair and Scratch': The Social Significance of Fighting in the Southern Backcountry." *American Historical Review* 90 (February 1985): 18–43.

Korstad, Robert, and Nelson Lichtenstein. "Opportunities Found and Lost: Labor, Radicals, and the Early Civil Rights Movement." *Journal of American History* 75, no. 3 (December 1988): 786–811.

Mayfield, Julian. "The Monroe Kidnapping." *West Indian Gazette and Afro-Asian Caribbean News*. Reprinted in House Un-American Activities Committee, "Testimony of Robert F. Williams," 144–48.

Norwood, Stephen H. "Bogalusa Burning: The War against Biracial Unionism in the Deep South, 1919." *Journal of Southern History* 63, no. 3 (August 1997): 591–628.

Quick, Amy. "The History of Bogalusa, the 'Magic City' of Louisiana." *Louisiana Historical Quarterly* 29, no. 1 (January 1946): 74–178.

Rony, Vera. "Bogalusa: The Economics of Tragedy." *Dissent* 13, no. 4 (May–June): 234–42.

Schultz, John. "An Interview with Robert F. Williams." *Studies on the Left: A Journal of Research, Social Theory, and Review* 2, no. 3 (1962): 51–62.

Thornton, J. Mills. "Challenge and Response in the Montgomery Bus Boycott of 1955–1956." *Alabama Review* 33 (July 1980): 163–235.

Tyson, Timothy B. "Robert F. Williams, 'Black Power,' and the Roots of the African Freedom Struggle." *Journal of American History* (September 1998): 540–70.

Dissertations and Theses

Crosby, Emilye. "Common Courtesy: The Civil Rights Movement in Claiborne County, Mississippi." Ph.D. diss., Indiana University, 1995.

Estes, Stephen Sanford, Jr. "'I AM A MAN!': Race, Manhood, and the Struggle for Civil Rights." Ph.D. diss., University of North Carolina, 2001.

Hill, Rickey. "The Character of Black Politics in a Small Southern Town Dominated by a Multinational Corporation: Bogalusa, Louisiana, 1965–1975." Master's thesis, Atlanta University, 1977.

Joyce, Thomas. "The 'Double V' Was for Victory: Black Soldiers, the Black Protest, and World War II." Ph.D. diss., Ohio State University, 1993.

Rich, Evelyn. "Ku Klux Klan Ideology, 1954–1988." Ph.D. diss., Boston University, 1988.

Umoja, Akinyele K. "Eye for an Eye: The Role of Armed Resistance in the Mississippi Freedom Movement." Ph.D. diss., Emory University, 1996.

Index

tion, 154–57; city officials and Klan comply with federal court orders, 157–59; and fall school boycott, 238–40; and "Bloody Wednesday" riot, 240–41; Bogalusa to Baton Rouge march, 251–53

Bogalusa, Louisiana, Deacons chapter: confrontations with Klan, 1–2, 13, 130, 251; founding by Jonesboro chapter, 103–6, 108; leadership, 109, 110; membership, 111; and Alton Crowe shooting, 140–44; and Deacons organizing in Chicago, 228–30; leadership jailed, 239; Bogalusa to Baton Rouge march, 251–53

Bogalusa Civic and Voters League: history prior to arrival of CORE, 83–84; leadership changes, 92–93, 99–100; wins concessions in spring campaign, 125–28; organizes march to defend right of armed self-defense, 153; fund-raising in North, 218–20; and Martin Luther King, 229. *See also* Bogalusa, Louisiana; *Hicks v. Knight*

Bogalusa Community Relations Commission, 83

Bogalusa Daily News, 84–85, 87, 89–90

Bond, Horace Mann, 78, 82

Boston, Massachusetts, Deacons chapter, 224

Boxley, Clifford, 203

Bradford, Percy Lee, 15, 32, 50, 53–55, 57, 71, 110

Bradley, Tom, 139

Brookins, H. Hartford, 138

Brooks, Fred, 32, 33, 35, 39–41, 43, 69

Brown, H. "Rap," 252, 258

Burke, Jimmy Dane, 121

Burkes, Herman, 210

Burris, Royan, 1–2, 110, 113–14, 213

Bussie, Victor, 125, 129

Bussie Committee, 125–29

Caine, Ed, 210, 212

Cambridge, Maryland: riot in, 260

Canton, Mississippi: Deacons activity in, 212

Carmichael, Stokely, 19, 246, 250, 256

Centreville, Mississippi, Deacons chapter, 210–12

Chambers, Leon, 212

Chance, Jerry M., 85, 101

Charleston, South Carolina: riot in, 260

Chicago, Illinois, Deacons chapter, 225–32; protects Martin Luther King, 231–32

Christenberry, Herbert W.: role in Bogalusa, 138–39, 150, 154–58, 240, 242

Christian Mothers of Bogalusa, 151

Christmas, Charles, 94, 157, 242

Citizens Council (Bogalusa), 125–26

Claiborne Parish Civic League, 171–72

Clark, Felton, 153

Clark, Jim, 125

Cleveland, Ohio, Deacons chapter, 224

Clurman, Michael, 237

Cockern, Virgil, 10

Coleman, M. M., 168–69

Collins, Leroy, 88, 112

Collins, Virginia, 181–82, 223–24, 256

Columbia, Mississippi, Deacons chapter, 212–13

Community Affairs Committee (CAC), 115, 129–30

Community Coalition for Black Power, 232

Community Relations Service, 85, 122; memorandum on Deacons to John McKeithen and Hubert Humphrey, 156

Jacobs, Elmo, 57, 76–77

Jefferson County, Florida: Deacons activity in, 214

Jenkins, Gayle, 83, 91, 100, 239

Jet: coverage of Deacons, 138, 148–49; importance in civil rights movement, 138, 162, 307 (n. 65)

John Birch Society: opposition to Deacons, 219–20

Johnson, Annie Purnell, 25, 36, 56, 65

Johnson, Bennett, 232

Johnson, Glenn, 66

Johnson, Harvey, 46, 62, 66, 70–71

Johnson, Kimme, 115

Johnson, Lyndon, 5, 41, 71–73, 112; intervenes in Bogalusa, 154–55; reluctant to counter Klan, 242–43

Johnson, Paul B.: orders National Guard into Natchez, 195

Joliff, James, 211

Jones, Archie, 204

Jones, Harlell, 224

Jones, Henry, 210–11

Jones, James, 19

Jones, Leroi (Amiri Baraka), 60, 221

Jones, Mike, 128

Jones, Sally: sings at Bogalusa fundraiser, 220

Jonesboro, Louisiana: early history of black community in, 10–14; Voters League in, 13; voting rights suit in, 14; mass meeting as control mechanism in, 14–15; conservative role of black church in, 15–16; positive role of fraternal orders in, 16; desegregation campaign in, 35–37; formation of Deacons for Defense and Justice in, 38–51 passim; school boycott in, 65–75; school boycott in settled by McKeithen, 73–75. *See also* Jonesboro, Louisiana, Deacons chapter

Jonesboro, Louisiana, Deacons chapter: and informally armed defense groups, 24–25; debates nonviolence with CORE, 26–29; formation of black police unit, 31–32; and desegregation campaign, 35–37; and Klan parade, 36–37; formation of Deacons for Defense and Justice, 38–51; officers, 50, 294 (n. 25); membership, 53–54; and Jackson High School boycott, 64–75

Justice Department, U.S.: claims federalism doctrine prevented it from protecting civil rights activists, 38, 154–56; files suits in Bogalusa, 124, 154–59; fails to act effectively against Klan, 243. See also *Hicks v. Knight*

Katz, Alan, 160

Katzenbach, Nicholas, 112, 124

Kennedy, John F., 81; fails to protect civil rights activists and counter Klan, 155–56, 242–43, 259; fear of black violence motivates civil rights agenda, 262–64, 331–32 (n. 22)

Kennedy, Robert, 263

Kilgore, Rev. Thomas, 138

King, Ed, 182

King, Martin Luther, Jr., 2–4, 6–8, 15, 19, 63, 238; strategy contrasted with that of Deacons, 63; condemns Deacons and armed self-defense, 144, 162, 249, 306 (n. 54); repudiated by Deacons, 162, 225, 230; federal intervention strategy, 197; accepts protection by Deacons, 206, 325 (n. 51); rejected in Watts, 235; and Meredith March conflict with Deacons, 245–50; and Black Power, 249–50; raises specter of black violence, 262–63; views on failures of civil rights strategy, 270–71; public versus private views on nonviolence, 279 (n. 14)

Kirk, Claudell, 227, 230

Kirkpatrick, Frederick Douglas, 35, 63–65, 75, 103, 110, 162, 168, 254; early history, 31; role in black police unit, 31–33, 36–42; commitment to armed self-defense, 45–48; and Bogalusa Deacons, 103–7; and Homer Deacons, 171–72

Knight, Claxton, 89, 93–95, 114, 135, 156–58, 240

Koonce, J. D., 65, 71, 73

Kosciusko, Mississippi: Deacons activity in, 206–7

Ku Klux Klan: confrontations with Deacons, 1–2, 130, 251; 18 July Bogalusa rally, 143; intimidation in Ferriday, 174. *See also* Original Knights of the Ku Klux Klan; United Klans of America

Ladner, Dorie, 197

Lambert, Don, 123

Landry, Lawrence, 232

Laurel, Mississippi: Deacons activity in, 207

Lawson, James, 18, 19, 26, 236

Lee, Howard M., 86–87

LeSeur, Ricque, 221

Lesser, Mike, 21, 29, 34, 43, 49

Levine, Anita, 116

Lewis, Frederick, 171–73

Lewis, John: commitment to nonviolence, 18

Lewis, Robert "Buck," 176

Lexington, Mississippi: Deacons activity in, 212

Lexington, North Carolina: riot in, 260

Liberty, Aaron, 212

Life: coverage of Deacons, 137–38

Liuzzo, Viola, 72–73, 76, 112, 116

Loe, Newt T., 22, 33–34, 36–37, 57

Lomax, Louis, 136, 152–53; raises

funds for Bogalusa movement, 217, 219

Los Angeles Times: coverage of Deacons, 134–37

Lott, Bill, 103

Louisiana Commission on Race Relations, 154

Louisiana Youth for Black Power, 179

Lowndes County, Alabama, Deacons chapter, 213

Lucas, Raleigh, 241

Lynch, Connie, 143–44

Lynch, Lincoln, 9, 179, 234

Lyons, Sidney J., 240

Madison County, Florida, 214

Magee, L. C., 115

Magee, Russell, 157

Major, Lou, 84–85, 87

Malcolm X, 59–60, 163; calls for black "rifle clubs," 223

Mallory, Mae, 221

Malray, Harvey, 172–73

Manhood ideal: and respect in armed self-defense movement, 8–9, 27–29, 265–68, 318–19 (n. 50); plays central role in Deacons strategy, 27–29, 76, 140–41, 149, 161, 192, 226; and patriarchy, 309–11 (n. 34)

Marshall, Burke: on fear of guerilla warfare in South, 159

Martzell, Jack, 126

McBride, W. D., 33

McComb, Mississippi: riot in, 260

McCoy, Ray, 228

McDaniels, L. C., 143

McDonald, Gable, 212

McElveen, Ray: arrested for murder of black deputy, 131–32

McKeithen, John, 90, 91, 99, 102, 112, 115, 119, 123–26, 156, 252; negotiations in Jonesboro, 73–75; criticism of and efforts to destroy Deacons,

112, 143, 152–53; on O'Neal Moore
killing, 131; secretly meets with Klan
in Bogalusa, 131; negotiations in
Bogalusa, 151–53
McKenzie, Elmo, 211
McKissick, Floyd, 246, 248
McLaurin, Charles, 19
McNeese, Dorothy, 159
Mellion, Willie, 32
Meredith March, 245–49
Meridian, Mississippi: Deacons
activity in, 212
Metcalfe, George, 184–85
Middle class, African American, 62–
63; and conservative nature of
black church, 15–16; and conserva-
tive nature of black teachers, 64–
65; black working class protests
against in Deacons' communities,
66, 172, 175, 238–39; role in civil
rights movement, 281–82 (n. 12)
Miller, Steve, 91–93, 96–99, 103–4,
117
Minden, Louisiana, Deacons chapter,
168–71
Mississippi Freedom Democratic Party
(MFDP): sponsors public meeting
for Deacons, 182; conflict with
Charles Evers, 188; in Natchez, 196–
97
Mitchell, Catherine Patterson, 21–22,
27–29, 32, 35, 40, 46, 73, 75–76
Mitchell, Danny, 12, 22, 24, 32, 40, 73
Mondy, Joshua, 101
Moore, O'Neal: murdered by Klan,
131–32
Moore, Ronnie, 20, 21, 27, 34, 48, 57,
76, 91, 104, 115, 160, 214; meets with
Bogalusa officials, 83–84; and
school boycott meeting, 120–21
Morris, Frank, 174
Morris, Herrod, 241
Morton, Leroy, 72

Moses, Andrew, 82, 83, 90–95, 99
Moses, Robert "Bob," 18–19
Muhammad, Elijah, 216

Najah (Ahmed Saud Ibriahim Kahafei
Abboud Najah), 178
Natchez, Mississippi: Metcalfe bombing and riots in, 184–87; history,
187–88; October 1965 demonstrations and arrests in, 195–96; success of boycott campaign in, 204–6
Natchez, Mississippi, Deacons chapter: founding, 190–95; officers, 195;
fund-raising, 203–4
National Association for the Advancement of Colored People (NAACP),
17; in Bogalusa, 82; opposes armed
self-defense in Natchez, 190
National States Rights Party, 150
Nation of Islam (Black Muslims), 216
Nealy, Sandy, 195
Nelson, W. J., 124
Newark, New Jersey: Deacons activity
in, 323 (n. 26)
New Orleans, Louisiana, Deacons
chapter, 179–81
Newsweek: coverage of Deacons, 147–
48, 230
New York Post: coverage of Deacons,
119
New York Times: coverage of Deacons,
56–58, 63, 112, 132–33, 160–62
Nonviolence: myth as driving force in
civil rights movement, 2–9, 258–64;
as pragmatic reform strategy rather
than philosophy, 2–9, 280 (n. 22);
as way of avoiding white attacks,
20; varying degree of commitment
to among activists, 20; and federal
intervention strategy, 20, 197;
appeals to conscience of enemy, 22;
use by CORE in Jonesboro, 22–23;
problems with application in United

States, 23–24; debate over between pacifists and local people, 25–29; discourages black male participation in civil rights movement, 27–29; limitations of, 236–38, 265–68, 270–71; imposed on southern civil rights movement by pacifists, 236–38, 325 (n. 6); ineffective without threat of violence, 258–64, 329 (n. 2), 330–31 (n. 17); defined, 280 (n. 23); and theory of "legitimating" power, 283–84 (n. 23)

Nosser, John, 189, 195

O'Keefe, Michael, 125
Organization for Black Power, 222
Original Knights of the Ku Klux Klan, 86; founding, 84; change name to Anti-Communist Christian Association, 86; members in police department, 87, 123; terror campaign in Bogalusa, 100–101; attack Ralph Blumberg, 102–3; violent response to Bogalusa concessions to Voters League, 129–32; leadership, 157; Justice Department suit against, 157, 242–43; in Ferriday, 176–77; in Natchez, 176–77. *See also* Hays Committee; *Hicks v. Knight*

Patterson, Catherine. *See* Mitchell, Catherine Patterson
Peevy, Adrian, 22, 31–32, 36–37, 41, 47, 73
Perez, Leander, 88, 181
Phillips, Abraham, 179
Pincus, Ed, 28, 191
Plaquemines Parish, 181
Pleasant Grove Baptist Church, 16
Plymouth, North Carolina: Deacons activity in, 214
Pointe Coupee Parish: and Deacons, 179

Poplarville, Mississippi: Deacons activity in, 212
Port Gibson, Mississippi: riot in, 210
Port Gibson, Mississippi, Deacons chapter, 207–10; forces disarmament with Klan, 209–10
Pounds, Randle C., 121, 158, 242
Powledge, Fred, 56–57
Princess Anne, Maryland: riot in, 260

Qualls, Ceola, 32

Radcliffe, Jones, 115
Rarick, John, 125
Reeb, James, 69
Reed, Roy, 160–62
Rester, Robert, 158, 251
Reuther, Walter, 262
Revolutionary Action Movement (RAM): arms blacks in Mississippi Delta, 19; relationship with Deacons, 60, 221–23, 255–56; calls for black "rifle clubs," 223
Reynolds, Isaac, 140
Rich, Marvin, 37
Richardson, Jim Warren, 239
Riots: importance of Watts riot, 235–38 passim; impact in South, 259–62, 315–16 (n. 9); impact in North, 264
Robinson, J. T., 199
Rogers, Nahaz, 226, 232
Rustin, Bayard, 17, 235, 261

St. Augustine, Florida: riot in, 260
St. Francisville, Louisiana, Deacons chapter, 168, 206, 315 (n. 58)
St. George, South Carolina: Deacons activity in, 214
Saints of St. George, 214
Sass, Frank, 98, 113, 242
Satcher, Olin, 67, 70

Savannah, Georgia: riot in, 260
Scott, Elmo, 209
Seale, Bobby, 218
Segregation: as basis of social order in South, 24
Sharp, James, 60
Shelton, Robert, 158
Shepherd, Bruce, 85, 87, 114
Shields, Rudy, 206–7
Shuttlesworth, Fred, Jr., 22
Sims, Charles "Charlie," 104, 113, 116, 180, 228, 240, 253, 257; background, 109–11; on nonviolence, 137; at CORE convention, 140; meets with John McKeithen, 152
Singleman, George L., 125–26
Skiffer, George, 241
Smith, Don, 138
Smith, Pam, 172
Smith, Vernon, 177
"Snipers" group, 178
Socialist Workers Party (SWP), 227–28
South, Wesley, 226, 231
Southern Christian Leadership Conference (SCLC), 17, 190, 226–27
Southern Regional Council (SRC): opposes Deacons, 147
Sparticist League, 220
Spiers, Arnold, 87, 89, 121, 156–58
Stanford, Max, 60, 221
Stewart, John, 131
Stokes, James, 62, 186–87, 195, 199–204
Stoner, J. B., 143–44
Student Nonviolent Coordinating Committee (SNCC), 17, 25, 155; debate over pacifist principles, 17–21; leader Bob Moses initially opposes local armed self-defense, 18, 283 (n. 21); advocates nonviolence in Natchez, 196–97; and federal intervention strategy, 197,

317–18 (n. 37); shifts to voter registration, 288–89 (n. 31)
Sullivan, Joseph, 86

Talley, Bascom, 85, 87–88, 90
Tallulah, Louisiana, Deacons chapter, 173–74
Taylor, Alcie, 104, 110
Temple, Margaret, 36
Terrell, Isaac, 195
Thomas, Earnest "Chilly Willy," 10, 218, 227–28, 246–49, 253; early life, 25; opposes nonviolence in Jonesboro, 25, 26–27, 39, 45; helps found predecessors to Deacons group, 25–27, 38–39; as Deacons leader, 48; arrested in school boycott, 67–69; helps found Bogalusa Deacons, 103–7; in *New York Times*, 132; in Minden, 169; trip to Cuba and China, 254–56. *See also* Chicago, Illinois, Deacons chapter; Deacons for Defense and Justice; Jonesboro, Louisiana, Deacons chapter
Tillman, Mississippi: Deacons activity in, 209
Tollivar, Earnest, 211
Tureaud, A. P., 154
Tuskegee, Alabama: Deacons activity in, 213
Tylertown, Mississippi: Deacons activity in, 207

United Klans of America, 143, 158; and 1965 "Mississippi Klan Panic," 243–45
United Rubber Workers Union, 188
U.S. Commission on Civil Rights: in Natchez, 184
Ussery, Wilfred T., 124

Van Beasley, James, 39–40, 68
Vicksburg, Mississippi: Deacons activity in, 206–7

Vivian, C. T., 226–27

Von Hoffman, Nicholas: on Deacons, 144–45

Voter registration: provokes less violence than desegregation protest, 29; CORE promotes over desegregation, 41; local people show little interest in, 175; intended to divert activity from desegregation protest, 288–89 (n. 31)

Voters Education Project (VEP): promoted by Kennedy administration to discourage desegregation protest, 288–89 (n. 31)

Walker, Edwin, 140

Walker, George, 207–9

Wall Street Journal: coverage of Deacons, 146–47

Walterboro, South Carolina: Deacons activity in, 214

Ware, Bill, 196

Warner, Sidney August, 101

Washington, Booker T., 64

Washington, D.C.: Deacons activity in, 224

Washington, J. D., 206

Washington, J. R., 65

Watkins, Hollis, 19

Weaver, Mike, 22, 35

Weaver, Robert, 34, 35

Webster Parish. *See* Minden, Louisiana, Deacons chapter

Webster Parish United Christian Freedom Movement (WPUCFM), 169–70

Wells, Ruthie, 22, 40

West, Gordon E., 103

Whatley, Charlie, 177–78

Whatley, David, 64, 174, 177–79

White, Charlie, 51, 67, 71

White, Lee, 37

Wilkins, Roy: condemns armed self-defense in Natchez, 190; opposes Deacons, 246–47

Wilkinson County. *See* Centreville, Mississippi, Deacons chapter; Woodville, Mississippi, Deacons chapter

Williams, Charles, 123

Williams, Charles Ray, 101

Williams, Delos, 96, 101

Williams, Hosea, 246

Williams, Robert F., 60, 222, 254, 266; relationship to Deacons, 220–21, 256

Wilson, Jerome, 129

Wilson, John, 78

Wisdom, John Minor, 242

Women's Civilian Patrol, 159

Wood, Aubrey, 179–81

Woodville, Mississippi, Deacons chapter, 210–12

Workers World Party, 221

Wyche, Zelma, 173

Wyre, Burtrand, 111

Yates, William "Bill," 22, 35, 40, 91–95, 103–4, 115, 117–19; tests public accommodations in Bogalusa, 91–95; attacked by Klan, 96–99, 118

Young, A. Z., 92, 99–100, 109, 119, 127, 129, 229, 253; confrontations with Klan, 13

Young, Andrew: sent to Natchez by SCLC, 190

Young, James, 185, 188, 195, 198, 200–201

Young, R. T., 124

Young, Whitney: opposes Deacons, 246–47

CPSIA information can be obtained
at www.ICGtesting.com
Printed in the USA
LVHW112245081020
668328LV00006B/265

9 780807 857021